COLUMBIA COLLEGE

D1566177

TELEVISION
TIGHTROPE

ENTERED DEC 0 6 2007

COLUMBIA COLLEGE LIBRARY
600 S. MICHIGAN AVENUE
CHICAGO, IL 60605

TELEVISION
TIGHTROPE

HOW I ESCAPED HITLER SURVIVED CBS AND FATHERED VIACOM

RALPH BARUCH
WITH LEE RODERICK

ProbitasPress

Published by Probitas Press
Copyright © 2007 by Ralph M. Baruch
All rights reserved.

No portion of this book may be reproduced in any form without
permission from the Publisher, except in the case of brief
quotations, which must be properly attributed to book.

Published in the United States by Probitas Press, LLC
2016 Cummings Drive, Los Angeles, CA 90027-1729
1-800-616-8081 or 323-953-9853 fax
http://www.probitaspress.com
Distributed by Chicago Review Press, Inc.,
Independent Publishers Group
http://www.ipgbook.com

Library of Congress Catalog Card No. 2006900695
Publishers Cataloging-in-Publication Data
Baruch, Ralph.
    Television tightrope : how I escaped Hitler, survived CBS,
    and fathered Viacom / Ralph Baruch with Lee Roderick. —
    Los Angeles, CA : Probitas Press, 2007.
        p. ; cm.
        ISBN-13: 978-0-9673432-2-8
        ISBN-10: 0-9673432-2-4
        Includes bibliographical references and index.
    1. Viacom Inc.
    2. Television broadcasting—United States—History.
    3. Television broadcasting—United States—Biography.
    4. Mass media—United States—History.
    5. Columbia Broadcasting System, inc.
    I. Roderick, Lee, 1941-
    II. Title.

PN1992.3.U6 B37 2007   2006900695
384.550973--dc22   CIP

Printed on recycled paper in the United States of America

To Jean

*Whose love and support continue to illuminate my life
and that of our family —
as well as all those around us
whose presence she touches*

Contents

ACKNOWLEDGMENTS

I have written this book in the belief that I have something worth saying, and to put in perspective a life that has been enormously eventful, challenging, and even dangerous at times, but always exciting and, on balance, richly rewarding.

Whatever successes I have enjoyed could only have come in America. A boy grows up in relative wealth in Germany and France. His family flees, leaving everything behind. He lands on these shores determined to create a future, with no tools except burning ambition, an eagerness to work hard, and a commitment to fair play. For me, as for millions of other refugees, the American Dream was and is very much alive—and that future has been splendid.

Communication has fascinated me since I was a boy in Paris, handing out copies of a gossipy neighborhood newsletter I typed with two fingers on a manual typewriter and ran off on a hand-cranked mimeograph machine. Things have changed a tad since then!

At this writing, communication technology is on the threshold of another sea change. Telecommunication giants are well along the road to going head-to-head with broadcast and cable television—the two industries that have consumed much of my life and are a major focus of this book. Lessons in these pages are a primer for the challenges now confronting all these players.

In whatever way audio, video, and the printed word are delivered into our homes, today and tomorrow, this reality will not change: People are largely indifferent to technology. What they hunger for is content that satisfies—emotionally, intellectually, culturally, spiritually. He who owns content owns the future.

For the content of this book, I have many people to thank, including the remarkably talented men and women who have been my mentors and professional colleagues through the years. Their names are in these pages. I am grateful for the guidance and invariably good sense of my publisher, Probitas Press, and its president, Yvonne Maddox. My able, longtime assistant at Viacom and beyond, Janice Levin, has demonstrated great patience with the many changes and rewrites that go into such an undertaking. Elizabeth Shaw, our typesetter/graphic artist, contributed significantly. Janet Allison of Coltrin & Associates and Holly Broome-Hyer kindly assisted with the photos and other visual images. Janet's boss, my friend Steve Coltrin, gave me timely encouragement that got the ball rolling.

A special thanks to two Probitas editors who helped shape the book—Scott Springer and Frank Johnson. Creative direction and graphic design were by Marie Woolf. My talented colleague Lee Roderick walked with me each step of the way in taking this book from concept to completion. Finally, to the notables who have read and endorsed *Television Tightrope*, I am flattered by your comments.

Ralph M. Baruch
April 2007

*America is a fabulous country ... it is the only place
where miracles not only happen,
but where they happen all the time.*

— Thomas Wolfe

INTRODUCTION

I n 1933 my father, held by the Nazis as a political prisoner in Frankfurt, escaped jail and we fled to Paris—my older brother Charles, my parents, and me, then nine years old. Four years later our family waited for the other shoe to drop. A German cloud was gathering over Europe, menacing everything beneath. The pleasant life we had rebuilt in the City of Light no longer seemed so safe.

That summer Mother and I went to see the 1937 *Exposition Internationale,* in the heart of Paris near the Eiffel Tower. It showcased the architecture, art, and technology of forty-four nations. Opening day was set back again and again by an embarrassed French government, faced with worker strikes and unable to complete a new art and science museum on time. It was a portent of France's unpreparedness for the war just around the corner.

Mother and I inhaled the sights and sounds of the fair. It was exactly what we needed. The whole world, it seemed, had been planted on the banks of the Seine for our diversion. There were a couple hundred pavilions, including exotic huts constructed for peoples from France's colonies in Africa and Indochina. Native artisans wove handiwork and hawked their wares beside totem poles and imported banana plants.

The United States, coming of age as a world power, built a towering skyscraper topped by an American flag. Inside were exhibits on President Franklin D. Roosevelt's New Deal—public works projects aimed at pulling the U.S. out of the Depression. France's humanitarian contribution was colorfully displayed throughout the fair. With many local artists nearly starving, France and the city of Paris had commissioned 2,000 of them to create works that decorated the pavilions.

A less innocent world also was represented. A month before the fair opened, Adolph Hitler sent German warplanes over Guernica, a small Basque village in northern Spain, for bombing practice. Villagers fleeing collapsing buildings were machine-gunned from the air. Sixteen hundred were killed or wounded in the terrorist assault. It was done in the name of fascist Francisco Franco, trying to topple Spain's government.

The atrocity moved Pablo Picasso, living in Paris, to create *Guernica*, a twenty-five-foot mural. Painted in an emotional fury of a few weeks, its haunting images include a dying horse, a fallen man with a broken sword, a baby's corpse, a weeping woman. It was the centerpiece of the Spanish pavilion and would become modern art's strongest antiwar statement.

Russia also intervened in the Spanish Civil War—on the side opposite the Nazis. The struggle intensified Germany and Russia's mutual hatred, evident at the fair. Their two pavilions faced and menaced each other from close range on the right bank of the Seine. The tall, stark Russian edifice supported heroic statues of a working man and woman, wielding hammer and sickle and glaring at the German pavilion. The looming German colossus was topped by an eagle with wings spread, head turned disdainfully, talons clutching a wreath encircling a swastika.

National rivalries were reflected inside pavilions as well. Modern countries strutted their latest technologies. Security guards were posted in each pavilion to prevent photographs, and printed information on processes and materials was almost nonexistent. Paris was abuzz over *Guernica,* the German-Russian architectural confrontation, and what it all portended for the future. What riveted my attention, however, was a French technological demonstration. A placard announced it as *"Television francaise."*

Television. Radio with pictures. Near the top of a four-foot-tall wooden cabinet was a small screen, perhaps nine inches square. Images on the screen danced in sync with the sound. The pictures were in black and white and unmistakable, though with a greenish tint. I cannot recall the specific images, but I have never forgotten the thrill. Imagine the possibilities!

Television was a startling discovery for me, but it had been germinating in scientific laboratories in Europe and the United States for years. France, Germany, and England put the first television broadcasts on the air. France built a television studio in the Eiffel Tower. The year of the Exposition, 1937, France began constructing the world's most powerful television transmitter in the Tower. Also that year Britain beamed Wimbledon and the coronation of King George VI to as many as twenty thousand English TV sets.

More than a half-century earlier a German named Paul Nipkow had taken out a patent on the first image scanner using a rotating disk. The device, barely workable, led early television down the dead-end path of a mechanical approach. (Someone labeled mechanical television "a stepladder to the moon.") Later it would be discarded in favor of electronic television.

Nonetheless, Hitler hailed Nipkow as the "inventor of television"—more evidence of the superiority of the German race. Although other countries, including the U.S., already had the key technologies, Germany declared television a state secret and kept its research laboratories under close surveillance.

There was no doubt that, if possible, Hitler and his propaganda minister Joseph Goebbels would use television to spread Nazi distortion. "Propaganda has only one object—to conquer the masses," said Goebbels. What better tool than television?

Vladimir Zworykin, a Russian immigrant to the U.S. and one of the inventors of electronic television, tasted Germany's hunger to exploit it. After delivering a lecture in Berlin and proceeding on to Hungary, Zworykin found himself face to face with the director of one of Germany's electronic labs. A "very important person" in Germany had been unable to attend Zworykin's lecture, the man told Zworykin, and wanted him to return to Berlin for a private audience.[1]

"He even offered to take me there on a military plane, which he had at his disposal," said Zworykin. "This was a flattering proposal, but

I had a very confusing impression from conversations with some of my German friends, so I declined the invitation. This refusal visibly upset the professor; it appeared that he was under orders to bring me to Berlin." The irony of being declined by a Jew could not have been lost on German leaders.

Television was not yet on the air in the United States. Industry laboratories raced to produce the best picture. A writer traveling in the U.S. in 1937 noted with deserved pride that a fellow Englishman, John Logie Baird, had given the first public demonstration of television a decade earlier. Britain also was the only country then offering a national television service. However, the writer, Scott Taggart, had a feeling the Americans would yet trump those achievements.

"In America television will burst upon the public," predicted Taggart. "In Britain it is oozing. In America apparatus and service will be perfected (after a fashion) before being offered to the public. In Britain we are trying our cookery on the dog as we go along. There has been a good deal of canine indigestion, but the [number of people affected] has been small. Few sets, comparatively speaking, have been sold."[2]

Two years later, at the 1939 New York World's Fair, daily television broadcasting was inaugurated in the United States. On April 20, David Sarnoff, head of the Radio Corporation of America, stepped before a television camera outside RCA's pavilion in Flushing Meadow Park. "Now we add sight to sound," he announced.

At the fair's opening ceremony ten days later, FDR became the first president to be televised. The next day RCA's broadcasting arm, NBC, began regularly scheduled television broadcasts several hours a day. RCA also offered television sets for sale at $600. There were few takers, however. That was about a third of the average annual salary of those lucky to be employed near the end of the Depression, when a car cost $750.

European television relied on government support, while U.S. television was a private affair. On the eve of World War II, when Britain, France, Germany, and Russia each had one quasi-government-run station on the air, private companies in the United States had more than a dozen experimental stations. Capitalist competition provided a fertile seed bed for eventual world leadership in the technology, business, and programming of television.

For me these developments were entirely out of sight and out of mind. When I saw television at the Paris world fair, crude as it was, I knew I had glimpsed something miraculous. I had no idea that one day it would dominate my life—nor that I would travel to many of the countries represented at the fair to help establish television and supply programming.

But first things first. Too soon the miracle my family and I need-ed most would be survival and escape from Europe. In the official gov-ernment report following the Paris world's fair, the French Minister of Commerce pronounced: "This great lesson in international cooperation will not be forgotten."[3] Less than three years later Paris would be under the iron boot of the conquering Nazis.

This book is a true adventure of how I and others took tele-vision around the globe. Among many encounters it describes bare-knuckle fights between competing interests in the television frontier of Australia, the powerful hold of the British Broadcasting Corporation on Europe, the peculiar protocols of the Japanese and the high costs of ignoring them, and the struggle to open world airwaves to U.S. program-ming.

The development of broadcast and then cable television in the U.S. was impeded by Washington, notably the Federal Communications Commission. It was lethargic when it should have acted, meddlesome when it should have restrained. Later, in the face of FCC rules against the three television networks, I prepared a detailed plan of what our network, CBS, should do if forced to cease certain functions. That plan became Viacom, a tiny company created and then spun off CBS under my leadership for the next decade and a half.

Giant CBS, jealous of its prerogatives, nearly strangled Viacom in its crib. Shoving the newly independent company out the back door, CBS unloaded some undesirable personnel on Viacom, strong-armed a series of oppressive agreements, and refused to hold Viacom harm-less from legal actions. Close observers—including CBS employees who dashed out and sold their Viacom shares—bet that Viacom could not survive.

Instead, overcoming adversity made Viacom strong and better prepared to succeed in a television world soon to become chaotic as other players rose to challenge CBS and the other two broadcast networks, NBC and ABC. Hitching its star to another infant, cable television, Viacom grew to become the largest entertainment company in the world. At the end of the century, Viacom closed the circle when it returned and bought CBS.

These pages show how we did it.

After working in broadcast television, I played a central role in the rise of its nemesis, cable television. I personally led the landmark battles in cable's long struggle against broadcast television and the FCC, which by then, many said, was in broadcasting's hip pocket.

One fight—to overturn blatantly unfair program restrictions—reached all the way to the U.S. Supreme Court. We won. Another historic struggle ended in the first major revision of the U.S. Communications Act in half a century. For the first time, cable television's rights and responsibilities were defined in U.S. law.

The fruit of our struggle is visible today in most American homes. In 1977 television viewers in the nation's biggest cities received seven channels at most. A decade later the number was thirty-eight—virtually all the difference coming from local and national cable channels. By 2002 most U.S. homes could get over one hundred channels, with cable again supplying nearly all the new ones. And today the most confirmed couch potato, cable snaking into his home and a thirteen-inch DBS satellite dish on the roof, can feast on a television smorgasbord of five hundred channels.

Television's watershed came in the 2003-04 viewing season. For the first time, more Americans got their television from cable channels than from broadcast channels. Cable has continued to widen the gap, including in the November 2005 Sweeps when ad-supported cable stretched its lead to seven share points over broadcast.

This is also a personal story. It follows my family out of Europe—a step ahead of the Nazis, who put a price on my father's head—

and into a new life in the U.S. Since that day long ago when our ship of refugees sailed into New York harbor, I have been extremely grateful to the United States. Bringing nothing but determination and a willingness to work hard, I believe nowhere else could I have found the opportunities and blessings America has given me and countless other refugees.

My gratitude could not be measured, but I hoped my life would reflect it. Most of all I wanted to give back more than I would take—to live worthy of the special trust Fate had handed me.

EUROPE IN TURMOIL

I was reared in domestic as well as national turmoil. Mother was a teenager when she married my father, a decade her senior. It was a stormy, unhappy union.

A wedding photo in our home in Frankfurt captured their differences—father stiff and dour in his World War I uniform, Mother modest in a simple white dress with fox collar.

Domestic and social relations were more complex for many German families following the Great War. Ordinary citizens paid the price for our country's aggression. Germany groaned under the harsh terms of the Treaty of Versailles, signed in 1919. It stripped Germany of considerable wealth at home—land, farms, factories—and its colonies and investments abroad. Even traditional German industriousness could not overcome the burden.

When Germany delayed payment of war damages in 1923—the year of my birth—French and Belgian forces invaded and occupied the Ruhr Valley, the most industrialized region in Europe.

With no monetary reserves, the German government resorted to simply printing more money. Almost all middle-class savings were wiped out in the hyperinflation that followed. The U.S. dollar equaled 7,000 marks at the start of that year. Within days of the occupation, the mark fell to 18,000 and kept plummeting—to a million, billion, and uncountable trillions.

My father, Bernard Baruch (not the famous statesman), prac-

ticed law. When a client came to the office, one of Father's first questions was "How will you pay—in foreign currency or German marks?" If
the answer was marks, my father would excuse himself and immediately
go to a shop to buy food or other necessities, concerned that within an
hour or two prices would be dramatically higher. Our nanny sometimes
received her wages and got on the streetcar to find that a month of toil
would not cover her fare.

Also in 1923 Adolph Hitler appeared on the scene, vowing to
reclaim Germany's place in the sun. Germany, he promised, would pros-
per again, would rebuild its armed forces, and would tear up the hated
treaty.

In November, at a public rally in Munich, Hitler proclaimed a
National Socialist Party revolution. The next day, leading 2,000 hooligans, he tried to topple the regional government in Bavaria as a prelude
to overthrowing the national Weimar Republic. In what history calls
the Beer Hall *Putsch*, police killed sixteen Nazis. Hitler was imprisoned
for treason and sentenced to five years. He had lit a fuse that would ig-
nite the Second World War.

Hitler's sentence was reduced to nine months, and he left prison
in December 1924. Meanwhile, Germany's economy steadily improved.
After years of progress, however, in 1930 the worldwide Depression
reached Germany's doorstep. Hunger and unemployment again spread
through the populace, now ripe for an all-powerful leader.

Adolf Hitler by no means was alone in his hatred of Jews. I
learned this at an early age when we traveled to Dad's old haunts. He
had studied law at Oxford and in Heidelberg before the war. In Germany, especially Heidelberg in those days, college students virtually had
to join a fraternity.

Dad affiliated with the only Jewish fraternity, called the KC,
and wore its cap and colored ribbons. That was like brandishing a yellow Star of David on your chest. Father fought seventeen first-disabled
saber duels and two pistol duels, all because of anti-Semitism. He had
ugly scars on his arms, chest, and face to prove it.[1]

Father was from the Rhineland, a region on the French-Ger-
man border that for centuries has been a prize of war. It was Germanic

at the outbreak of World War I. Although he disliked all things German, Dad was drafted into its army and wounded three times. Despite being a Jew and contrary to all custom, he was appointed a judge in the military Court Martial.

A case Dad was involved in illustrated the feelings of many Germans toward Jews. A merchant with a Jewish name appeared before the court on which Father sat. The man was accused of falsifying the label on the soup he was selling in the midst of a severe food shortage. The label said "Chicken Soup," but it bore evidence of horse meat. The accused finally admitted using horse meat, but explained he had used equal amounts of each—"One chicken, one horse"—to the merriment of all.

When Father and the two other judges retired to deliberate, one of the others made an anti-Semitic remark to which Dad strongly objected. Unnerved, the judge did an about-face, claimed he was misunderstood, that he was not convinced of the man's guilt, and would vote to acquit. The second judge joined him, over my father's strong objection that the man obviously was guilty.

The defendant was acquitted and surely told others of his good fortune in having a friendly Jewish judge on the panel who helped him beat the charges.

We lived in a spacious, nicely furnished apartment in a small building facing a park. It had a sunken living room, a dining room filled with guests on many evenings, and two bedrooms, one of which I shared with my brother Charles. We had a cleaning lady and Regina, our nanny, who watched over us like a mama bear. Our own mother was delightful—gregarious, witty, with numerous friends—and a good counterweight to my father.

Her father was a banker and he and my grandmother owned a large house in a wealthy district of Frankfurt. Dad apparently was told by my grandfather that in marrying Mother he would get a large dowry. It never materialized. My parents fought frequently over the dowry and over her parents, especially Grandmother, who in those difficult times still insisted on four-horse-carriage rides.

Father seemed to relish moving Mother to tears. On one occasion he hid a diamond pin and taunted Mother, accusing her of losing it. He was intellectually bright, and perhaps contrived such pranks out of boredom.

Father was strong, physically and temperamentally, and completely dominated her, as he dominated the entire household, terrifying the cook and nanny. The fights were dreadful. He would yell at Mother: "Why don't you go back to your parents' house!" As a child, this filled me with terrible fear of being left motherless. Occasionally she would start to rebel, sparking even more battles. Her friends and relatives knew of their fights, and she evoked a lot of helpless sympathy.

When Father became angry and exploded—often at me—she would come to the rescue, dismissing me to my room or the playroom to get me out of harm's way. I remember being unhappy a lot. At the age of seven or eight, without telling my parents, I left home to visit an aunt, across the river in Sachsenhausen. I walked for about an hour and a half to reach her apartment. My parents were frantic until my aunt called and told them I was safe.

My brother Charles, two years older, was a model student and a good friend. I was the devil who made his life difficult. We had similar handwriting and many times Charlie did my homework. During a sibling argument I threw a flashlight that hit him behind an ear, requiring stitches and incurring, for once appropriately, the wrath of my father, who beat me.

Most times I felt that he singled me out arbitrarily for ridicule and spankings. Father favored Charlie and did not pretend otherwise. Charlie was brilliant and responsible beyond his years. He even looked like Dad. I was small for my age and looked more like Mother.

When I was young my parents routinely took Charlie with them to vacation on Belgium's beaches, leaving me with our nanny who took me home to her family farm. When I was four or five I remember taking it upon myself to "help" with chores. Dressed in a tiny white suit, I got a bucket of water and a hoe and proceeded to clean the cows' mucky rear ends. I guess I wanted to feel useful.

Frankfurt was Germany's transportation hub and a center of

commerce and banking, second only to Berlin, the capital. Much of my father's law practice was before the International Court of Law in the Hague; living in Frankfurt eased his travel.

Father was well-educated and spoke several European languages expertly. He was also fluent in Latin and Greek. Dad belonged to an organization called the *Schlaraffia*, an elite group of intellectuals who improvised poetry, held performances by artists, and dabbled in other cultural things.

Ours was a most unusual and eclectic home. My parents' friends came from many walks of life—singers, actors, lawyers, students, travelers passing through. It was a constant parade of the most colorful human beings, one that Charles and I greatly enjoyed. Charlie could multiply two six-figure numbers in his head and quickly give the result. My parents often hauled him out when entertaining, and invited guests to stump him with questions. What is the capital of Madagascar? Where is the largest volcano in South America? Which is the largest ocean, and which the smallest? Charlie rarely missed.

One New Year's Eve a singer from the Frankfurt Opera came to our house, wearing a fur-lined overcoat. As he prepared to depart my father helped him into it, commenting that "This is a very heavy coat; what have you got in there?" The inner pockets were examined and found to contain some of our family's silver. It had been hidden there by the maid on Father's instructions. After a momentary embarrassment everyone had a good laugh.

An Austrian comic named Fritz Gruenbaum was a close friend of Dad's, and visited us often. One time he sent a telegram announcing his imminent arrival and adding, "Please extend yourselves." Years later, after Germany seized Austria, Gruenbaum was arrested for anti-Hitler and anti-Nazi jokes. He was put in a concentration camp and forced to shine shoes while yelling "Ein Volk, ein Reich, ein Führer!" He obeyed, but between each cry spit on the shoes, defying his captors. Finally they beat him to death.

Dad visited his friends backstage at the opera house, whispering jokes to the singers on stage. In *The Walküre*, for example, as the tenor approached the part in which he was to sing "Weiche, weiche," which means "Leave, leave," my father and his mischievous friends would say softly to him: "How do you like your eggs?" The tenor, of course, answered "Weiche, weiche," which had the dual meaning of "Soft, soft."

By 1932 the noose of Nazism was tightening on Germany. I was nine years old. On the way home from school one day I was attacked by a group of twelve- or thirteen-year-olds who wore black short pants and brown shirts—the standard Hitler Youth uniform. Some had knives. They screamed anti-Semitic insults as they beat and slashed at me, leaving a scar on my knee I would carry the rest of my life. A year later the government by decree forced us Jewish students to leave state public school and attend all-Jewish schools. For me it was a devastating change. I lost all my friends.

That same year my father was persuaded to help the Social Democratic Party and defend a man in court pro bono. The plaintiff produced a witness who, though illegal at the time, appeared in court in a brown Nazi uniform and promptly insulted my father as a Jew. Dad nodded to the judge to rebuke the witness, but his honor just smiled.

With that, Father took a few steps forward and slapped the Nazi in the face. The witness, supported by the Nazi Party, filed suit against my father, but in every instance it was thrown out because Father had been provoked. This slap would have serious consequences for our family.

Germany was in its last months as a democratic republic in 1932 when three candidates, including Hitler and eighty-five-year-old incumbent Paul von Hindenburg, ran for president. They split the votes, none winning a majority.

In a run-off election Hindenburg won an outright majority, but Hitler polled 36 percent—enough to make him a legitimate political figure in Germany and on the world stage. Hindenburg named Hitler chancellor. Upon the old man's death two years later Hitler proclaimed himself Germany's leader and installed his henchmen in the cabinet. His takeover of Germany was complete.

Days after Hitler rose to undisputed power in 1933, two men from the Gestapo—the secret police—came to our house and took my father into custody "for his own protection." He joined Jewish attorneys, doctors, and other professionals behind bars. The Nazis kept him in jail six weeks, knocking out some of his teeth.

Hitler issued laws restricting Jews from universities, the professions, and public service. While the wholesale slaughter of Europe's Jews would come later, several thousand were beaten, robbed, and murdered in the first months of Nazi rule. Judges did little, fearing for their own lives if they moved against individual Nazis.

On April 1, 1933, Hitler decreed a day of boycott of all Jewish businesses. SA guards were posted at the front of every Jewish store to discourage customers from entering. That same day the Nazi judicial system put Father on trial for the slap. The courthouse was mobbed by some who had lost cases to him, yelling "Today we're going to get you, you Jew bastard!" And get Dad they did, giving him a long prison sentence—for attempted murder.

Early one morning soon afterward Mother woke me and said we were going on a trip, and we would begin by walking very quietly to the train station. I did not know that once the verdict had been announced, my father, with inside help, broke out of jail. Assisted by a fraternity brother, he and Charlie left Frankfurt by auto, after stuffing money between a tube and tire.

Traveling separately, our whole family crossed the German border on the same morning, leaving all of our possessions behind forever. It seemed a cruel twist of fate at the time, but the forced flight put us beyond Hitler's reach for the moment and probably saved our lives.

After the train ride and short recuperation in neutral Saarland—between Germany and France—we went on to Paris. I thought of our escape as an adventure, but soon discovered the realities of a changed life in a country where I could not understand the language, even to decipher the "chaud" and "froid" on bathroom faucets. We were thrown from a life of relative ease to one of poverty, temporary but real nonetheless. My parents were discouraged—glad to have left Germany behind, but wondering how we were going to live.

The French Refugee Committee found us temporary quarters in

a small hotel in Montmartre. It lacked dining facilities and other amenities, so we took our meals at a nearby restaurant, paying with coupons from the committee. The food was dismal, including white beans that turned rancid if not eaten quickly. I stuffed my pockets with bread each day. One summer night our room was so hot that Charlie and I slept on the balcony, catching severe colds.

During the early months Mother helped support us by giving foreign-language lessons; she was fluent in French, German, and English. My parents were anxious to have me attend school at the beginning of the October term.

They found a tutor in the Latin Quarter, and I took French lessons six hours a day, followed by substantial homework. With that regimen I refused to continue piano lessons. I hated the structured lessons anyway, and improvised the music. The piano teacher told my parents that I played nicely, "but it does not come close to what is on the sheets."

Father opened an office at No. 10 Avenue de l'Opera and things began to look up. We moved to a furnished apartment, then to our own unit in Passy, the fashionable Sixteenth District.

Paris, where I would spend my formative years, was captivating. The easy-going French were a welcome, if sometime frustrating, contrast to the hurried, precise Germans. Paris had it all—breathtaking vistas, numerous art galleries and other cultural offerings, urban forests shading corner cafes and small shops throughout the city. There was a continual electricity in the air—a feeling that something important was about to happen.

"If you are lucky enough to have lived in Paris as a young man," wrote Ernest Hemingway, "then wherever you go for the rest of your life, it stays with you, for Paris is a moveable feast."[2] The last three words in Hemingway's letter to a friend provided the title for a slim memoir he wrote of his years there from 1921 to 1926. Paris obviously stayed with Hemingway, as *A Moveable Feast* was not written until three decades later and published after his death.

Hemingway and his first wife, Hadley, were poor in Paris, living on $5 a day. But, he noted, "In Paris, then, you could live very well on almost nothing and by skipping meals occasionally and never buying any new clothes," and diluting wine with water.

It was a legendary era in Paris. Its bookends were the close of the First World War in 1918 and the start of the Second in 1939. A popular bibliography of Paris in the 1920s and 1930s suggests the spirit of the time: *Geniuses Together: American Writers in Paris in the 1920s; The Crazy Years: Paris in the Twenties; Fireworks at Dusk: Paris in the Thirties, and The Glamour Years: Paris 1919-1940.*

Hemingway, a newspaper correspondent who had yet to write his first book, was one of many creative vagabonds drawn to Paris following the Great War. Others in the 1920s included writers F. Scott Fitzgerald, James Joyce, Gertrude Stein, and Ezra Pound. Spain's Pablo Picasso found much of his inspiration in Paris and France, arriving as a teenager around the turn of the century, waiting out Germany's World War II occupation, and dying there in 1973 at the age of ninety-one.

The romance of the Bohemian life largely died in the crises of the twentieth century. The Wall Street crash of 1929 deflated the pockets and sobered many expatriates. Henry Miller, Vladimir Nabokov and others regrouped in the 1930s, but the nomadic life in Paris never again would be so alluring.

France weathered the early period of the Depression better than the U.S., Germany, and Great Britain. Although its economy did not sink to the depths of the others, the downturn lasted longer in France. As its economy stagnated, citizens migrated to Paris and its suburbs, hunting for work. Jobs declined sharply in agriculture, mostly small farms with a lack of mechanization, and productivity well behind that of Germany and Britain.

The French government was notoriously unstable. Its leaders still had not absorbed a lesson from the French Revolution a century and a half earlier: Lack of bread for the people leads to political fractures.

Beneath the surface calm in France ran a deep current of remorse over World War I, which ended in a pyrrhic victory. Among combatants from all warring countries, one in every five was killed. Millions more were maimed or wounded. France suffered the most. Already experiencing demographic downturn, France lost 27 percent of men aged eighteen to twenty-seven. The resulting decline in marriages and births produced a smaller labor force and fewer soldiers for the next war.

In October 1933 I entered the Lycée Janson de Sailly and was relieved to find I could compete well. School, in fact, came easy. My English teacher, M. Lebêtre, was intelligent but especially strange. Exams were long—eight to ten pages. He would give us back the corrected tests. The student with the highest mark would have to copy the corrected version once, the student with the second highest mark would have to copy it twice, and so on until it came to the twenty-fifth or twenty-sixth student, who had to write out the entire exam that many times.

On one occasion I omitted the "s" when conjugating a verb, and Lebêtre made me copy the correct word *two thousand* times.

M. Lebêtre arranged class seating according to our marks. The top student would sit on his right-hand side in front, and from there we went across, row by row, according to our standing. Obviously those in back were the worst students. Once in a while Lebêtre called on a student in the rear of class. "You back there, what is your name?" he would say. "Oh yes, yes, can you answer the question?" He would wait a couple of seconds and provide the answer. "Of course not, you can't, that's understood. Please sit down; go back to sleep." After a year or so, I made it to the front row.

I joined the French Boy Scouts and went camping with my troop, first in the south of France near Toulon. On coffee duty early one morning in pouring rain I could not start a fire. Finally I threw a large lump of butter into the newspaper at the base of the wood. Flames roared up like a rocket, setting the trees ablaze and forcing the scout master to call the fire department.

My scout patrol took a walking trip on the Isle of Wight, the southern coast of England. I was the youngest of a group of four and had great difficulty keeping up with the rest of the boys. Each evening when I took my boots off I found large blisters on my feet. The third or fourth day of hiking ended in the dead of night. After a meager supper we groped around in the dark for a level spot to pitch the tent. Finally we located an ideal place, raised the tent, and dug the prescribed ditch around it to carry away water in case of rain. Exhausted, we wrapped our blankets around us and fell asleep.

Early next morning, just after dawn, a gentleman wearing a black suit and tie and bowler hat stormed into our tent, shaking its center pole and screaming uncontrollably. I had difficulty understanding the English but knew from his face, red as a tomato, that something was dreadfully wrong. He stabbed the air toward our tent opening, until we all poked our heads out. That was when we realized we had planted ourselves and dug a trench on the seventh green of a golf course. Like little Indians, we struck the tent and stole quickly away.

One day in 1934, sitting in the Café de la Paix in Paris, Dad assisted the next table's occupant, a young American who spoke little French. He identified himself as Rabbi Julius Mark. They talked at length, the Rabbi having just toured Germany to learn the true status of Jews and German attitude toward them. He was appalled, even though the systematic persecution was in an early stage. The Rabbi cited the case of an old woman whose attorney-son had fled Germany overnight. The Gestapo hauled the woman in repeatedly for questioning, until they were satisfied she had no complicity in his disappearance.

"Where does the poor woman live?" asked Dad.

"Frankfurt," answered the Rabbi, "and her name is Baruch." She was my father's mother.

Rabbi Mark became a chaplain in the U.S. Navy and eventually ended up as Rabbi of Temple Emanu-El in New York City, one of the most prestigious Reform synagogue congregations in the United States. After that first meeting, when traveling in France, he always visited us.

In the spring of 1936 Charlie was riding his bike home from the Lycée Janson we both attended. He was brushed by a car, fell, and broke the neck of his thighbone, the femur. Charlie was admitted to the Hospital Boucicot in the fifteenth *arrondissement*. A few days later I heard his screams way down the hall before reaching his room. Doctors had set Charlie's leg badly. They cut open the cast, which reached to his upper torso, and reset the leg, easing the pain.

That same year my father's mother, sister, and the sister's daughter and stepson decided they must leave Germany. The stepson, my cousin Richard, was American by birth. His father was American. They passed through Paris, leaving my grandmother with us, and went on to New York. Grandmother, in her late 70s, lived with us from then on.

Charles was at home, recuperating from his injury. One night he moaned in pain and vomited blood. Doctors rushed to our home, where they performed a crude transfusion between my father and brother. They took Charlie back to the hospital and found that his leg was infected from the pin holding it together. The infection spread, and antibiotics to stop it did not yet exist.

Sadly, on September 19 at the age of fifteen, we lost Charlie. His had been a most promising life. The *École Polytechnique* and the *École St. Cyr,* one for civil officers of France and the other a renowned military school, had begun to recruit him. But it was not to be. At his funeral I had to throw dirt on his coffin. It shocked me greatly.

Father's birthday was a week later. I looked for a gift to cheer him up, and realized we had no pictures of Charlie in our home. I took a passport photo to a special store and had it enlarged, then bought a nice frame. On Father's birthday I presented it to him. Instead of thanking me he became extremely angry and chased me around the house, hitting me with a shoe. I was dazed and distraught. Was it simply grief giving vent? I never knew.

Through a friend in the government my father met with Air Ministry officials. He told them he had learned from good sources that the Germans were building airplanes which could be converted to bombers in one to two days. He had photos to prove it. This was illegal under the Treaty of Versailles, which strictly limited German armaments production. But the French seemed annoyed and told Dad "Look, *Maître,* why don't you just practice law and let us worry about these things." They had no interest in pursuing it.

That year, 1936, Germany formally renounced the Versailles treaty, formed an alliance with Italy, and signed a pact with Japan, creating the Axis powers. It re-occupied the Rhineland, putting German troops on the French border—another clear treaty violation. Some French leaders wanted to push the Germans back, but others feared that would lead to all-out war. In the end France and Europe did nothing.

The French Republic, with continuing economic stagnation, had been in political turmoil for years. Five cabinets were dismissed in 1933 alone. Now, under Prime Minister Leon Blum, a fervent Socialist, France was concerned with little else but France. While Germany and Italy supported General Franco in Spain's civil war, and the Soviets backed the Popular Front, Blum's government remained neutral—further alienating his own Socialist party and Communist supporters.

I turned thirteen in 1936, traditionally a Jewish boy's coming of age as he celebrates his bar-mitzvah. For Charlie's we had had a wonderful party in one of Paris's most elegant hotels—scores of guests, great food, and an orchestra for dancing. But not for me. "Your brother just died. This is no time to celebrate," explained my father. My bar-mitzvah would be postponed for a year.

Even in death my brother had taken the spotlight and I was shoved into the background. I was terribly disappointed. A year later I had a modest bar-mitzvah following a religious service.

I was rather small. My first date, at fourteen, was with a girl considerably taller. Father recommended an elegant restaurant near the Palais Royal. Uncharacteristically, he even arranged to have the bill sent to him. I was nervous but everything went smoothly—until part way through dinner when I excused myself to go to the men's room. Apparently more uptight than I realized, I walked smack into an enormous glass door. It shattered, raining a thousand pieces on me. A couple of restaurant employees came running, but I was all right. I sauntered back to the table as if nothing had happened.

Later I told my father that in addition to the expensive meal, he would be getting a bill for the glass door. To my surprise, he was quite gracious.

I made many friends at the Lycée, especially Bert Jonas and Jack Aufricht. We decided to pay a visit to the most elegant brothel in Paris, on the rue Blondel. It was known to be expensive but well-inspected by authorities. Jonas and Jack were much taller than I was, but all of us casually sauntered in. To my horror the madam at the entrance asked me, "How old are you?"

"Seventeen," I stammered, lying my head off.

"You are *not* seventeen," she barked, "and you are much too young for this. Wait outside." I was shown the door, while my friends stayed and were initiated into manhood. Later we laughed a great deal about this episode, but at the time I was mortified.

Dad used his international connections to help refugees flowing out of Germany and the occupied areas. Among other things he helped get some of their money out; the Nazis would allow them to leave with only a pittance.

Appeasement of Germany, notably by France and England, continued to prove disastrous as Hitler systematically carved *lebensraum*—living space—for Germans from the rest of Europe. In 1938 German troops seized Austria, Hitler's homeland, and in September four leaders signed the infamous Munich agreement to sever the Sudetenland from Czechoslovakia—a fifth of its land and most of its industries—and give it to Germany.

Hitler called the Sudetenland "the last territorial claim I have to make in Europe." Signing the accord, along with the Fuehrer, were his ally Benito Mussolini of Italy, Edouard Daladier, who had replaced Leon Blum in France; and Neville Chamberlain, who declared they had bought "peace for our time." Many of our neighbors celebrated the Munich accord. I went to one friend's house where champagne was on big blocks of ice in the bathtub. When I suggested their celebration should have been a funeral service, I was practically asked to leave. The French lived in a world of illusion and delusion.

As war drums beat louder and Britain, the other regional power, prepared to fight, France, crippled by internal dissension, was indecisive. Unlike 1914 when war was met by a patriotic fervor, memories of wholesale slaughter were fresh and there was little heart or stomach for it this time. Frenchmen forty and fifty years old were called up in place of the generation decimated in the First World War.

The French general staff bet the country's future on a passive defensive strategy centered on the Maginot Line—a fortified defensive line across France's eastern frontier, named for a former minister of war. However, even after Belgium declared its neutrality in 1936, France inexplicably did not extend the Maginot Line to cover the Belgian frontier. The cost of France's lethargy and bunker mentality would be incalculable.

In 1938, unbeknown to me at the time, a Frenchman named Cerf came to see my father, citing his accurate warning two years earlier that Germany was building warplanes. Cerf said that the *Deuxième Bureau*, France's counter-espionage apparatus, lacked agents, and he asked Dad to help organize a better network of informants. As a native German, Father of course spoke that language perfectly, and with the dueling scars on his face and head, he looked quintessentially German. There would be no pay. His only reward—if he survived—would be to see democratic Europe better prepared for the inevitable showdown with Germany.

Father began making regular trips to Germany. I was simply told he was away on business. Only later did he give me a small peak into his secret world. Some of the people he recruited were caught and forced to reveal names, including his, so from time to time his false passport had to be replaced. I pressed him for other details of his spy missions but he refused to discuss them.

In the autumn of 1938 an incident in Paris led to another turning point for Nazi Germany. A German Jewish refugee, just a couple of years older than I, shot and killed the third secretary of the German Embassy, Ernst vom Rath. The killer, Herschel Grynszpan, apparently acted to avenge his family and other German Jews suffering persecution. The Nazis seized the isolated incident as an excuse for the worst pogrom yet in Germany.

"Spontaneous" demonstrations of the German people—actually led by Nazi leaders as documents later proved—culminated in *Kristallnacht,* or Night of the Broken Glass. Across Germany and German-occupied Austria on the night of November 9-10, thugs smashed the windows of hundreds of Jewish homes, shops, and synagogues, torching many of them. A number of Jewish men, women, and children were shot while fleeing the burning buildings; 20,000 other Jews were arrested.

"On the flaming, riotous night," wrote eyewitness journalist William Shirer, "...the Third Reich had deliberately turned down a dark and savage road from which there was to be no return."[3] Some historians mark this as the start of the Holocaust, the Nazis' "final solution" for the Jews.

The peace for our time promised by Neville Chamberlain and Edouard Daladier at Munich lasted not quite a year. In August 1939 Germany and Russia signed a nonaggression pact. On September 1 Germany invaded Poland, finally moving France and England to declare war on Germany. World War II had begun. Before its end, sixty million people would be killed.

Life for me did not change much with the start of war. But the world was being turned upside down for many others. A friend of ours, a conductor from Hungary who lived in Paris, invited our family to concerts he performed with the French Radio Orchestra. He had recently conducted one of Wagner's operas in Germany. When he went to the podium and opened the score, he discovered that the music had been cut to bits, and a placard placed in front of the pieces: "Today we'll get you, you Jew bastard." He conducted the entire opera from memory.

On New Year's Eve 1939 two friends and I donned tuxedos and went to dinner at a Chinese restaurant in the Latin Quarter, then hit the town. At the restaurant we met a member of a band playing in one of Paris's poshest night clubs, the Scheherazade, and he invited us to drop by for a good time. Sure enough, we went there, picked up girls, and had a great time. Early in the morning we returned to the Latin Quarter and strolled up and down Blvd. St. Michel belting out German songs. People just smiled at our boyish prank and seemed to enjoy our levity despite the war. But our carefree life was about to change.

After the German assault on Poland came eight months of little fighting between Germany and western Europe, the so-called "phony war." That changed suddenly on May 10, 1940, when the Germans invaded Belgium, Luxembourg, and the Netherlands. Two days later they made an end-run around the Maginot Line and poured into France.

2
NAZIS ON OUR HEELS

Dad was on another volunteer mission in Germany as the war reached France's doorstep. He returned safely, and we all breathed easier. Father took me aside and explained that yet again he had had to change the name on his false papers.

One of his contacts was caught and father's name tortured out of him. The Germans had put a heavy price on Father's head. If caught, there was little doubt our whole family would be executed.

May passed into June and the war was not going well. Luxembourg had fallen in a day, Holland in five, and near the end of May the King of Belgium surrendered his army and was taken prisoner. The French government ordered German-born people to report to authorities to be interned in detention camps. We were exempted because of my father's work with the *Deuxième Bureau*.

"France will never lose this war," Father insisted. I reminded him that in 1870 France lost Alsace-Lorraine, his homeland, and as a result he was drafted into the German army. He again assured me of the outcome, but this time he did not seem quite as confident.

The news increasingly worried me. Many of our friends were leaving and the government had already moved south to Tours and then Bordeaux. Why were we still in Paris? One afternoon early in June a strange thing happened, which I never saw reported, yet hardened my resolve. A clear sky suddenly turned gray and millions of tiny ash particles floated to the ground. That night the radio reported that a battle had been fought near Rouen, about sixty-five miles west of Paris; German troops had used fogging devices but had failed to cross the Seine. I became frantic. The Germans were trying to encircle Paris, and with their military superiority it would only be a matter of time before they succeeded.

Early the next morning I begged my father to get us out of Paris. For the first time he wavered. There was no gasoline to be had, so I went to two large train stations to purchase tickets. The crowds were enormous—thousands of panicked people trying to get out of Paris before the Germans arrived. It seemed obvious that, with my eighty-two-year-old grandmother, fighting the crowds would be impossible.

Desperate, I bought a two-wheeled wooden pushcart and pushed it to our house in Neuilly. Father shook his head and asked why I had purchased such primitive transportation. I had no time to argue, and simply gave an ultimatum: either he would join me, along with my mother and grandmother, and we would all leave together, or I would go alone. But go I would. After more arguing he agreed.

I had a plan. Paris's subway system, the Métro, had just been extended above ground to the south into the far suburbs. I intended to get us and our pushcart on a subway car, if at all possible, and travel south as far as the line went. That is exactly what we did. The French subway agents at this anxious time were quite lenient. With my elderly grandmother along, I suppose they took pity on us. We took just two suitcases—one filled with the family silver, money, and jewelry, and the other with clothes and other personal items.

The German onslaught in the north—far worse than reported in the media—set in motion a mass exodus of an estimated six million people. As the Germans neared Paris, another two million joined the grim parade.

The first leg of our odyssey took us about twenty miles south of Paris. At the end of the subway line we walked to the nearest highway. We were shocked. As far as the eye could see there were ragged lines of people—on foot, in cars, on horse-drawn wagons; pushing baby carriages, carts, or bicycles. They were laden with luggage, boxes, bundles. We joined the throng, Dad and I taking turns pushing Grandma on the cart. Along the roadside, French farmers were selling water at exorbitant prices.

Any car that broke down and blocked the road was pushed into a field, over the owner's protests. There were frequent fights. Slowly, so slowly, the lines snaked to the horizon. As evening approached our family left the road and walked to a nearby farm. I knocked on the door and asked the farmer if we could stay the night. He agreed, for a price, allowing us to sleep on hay in the barn. Grandmother could not understand why we didn't just check into a nice hotel with good food and a hot bath.

Next morning we managed to buy bread and milk from the farmer, and were on our way. We hiked much of that day and in the afternoon arrived exhausted near a place called Dourdan. We stopped to regain our strength and were eating the bread when we heard airplanes in the distance. Suddenly their whine was punctuated by the explosion of ordnance. We pushed Mother and Grandmother under a truck. Moments later three German planes came over, dropped several bombs, and circled back to machine-gun the massed refugees.

Screams pierced the morning air. The planes roared away in a black cloud of exhaust, leaving several dead and many others injured and moaning. The road was strewn with clothes, pots and pans, and other debris. At least two victims lay in their own blood. It was a ghastly sight. I understood for the first time what war was really like. The German aim was to spread panic and impede the movement of the French army on the roads.

With the planes gone, we quickly went to the railroad station in Dourdan, on a slim hope that a train might come by. Minutes later a train of cattle cars arrived, filled with Belgian refugees. We abandoned the pushcart and threw our two suitcases into one of the cars. Those inside hoisted us aboard. There were about twenty people in the car sitting on straw, surrounded by boxes and suitcases. An overcoat in a corner covered a spot used as a toilet.

Others from the road also struggled aboard. The train departed and for the moment we rested as we put distance between us and the advancing German army. We had no idea of the train's destination but it must be heading south, and that's all we cared. In the middle of the night, as the train rattled on, scare replaced slumber. Grandmother must have suffered a small stroke. She started babbling in perfect German. Other refugees eyed us suspiciously as we hurriedly explained that we were Jews who had escaped Germany. Hostility melted, but sleep came hard.

At midmorning our train slowed to a crawl in the countryside, switched to another track, and rolled to a stop in an open field. Soon we saw our locomotive, disconnected, speeding off in the direction we had just come from. Some refugees, seemingly unconcerned, gathered wood and built fires for morning coffee. Father and I walked to a nearby village where we saw a line of flatbed trucks. It was a convoy of French soldiers, headed south with airplane engines. Dad approached the commander, explained our situation, and showed him papers. The officer told us to come back within the hour and he would try to take us with them.

We retrieved Mom and Grandma and returned to the trucks. They sat Grandmother beside a driver. There was no other room inside a cab, so Mother and Father sat outside on the bed of a truck and I perched on top of an airplane engine. Off we went southward. Dad had a bottle of wine to help cool us. He and Mom would take a swig, then hand the bottle up to me. After awhile the wine and the scorching sun made me light-headed. I started to sway, but fortunately held on. After a few hours we rolled into Tours in central France.

The town square was a cacophony of cars, trucks, bicycles, bundles, boxes, and frenzied families hustling in every direction. Everyone, it seemed, was trying to get out of Tours. Dad and I wandered around and spied a bus, black with a green roof, whose driver was sitting on the doorsteps smoking a pipe. We asked if he would take us to Bordeaux, about 200 miles away, if we could find others to share the cost. To our relief, he agreed.

We rounded up the women, found several others who wanted to go, and boarded the bus. The government had evacuated to Bordeaux, so we figured the city must be relatively safe. As we continued south, German troops were overrunning France in the north. They had invaded through Belgium on May 12 and launched a major offensive June 5. Paris was surrendered and declared open to spare it bombardment. Hitler's troops entered the city on June 14. We had escaped by a bare few days. Our objective was to reach the border in the southwest corner of France and cross into neutral Spain. How to do so remained a puzzle.

Traffic in Bordeaux was clogged in every direction with anything that could walk or roll. The city was brimming with government officials, hangers-on, refugees. We left the bus and took a taxi to the railroad station. Pandemonium. Masses of people shouting and surging helter-skelter. Train schedules no longer meant anything.

We were dead tired but the hotels were filled. After eating in a small restaurant we joined scores of others camping on the cold marble floor of the railroad station. Enemy foot soldiers apparently were not in the vicinity, but Germany's air force, the Luftwaffe, certainly was. It was a difficult night, filled with the drone of planes and staccato of anti-aircraft fire. Next morning, after coffee and croissants, Dad and I set out to find temporary lodging while we figured out what to do next. After a long search, a woman rented us a room for a few days at an exorbitant price.

That night was the scariest of my life. To force France to its knees, Germany was massively bombing Bordeaux. Soon after we went to bed sirens screamed the alarm. Then came the whistling and explosion of bombs that shook our building. Convulsions continued. We crawled under our beds in case of falling debris. Before long we heard a peculiarly loud, terrifying screech from the sky. It ended in an enormous detonation which violently rocked the building. Windows shattered, plaster fell. I thought the end had come.

But, though scared to death, we were uninjured. After a few more minutes sirens sounded the all-clear. Brushing off our beds, we climbed back in, sleeping fitfully the rest of the night.

Daylight revealed an awful sight. Buildings were missing windows, siding, and chimneys. The one right across the street from ours had disappeared altogether, with only a huge hole where it had stood. Through windowless frames we saw dazed families sweeping debris from their houses. Bordeaux had been savagely attacked.

We went back to the train station but again learned little. Railroad agents shrugged and all gave the same answer to each unanswerable question: "Monsieur, nous sommes en guerre." ("Sir, we are at war.") We ended up again in our rented room, where we finally got a decent night's sleep.

Next morning we heard a rumor of a train going to Bayonne, the French side of the Spanish border. We quickly gathered our belongings and returned to the station. Sure enough, there was the train, with a big sign on its side: "Bayonne and Bilbao [Spain]." We boarded and felt in luxury to be in comfort on a passenger train. When we arrived in Bayonne, however, everyone was ordered off the train. Though marked for Bilbao, apparently the Spanish border was closed.

We took a taxi to the local préfecture de police. The rest of us waited outside while Dad went in and inquired how we could get into Spain. Coming out, he put a finger to his lips to hush our questions. We took the cab to a cafe, where he quietly filled us in. After identifying himself as a member of the Deuxième Bureau the police told him confidentially that an armistice was to be signed that very day, June 22. A new French government acceptable to Hitler would be led by 84-year-old Philippe Pétain, a hero of World War I and former Commander-in-Chief of the French army.

Marshal Pétain had made a pact with the devil. The Germans would rule the northern and western portions of the country, including Paris, leaving Pétain to govern the mostly rural southeastern portion from Vichy. Once established at Vichy, a resort area, Petain's government instituted its own anti-Jewish measures. Jews were required to register with the police. Many lost their jobs or were imprisoned.

Pétain was urged on by Pierre Laval, a right-wing politician and admirer of Germany. Two years later, at Hitler's insistence, Laval became head of the French government. Laval ordered the police to round up Jews, sent skilled laborers to Germany in exchange for French prisoners of war, and gave the Gestapo permission to hunt down members of the French resistance in unoccupied France. (After the war Pétain and Laval were tried for treason. Laval was executed and Pétain imprisoned. France's hopes rested instead with General Charles de Gaulle, who fled to London rather than surrender, and from there led a movement called Free France.)

Father was told that Bayonne, where we stood, was to be occupied imminently by the Germans. Already the Gestapo was arranging to find those whose names appeared on their lists. The police advised us to go toward the interior of France, beyond the occupied zone. We hired a car and driver and hurriedly left. We drove a couple of hours east, into a mountainous region, and stopped for the night at a small inn. A couple hours after we were asleep, someone banged on our doors.

"You've got to go! Hurry!" they yelled. "This place is going to be occupied by the Germans, and they are on their way!" We had not gone far enough. Dressing quickly, off we sped into the night. When we reached Accous, a small Basque village, our driver left us. We found ourselves among scores of others who also had come inland from the west.

The Basque people were extremely kind. The mayor came among us and said he was trying to find accommodations for everyone. Meals were available in the town recreation hall. We were assigned a tiny house right outside the village, for a month maximum. But we had no intention of staying that long. That first night I started shivering uncontrollably and made frequent trips to the outhouse. In the morning a doctor diagnosed dysentery. Despite the liquids and pills he prescribed, I felt awful for a week.

A French soldier who had left his unit heard of my illness and brought a fresh trout he had caught. Despite my terrible aversion to fish, Mother cooked the trout and I ate it—the first solid food I had had since taking sick. A few days later I felt well enough to travel and we were on our way.

We went by bus and train to Marseille, the storied maritime city on the Mediterranean Coast. It swarmed with people from all over Europe—shoving, surging, and shouting in various languages. Like us, many were desperate to escape Europe. We were fortunate to get two rooms in a hotel, and immediately cabled my aunt in New York. The next day she cabled back, relieved we were alive. Every effort was underway to help us, she wrote.

The local refugee committee helped us find lodging within a trolley ride of downtown Marseille. Though it was a sixth-floor walkup, and thus Grandmother's prison for the moment, it suited us fine. A café was a hangout for many refugees from Paris. There one day we found our Paris neighbors, the Brombergers. We told them in strictest confidence of our plans. They were dubious. Going to America was too risky, they insisted. Their family planned to return to Paris, which they believed was peaceful.

After the fall of France, President Roosevelt—at his wife's prodding—ordered the State Department to issue some 500 visitors' visas to Europeans "of superior intellectual attainment, of indomitable spirit, experienced in vigorous support of the principles of liberal government and who are in danger of persecution or death at the hands of the autocracy."

The State Department dragged its feet, worried about possibly importing spies, and the crushing burden represented by the world's displaced persons. Eleanor Roosevelt spurred her husband with strong notes and phone calls. Finally he insisted and State issued the visas. Our lives depended on getting four of them.

We idled away the rest of July and part of August in Marseille, an absorbing city rich in culture, art, and science. France's largest commercial port, it is also the country's second largest city and its oldest—founded by Greek sailors in 600 B.C. Each night from a small radio in our apartment we secretly listened to the BBC. Doing so had been strictly forbidden by the Pétain government and had severe penalties. But we could not wait to hear the nightly pealing of Big Ben, followed by "This is London."

A colossal air battle was in progress over the English Channel and England. The brave fliers of the Royal Air Force were accounting themselves magnificently. The next day we would read quite a different version of the same battle in censored French newspapers. England, now under Winston Churchill as prime minister as well as war minister, was resisting heroically. Europe's hope—and the world's—hinged on England's victory.

My aunt in New York hired an immigration attorney and contacted an organization called the Emergency Rescue Committee (later known as the International Rescue Committee, or IRC).[1]

The organization was started seven years earlier in New York at the request of Albert Einstein, himself a refugee from Germany, as the American branch of a European-based relief agency headed by Einstein. The organization's purpose was to assist those in Hitler's path, however possible: send money to besieged families, resettle those who escape the Nazis, smuggle democratic leaders out of Europe.

In 1933 the Third Reich had denounced Einstein as a traitor and burned his books. Fortuitously, the Nobel laureate was in California when Hitler came to power. He stayed in the U.S. and accepted a position at Princeton University. There the great genius would live out his life, becoming a U.S. citizen in this same year, 1940.

We visited the Marseille office of the IRC. There we were told that we would be given four emergency visas to enter the United States, and to report to the American consulate.

We took the trolley to a Marseille suburb and spotted the consulate on a hillside. Getting Grandmother up to it presented yet another challenge. As we trudged toward the building, a large black American car stopped in a cloud of dust. A man emerged and gave the women a ride to the consulate. He was Vice Consul Hiram Bingham IV. Despite State Department disapproval, Bingham risked his career—and years later sacrificed it—to help endangered Europeans.

The consul issued us a "Certificate of Identification," a large, white piece of paper. Across the top was printed in bold letters: "The United States of America," with a seal of the U.S. from which two large red ribbons protruded. An impressive document. We were advised to obtain Spanish and Portuguese transit visas.

Elated, we took a taxi back to the cafe, telling the Brombergers of our good fortune. Visitors' visas to the United States were risky, they insisted. "What if the Americans refuse to renew them and deport you back to France?" We considered that unlikely. The Bombergers returned to Paris. Months later the Nazis shipped them to Poland. There, with so many other French Jews, they perished.

The problem of the border crossing remained. France required exit visas but we hesitated to approach the Petain government for them. Instead we were told to contact an American named Varian Fry, who represented the Emergency Rescue Committee in Marseille.

Lost to history for decades, Fry would one day be called "America's Schindler" for helping to save hundreds of refugees, including artists Marc Chagall and Max Ernst, sculptor Jacques Lipschitz, philosopher-writer Hannah Arendt, and others who would rise to world prominence.[2]

We met with Fry, a young Harvard-educated journalist, who was helpful indeed. Fry had dark hair, glasses, and a serious, scholarly demeanor. He was energetic, effective, and in constant danger during the thirteen months he assisted refugees to escape the Holocaust. Fry arrived in France in August 1940 with a list of two hundred of the most imperiled refugees taped to his leg. He was not trained for undercover work, but made up in courage what he lacked in experience.

Operating under the guise of a humanitarian mission, Fry hired artists to forge documents, bribed passport officials at consuls, and found secret routes for refugees to take into Spain. Such activities put Fry at odds with isolationist Washington as well as with Germany and Vichy France.

Fry warned us not to apply for French exit visas. Under the Hitler-Petain armistice, the Vichy government turned over any former German refugees demanded by the Gestapo. By applying we would reveal our presence and almost certainly be turned over.

Under pressure from Vichy, the U.S. refused to renew Fry's

passport. He was expelled from France in September 1941. Fry returned to the United States, unfortunately to an unhappy life. He apparently suffered from depression. Fry divorced his wife, had a stormy relationship with a second wife, and lost a series of jobs. He died in 1967.

His own country shamefully ignored Fry's heroism. A few months before he died, France awarded him the Croix de Chevalier de la Legion d'Honneur. Today thousands of men and women are honored at Yad Vashem, Israel's Holocaust Memorial, as "Righteous Among the Nations." The first American given the honor was Varian Fry.

Fry instructed us to take a train southwest to a border town near Spain and sit in a certain café. Mother was to have a newspaper under her arm. We arrived at our destination at midday and immediately went to the café. A couple hours later a man with a bushy mustache, dressed as a peasant, entered, carrying a stout walking-stick. He identified himself and sat down. Fry did not tell him our family included an old woman—an omission that rattled our new friend. A long mountainous hike was involved, he explained.

Evening came and our guide reappeared. We piled into his car and drove westward for an hour or so. Suddenly the headlights revealed a French checkpoint. Frightened, we presented our American documents. Incredibly, the guards let us pass. At a second checkpoint a guard barely glanced at the papers, put an index finger to his cap, and waved us on.

About a half-hour later our driver stopped in the foothills of the Pyrenees Mountains. He led us to a trail, pointed the way from there, and disappeared. We began hiking upward but in no time Grandmother was exhausted. I hoisted her onto my back; she protested but there was nothing else to do. We continued on the path to a small lean-to filled with straw, where we spent a cold, anxious night.

Next morning we continued our climb over the mountain and descended toward the Spanish border near Figueras. Through the trees to our right we could see the French border station. To our left the Spanish flag flew next to a small building. We approached the

Spanish enclave. The border agents seemed impressed with our papers but asked for French exit visas. We said we did not require them to cross into Spain. They disagreed. They put us in a room with bars on every window, bare except for a couple of wooden benches and a table.

Dad explained our dilemma to the senior officer. After a lengthy discussion he softened. A bribe was not mentioned directly. Rather, there was a mild disagreement over the cost of a car to take us to the train station. Finally we paid what was asked and a taxi was called. At the station we went by rail to Madrid, Spain, and on to Lisbon, Portugal. At the border the Spanish let us out without incident, and the neutral Portuguese let us in. We felt safe at last.

My father's cousin in Lisbon, Max Azancot, took us to his family home. I can still taste the delicious hard rolls and real butter they gave us for breakfast, along with real coffee. They got us rooms in a boarding house.

We were in Lisbon from September through November, recovering from the arduous trip and the tensions of recent weeks. Azancot, an attorney, arranged passage for us on a small Portuguese ship called the *Nyassa*, built to carry two hundred passengers. We got an inside cabin for four at $450 each, a huge amount at the time. The enterprising owners had placed cots on the first level of the cargo hold to accommodate hundreds more. At the end of November the *Nyassa* sailed from Lisbon with over a thousand passengers.

As soon as we hit open water I got seasick and remained so for the ten days of the crossing. The food, including rotten fruit, was awful; the stench from inadequate toilet facilities down below suffocating. We crossed the Atlantic on a fully lighted ship, when German submarines were stopping and boarding civilian ships and seizing passengers on their lists. Three days out of New York the *Nyassa* listed and china slid off the tables. The ship made a complete circle. Its automatic steering had broken down, and for the remaining days of the journey they steered it manually.

Early in the very cold morning of December 4, 1940, I stood

on deck as our overburdened ship slowly passed the Statue of Liberty. Our six-month odyssey had come to a happy end. Somehow we had been delivered, while so many others remained behind in a Europe on fire. We were exhausted and joyous. Against all odds we had even managed to bring my elderly grandmother to safety.

At last we were free.

3
STARTING OVER IN AMERICA

W e docked in Hoboken and were met by my aunt, who brought us sweaters, coats, and other warm clothing. She had made arrangements with the American Jewish Congress for us to stay at Congress House.

Located in the West Sixties of New York City, it was a series of old brownstones converted for multiple tenancy and occupied by about a dozen families waiting to find more permanent accommodations. Grandmother stayed with my aunt. A few months later her heart finally gave out. Mother and Father had serious health problems that required immediate medical care. She had heart trouble, apparently an aftermath from diphtheria as a child, and he entered Mount Sinai Hospital with ulcers.

Such cares soon melted away. We were free to begin a new life in a wonderful new country. We were extremely blessed to have escaped Hitler and the Holocaust. To our knowledge, all of our immediate and more distant relatives were eventually exterminated. Our joy at being safe was tinged with sadness for them and other millions trapped across the Atlantic.

A huge majority of desperate supplicants at America's door were not as fortunate as we were. The German steamer *St. Louis*, out of Hamburg, for example, in 1939 carried over nine hundred German-Jewish refugees to Cuba and then Florida, where the U.S. Coast Guard refused to allow them to enter American waters. The ship was forced to return to Europe, to the Nazis' delight, and its passengers suffered the same fate as other Jews.

After a few weeks at Congress House we moved to an apartment in a section of Manhattan full of German refugees, ironically called the Fourth Reich. It was in Washington Heights, at 168th Street and Broadway, opposite Columbia-Presbyterian Hospital.

Now broke, we had two rooms and shared the rest of the apartment with a cattle dealer and his wife who also escaped Europe. A squat, uncouth man with a grating German dialect, he often screamed at his wife, who screamed back. After a few months of unhappy cohabitation, we moved to an efficiency on West Ninety-Third Street. My parents slept on a fold-out bed; I slept on a cot in the tiny kitchen.

Through a contact of my father's I landed a job in a local shoe factory, Recordia, which employed only German refugees. Everyone earned the same thirty-five cents an hour, fourteen dollars a week, whatever their job. Not a lot, but five cents bought a carton of milk or a subway ride. A ham sandwich cost twenty-five cents.

After months of lugging around cardboard boxes filled with shoes, I was taught to make sandals. I'm not adept at manual labor, however, and one day inserted my thumb between the leather upper and the sole, riveting the three together. I was sent to a nearby hospital where the rivet was removed and my finger patched up.

With both parents in poor health, I was our family's sole source of income. The money at the shoe factory was not enough to support us, so I also took a part-time job as an usher at the Apollo Theater on Forty-Second Street, then part of the Brandt chain of movie theaters. I worked Saturdays and Sundays, two full nine-hour shifts, for about six dollars a week.

The Apollo in those days showed mostly French or Russian movies with subtitles that helped me learn English. The theater assisted charities, often the USO. We were given cardboard coffee containers with a slit in the top to pass along the rows. Backstage on my first charity drive I was asked by other ushers: "How much did *you* make?"

"What do you mean?" I answered.

"How much did *you* make?" they repeated.

"I didn't make anything," I stammered, puzzled.

Suddenly two of the larger ushers grabbed and turned me upside down, and proceeded to shake me. "Baruch is holding out on us!" they insisted. It seems that during the travels of the coffee container, a good part of its contents routinely went into the ushers' pockets. The amount left for charity was quite meager. When no coins tumbled from my pockets, they let me down.

The following year, 1942, I went to work at Cosmos Footwear in Brooklyn. The factory was unionized and had about three hundred workers, virtually all Italian-Americans except me. I felt quite alone, though the owner, a Mr. Klauber, was kind and occasionally came over and said a few encouraging words.

Over time barriers melted and I felt accepted. My outlook brightened further when I found my old friend Jack Aufricht from Paris, who also had escaped and was living on the Upper West Side. Jack and I got together quite often, but now we had adult responsibilities in a harder world, and the carefree excitement we felt in Paris was gone forever.

As Dad's health improved he got a job with the War Department in New York. Mother went to work in a dress factory, despite continued heart problems. Our visitor's visas issued by the American consul in Marseille were routinely renewed, but we could not apply for citizenship without formal immigration status. The State Department arranged for us to be pre-screened and instructed us to take a trip to Montreal, obtain immigration visas, and return to the United States. We did so, and were given permanent status.

Although preoccupied with keeping our family financially afloat, I was not too busy to keep an eye out for attractive girls. One who intrigued me lived in our apartment building. She was very pretty—slender, about five-foot-seven, with dark blonde hair gathered at the sides or worn in a ponytail, a prominent but not unattractive nose, and an air of confidence that seemed to say "Watch me—I'm going places!" She often wore high-heels, accenting her long, shapely legs.

Soon after moving into our tiny apartment, I was walking outside it one day with Mom and Dad. A distinguished-looking man and this girl were coming our way. The three adults broke into shouts of recognition and he introduced his daughter to us.

They were also Jewish refugees from Germany—the father, Berthold Bachrach, daughter Elizabeth, and mother Lucy, somewhere else at that moment. Years earlier my father had done some legal work for the Bachrachs in Frankfurt, where Berthold was a medical doctor. By coincidence, the woman who had cleaned his office there was Regina, my former nanny, who had told the Bachrachs all about the Baruchs. Dr. Bachrach had been studying for his American medical board exams in dermatology.

The Bachrachs had immigrated to the United States in 1938, after Dr. Bachrach had been imprisoned for several months at Dachau, the first regular Natzi concentration camp. Built in 1933 near Munich, Dachau in the early years was a camp for political prisoners, including Jehovah's Witnesses, Roma (Gypsies), homosexuals, and repeat criminals.

Dr. Bachrach was fortunate. Relatively few Jews were interned at Dachau in the early years, unless they belonged to one of the targeted groups. His family had applied for visas to both the U.S. and Britain. When the British visa came through first, the Nazis allowed him, Lucy, and Elizabeth to go to London—without money or valuables, of course. Later, when their U.S. visas were issued, they proceeded on to New York.

Elizabeth—nicknamed Lilo (pronounced Leeloe)—and I started dating. We had a lot in common. Both of our families had narrowly escaped the Holocaust. More important, we both belonged to dysfunctional families. My parents had a bad marriage and so did hers. In Lilo's case, however, the difficult parent was her mother. Lucy was about twenty years younger than Berthold, and seemed immature and erratic.

Lilo was closer to her father. Both were highly intelligent. Lilo, sixteen, attended George Washington High School, where she had a full load of science classes. She had already read most of her father's medical textbooks and planned to follow him into medicine, a prospect that thrilled her parents.

We had little money to date, but Lilo was happy with inexpensive entertainment. She devoured nonfiction and the classics. We listened to classical music on the radio, walked to Central Park Zoo, and occasionally went to concerts at the old Lewisohn Stadium, no longer in existence, where twenty-five cents bought us concrete seats. We had no car or money for taxies or eating out. When our destination was far we took the subway. Both of us loved movies.

A favorite date was to Radio City Music Hall, which gave us a lot for our money: a stage show with the famed Rockettes, an orchestra that rose on a platform from below to stage level, as well as recitals on its world-famous organ, and a movie.

Like most of the country, we were taken by "Mrs. Miniver," with Greer Garson in her Oscar-winning portrayal of British determination against Nazi aggression. Her husband, played by Walter Pidgeon, takes a small boat to the beaches of Dunkirk, where the British narrowly escaped mass slaughter or surrender; a daughter-in-law dies in an air raid; a son joins the Royal Air Force.

The 1942 MGM masterpiece of wartime propaganda was so powerful that President Franklin Roosevelt had the speech in the final scene printed and air-dropped over Europe. British Prime Minister Winston Churchill called "Mrs. Miniver" "more powerful to the war effort than the combined work of six military divisions."

From Ninety-Third Street our family moved to a second-floor walk-up on Ninety-Second, where at last I had my own bedroom. I was restless at the Cosmos shoe factory and looked around. I wanted to serve my adopted country, and was examined several times by armed forces personnel. However, they turned me down for medical reasons. As a child I had had a mastoid operation, cutting back the bone—there were no antibiotics in those days—leaving me with a perforated left eardrum. I was classified unfit for military duty.

My friend Jack Aufricht had taken a course to become a recording engineer, and I wanted to also. Mass communication had been a lifelong interest. As a boy I wrote a "newspaper"—a typed sheet distributed to friends—and often was glued to the radio.

I could not afford the engineering course, but when Jack landed a job at a recording studio he lent me his books and I devoured them. I quit my job at Cosmos shoes and hit the street, determined to become a recording engineer. Jobs were scarce. I made the rounds for weeks with no luck, until one day a company on Fifty-Seventh Street offered me a job as a fill-in recording engineer.

As soon as I took the job, Lilo and I secretly got married, not telling our parents. We had dated for a year and were deeply in love. I was nineteen, she was seventeen.

When they found out, both sets of parents protested vigorously. My parents, steeped in old-world thinking, felt I had married beneath our station in life. Lilo's parents saw the end of their ambitions for her. Bitterly they accused me of abducting their child. By then Lilo had graduated from high school and taken several pre-med courses at New York University. When we married she dropped out of college.

Her parents' unyielding objections broke Lilo's heart and foreshadowed the depression that would visit her periodically for months at a time from then on.

Rudolph Steiner owned the recording studio. His partner had previously managed a large recording company in Paris named Polydor. I worked many weekends, and also did part-time recording for orchestra leader Raymond Scott, an electronic genius but quite eccentric. He had befriended Dorothy Collins, a singer on the radio show "Your Hit Parade." Scott coached her hour upon hour at his recording studio on Sixth Avenue, until she would be practically in tears from weariness and frustration.

In 1943 I landed a job at Empire Broadcasting, a large recording operation run by three partners who employed eight recording engineers. I was a mixer, taking sounds from different sources and combining them to make a final recording. Some sessions were with musicians unfamiliar to me who would become household names: Dizzy Gillespie, Charlie Shavers, Della Reese, Benny Goodman, and others.

Tape was unknown in those days, so recordings were put on acetate, with one or two masters recorded on sixteen-inch records at 33 1/3 rpm. Dubbing from the original was quite a challenge. The business was built primarily on revenues from record companies, advertising agencies, and radio spots. They underpaid us considerably, so when several of us were approached by Local 1212 of the International Brotherhood of Electrical Workers union, we signed promissory cards to join.

Meantime Jack had progressed to the National Broadcasting Corporation, where he became a producer for NBC Radio International. In those days NBC and CBS had radio broadcast outlets in both short- and medium-wave in Central and South America. They used the stations to broadcast radio documentaries, news, and cultural programs. NBC needed a multi-lingual producer for its Latin America broadcasts and Jack got the job.

One of his assignments was to produce the NBC Symphony concerts for Latin American consumption. CBS had been broadcasting the New York Philharmonic concerts on Sunday afternoon for many years. RCA, to burnish its own reputation, attracted world-renowned maestro Arturo Toscanini to New York, and hired an entire orchestra for him—the NBC Symphony.

Toscanini was a schizophrenic music-maker, beloved as well as feared by orchestra members. One time he became so exasperated with the orchestra's performance that he took out his gold watch and flung it to the floor, smashing it to pieces. Near retirement years later, the musicians chipped in and presented him a new gold watch.

Jack knew I loved music and invited me to a Toscanini rehearsal. The NBC International control room was adjacent to NBC's standard control room in Studio 8H at Rockefeller Center. I was told it was built primarily for Toscanini and the NBC Symphony. Toscanini determinedly strode in—a short, thin man with a shock of white hair. He mounted the podium and began to conduct, periodically stopping the musicians to comment.

At one point he asked them to continue playing a Richard Wagner piece as he went into a control room. Toscanini listened awhile, shook his head, and grabbed the talk-back microphone connected to the studio. "Stop-a! Stop-a!" he yelled in thick Italian. The orchestra stopped promptly.

Toscanini grabbed the sleeve of the mixing engineer, who towered over him, dragged the man through the control room into the studio, and called, "Giv-a me a chair." A chair materialized, he pushed the engineer into it, then mounted the podium and began to conduct the same piece. After awhile he stopped the orchestra and turned to the engineer. "You see, that's-a the way it ought to sound."

Back at my own job, one day a young man came in to record songs, coached by his manager, a nice gentleman with a crippled arm. The singer, in my judgment, was not very good. He recorded "Tonight We Love," claiming part authorship. I replied with a quip which probably could have cost my job: "I thought Tchaikovsky wrote it." The song was based on Tchaikovsky's First Piano Concerto. The singer was Dean Martin, who later dismissed the manager and no longer needed us either. The rest is music history.

In May 1944 Lilo and I were on Riverside Drive watching the Memorial Day parade. I playfully mentioned she had put on a little weight.

"Yes, Ralph, we're going to have a baby."

Startled, I asked: "How long have you known?"

"About six months."

She had shown no outward signs, and kept it an absolute secret even from me. Less than two weeks later, on June 5, surprise turned to shock when Lilo was rushed to Leroy Sanitarium and gave birth to a baby girl, seven weeks premature.

Lilo's parents were dismayed—even more so when they learned there were no apartments to be had in wartime New York, at any price, and the only option was for us to move in with them. They had already taken in Dr. Bachrach's sister. By then he had his medical license and was practicing out of their ground-floor apartment at 910 West End Avenue. The living room was also the waiting room.

Our baby, Eve, was not quite three pounds at birth. For weeks she remained in the hospital, to which we regularly delivered breast milk in iced containers from our apartment on the far west side of the city. Finally we took Eve home to the Bachrachs, where she slept in our room.

The arrangement was tough on everyone. We had to be quiet when a patient came to the office, but maintaining silence with a baby down the hall was very difficult.

Eve once developed a terrible cold, including a high fever and seizures. We rigged up a humidifier by putting a burner and pan of water on the floor of our cramped room. Getting out of bed one morning, groggy from a bad night's sleep, I kicked over the steaming water, severely burning my feet. I got very little sympathy from my father-in-law the doctor.

Despite the awkward living arrangements, Lilo at first seemed to adjust quite well to motherhood. Several weeks after bringing our baby home, however, I returned from work to find her slumped on the living room couch, crying. When she couldn't articulate why, I rushed into our bedroom. There, to my relief, was Eve, sleeping peacefully.

I assumed Lilo's strange behavior would soon pass and be forgotten. But it went on, with occasional interludes, for five or six months. My beautiful wife, in reality so intelligent and capable, seemed overwhelmed by a shadow she couldn't explain. Her doctor-father, a dermatologist, also was baffled. Lilo was happier when I was with her, but, of course, I was at work on weekdays.

When the war ended the following year, we found our first apartment as a little family. It was on Morningside Drive near Columbia University, on the third floor overlooking a park. The neighborhood was spotty, however, and at night I hesitated to cross the park to reach the subway.

Lilo did not work outside our home, and I was not making enough to cover our needs. To supplement my income we took in piece work—such as pasting feathers on ribbon for a manufacturer, who paid us ten cents an hour. We also had a succession of boarders. The first one was from South Africa—a terrible slob. When he left after about six months, we found banana peels and moldy bits of food behind his bed. By being frugal we made ends meet.

After a few years on Morningside Drive we moved to a two-bedroom apartment on West Eighty-Second. The neighborhood was a little better, but our ground-floor apartment was dark. Lilo became pregnant again. She was uncommonly happy during this term. We were in our own place, my job was going well, baby Eve was delightful and growing fast, and Lilo generally had made peace with her parents. Life was good, and I was confident that whatever had ailed Lilo after Eve was born, no longer was a concern. But I was wrong.

On June 5, 1948—exactly four years after Eve's birth—Lilo was due to deliver our second child. That Saturday morning the Salvation Army Band—forty to fifty musicians—came to record in our suddenly cramped studio. It was a logistical challenge and my technical knowledge was about zero, but I hung a microphone from the ceiling and successfully recorded the band.

While alone at the audio controls I was informed that Lilo was about to give birth. I faced a lose/lose choice: Leave the studio, the band would sue the company, and I would lose my job. Stay and my family might be equally upset. I chose to save my job, and Lilo forgave me. She gave birth to our second beautiful daughter, Renee.

Once again Lilo seemed to relish being a new mother. But after about a month her mood again spiraled downward. She became tired most of the time, had a hard time eating, and no longer seemed able to find respite in favorite activities such as listening to music or burrowing into a good book. She also had difficulty making routine decisions. When not preoccupied with our two daughters, Lilo would lounge on the couch or bed, looking dejected or sobbing for no apparent reason.

Research told me it was common for women to feel blue for a few hours or days after giving birth. Lilo's depression, however, did not set in immediately after birth and, once arrived, did not depart for many months. I found little in medical literature to help us understand what was happening or what to do about it. Anti-depressant medications were not yet available. In the coming decades a lot of studies focused on what would be called postpartum depression, doubtless what Lilo suffered.

In retrospect I could identify a number of likely causes of Lilo's PPD. Her self-esteem suffered when she dropped out of college—magnified by her parents' refusal to accept her life path as a mother and homemaker. Lilo was self-conscious over her German-accented English.

Languages came easy to me, and I spoke English almost without an accent—which she envied.

Lilo's mother Lucy was not too stable, and a family history of psychiatric illness can be a major factor in PPD. Life stress in general can be a cause, and as a young couple our finances were tight and sometimes worrisome. Marital stress can also be a cause. While Lilo and I usually got along well—making most major decisions together—our private relationship was not as warm and affectionate as I would have liked. At any rate, for whatever reasons, Lilo ached from postpartum depression, and I ached for her.

Jan August, a gifted instrumentalist who played the piano as one did the xylophone—hitting the notes at machine-gun-like speed—came into the recording studio flanked by a trio of guitar, bass, and drums, for a little-known company, Diamond Records. With August's wife sitting beside him on the piano bench for encouragement, we recorded two sides, "Babalou" and "Miserlou." The session started at 6 p.m. and went until 4 a.m., when everybody was exhausted. Days later we mixed parts of one take with parts of another, then dubbed the ending from yet another take. Finally the deed was done. The record became a big hit.

I recorded commercials for General Foods, voiced by Dan Seymour. Years later Seymour became CEO of one of the world's largest advertising agencies, J. Walter Thompson. I also recorded world-famous violinist Ruggiero Ricci. His playing was superb and, to me, inspiring. Ricci had deep scars on the left side of his neck from the constant pressure of the violin.

Another intriguing assignment was with a man named Allen Funt. He wanted to secretly sound-record purchases of women's underwear by soldiers in a department store. Someone on his payroll impersonated the salesperson. It would have been cumbersome to transport recording equipment, so Funt experimented with a 35 mm film loop on which the voices were barely audible. We spent day after day at the department store, but the tests were only moderately successful.

Then sound recording on tape was invented, and soon afterward the ABC Radio Network announced Allen Funt's *Candid Microphone*. Later, Funt's *Candid Camera* spun off the radio program, airing on and off from 1948 to 1990, when his son carried it on. Allen Funt was a pioneer who created what became an entire programming genre, symbolized by the phrase "Smile! You're on Candid Camera."

Perhaps inspired by such creativity, Jack Aufricht and I set out to produce a radio soap opera. It was right after the end of World War II and we had a script written and produced, a half-hour pilot called "Going Home." A soldier returns from the war to find his family life in turmoil—a typical soap. The actors and organist agreed to do it on spec, and one night we recorded. The end result was actually quite good, and we submitted it to advertising agencies. None picked it up.

A technical journal asked me to write some human-interest articles. Our chief engineer agreed I could freelance. The first interview I sought was with someone rumored to have developed a new kind of record. He was the brilliant Peter Goldmark, CBS's resident inventor. I went out to the CBS labs in Stamford, Connecticut, and interviewed Goldmark at length about his project: a new record with ultra-fine grooves which could record forty minutes or more on each side, with extremely good fidelity. It was the prototype of the long playing (LP) record. My article was published and some readers wrote complimentary letters to the magazine.

The article helped set the stage for a fascinating exchange down the road between two industry giants: Frank Stanton, president of the Columbia Broadcasting System, and General David Sarnoff, head of arch rival Radio Corporation of America (RCA) and its network, NBC. Years later Stanton filled me in on what happened after Goldmark's LP was perfected.

CBS and RCA were fierce competitors. CBS eventually got the upper hand with programming and talent—much of it lured away from NBC—but RCA usually led in technology. A notable exception was the next generation of longer playing records. RCA was working hard on the small 45 r.p.m., even though it could only hold a few minutes' more music than the old shellac, breakable 78 r.p.m.

When the Goldmark 33 1/3 r.p.m. was ready for roll out, Stanton invited Sarnoff over to CBS for a private luncheon, hoping to head off a rivalry between RCA's 45 and CBS's LP. Stanton typically left nothing to chance. He stocked up on the General's favorite cigars and ordered the best RCA speakers and 33 1/3 player (these were available because all large sixteen-inch records for transcription purposes were recorded on 33 1/3). The equipment was set up in a comfortable room adjoining Stanton's private dining room. All through the meal Sarnoff tried in vain to learn why Stanton had asked him over. The meal ended with its purpose still a mystery.

Stanton asked the General to step into the next room for a cigar and more chat. Sarnoff, usually no-nonsense, followed, somewhat reluctantly. He plopped down in an easy chair obviously hoping to get to the point of the luncheon. Lovely music played in the background. They exchanged a few more pointless pleasantries, then Sarnoff asked what the music was.

"Oh, I don't know," said Stanton, "but we have at least forty-five minutes to find out." Suddenly realizing he was listening to a new LP record, Sarnoff nearly swallowed his cigar, Stanton told me. Stanton urged Sarnoff to compromise and adopt the 33 1/3 system as the standard for future records. Sarnoff refused and said RCA would go its own way.

New record players had to adopt to both speeds. A spindle in the center was manufactured to accommodated RCA's smaller 45 record, then was removed to play CBS's 33 1/3 LP, which ultimately became the industry standard.

One of Empire Broadcasting's clients was the U. S. Navy. Since I was not yet an American citizen I was asked not to work during the hours when the Navy came in to record flying instructions for pilots in its new fighter planes. Instead I took the night shift. Most afternoons when I arrived for work, there sat the sixteen-inch records the Navy had made. So much for national security.

One night on this shift in 1947 I received a call from an announcer at WMCA, a New York radio station, asking me to record his program from midnight to 1 a.m.

"I'm sorry," I told him, "but we close at midnight."

"Please, please," he persisted, "I have no other way of doing this, it is ten o'clock already and I cannot line up another studio to record this." I gave in but explained "I must make out a worksheet, and I'm sure the company will charge you a substantial sum for overtime."

"No problem. Just record it, and I'll pay whatever the costs may be."

I recorded the program, made out a worksheet, and in big letters at the top wrote "NOTE OVERTIME, 12 TO 1 A.M. BILL AC-CORDINGLY." He came in, paid the bill, and left me an envelope with a ten-dollar tip.

A few days later the owner summoned me to his office and accused me of being bribed to do that work and of writing outside articles without the company's consent. (Obviously they also resented my activities on behalf of the International Brotherhood of Electrical Workers.) I explained that the man left me a tip simply because he was grateful I stayed late to do the recording. As for the occasional articles, the chief engineer had given me permission.

"Ralph, we want you to resign," said the owner.

"I will not resign. I have no reason to resign. I was not bribed." With that I went home. Next morning I received a registered letter firing me. Immediately I went to see the union. Charles Kalame, business manager of Local 1212, just shrugged his shoulders: "You know, Ralph, this is a very small local. Empire Broadcasting has only eight engineers and I really don't want to create a big problem." I was stunned and insisted that I appear before the union board, where the result was the same.

Determined not to take it lying down, I attended the next open membership meeting, held at the Hotel Diplomat. It was quickly apparent that the outcome had been pre-arranged. After routine business the floor was opened for members. I stood and began to state my case. Someone in the back of the room yelled "Shut up! Sit down!" That refrain echoed all over the ballroom, drowning my complaint. It was no use and I left.

A few weeks later I received a withdrawal card from the union which entitled me to take any open job under IBEW control. I wrote back: "Your complete lack of support in my unjust dismissal from Empire Broadcasting has certainly shown your lack of concern for your union members. It will be a dark, cold day in July before I will again take a position controlled by your union." No one replied. In later years I was able to give Mr. Kalame and his union local a small taste of their own medicine.

As I languished as a recording engineer, one day I saw an ad for the American Association of Advertising Agencies about an aptitude test to be given at the old Roosevelt Hotel. It was quite expensive but I felt it would help determine where my abilities could best be used. The all-day test was demanding. Two weeks later I received the results. Every person reviewing my papers felt that I had little talent on the creative side but great potential as a salesman. That was the final impetus to change directions.

I decided to branch out and get into radio more directly. SESAC, a music-licensing organization similar to ASCAP and BMI, had an opening for a field representative and general executive. I applied and was hired. Unlike the other licensing organizations, SESAC (the Society of European Stage Authors and Composers) was privately held and tightly controlled by a husband-and-wife team, Paul and Ruth Heinecke. Licensing gave composers additional royalties, but many stations simply refused to pay for music they could play for free, with few or no consequences.

The Heineckes had begun by using a repertory of primarily European composers to license radio stations. Their contract gave radio stations the right to use any music of composers and arrangers controlled by SESAC. The agency also issued a transcription library of music which was sold individually to radio stations all over the country.

I sold the transcription library quite successfully, and soon became troubleshooter for radio stations from which the field staff was unable to obtain music licenses. Working out of New York City put me at a disadvantage, however, since SESAC paid me the same flat expenses per week as the field men, even though I had to travel long distances in my old car. Otherwise I loved the job and, besides, I had a wife and two children to support.

While on the road constantly for SESAC, my mother's heart condition grew progressively worse. Medical insurance was virtually unknown then, and my father felt he could not afford standard care for her. Out of desperation he turned to refugee doctors. They had not yet been licensed as physicians in the United States but claimed they knew how to treat Mother.

In August 1949, as I visited a potential radio licensee in Springfield, Massachusetts, I received a call from Lilo, who delivered the news I had long dreaded. Mother had just passed away, at the young age of forty-nine. I drove home in tears. We started to include my widowed father in our family circle, having him over for meals and special occasions.

One day I found myself negotiating with Walter Benoit, head of Westinghouse Broadcasting, headquartered in Washington, D.C. SESAC had been unable to conclude a contract with Westinghouse. Still in my mid-twenties, I was sent in to negotiate with Benoit, a dignified, white-haired gentleman in his sixties. Benoit and I bargained, sometimes heatedly, throughout the morning. He then looked at his watch. "I think we should break for lunch."

"Fine, Mr. Benoit, when would you like me to return for the rest of our discussion?"

"No, no, you seem like a nice young man. I will take you to lunch. Because we disagree on business does not mean that we cannot eat together." And so we did. After lunch we resumed our intense discussion and a few days later the contract was signed. It was a personal triumph and was well received at headquarters.

SESAC asked me to visit a radio station in Culpepper, Virginia. I went by rail to Culpepper, took my suitcase off the train, and stood there in shock. At the side of the station were two signs: "Restrooms— White," and "Restrooms—Colored." They evoked troubling memories of Europe under Hitler. I checked into a small hotel. My pants were wrinkled and so I took them to a cleaner.

"I would like to have these pants pressed, please," I said.

"It'll take a week," the middle-aged woman replied, barely looking up.

"I'm sorry, I don't have a week. I just want them pressed."

"We don't press Yankee pants in less than a week," she said coldly. "You'll have to take them elsewhere."

That was my introduction to the segregated South.

Lilo, the two girls, and I were settled in our apartment on West Eighty-Second Street—a fairly dismal place. My old 1941 Oldsmobile had broken down for good, and without it we could not get away from the city on weekends. I urgently needed a car for my job as well, and asked my father-in-law if he would help us buy one. He agreed, with Lilo's aunt also contributing. I supplied the rest of the money and soon we were the proud owners of a brand-new, blue 1949 Chevrolet. No frills, but we were thrilled. We celebrated by driving to Florida for a warm year-end holiday vacation.

My SESAC years left indelible memories. Clair McCullough, general manager of WGAL-TV in Lancaster, Pennsylvania, a respected figure in the industry, despised SESAC and politely asked me to leave his office, but also fixed a parking ticket for me. In Fall River, Massachusetts, a radio station manager threatened to throw me down the stairs.

I represented SESAC at the 1949 National Association of Broadcasters (NAB) convention in Chicago, again on a flat expense account. I drove about nine hundred miles to Chicago, attended the convention, and one night got in a poker game with some industry leaders, including the president of Storer Broadcasting and the manager of its radio station in Toledo. That night I lost six months' salary at the poker table. I was sick, and vowed never to gamble again.

On the last day in Chicago I received a note from SESAC, asking me to go to Indiana. I arrived there and negotiated with a radio station, then was redirected to two or three other places, all on my limited expense account. I finally got back to New York, knowing this could not continue.

I called Ruth Heinecke, one of the owners, who asked me to come and talk with her at their country home in Pine Hill, New York.

After I explained the situation she said, "Ralph, I think the best thing is for you to resign." Despite bleak personal finances, I answered, "Very well, what date would you like me to put on my resignation?" My firm reply caught her off-guard, and she asked me to explain the problem again. Nothing was resolved except my determination to leave SESAC.

In January 1950 I walked past an appliance store on Broadway. Several dozen people pressed against a window, watching a small black and white moving picture in a box.[1] It was a wrestling match, made more visible by a piece of magnifying glass in front of the screen. Hours later I passed back by the same store. A small group still stared inside—at a test pattern.

The fascination I felt when first seeing television at the Paris world's fair a dozen years earlier came flooding back. This time I resolved to seriously investigate this amazing invention, which transmitted pictures as well as sound, and had the power to mesmerize people.

4
EARLY TELEVISION

My awakening to television as a possible career scarcely could have been better timed. Television the invention had developed over decades, but television the industry was an infant.

The name *television* comes from the Greek word *tele,* meaning far, and the Latin *videre,* to see. Thus television means to see far. Pictures and sounds are sent on signals called electromagnetic waves that a receiving set changes back into pictures and sounds.

Two prolific geniuses in the United States were the principal inventors of electronic television. Utah-born farm boy Philo T. Farnsworth in 1922 developed an electronic scanning system, and a year later Russian emigre Vladimir Zworykin (see Introduction), working for RCA, invented the "iconoscope" and "kinescope"—cathode ray tubes used respectively for sending and displaying television signals. Farnsworth later won a patent for electronic television that, in an extremely rare instance, brought mighty RCA, hat in hand, to his doorstep.

Another brilliant inventor, Allen B. DuMont of Montclair, New Jersey, simplified and improved cathode ray tubes. Until his discoveries in the 1930s, expensive tubes that burned out after twenty-five hours or so were imported from Germany. DuMont's tubes lasted a thousand hours and helped make television economically feasible. Two other men—entrepreneurial wizards David Sarnoff of RCA and William S. Paley, founder of CBS—guided television into the most powerful communications tool the world had seen. DuMont and Paley both figured importantly in my future.

In 1923 Sarnoff wrote a visionary memorandum to his RCA board of directors describing what he called "seeing by radio." Wrote Sarnoff: "I believe that television...will come to pass in due course...we shall be able actually to see as well as hear in New York, within an hour or so, the event taking place in London, Buenos Aires, or Tokyo."[1] A few years later he told *The Saturday Evening Post* that, among the coming benefits, "A scientist can demonstrate his latest discoveries to those of his profession even though they be scattered all over the world."

RCA teamed with Westinghouse and General Electric to form the first radio network, the National Broadcasting Company (NBC), in 1926. A year later the British Broadcasting Corporation (BBC) appeared, followed in 1928 by the Columbia Broadcasting System under William Paley. CBS dipped its toe into experimental television broadcasting, while NBC plunged in, spending $10 million on research, then launching America's first regular telecasts at the New York World's Fair in 1939.

NBC's programs were largely for show, however. "In the early days of television, in New York," wrote Burke Crotty, one of NBC's first producers, "there weren't more than 120 [sets] in all the city, and the majority of those were in one of two places—RCA executives' homes or bars." RCA's first set, the TRK 660, was over four feet high. The picture was viewed by lifting a lid. Inside was a mirror that reflected the image, coming from a large kinescope picture tube.

Inhibiting while trying to enable the U.S. industry was the Federal Communications Commission (FCC), which initially prohibited sponsored television programs. Charles Jenkins, an inventor, in 1930 broadcast the first television commercial—and was promptly fined by the Federal Radio Commission, predecessor of the FCC. In 1939 the agency reversed itself—a routine occurrence—accepted the inevitable, and voted to authorize commercial television.

As Washington bureaucrats fretted over how to control the would-be giant, television enterprises sprouted abroad. Canada's first television station, VE9EC, started broadcasting in Montreal in 1931.

Three years later Germany began filmed television service three days a week, and France started broadcasting from the Eiffel Tower. Television was still largely a novelty, however, with only about two thousand sets in use around the world by 1936.

On September 1, 1939, several thousand Brits were watching Disney's Mickey Mouse on their crude sets. As German troops stormed into Poland, igniting World War II, the BBC abruptly stopped the broadcast mid-cartoon. When peace returned in 1945, the BBC resumed the cartoon at that same point. TV broadcasts in the U.S. mostly lapsed after the nation's entry into the war in 1941 until its end in 1945. Technical developments also were largely suspended, as nations devoted their scientific and engineering prowess to the worldwide struggle.

With the end of war, pent-up consumer demand exploded, especially in the United States. In 1945 there were probably fewer than 10,000 television sets in American homes and businesses. Although exact estimates vary, the numbers increased exponentially: about 44,000 in 1947, 350,000 in 1948, 7,000,000 in 1950.

Television was well on its way to becoming the most influential medium of the twentieth century. It would transform everything from business practices to political campaigning to social life to the way furniture was arranged in huts and homes across the globe.

Commercial interests followed suit. With a coaxial cable interconnecting New York, Philadelphia, and Washington, D.C., the number of television advertisers on CBS alone increased six-fold in a year, from about thirty in 1946 to more than one hundred eighty in 1947. Its network programming climbed from ten hours a week in 1946 to thirty-eight hours in 1948. There were so few stations on the air that, to meet sponsor demand for programming, most stations affiliated with more than one network. The number of television sets manufactured in the U.S. in 1948 increased five-fold over the previous year.

NBC, CBS, and ABC had a head start on DuMont. All three had radio networks, many of whose member stations were eager to catch the television wave sweeping the country. NBC, backed by its wealthy parent RCA, launched its television network in 1940, the only one in the U.S. before it entered the war. The ABC and DuMont television networks followed in the mid-'40s, and CBS brought up the rear in 1948.

CBS had been preoccupied for years developing a color television system, but under the hard-charging Bill Paley CBS soon reached network parity with NBC. Both had twenty-five to thirty TV affiliates by the end of 1948, and another fifty indicated they would join CBS.

But a funny thing happened on the way to the bank. On September 30, 1948, the Federal Communications Commission announced a temporary freeze on the granting of television station licenses. The freeze was to last until the FCC decided on a plan to allocate frequencies in a way to avoid broadcasts from one market interfering with those in another. The action followed hearings earlier that year on frequency allocation and other television issues.

When the freeze was ordered, 37 television stations were on the air, 303 station licenses were pending, and construction permits were in process for an additional 86 stations.

The FCC estimated its freeze on TV licenses would last a couple of months at most. In fact, it lasted four long years—and helped rearrange the nation's television landscape. "In its absolute authority over a great natural monopoly, and in the immense impact of its decisions on the national economy," wrote one observer a year after the freeze began, "the FCC is comparable in importance only to the Atomic Energy Commission."[2]

The commission is an independent government agency which is to regulate interstate and foreign communications in the public interest. It was established in 1934, replacing the former Federal Radio Commission. The FCC is presently directed by five members appointed by the President and confirmed by the Senate for five-year terms. Only three commissioners may be members of the same political party. The agency has a long history of vacillation on key issues of critical importance to the public and communication industries. Many of its members have come from—and later returned to—the ranks of the industries they are pledged to regulate.

"In youth they are vigorous, aggressive, evangelistic, and even intolerant," wrote economist John Kenneth Galbraith of regulatory agencies. "Later they mellow, and in old age—after a matter of 10 or 15

years—they become, with some exceptions, either an arm of the industry they are regulating, or senile."[3]

FCC commissioners sometimes are accused of conflicts of interest. Their greatest impacts for good or ill, however, have stemmed
not from personal conflicts but from allowing the clear conflicts of other
powerful individuals and organizations to weigh decisively in defining
the public's best interest.

The long struggle between entrenched broadcast television and
then-upstart cable television, as I personally lived and witnessed it at
close range, is a classic example of how the FCC sometimes serves one
industry to the clear detriment of another, with citizen interest counting
for little.

Occasionally commissioner conflicts of interest have proved to
be more than suspicions. In 1957 the U.S. House Committee on Legis-
lative Oversight appointed a New York law professor named Bernard
Schwartz to investigate the FCC and other federal agencies for possible
improprieties. Schwartz learned that FCC Commissioner Richard A.
Mack, appointed by President Dwight Eisenhower three years earlier,
had secretly been paid by an influential Miami businessman for Mack's
support of an applicant for Miami's Channel Ten. Facing impeachment,
Mack resigned early in 1958 and was later indicted by a federal grand
jury.

Commissioner John C. Doerfer, a protege of Senator Joseph
McCarthy and also from Wisconsin, was a favorite of broadcasters after recommending that the FCC make broadcast licenses permanent.
(In theory a license is to be granted or renewed only if a broadcaster
operates in the public interest. In reality the public interest has never
been defined clearly enough to grade a broadcaster on compliance. The
upshot is that it is virtually unheard of for a license not to be renewed.)
Pressured by broadcasters, President Eisenhower in July 1957 elevated
Doerfer from FCC commissioner to chairman.

Professor Schwartz dug under Doerfer and again uncovered
highly questionable behavior. Doerfer and his wife in earlier years traveled and vacationed on the dime of private broadcast interests. He also

partied on a yacht owned by George B. Storer, chairman of Storer Broad-casting, at a time when Storer had a case before the commission.

Other commissioners likewise were embarrassed when Schwartz listed their freebies from those they were supposed to regulate: lunches, Christmas turkeys, color television sets. (Doerfer argued that the sets were needed to monitor the TV industry.)

Schwartz's efforts exceeded Congress's expectations—and he was promptly fired. In a scathing speech at Harvard Law School shortly afterward, he charged that the FCC and similar federal agencies had become a "political dumping ground for lame-duck congressmen" who make decisions "not based on the law or the facts, but on how heavy a pressure is brought to bear" on them.[4]

In fairness, it should be noted that the networks had their share of scandals in the period. A popular game show, CBS's *The $64,000 Question*, was canceled after it was shown that contestants were fed answers in advance. NBC's competitor, *Twenty-One*, also fell into disrepute after Columbia University Professor Charles Van Doren, after winning more than $100,000 and appearing on the cover of *Time,* admitted to fraud before a congressional investigating committee.

The FCC, after freezing television channel allocations in 1948, faced a daunting task. On occasion it had proven decisive in adopting measures essential for the television industry to develop. Notably, in 1941 it approved technical standards recommended by a group of in-dustry engineers and executives called the National Television Systems Committee (NTSC). Those standards, for line frequency, bandwidth, and frames per second, comprise the system television still operates on more than a half-century later.

In 1948, however, a maze of interlocking technical issues were before the FCC. Their outcome would spawn a future for some busi-nesses, destroy others, and largely determine the quality of television available to viewers for decades to come.

Allocating frequency plans for thousands of communities, to avoid interference from neighboring markets, was the cornerstone of the FCC's deliberations. Other issues included color television, the use of both the VHF (very high frequency) and the weaker UHF (ultrahigh frequency) bands, and uniform engineering standards—all while under immense pressure from industry and Congress, and under a mandate to act in the public interest.

Allen DuMont recognized that the FCC decisions had the potential to doom his network. ABC, CBS, and NBC television had VHF affiliates ready to roll in each major market, through longstanding radio relationships. DuMont had no such ties. His network would have to affiliate with mostly new stations in the weaker UHF band, whose signals reached thirty to forty miles, compared with VHF's reach of sixty to eighty miles.

By 1952 there were over twenty-five million television sets in the U.S., practically none of which could receive UHF. DuMont urged the FCC and other government bodies not to mix VHF and UHF channels in the same markets. But his arguments fell on deaf ears.

In April 1952—four years after imposing a "temporary" freeze—the FCC issued an order establishing 1,770 commercial television station assignments. They included 500 VHF stations, limiting to three the number of these stations in most major markets. Despite DuMont's strong opposition, they also included 1,270 UHF stations, many in the same cities as the VHF stations.

The FCC decision meant that in many markets assigned three VHF stations, the stations would affiliate with ABC, CBS, or NBC. DuMont would have to affiliate with a UHF outlet, which in essence meant no audience because almost none of the millions of televisions in use could receive UHF. The following September the first UHF station began broadcasting, in Portland, Oregon. With a lack of UHF-equipped television receivers and consequently an absence of audience, the station eventually folded.

Television was about to change my life forever. After some career dead-ends, I was determined to get in on the ground floor of this fascinating new industry. It was a great time to climb aboard. Television was about to reach critical mass right as I stood on that New York sidewalk in 1950, astonished by its unique ability to enthral people.

Growing evidence confirmed my feeling. In 1948 more than nine hundred sponsors had bought TV time—500 percent more than the previous year. National sponsors were fleeing radio for television at record rates. In 1950 *Variety* called the exodus "the greatest exhibition of mass hysteria in biz annals."[5]

Shortly after my fruitless talk with the owner of SESAC, I went to the DuMont Television Network on Madison Avenue, where an older gentleman interviewed me. I then met with the head of sales, Ted Bergmann, and was hired to sell advertising spots, time, and programs for WABD, Channel Five, the station DuMont owned in New York. DuMont also owned two other stations, WDTV in Pittsburgh, and WTTG in Washington.

Our primary job was to sell commercial time and programs in New York City to advertisers and ad agencies. It was a tough sell against other strong New York competition, which included affiliates of each of the other networks. DuMont lacked the kind of clout enjoyed by ABC, CBS, and NBC, which had deeper pockets and radio affiliates ready to be licensed as television stations once the FCC freeze was lifted.

We were still creating commercial television, and our small staff was involved in talent and programming as well as sales. In the earliest days there were no teleprompters—electronic devices that, unseen by the audience, unroll a prepared script line by line for the talent—or even cue cards (irreverently called "idiot cards").

Those in front of the camera's unblinking eye had to memorize or make up everything. Live television was a high-wire act without a net. There was no trans-continental transmission, so programs were recorded on a film called a kinescope (same name as the TV receiving tube) and shipped to the West Coast for rebroadcast. The resulting TV picture usually was fuzzy and sometimes distorted.

Allen DuMont, the inventor and founder, was a bald, round-faced man with light blue eyes and an unpretentious manner. We called him "Doc." At the age of eleven in Brooklyn he was stricken with polio and spent almost a year in bed. Later he called that year "a blessing in disguise." Allen tinkered with a crystal radio set his father gave him, buried himself in books studying the principles of radio, and built a receiving and transmitting set before returning to school. His course was set for a life of discovery and achievement in electronics.

DuMont, whose company was the primary U.S. manufacturer of cathode-ray tubes and also manufactured TV sets, became the television industry's first millionaire.[5] But some felt that Doc, for all his brilliance, lacked business acumen.

The former head of the DuMont Network told me what happened in 1938 when Doc wanted to manufacture television tubes and looked around for a facility. He found an old pickle factory in Clifton, New Jersey. It was large and seemed perfect for the creation of a production line. Doc needed about $200,000 to purchase the factory and used a Wall Street financier, Morton Lowey, to introduce him to Paramount Studios. Paramount agreed to pay DuMont slightly over $200,000 for all of the class-B common stock in the Allen B. DuMont Laboratories— approximately 29 percent of the company.

Lowey was so happy he called Doc from a pay phone and reported he had made a deal for $200,000. DuMont immediately—somewhat naively—called a real estate broker and signed a contract to buy the pickle factory. When papers for the purchase of the B stock were drawn up, a meeting was arranged with Paul Raibourne of Paramount and people at DuMont, including Lowey. As they got down to business, so the story goes, Raibourne said, "Here's the check, but first you have to sign this."

"What's that?" asked Lowey.

"It's the loan agreement," said Raibourne.

"What do you mean 'loan agreement'? We're giving you 29 percent of the DuMont stock."

"Oh no," Raibourne shot back, "the stock is the cost of making you the loan; now you owe us $212,000."

Lowey called Doc, who was, well, in a pickle. But he agreed to pay the money and the stock. So Paramount acquired 29 percent of DuMont for absolutely nothing. When the stock was later sold they got tens of millions for their share of the DuMont Broadcasting Company. That is how Paramount became part owner of the DuMont Television Network and the three DuMont-owned television stations.

The national networks, all based in New York, returned to the air shortly after the war. Initially there were only nine television stations in the U.S.—three in New York City, two each in Los Angeles and Chicago, and one each in Philadelphia and Schenectady, New York.

The other television networks had revenues from their radio operations to help finance prime-time shows that could deliver large audiences. DuMont lacked outside financing, save for the stock sold to Paramount before World War II, and its program budget was much smaller than those of its competitors. When DuMont developed a ratings winner despite its modest budget, often the program was stolen by NBC or CBS.

Television programming initially copied the old radio formats, with a single sponsor per show. In January 1948 the DuMont Network put the first fully sponsored one-hour television show on the air—*The Original Amateur Hour,* sponsored by P. Lorillard for Old Gold Cigarettes. The show aired on Sunday nights and about fifteen stations out of the nineteen then existing carried it. Other TV programs soon followed, including *Arthur Godfrey's Talent Scouts* and *Studio One,* with original live drama.

The first television sports extravaganza—the Joe Louis-Billy Conn heavyweight fight at Yankee Stadium—was staged successfully by NBC and Gillette in 1946. An estimated five thousand sets carried the fight, many in bars, with an average of thirty viewers each, for an estimated audience of 150,000. Many viewers were seeing TV for the first time. NBC's *Howdy Doody* in 1947 expanded television's scope to children in a daily and Saturday show.

Though commercialism has dominated television from the start, TV early on proved its public affairs potential. In 1947 NBC debuted *Meet the Press,* still going strong more than a half-century later as the longest-running program on television. In 1948 all four networks televised the national political conventions from Philadelphia, with NBC servicing stations in seven cities and the other three networks splitting an additional eleven cities.

Two years later a special U.S. Senate committee, chaired by Sen.

Estes Kefauver (D-Tennessee) held a series of field hearings on organized crime, televised and viewed by an estimated thirty million citizens, resulting in 250,000 pieces of mail to Washington.

CBS's Paley proved a worthy match for RCA/NBC's David Sarnoff. "If Sarnoff was the visionary of television broadcasting," notes one industry historian, "Paley was the visionary of television programming."[6] CBS never caught up with the larger, richer NBC in technical development. But Paley knew instinctively that no matter how sharp the picture, it was of little value without sharp programming.

In 1948 Paley caused the biggest convulsion in broadcasting since buying CBS Radio twenty years earlier. Blithely ignoring a gentleman's agreement with Sarnoff, Paley massively raided NBC's superior stable of talent.

Some NBC stars were lured to CBS by an innovative tax loophole. The talent incorporated themselves as businesses. The proceeds they got when CBS purchased them was taxed by the IRS as a capital gain—25 percent—not the hefty 77 percent on personal incomes above $70,000. The programs aired first on CBS Radio; most went to CBS television as well.

First to make the jump to CBS were Freeman Gosden and Charles Correll, two white actors and the creator/voices of the situation comedy *Amos 'n' Andy*. The show had been on NBC Radio for nineteen years, but its migration to television was problematic. The revised show—the first TV series to feature an all-black cast—cost CBS $2 million plus a share of future profits. Following its first show in 1951 the NCAA and other African-American political groups denounced the program as insulting to blacks. Sponsors grew skittish and, after two seasons, *Amos 'n' Andy* was canceled.

Most pirated shows did well for CBS. As Paley preened and Sarnoff screamed, CBS proceeded to pick off much of the rest of NBC's most bankable performers: Jack Benny and his co-stars (for $4 million), George Burns and Gracie Allen, Edgar Bergen, Red Skelton. Bing Crosby had debuted on CBS in February 1951, then migrated to NBC and ABC, from where Paley brought him back to CBS.

Almost overnight, Paley's radio network—and soon his television network—had assembled an unbeatable prime-time lineup. *Variety* called his coup "Paley's Comet." CBS, on a roll, also established a permanent presence in Hollywood, the nation's creative capital. In November 1952, CBS dedicated a new office and production facility, Television City, designed by two of the nation's premier architects, Jim Langenheim and Charles Stanton.

CBS was stumped, however, in its quest to develop a variety show competitive with NBC's Milton Berle, the zany and wildly popular master of ceremonies on Texaco Star Theater. Other CBS brass flatly rejected a suggestion by their program development chief that they hire an awkward, stoop-shouldered Broadway newspaper columnist to emcee a new variety show and recruit talent for it.

But Chairman Paley, literally minutes after hearing the proposal, overruled his colleagues and ordered him signed. The show debuted as *Toast of the Town* and eventually was named after its emcee, *The Ed Sullivan Show*. It stayed on the air more than twenty-three years, from 1948 to 1971. Berle lasted eight years, until 1956.

Paley also assembled the legendary journalists who would invent television news and set the standard by which all future broadcast news teams would be judged. Edward R. Murrow already was a household name after his dramatic on-the-scene radio broadcasts from London as the Germans bombed the city. In 1950 CBS hired another former World War II correspondent to cover the Korean War for the network. One day he would be considered the most trusted man in America: Walter Cronkite.

Given the obstacles, DuMont made a pretty good account of itself. Our shows included *Cavalcade of Bands* and *Cavalcade of Stars*. The latter show starred Jerry Lester, but the sponsor was unsatisfied, so Lester stepped aside for a friend of someone on the production crew named Jackie Gleason, who was hired starting at $750 a week. Gleason, of course, was destined for bigger things later at CBS.

Back then advertising agencies owned some programs, and both *Cavalcade* shows were owned by the Ed Kletter Agency and sponsored by a drugstore chain. Such a sponsor could require a company to purchase a TV spot before stocking its product. DuMont also had Captain Video each weekday, whose weekly prop budget was all of $25! It was sponsored by General Foods out of Benton & Bowles, a leading ad agency.

DuMont also launched *Life Is Worth Living*, a half-hour television show featuring the Reverend Fulton J. Sheen, Catholic Auxiliary Bishop of New York. The show was shot on a set simulating his office. Bishop Sheen was a phenomenon, belying a belief that television personalities could not be both morally compelling and commercially successful. He attracted sizable audiences for us—even opposite "Mr. Television" Milton Berle on NBC—while delivering a ton of food for thought.

Bishop Sheen reviewed current events and how they affected the social and ethical prospects of peoples throughout the world. No commercials were allowed within the program; all were positioned before or after the show.

A half-hour before start time, he meditated in a small room behind the studio, then went on the air live, without notes, for nearly twenty-seven minutes. Someone would give the Bishop a three-minutes-to-end sign, followed by two-minute and one-minute warnings, and he would always complete his talk right on the mark. An amazing performer. On one program Bishop Sheen vehemently denounced communism in general and Joseph Stalin in particular, likening him to Brutus. Not long thereafter the Russian dictator had a stroke and died.

It was the era of *Night Beat,* a daily, 11 p.m. program hosted by a young Mike Wallace, who sat on a stool interviewing celebrities and public figures in his tough, inimitable style.

Boxing was a TV institution in the late forties and early fifties. Boxing was especially attractive to DuMont. It was cheap to produce, since camera coverage only had to include the ring, and the greater New York area had a half-dozen arenas, reducing travel costs. Dennis James announced our boxing and wrestling programs when I arrived at DuMont. He was followed by Ted Husing from Eastern Parkway, way out in Brooklyn, known as the "House of Upsets" for all the high-ranking fighters beaten there. We often took clients to the fights. Husing in turn was followed by a young Chris Schenkel, who became one of America's best-known sports announcers.

I was a sponge, soaking up everything I could about television. I simply couldn't get enough—devising new ways to sell shows, cheering on talent, even one time tracing rumors that a bowling show which appeared on one of the local stations was fixed and the results known to some innovative people.

At last I was home.

5
DuMont and CBS

"**I** want to be a salesman when I grow up!" That sentiment probably has not tripped off the tongues of many boys. And it had not been my ambition. But communication has fascinated me, from the time I typed out a crude news sheet as a boy and circulated it to friends.

When I joined DuMont in 1950 another stage caught my attention. In February 1949 Arthur Miller's Pulitzer Prize-winning play *Death of a Salesman* had opened on Broadway. Traveling salesman Willie Loman has spent his life "riding a smile and a shoeshine," proud of his ability to sell anything to anyone and take care of his family. Now, at the twilight of his career, he is forced to confront his failures. Willie has lost his job, the respect of his sons, and finally hope.

It is not supposed to end this way. Willie Loman desperately wanted his family to live the American Dream. I did too. When I joined DuMont I was the father of two young daughters, to be joined by a third within a year. Mindful at some subconscious level of how fleeting life and notions of self-worth can be, perhaps a legacy of my turbulent childhood in Europe, I would take nothing for granted. I failed to see then that my single-minded professional climb in the coming years would take me away from home too often, eventually exacting a heavy toll on my relationships with some of my children.

Miller's exposure of everyman's psyche struck a deep chord, which proved universal as *Salesman* was performed around the globe in coming years. Surely it applies to many professions. But, tellingly, Miller applied it to the peddler, the butt of countless jokes, whose profession historically has been belittled. *Am I as good as I must be? If I cannot sway others, my family and I will not eat.* I suspect that deep within many, if not most, salesmen lurks that concern.

In my case a certain natural hubris kept the possibility of failure below the surface. Nonetheless I was acutely aware that television was the opportunity for which I had long prepared. With no on-air talent or production experience, selling was my ticket inside television's small tent. If I were to remain inside, I had no choice but to succeed at it. Only later would I learn the happy truth that most top leaders in television also began in sales.

Television advertising has been refined over the years but the principles remain the same. Advertisers buy time in several ways. National advertisers whose companies and products are available across the country typically purchase network time. While the overall costs are relatively high, the per-viewer cost is low.

Syndication—the selling of programs directly to TV stations for their own scheduling—usually is less expensive, but the advertiser loses some control over when and where the ads will run. Advertisers can also target their products to selected cities or regions by purchasing "spots" to air just in those places.

Networks and individual television stations all have sales representatives to handle this side of their business. Individual companies have their own marketing and sales forces, and national corporations also retain advertising agencies and media-buying organizations to help create ad campaigns and place them with TV programing that will deliver buyers. Today advertising is a multi-billion-dollar business, and some ad agencies are better known within the television industry than the companies and products they represent. Back then some of them created programming as well.

At DuMont, with a small guarantee against commissions, I was assigned a number of ad agencies. However, I was surprised to find that one veteran salesman hoarded a list of agencies that included all the major ones. He hesitated to even leave his office because of frequent phone calls he got from those agencies. They included J. Walter Thompson, the Biow Company, Dancer Fitzgerald Sample, BBD&O, Benton & Bowles, and many others.

His cache was the subject of sales meetings shortly after I arrived at DuMont; some of the agencies were removed from his list and given to other salesmen. I was assigned Benton & Bowles.

I went to see the chief time buyer for Best Foods at Benton & Bowles, a lovely lady named Mary McKenna. Mary gave me a budget for a trial campaign in New York on WABD, using Best Foods products to test the advertising. She gave a competing station—then WNBT, Channel Four—the same proposal. After research I decided a Sunday afternoon motion picture program running two hours would give Best Foods the ideal opportunity to present their many products.

The emcee of the proposed show was to be Rex Marshall, a veteran on-camera announcer. I learned, much to my distress, that my commissions would be calculated after subtracting Marshall's substantial fee, as well as the motion picture license fees.

Competition for the Best Foods business was fierce. I was up against Channel Four's "Operation Lightning" offer: An advertiser spending above a certain amount got coveted aisle-end displays for his product through a tie-in with a number of supermarkets in the New York metropolitan area. Through sheer persistence, I won the contract. Our first program featured the English classic, "One of Our Aircraft is Missing."

Channel Four's manager, Ted Cott, did not take defeat lying down. He phoned and asked me to come see him, without saying why. At the appointed time I arrived outside Cott's office at NBC in Rockefeller Center. Without explanation I was kept waiting forty-five minutes, then was ushered into his cavernous office and presented myself in front of Cott's desk. He continued writing as I stood there for what seemed an eternity, but must have been only a minute or two. Finally Cott looked up and said curtly, "Well, what do you want?"

"The first thing I want is to be offered a chair," I shot back. Then and there I knew I could never work for that man. Sure enough, Cott wanted me to join NBC sales. I said I would think it over. A few days later I called and declined.

One of my agencies at DuMont, J.M. Mathes & Company, developed a show on behalf of Canada Dry Ginger Ale, called *Terry and the Pirates,* which aired at eight-thirty on Tuesday evenings, following Bishop Sheen's *Life is Worth Living.* I wanted to sell the spot between the two shows to Ogilvy and Mather, one of New York's largest ad agencies, and one of its clients, Sunoco. I did everything I could think of to sell this enviable advertising position to the time buyer and Sunoco, to no avail. She was convinced *Terry and the Pirates* appealed primarily to children, who don't buy oil and gasoline.

Finally I contacted the *New York Daily News* and got the demographics for the newspaper comic strip of the same name. It showed what I hoped: *Terry and the Pirates* was not a children's comic strip show, and a petroleum commercial would be ideal between the two adult shows. Armed with the analysis I returned to the agency and won the business.

My DuMont colleague who previously had nearly every major New York agency in his portfolio became sales manager. His girlfriend was named our weather girl. At every sales meeting he pushed her program.

At about the same time, General Foods was anxious to get *The Red Buttons Show,* then on CBS, cleared on WDTV in Pittsburgh—DuMont's station and the only one in town. A time buyer at Benton & Bowles proposed to me that in exchange for clearing *Red Buttons* on WDTV, General Foods would make a substantial purchase on DuMont's New York station. I refused to even discuss it; this was tie-in buying, or tie-in selling, depending on which side of the desk you were on, and I was not sure it was even legal.

A few days later our sales manager informed me that General Foods was buying sponsorship of the weather girl, seven days a week for fifty-two weeks, firm. I had a pretty good idea how this had come about, confirmed in my mind when *Red Buttons* was then cleared to air in Pittsburgh.

A few days after getting this order, Benton & Bowles called me, asking if the weather girl was willing to do live commercials. I turned to the sales manager and asked, "Will Janet do live commercials?"

"Who is it for?" he asked.

"General Foods."

"Yeah, sure," he said. My client asked if there would be any extra charge, and the sales manager said no. A few weeks after the program went on the air, I received a call from Tom McDermott, the powerful and talented head of radio and television programming at Benton & Bowles. Using the foulest language, he shouted "Ralph, I just got a call from some broad who's the weather girl on your channel, asking for more money. What the hell is this all about?" Talent just did not call an agency directly. I told Tom I'd look into it and get back to him. "Get her off my back!" he demanded. I promised I would.

The sales manager said his girlfriend was asked to do a different commercial every day, something he had not anticipated. "There will have to be an extra charge," he said.

Management and I were called to a high-level meeting at Benton & Bowles. I was asked what the understanding was, and I conceded the weather girl had agreed to do live commercials and my supervisor said there would be no extra charge. That ended the meeting. I had told the facts, but of course had not endeared myself to the sales manager. The station had to make good on its offer to have the weather girl do live commercials at no additional cost.

I conceived the idea that ten-second spots could be used to give weather forecasts and the latest news. We'd display a large card on the screen through a special projector, with the latest news headline and the weather typed in at the bottom, as a jingle played in the background. I arranged lunch with Ted Bergmann, head of sales at DuMont and an account supervisor at Benton & Bowles to explain the idea and suggest he propose it to a client, Carlings Beer.

The supervisor, Ted Steele—who later became chairman of Benton & Bowles—was intrigued by my proposition, so I brashly proposed that his agency buy fifty ten-second spots a week for fifty-two weeks for Carlings Beer. He was surprised by the size of the request, and asked how we would project the spots on the air.

I told him a special projector called a telop could be used to display the picture. On the bottom of the card we would type in the news headline and the latest weather, and project the two, as a recording of the Carlings jingle played in the background.

Steele soon came back from Cleveland—headquarters for Carlings Beer—to tell me they would not buy fifty-two weeks of spots but would buy thirty-nine weeks at the rate of fifty spots a week. I was elated, dollar signs from the substantial commissions dancing in my head.

I met with people in DuMont's program department and outlined the need for the telop and an operator to type in the headline and weather. They exchanged embarrassed looks.

"What's the problem?" I asked. "We don't have a telop machine," one said. It was a standard piece of equipment for almost every major TV station in the country. My commissions in peril, I tramped Madison Avenue seeking a solution. Finally I found something called a varytyper, a new kind of typewriter. If its smallest font was used to type the news headline and weather on a piece of cellophane, to be superimposed on a slide, it might work. And it did.

In May 1951 our third child, another beautiful daughter, was born. I rushed Lilo to the hospital in Manhattan, making it barely in time for the birth. It was a relatively easy delivery. We named our baby Alice in memory of my mother. This time we were more mentally prepared for the depression we assumed Lilo would suffer, and which unfortunately she did. A slight comfort this time was the knowledge from experience that Lilo would overcome the PPD in a matter of months, which she also did.

Dad asked what I would think if he were to marry again. I assured him Lilo and I would be delighted. He introduced us to Elsie Lowenberg, whom he married that year. Elsie was one of three sisters and had always been single. She and Dad seemed happy together; they moved from an apartment in Manhattan to one in Queens. He retired and they traveled extensively.

Father had worked for the U.S. War Department in New York until World War II ended. He held a variety of other jobs, culminating at the Museum of Natural History in a project that was a pure labor of love: writing a bibliography of prehistoric South America, a favorite interest.

Always proud of his academic accomplishments, especially his doctoral and law degrees, Father became progressively more annoyed with phone calls, mail, and telegrams he received that omitted reference to his Ph.D. He refused to accept the American custom of reserving the title of "Doctor" largely for those with medical degrees, and insisted on being called "Dr. Baruch." If someone said "Mr." instead, he would often answer,

"As long as we are being that familiar, why don't you call me by my first name, Bernard."

The noted American financier and statesman, Bernard M. Baruch, a daily fixture on a Central Park bench, was not listed in the phone book, except for his business number on Madison Avenue. Above him my father was listed as Bernard Baruch on West Ninety-Second Street. This led many a panhandler or would-be investor to mistakenly contact my father for money.

In 1952 Dad was the subject of a column in a New York newspaper by John Cameron Swazy. Dad had written to Bernard M. Baruch, asking him to take whatever steps he could, including changing his phone number if necessary, to stop the flood of misguided solicitations. He received a letter back that was quite self-serving. It did nothing to help the situation and Dad continued to receive mail and phone calls for his namesake until the financier died.

On occasion Dad extracted a bit of poetic justice. A telegram came from the White House that read something like this: "Please state if you have any objection if [name deleted] is named Assistant Secretary of State." Dad wired back, "No objection whatsoever," and signed it Bernard Baruch. When I asked him about it, he said "How could I object? I don't even know the gentleman."

DuMont was a pleasant, stimulating place to work. The atmosphere was friendly but efficient, a tone set by Allen DuMont himself, whose office was in New Jersey. He dressed indifferently—a slide rule invariably sticking from a jacket pocket—and Doc's battered office furniture looked as though it had been picked up in a garage sale, even though by 1951 the company was grossing about $75 million a year.

Chris Witting was Dumont's managing director. One day Chris was at his dentist's office out in Connecticut when the dentist said his brother, an attorney, would love to get into television. That led to the brother, Donald McGannon, being appointed head of DuMont's owned and operated stations. Years later he would play a major role in U.S. television and radio broadcasting, including helping the FCC write rules reining in some network practices.

Soon after he arrived, McGannon called me in to his office and asked how one goes about selling television advertising. Although rather green myself, I spent considerable time explaining all the details I had learned, as he took copious notes. That was the start of a long and pleasant professional friendship with Don, who was one of the most decent, hard-working, forward-thinking people in communications.

Chris Witting left DuMont to become president of Westinghouse Broadcasting. After Witting resigned, Allen DuMont asked sales director Ted Bergmann to his office. There, Doc asked him to be the new head of his network. Ted was shocked. "Doc, I'm flattered," he reportedly said, "but I need to point out something that may change your mind."

Ted reminded DuMont that our business depends on sales to advertising agencies. Except for the Biow Company, no other agency was headed by a Jew. "As a matter of fact," Ted added, "most ad agencies don't even like to do business with Jews, and this may make it difficult for us to work with these agencies."

"Mr. Bergmann," DuMont replied, to Ted's pleasant surprise, "if that's the way they feel, then I don't want their business anyway." Standing up, Doc extended his hand to Ted. "Congratulations. You're head of my network."[1]

Witting was asked to fulfill Westinghouse's longtime ambition to own a television station in its hometown of Pittsburgh. He negotiated with Don McGannon, and purchased our company's Pittsburgh station, WDTV, for slightly over $10 million. Perhaps as a reward for pulling that off, Witting was named vice president for consumer products at Westinghouse Electric. Eventually McGannon became head of Westinghouse Broadcasting.

Under Don's capable leadership, Westinghouse became one of the most powerful companies in television, eventually owning five stations in major markets. He initiated the production and syndication of two successful Monday through Friday programs, *The Mike Douglas Show* and *The David Frost Show*. They also produced a daily one-hour news magazine program called *PM*. Some of these and other shows started under Don continued for many years.

In the 1951-52 season, television became a true national entertainment and public affairs medium. Just before the start of fall shows,

AT&T completed a coast-to-coast coaxial cable. Until then, fewer than 50 percent of the nation's TV homes could receive live network television; now 95 percent could do so.

CBS and NBC—and to a lesser degree ABC—for the first time made more money from their television operations than their radio operations. They ate the lunch of other forms of mass entertainment: In cities with access to television, radio use shrank and movie theaters were closing, attendance typically down by 20 to 40 percent.

Wide access to television created new social and political patterns. Politicians aired the first televised campaign ads in the 1952 election. Democrats bought a half-hour slot for a speech by presidential candidate Adlai Stevenson—who was bombarded by hate mail for preempting a broadcast of *I Love Lucy*. Republican Dwight Eisenhower bought twenty-second spots and drubbed Stevenson at the polls.

In opinion polls that year, Borden's Elsie the Cow edged out actor Van Johnson and U.S. Senator Robert Taft as one of America's most recognized faces.[2] Magazines began routinely to offer homemakers tips on arranging furniture for the best television viewing. TV even got its own saint. Pope Pius XII announced that Saint Claire of Assisi was the patron saint of television. Placing an icon of her on the TV set was said to improve reception.

One of the most popular TV programs was *Texaco Star Theatre*, with Milton Berle. *Philco Playhouse* and *Goodyear Playhouse* alternated Sunday nights on NBC, which also began *Your Show of Shows*, a ninety-minute variety program with Sid Caesar and Imogene Coca. *Toast of the Town* with Ed Sullivan continued strong. *Kukla, Fran & Ollie,* and *Garroway at Large* were two of the handful of shows originating from Chicago. Mornings would never be the same once NBC inaugurated a new 7 a.m. two-hour news and talk program called *Today. Tonight* and a daytime *Home* program soon followed.

The blockbuster of them all was *I Love Lucy,* which premiered in October 1951 and was an immediate sensation. (Utility officials in Toledo, Ohio, reported a sudden, vast increase in water usage during *Lucy* commercials.) The antics of America's favorite redhead Lucille Ball, with her real-life husband Desi Arnaz and neighbors played by Vivian Vance and William Frawley, made the situation comedy the most popular show in television history.

In 1952 Paramount Theatres purchased ABC. Although Paramount owned an interest in my employer, DuMont, it was betting its future on ABC instead. Obviously Paramount's resources were going to flow to ABC, making DuMont's position ever more fragile. The writing was on the wall for DuMont when the FCC ended its freeze that year and announced that VHF and UHF signals would be mixed in the same markets. DuMont would be stuck with UHF stations and their minuscule audience. The end of its network was now just a matter of time.

The coming collapse of DuMont propelled ABC's quest, ultimately successful three decades later, to catch up to industry leaders CBS and NBC. FCC concern over monopolistic radio had led to ABC's birth in 1943. RCA had two networks, NBC Red and NBC Blue, and the FCC ordered RCA to sell one of them. The Red network was more commercial and profitable, with the Blue carrying many cultural and public affairs programs. RCA, of course, sold the Blue. Purchaser Edward Noble, a Lifesavers magnate, changed its name to the American Broadcasting Company.

ABC remained a minor player until purchased by Leonard Goldenson of Paramount in 1952. Goldenson had a Harvard law degree and was modest and approachable. While not as famous as Sarnoff of NBC or Paley of CBS, Goldenson was as instrumental in building his network as they were in building theirs. Goldenson's takeover of ABC gave him five stations and a minor network. In 1954, ABC had just forty primary affiliates of the more than three hundred stations on the air.

Over the next thirty years, Goldenson built ABC by going where CBS and NBC neglected to go. ABC was the first network to air movies made for television, and miniseries—"Roots" was a memorable example. Goldenson partnered with Walt and Roy Disney in building Disneyland, getting a weekly one-hour show of the same name in the bargain.

Sports broadcasting pioneer Roone Arledge played a major part in putting ABC on the map. He headed its sports division starting in 1968, becoming president of ABC News in 1977.

DuMont's untenable position led me to consider other options. A subsidiary of the *Los Angeles Times* called Consolidated Television Film Sales invited me to join them. The *Times* also owned KTTV, Channel Eleven, in Los Angeles, which had no network affiliation. Since there were not yet transcontinental lines, programs for western stations were supplied by the eastern-based networks on kinescopes, or stations had to buy separate programming on film. As an independent, KTTV had little opportunity to buy programming, so the station decided to produce programs and distribute them nationally. Consolidated was its sales vehicle.

The *Times* had a business partner in this new venture, oddly a manufacturer of small diesel engines. The head of the *Times* subsidiary had devised an ingenious package of television shows called the "Station-Starter Package." It supplied a number of programs at a reasonable price to newly licensed television stations, which enabled them to begin broadcasting.

Early in 1953 I left DuMont and joined the *Los Angeles Times* subsidiary, distributing its programs in the eastern United States. Two years later, to Allen DuMont's great sorrow, his network and company were dismantled and sold off piece by piece. The last program to air on the DuMont Network was a boxing match from St. Nicholas Arena in August 1956. DuMont Broadcasting became Metropolitan Broadcasting Company, and later Metromedia, Inc. Ultimately these stations were sold to Rupert Murdoch and formed the nucleus for the Fox Network.

I traveled a great deal in the East and sold numerous programs to new TV stations. With a rewarding new job our family made domestic changes. The five of us left our dreary two-bedroom apartment on West Eighty-Second Street and moved to a three-bedroom unit in outer Queens, near the end of the subway line. We traded in our Chevrolet for a new Dodge Dart, green with air conditioning—a godsend in steamy New York.

Lilo and I took a trip to Europe to see my childhood nanny, Regina, still living in Frankfurt. Regina knew us both. She was my nanny and later cleaned Lilo's father's office in Frankfurt. We had sent her many packages through the years. Over dinner Lilo and I were shocked to get Regina's reaction to the war. It was an evening-long tirade against the "terrible Americans" who bombed Frankfurt, killing thousands of people and leaving others to suffer. Disillusioned, we stopped all contact with her.

The National Association of Broadcasters (NAB) held its convention on the West Coast in 1953 and the staff of Consolidated Television Film Sales gathered in Los Angeles, headquarters of our parent company, the *Los Angeles Times*. The next day Norman Chandler, owner of the *Times*, invited us for cocktails in the elegant penthouse of the newspaper's office building.

Later we went to the Beverly Hills home of a company executive. There I witnessed a strange thing. After a couple rounds of drinks, the Times' partner had to be helped out and taken home—apparently a routine occurrence. It gave me an early taste of what too often passes for professionalism in Hollywood, a blighted world I would increasingly distrust.

Consolidated Television Film Sales, while extremely successful by most measures, did not bring the kind of returns *Times* owners were used to. Late in 1953 they sold it. The new owners came to New York to check out our operation and employees. Their leader glided in wearing a paisley shirt, a large gold chain with a medallion dangling from his thick neck, and more gold around his wrists. I took one look and knew this was not for me.

I had made a mistake by joining the *Los Angeles Times* subsidiary. I let myself be seduced by the charm of the man who became my boss at Consolidated. The end result was that I gained little experience that proved valuable, and wasted more than a year of my professional life. I should have stayed at DuMont until something better opened up.

I was approached by Charles Wick, an agent for singer Frances Langford and other talent. Wick had acquired the rights to a British program called *Fabian of Scotland Yard,* a series of thirty-nine half-hours, but did not know how to distribute it. Charlie, who later moved to California and played an important role in the Reagan administration, hired me part-time to sell the program.

Among job prospects was CBS, the most desirable of all broadcast organizations. It was the leader and trend-setter in radio and television, and a job there was coveted. In April 1954 I was interviewed by a nice gentleman who headed CBS Films. We shook hands and my career at CBS began. It was a move I never regretted, despite many problems with CBS later on. Working for this great company would be one of the best experiences of my life.

6

THE TIFFANY NETWORK

Capsulizing the history of the Fifth Estate in the twentieth century, *Broadcasting & Cable* magazine named William S. Paley broadcaster of the century. Paley, it explained, "created the greatest broadcast organization the world has ever seen."[1] CBS was widely known as the "Tiffany Network." Such was the esteem in which my new employer came to be held.

The CBS story began in 1928 when twenty-seven-year-old Bill Paley persuaded his father, a Russian emigrant and cigar maker, to purchase controlling interest in a radio network for a half-million dollars. Paley, handsome and charismatic, aggressively built the Columbia Broadcasting System, from twenty-two affiliates when he bought it, to forty-seven by the end of 1928.

With a keen eye for programming and news talent, shrewd business sense, and the guts and instincts of a high-stakes gambler, Paley became a legend. *Broadcasting & Cable* said simply that "he was to American broadcasting what Carnegie was to steel, Ford to automobiles, Luce to publishing and Ruth to baseball."[2]

Equal credit for what CBS became must be shared by Frank Stanton, recruited to the network by Paley right after Stanton earned his Ph.D. in psychology at Ohio State University. The elegant Stanton, a pioneer in audience research, ran CBS as its longtime president starting in 1946, under the watchful eye of Chairman Paley. Stanton became the unofficial spokesman for the broadcasting industry as well. His steady temperament and intellectual and organizational skills complemented Paley's strengths. Together they were the most powerful and effective leadership team in broadcasting. Though at that time my own humble office was well removed from theirs, I was thrilled just to be part of such a first-rate organization.

Senator Joseph McCarthy was still witch-hunting. The Wisconsin Republican had brandished lists of alleged Communists and Communist sympathizers in the U.S. and charged, on the thinnest of evidence, that they had infiltrated Washington and sensitive industries including broadcasting. In response, CBS, among other organizations, over-reached by requiring its employees to sign loyalty oaths and calling some on the carpet to explain past associations with left-leaning groups.

Several years later, however, CBS became the first television outlet to publicly and systematically take on McCarthy. In March 1954 Edward R. Murrow, in a *See it Now* program, promised "We will not be driven by fear into an age of unreason...." He ended by saying, "This is no time for men who oppose Senator McCarthy's methods to keep silent... The actions of the junior senator from Wisconsin have caused alarm and dismay amongst our allies abroad and given considerable comfort to our enemies."

It was the beginning of the decline of McCarthy's influence. The Senator demanded and received equal time on CBS. He attacked Murrow for supposed communist connections earlier in his career, but his rejoinder was quite ineffective.

I joined CBS the following month. Shortly afterward I took a prospective client to lunch at the Barbary Room at the Berkshire Hotel, in those days a hangout for media types—quiet, elegant, expensive. Nearby was Murrow with some associates. After lunch I went over and congratulated him on his work.

Trademark cigarette dangling from his mouth, he answered, "Oh, thank you very much. What is your name?" I replied, "That doesn't matter, Mr. Murrow, just let me tell you how proud I am to be working in the same company as you." He grinned and I went on my way.

That year, 1954—my first at CBS—the company became the world's single largest advertising medium, a distinction it would hold for ten years in a row.[3] Agency time buyers knew they had to be on the CBS network or an affiliated station to get maximum exposure for the companies and products they represented. Selling time, national or local, became relatively easy for most CBS salesmen. They visited the agencies, requested that a substantial portion of their budgets be allocated to the CBS network or station, and agencies usually complied.

Not everything CBS touched turned to gold, however. The company was virtually unbeatable on its own turf. But over the coming decades CBS repeatedly milked its cash cow—broadcasting—to invest in other businesses, only to watch most of them drown in red ink.

No venture would be more costly than Bill Paley and Frank Stanton's gamble much earlier on a manufacturing company called Hytron Radio and Electronics. I assume they wanted to emulate RCA, and compete on the manufacturing turf of their arch-rival. The two main owners were brothers Bruce A. and Lloyd H. Coffin. CBS paid an exorbitant $17.7 million in stock for Hytron—a quarter of all CBS shares. Paley and other CBS leaders figured they might as well produce and profit from the electronic tubes and television sets which delivered their programs.

Serious manufacturing and marketing mistakes were made, however, and CBS learned too late that it could not match higher quality sets produced by others. In 1961 Paley finally put a tourniquet on the hemorrhage. By then CBS's losses had reached an estimated $50 million, in addition to the shares of stock still held by the Coffin brothers. The intriguing postscript to this saga is that CBS generated so much profit that the Hytron calamity was largely buried in the thick columns of black ink on the ledger.

CBS Films offered me a small guarantee against commissions. I was assigned the territory of eastern Pennsylvania, New Jersey, and greater New York City. My first trip was to Wilkes-Barre/Scranton, Pennsylvania, an area I approached with apprehension. The man I replaced wrote that there was no business to be had there. He said the area had only tiny stations in an all-UHF market, and recommended that CBS Films not even try to sell programs there.

Nevertheless I went, and discovered that my predecessor had

never actually made a sales call in the market. I learned, in fact, that he did not visit any small markets in his territory, apparently considering them beneath him. He was single, drove a sports car, and lived, I assumed, off padded expense accounts submitted to CBS. I was a hungry salesman with a family to support, and within six months I was sold out in Wilkes-Barre/Scranton.

That mountainous region in eastern Pennsylvania relied solely on UHF, one of the few such markets in the country. Television sets were unable to receive UHF directly, but through cable hook-up viewers were able to watch programs, including those on CBS and the other networks.

My sales in that market alone covered the guarantee the general manager of CBS Films had offered for the first few months of my tenure. Next I went to Harrisburg and York. They too had rarely if ever been visited by anyone from CBS Films. Shortly I was almost sold out in Harrisburg.

I returned from the first trip to Pennsylvania and carefully filled out an expense account. Somehow other salesmen became privy to the record, and a group of them came to see me. They expected me to spend and report significantly more, they said, or their own jobs could be threatened. It reminded me of my movie theater experience, when some ushers routinely stole donation money. This was another form of stealing, I felt, but I went along with them in a limited way. Over a half-century later the memory still leaves a bitter taste in my mouth.

We were directed to sell thirty-nine episodes of *The Gene Autry Show,* produced by Flying A Productions. Thirteen new episodes a year were released on the CBS Television Network, sponsored by Wrigley Chewing Gum out of Chicago. The new shows were rerun repeatedly in combination with older ones. Apparently Autry had a close relationship with Mr. Wrigley and the general manager of the CBS station in Chicago.

During my first sales call in Philadelphia for the show, newspapers reported that Autry had fallen off his horse at a Texas rodeo. Some suggested alcohol was involved. The incident put a dent in the squeaky-clean image of America's singing cowboy and made it difficult to sell his show.

In 1955 CBS tangled with my old friends at Local 1212 of the International Brotherhood of Electrical Workers, particularly business agent Charles Kalame, over terminating CBS's union contract. This was the same local with the same leaders I had appealed to when I was fired at Empire Broadcasting, and who had refused to hear my side. It was pay-back time.

As the possibility of a technicians' strike loomed, CBS required the managerial staff to learn how to operate the studio. I was to handle audio portions of various broadcasts—familiar territory to me. My first assignment was CBS's morning broadcast, airing at 7 a.m., for which I had to be in the studio at five-thirty. This meant getting up at four in the morning, going to the studio for rehearsals, then operating the audio portion of the live television broadcast.

The Guiding Light, a live soap opera at one in the afternoon, was my last daily program. I spent some time in my office on routine work, then went home for an early dinner and bed at eight o'clock, prepared for the same schedule the next day.

Finally, on a Friday afternoon about ten days into the strike, the union blinked and it was settled. I went home elated. That Sunday morning a deliveryman rang our doorbell with a letter from CBS. I thought to myself, *Holy smoke, the strike is on again.* But it was a personal note from company president Frank Stanton, thanking us for going the extra mile during the strike, and enclosing a bonus check, taxes already deducted. The CBS accounting department must have worked much of the weekend to pull that off. It was a typical Stanton operation that reflected his class and appreciation when a job was well done.

Philadelphia was one of my main sales targets—a large and difficult but potentially lucrative market. Its three television stations were each affiliated with a network. CBS's partially owned station, WCAU-TV, produced a weekly network circus show for us. I sold them thirteen episodes of *Range Rider,* which WCAU ran at 1:15 a.m. Sunday, essentially throwing it away.

A powerful second station, WFIL, was affiliated with ABC and owned by Walter Annenberg, publisher of *TV Guide.* WFIL produced a daily disc-jockey dance show for which long lines formed outside the studio. It was hosted by an unknown youngster named Dick Clark.

WFIL wanted to strengthen its late-afternoon lineup. I got an idea. We had a number of westerns—*Autry, Range Rider, Buffalo Bill, Jr.* and others—and I proposed that WFIL schedule them back-to-back from five to six in the afternoon, with an emcee. They liked the idea and chose a young woman, nicely named Sally Starr, to host the hour, calling it *Starr Theatre*. One piece was missing, however—the thirteen episodes of *Range Rider* sold to WCAU. After considerable persuasion, WCAU sold us back the episodes. This was an early example of Monday-Friday programming, one of the first of what the industry calls "strip" shows.

Then, like a weapons merchant, I called on the third Philadelphia station, WPTZ, owned by NBC, and proposed they rerun CBS-produced *Amos 'n' Andy* opposite *Starr Theatre*, which I had just helped create. It was awkward on both sides for an NBC-owned station to buy a CBS program. Nonetheless, WPTZ finally agreed. I typed up a program order, had it signed by the station's general manager, and submitted it to CBS.

Eyebrows arched. Here was an NBC-owned station scheduling a CBS-network rerun opposite the station in which CBS had a substantial interest. But there was no way out; CBS swallowed hard and honored the sale.

A small New York ad agency named Emil Mogul wanted to replace its local show which ran each weekday at 7 p.m. on NBC-owned WNBC. I heard rumors that *The Honeymooners*, completing its original run on CBS, would not be renewed. Needless to say, it was a fabulous hit. I took my courage in two hands and called on Emil Mogul, offering them thirty-nine episodes on a first-rerun basis at an exorbitant price. They agreed it would be a wonderful vehicle for their client, Ronzoni Macaroni, and signed the program order.

Now the trick was to get CBS to honor the commitment, if and when *The Honeymooners* ended on our network. Some CBS brass by now considered me a bit of a scamp, but the price offered by WNBC was so high they agreed to the sale.

Another station near Philadelphia was WDEL in Wilmington, Delaware. Storer Broadcasting bought it to make Wilmington-Philadelphia one advertising market. Storer named the manager of its Atlanta station to lead WDEL, and I traveled to Wilmington and met with him. The man slumped in a chair behind his desk and planted his feet atop it. I was forced to constantly move my head around his feet to maintain eye contact. To a lowly salesman on commission, this was supposed to put me in my place. He was not interested in what I had to say and spent the time bragging about his success in Atlanta and his horses.

In truth, running a network-affiliated station in Atlanta was no great accomplishment, as the audience came automatically. WDEL failed as a commercial station. It was eventually given away, later becoming the educational outlet in Philadelphia, to this day a PBS affiliate. It was a typical Storer mistake. The station could have been enormously successful. But there was no vision, no long-term planning. Each day after lunch the station manager hit the golf course.

I took a much-needed break from work in 1957 for a family European vacation. Since joining CBS three years earlier and hitting the road to sell programming, I had gone all-out to prove myself to CBS. It felt natural; I relished the challenge and saw great opportunities ahead in our high-flying company.

CBS had gotten the lion's share of my time and attention. I frankly had neglected Lilo and our daughters and, in reflective moments, felt guilty about it. The girls were growing fast and I was missing too many of their special moments. Eve was now a teenager at thirteen, Renee was nine, and Alice six.

Lilo was a very conscientious mother—perhaps too conscientious. Our daughters were almost her whole life, though on occasion old friends from high school would drop by. Lilo read to our girls and helped with their homework. As a result they did excellent in school and seemed happy. On weekends she drove the girls to tourist sites in the greater New York area; I joined them as often as I could. Lilo was a good homemaker who often cooked traditional German dishes such as pot roast, corn beef, or breast of veal.

She was also a great asset in my work. Once or twice a week she joined me when I met with clients. Lilo put them at ease and carried a conversation beautifully. She enjoyed these occasions a lot.

The European vacation in 1957 was a special time together and something we all needed. We bought a Volkswagen, crammed the five of us into it, and toured France and Switzerland. It was a chance to show our daughters places that were important to me as a boy. I was told a Swiss village named Wengen would be a good place to stay. Cars were not allowed in town. We parked outside it one evening and rode a quaint little train up to Wengen.

In the lobby several elderly women were knitting and an old gentleman was asleep in an easy chair. Not the cheeriest of welcomes. It got worse. Guest rooms in Switzerland usually are cozy and immaculate; ours was not. The walls were clammy and, probing between the sheets, I found that the bed also was somewhat damp.

It was disconcerting, but at least they agreed to serve us a late dinner downstairs. The food likewise was marginal. We pacified our sleepy girls by noting the menu included a dessert called "egg surprise." It turned out to be a little scoop of rice pudding with half an apricot on top.

We put the children to bed and Lilo and I were discussing whether to stay, when I got a call from New York. Although it was un-related business, I used it as an excuse to check out of the hotel the next morning. We paid for the three days of our reservation and were off again.

For years I had heard about a place called Pontresina. Lilo skied there as a girl, and we decided to check it out. We took a long drive over mountain passes, one of them so obscured by fog that I kept stopping and getting out of the car to see where the road was. Several tedious hours later we arrived in Pontresina. It was August 1, a Swiss national holiday. Lilo and I walked wearily into what was called the best hotel in town, the Grand Hotel Kronenhof.

We approached the desk clerk and I blurted out our sad tale. "I know it is high season, and space is tight. But we are worn out and desperately need a place to stay, and—" The young man cut me off, grin-ning, and raised his hands to signal "I surrender!" He had a lovely suite for us. It had a large living room and a bedroom on each side, one for the children and one for us.

We had a marvelous time in Pontresina, and to this day our family continues to spend delightful summers at the Hotel Kronenhof.

CBS Films, my division, had a number of management changes in the mid-fifties, and a stronger effort to take the high road in television programming. Sam Cook Digges, general manager of Channel Two, the CBS outlet in New York City, reigned over a station with huge audiences. *The Early Show,* late afternoon movie programming, was enormously successful, as was *The Late Show,* movies after the late news. Most other CBS stations had similar programs, making the company perhaps the leading buyer of motion pictures.

Digges launched an early-morning educational program called *Sunrise Semester,* working with New York University. Serious viewers could earn college credits—an early example of distance education that would not become widespread for decades. The show aired at 6 a.m. and did well given its cerebral nature. *Sunrise Semester* simply consisted of a professor in a tall chair discoursing on philosophy, literature, or other esoteric subjects.

Digges' pioneering efforts won national acclaim. In 1956 he was named administrative vice president of CBS Films, my division.

CBS Films moved to 477 Madison Avenue, next to CBS headquarters. Digges custom-ordered a corner office with red-tile floors, elegant black furniture, and a maritime clock on the wall. On his transfer from Channel Two, he was given the high chair originally used by the professor on *Sunrise Semester.* To use it, Sam ordered a stand-up desk, also in black. On the cocktail table sat an enormous aluminum sculpture shaped like a rocket. Sam's office became known at CBS as the embodiment of bad taste.

One of the first tasks of the sales staff under Sam, predictably, was the syndication to local stations of *Sunrise Semester.* It was not well received, and was followed by the syndication of *Omnibus,* one of commercial television's most critically acclaimed cultural series, hosted by Alistair Cooke. *Omnibus* was a ninety-minute show subsidized by the Ford Foundation, and had run at different times on all three networks, including CBS on Sunday afternoons.

A handsome brochure was prepared to help market *Omnibus,* but sales were disappointing. No surprise: During five years on the air, *Om-*

nibus had attracted $5 million in advertising but had cost $8.5 million to produce.[4] (Nearly a half-century later, before his death in 2004, Cooke's *Letter from America* to BBC radio listeners was the world's longest-running talk radio program.)

Leslie Harris, from the McCann Erickson ad agency, joined CBS Films as vice president for programming. He was most likable, often tugging at the shirt cuffs under the sleeves of his jacket while chirping, "My dear boy, when you are with me you are in God's right-hand pocket."

I became a sales supervisor.

Our next challenge was *Robert Herridge Theater,* also with an intellectual bent. Episodes ranged from esoteric to downright strange, and the series likewise was difficult to peddle. As a supervisor it was my job to motivate the salesmen to move more programs, a tough task with the more intellectual fare.

Complaints about the quality of television programs have been around for as long as TV has been around. They are not groundless. But through personal experience I learned how tough it is to sell shows that require the viewer to think. Debuting the same year as *Omnibus* in 1951 was *I Love Lucy. Omnibus* had to be subsidized, while *Lucy* was the number one-ranked TV show in the nation for four of its six full seasons.

Our sales team was anxious to obtain CBS shows like *Lucy* for syndication, and the network was just as reluctant to give them up. *I Love Lucy* had ended its night-time run on CBS. Rather than release it to CBS Films for syndication and pay us a commission on sales and reruns, the CBS network division ran it on weekday mornings, where again it was extremely successful.

We claimed the CBS reruns would hurt eventual syndication, but we were wrong. *I Love Lucy* is probably the closest thing there is to television immortality. When *Lucy* was finally released on a market-by-market sale, it was just as successful. At this writing a half-century later, Lucy is *still* rerunning and still getting respectable ratings. Such comedic classics as *Lucy* and *The Honeymooners* show that good writing and good chemistry do not become stale with the passage of time.

In 1957 the first CBS Films-sponsored production under program leader Leslie Harris came off the line. *Assignment, Foreign Legion* was produced by Tony Bartley and starred Merle Oberon. Bartley, a World War II ace in the Royal Air Force, was married to film star Deborah Kerr, and sold CBS programs in the United Kingdom.

He crossed the Atlantic to show us a pilot of *Foreign Legion* prior to a luncheon at "21," at which Miss Oberon was special guest. She was best known for her role opposite Laurence Olivier in the 1939 release of *Wuthering Heights.* Producer Alex Korda cast her in several major dramas and then took her to the altar to become Lady Korda.

Miss Oberon was a big hit at our event, fluttering her bedroom eyes at everyone in sight. She had silky light-tan skin, classic high cheekbones, and full lips—a beautiful woman. Unfortunately, the pilot of *Assignment Foreign Legion* was awful. Bartley had never before produced anything on film, let alone a television series. Twenty-six episodes were made, which we sold to U.S. stations with considerable difficulty. I wasn't privy to the numbers, but the series must have been a financial disaster.

Les Harris's next venture was a program in cooperation with the U.S. Navy called *Navy Log,* by veteran producer Sam Gallu. Sam was short and stocky, with a cheery disposition and a resonant tenor voice he loved to show off. *Navy Log* was a good production and a bargain to make. The pilot was completed and CBS scheduled it Tuesday evenings opposite the last half of the smash hit *Milton Berle,* beginning in September 1955.

The program went into production the previous spring, and thereafter a story circulated widely at CBS and passed into network folklore. Lilo and I took a vacation that same spring. We spent about ten days in France, toured Monaco and Monte Carlo, and ended up on the French Riviera. It was a lovely spot and out in the distance we could see the U.S. Navy ships engaged in producing *Navy Log.*

Sam and Les took a break from production and spent a weekend on the Isle of Capri, the famous resort. They picked up female company, had a few drinks, and after midnight strolled the narrow streets of Capri, Sam singing at full tilt.

They walked, or stumbled along for quite awhile. Then suddenly a light went on in a top room of a small hotel, a louver flew open, and a man, his face undetectable with the light at his back, shook his fist at Sam and Les and yelled down, "I'm going to tell Bill Paley about you two!" The shades promptly closed and the light went out. Until now nobody knew who that mystery man was. I had great fun pretending to be angry at my colleagues that memorable night.

Navy Log was on CBS for one year; it ran on ABC an additional two years and then was sold in syndication. Despite its relatively low income from CBS and ABC, Les Harris assured CBS management there would be substantial profit from the reruns in syndication. However, not only were the revenue targets missed, CBS suffered large losses from *Navy Log*, and Harris was forced out of CBS Films.

By the mid-fifties CBS Films sold CBS News coverage of global events, express-shipped daily to TV stations in the U.S. and abroad. Our popular reruns included *Our Miss Brooks, Gene Autry, Gunsmoke, Brave Eagle, Champion, The Honeymooners, and Navy Log*. Walter Cronkite narrated *You Are There*, recreating chapters from history such as Joan of Arc and Caesar.

The CBS network commissioned a pilot from Desilu Productions, a partnership of Lucy and Desi Arnaz, later acquired by CBS. *Whirlybirds* was an adventure series that used a helicopter for rescues and chases. CBS could not find a slot for it, however, so I was asked to sell it in syndication.

I called on Benton & Bowles, which pitched it to Continental Oil, better known as Conoco, and had almost convinced them that *Whirlybirds* was a good show with a lot of potential for licensing and product merchandising. But just before Thanksgiving, CBS brass called and wanted the show back for the network to run Saturday mornings.

Tom Moore, the new head of CBS Films, and I went to CBS Television president Merle Jones. We told him Conoco was actively considering the show, and to withdraw it at that point would be a terrible embarrassment. Could we keep the show until after the week of Thanksgiving? Merle agreed.

That weekend we worked frantically and voilà! we won an order for *Whirlybirds*, sponsored by Conoco for about fifty markets. *Whirlybirds* stayed on the air three years—1956 to 1959—for one hundred-eleven episodes. I got substantial commissions. Moore left CBS Films to be head of programming and later head of sales at ABC. Eventually he headed the ABC Television Network.

By the end of the fifties we distributed twenty-four major programs, all on videotape—a revolutionary invention that replaced unwieldy kinescopes. Programs included one of CBS Films' own productions, *Border Patrol,* in cooperation with the U.S. Border Patrol.

Strangely, the star of the show began to fantasize that he was an actual U.S. agent. On a commercial flight to Florida he identified himself as a Border Patrol agent and asked that another passenger be arrested as a smuggler. At the end of the flight everyone was identified and, of course, the purported suspect was not a smuggler. The program ended after thirty-nine episodes.

In 1958 CBS Television split into two divisions—CBS-owned stations and the CBS Network—led by two company veterans, Merle Jones and Jack Van Volkenburg, respectively. Merle had been with CBS since 1936 and was close to both Paley and Stanton. He had once been president of all CBS's television interests, and now was given first choice of running the network or the stations division.

Wisely Merle chose the latter. CBS's stations were enormously profitable. For every dollar in sales, nearly fifty cents went right to the bottom line. The network, though dominant, was at the mercy of ratings by fickle viewers.

My unit, CBS Films, was a subsidiary of Merle's stations division. It was unpopular with the network, whose program department considered our production efforts competition. More grating, CBS Films received a distribution fee of 35 to 40 percent, free and clear, while the network bore all costs of distribution.

Network resentment was intense, especially after Jim Aubrey became CBS Network president. A slender six-foot-plus with ice-blue eyes and tight smile, Aubrey reached the top rungs at CBS after developing a long string of commercially successful programs for the network, then spending three years at ABC before returning to CBS. His contributions included *The Dick Van Dyke Show* as well as such rural comedies as *The Beverly Hillbillies, The Andy Griffith Show, Mr. Ed,* and *Petticoat Junction.*

Merle and I met with Aubry and others on the stalemate during an unpleasant dinner. Aubrey casually crossed his legs, extended them far out from his chair, and lambasted Jones, a much older CBS veteran, who did not respond effectively. The head of network business affairs suggested terms be turned around—that CBS Films get 60 percent of the money from distribution, bear all costs, and remit 40 percent to the network—but we said this was unacceptable. Nothing changed except to harden the network's dislike of CBS Films. To the outside world CBS appeared a polished organization, but inside the wrangling was fierce and sometimes disruptive, to the detriment of the company and its shareholders.

His efficient, ruthless manner earned Aubrey the moniker "Smiling Cobra." A specialty was coldly firing aging stars including Jack Benny. On one occasion a seasoned program head named Hubbell Robinson, once higher than Aubrey in the CBS pecking order but now reporting to him, was briefing Aubrey on the upcoming season. Midway through his rundown, Robinson told me, Aubrey interrupted and quietly said "You're through, Hub."

"But I have a few more things to bring up," Robinson responded.

"No, I mean *you're* through."

Robinson now got the drift and said he would go talk to Paley. "I've already talked to Paley," said Aubrey. "We accept your resignation."

After a series of programming failures, CBS Films created the new position of vice president for programming, and hired Robert Lewine to fill it. He had held the same position at both ABC and NBC, and was a gentleman and first-rate producer. But he was doomed to disappointment. Lewine's new position duplicated what CBS's television network already did: create television programs.

One of Lewine's first ventures for us was a half-hour situation comedy starring a fresh young star, Annie Fargé, in *Angel,* about a French girl acclimating herself to America. The CBS Network reluctantly took the show. Not about to help a competitor to its own program department, however, the network scheduled *Angel* in a tough time period. It ran for one season and was canceled.

Bob produced a number of additional pilots, most of which were outstanding, but could not sell them to CBS, NBC, or ABC. In desperation, Bob asked me to meet with him. We went to a nearby eatery.

Sliding into a booth and ordering coffee for two, he asked, "Ralph, how come I can't sell my pilots?"

"This is a problem you should have thought about when you took the job," I answered.

"What do you mean?"

"Well, look at it this way. You produce a pilot. Of course, you must first present it to CBS. The network program department looks at your pilot, and if they like it, somebody will ask why they didn't come up with something as good. Let's say they like it enough to put it on the air. Since it's not their creation, they will give it a time period in which it has little chance to succeed. After it fails they'll say it was a nice pilot but the idea didn't catch on."

Bob stared silently into his coffee as I continued. "Take the other alternative, that they don't like it. To recoup your investment, you must take it either to NBC or ABC. Of course, the people at the other networks know that CBS already has seen the pilot and doesn't want to air it. So NBC or ABC will screen the pilot and will either tell you they don't like it, or that they like it and they will put it on the air."

"If they put it on we win!" Bob said, brightening.

"Not so fast," I said. "Either the show will succeed or it will fail. If it fails the CBS program department will say they told you it wasn't any good. But let's say the show succeeds. That's the worst of all possibilities, because now a CBS subsidiary is producing a show that is running on ABC or NBC and beating the hell out of CBS in its time period. This could cost CBS a great deal of lost audience and money."

Lewine looked as if he had been shot. "Oh my god, why didn't I think of that before? You're right, we *cannot* succeed." CBS Films' production efforts indeed did not succeed. The pilots, costing millions of dollars, all had to be written off. I well recall an emergency evening meeting in 1959, called by an anguished Merle Jones, head of the stations division, who asked how these losses had happened. It was a terrible time for CBS Films.

That year my boss, Sam Digges, said CBS had new plans for me. The company was doing reasonably well overseas, but wanted to do better. Sam asked if I would take over CBS's global sales operations. It was not an easy decision. Lilo's health was somewhat fragile and I needed to help more with our children. I made an excellent salary plus commissions, and would earn substantially less in the new job. CBS offered other incentives, however, including corporate profit-sharing.

Sam and I finally agreed on a modest starting salary and shook hands to seal the deal. I had come full circle since arriving in the United States nearly two decades earlier. Once more my future depended on doing well abroad.

SELLING CBS ACROSS THE GLOBE

Television developed more slowly abroad than in the United States. Usage was reaching critical mass in the U.S. in 1950, when there were seven million sets in the country—compared with a third of a million two years earlier. The rest of the world combined did not have seven million sets until 1954.

But then foreign television took off: 10.5 million sets in 1955, double that number—21 million—three years later.[1]

Hollywood paved the way for U.S. television programs abroad. Movies made here had dominated theaters across the globe for decades. A ready-made audience awaited similar television fare. In 1956 over a hundred different American TV programs aired weekly in forty-three foreign nations.[2]

But Hollywood's legacy was a two-edged sword. Leaders of some countries vowed not to have American culture—especially its emphasis on sex and violence—dominate their television screens as it dominated their movie screens. The proud French, who I knew best, aired the fewest American TV shows—just three.

When I took over CBS's foreign sales in 1959, governments tended to tightly control their countries' fledgling television systems, limiting on-air hours and hence opportunities for program sales. In December that concern led CBS, ABC, NBC, and William Morris, the international talent and literary agency, to form the Television Program Export Association (TPEA) to press for open markets abroad. The Hollywood studios already had a parallel organization—the Motion Picture Export Association (MPEA).

Just as the FCC was unable to keep a lid on the growth of TV in the United States, other free-world governments one by one likewise were forced to bow to public demand for commercial television. By October 1961 the number of sets outside the United States—fifty million—essentially had caught up to the U.S. As we hoped, the likes and dislikes of foreign television audiences mostly paralleled those in the U.S. A notable exception was situation comedy, which tended to be purely American in taste, with the interesting exception of Japan.

Late in 1960 *Business Week* reported: "Foreign television has moved away from government supervision and...toward commercial operation. On both the sending and receiving end, television abroad is coming to look more like television in America...U.S. programs, suitably dubbed for the local market, provide the bulk of the most popular fare on foreign stations."[3]

The U.S. industry also looked abroad to bolster profits because the domestic television market had become saturated. In 1960, my first full year leading CBS's worldwide distribution, an estimated 90 percent of American homes had at least one TV set. By then the U.S. industry's combined revenue from foreign sales was $30 million annually—20 percent of total sales—rising to $50 million in 1962.

Opportunities abroad were tantalizing, but I was discouraged by CBS's international sales operation and agreements I inherited. In Japan, for example, we paid a 35 percent commission to the company that represented us, when CBS Films only received 35 or 40 percent from the CBS Network. At times distribution in Japan made no money at all for us.

In Australia—a market with tremendous potential—we dealt exclusively with an agent located in New York for Channel Nine in Sydney. Television in Latin America as a whole had less government interference than any other market, but we were not capitalizing on it. Our agent for the region bought the rights to our programs cheaply and kept all income from selling them—a bad deal for CBS.

In Canada we were represented by Spencer Caldwell, who started the Canadian Television Network (CTV). Obviously he had a conflict of interest running one network and representing another network's program sales organization. CBS brass had made one decision favoring my division, CBS Films: To air on the CBS Network, all programs had to cede their domestic and international syndication rights to CBS. This bolstered our international sales catalogue, which was enormous.

My first priority was Europe. Each continental country had just one network, mostly run by the government. Michael Burke, head of all CBS operations in Europe, seemed much more interested in producing programs over there—the glamorous side of television—than in the crass but far more profitable business of selling them.

Burke fit the CBS mold: over six feet tall, slim, still athletic two decades after playing football for the University of Pennsylvania. He had stylish grey hair and wore striped shirts with French cuffs. By now it was obvious to me that such a striking personal appearance was virtually a prerequisite for high-level status at CBS. The company's leadership ranks were peopled with men who all could have posed for GQ ads. I had seen bright, talented men fail to advance, seemingly because they were too short or too heavy.

Burke, whom I had not met, had something important in common with CBS Chairman Bill Paley. During the war Paley assisted the allied propaganda effort in the Office of Strategic Services, forerunner of the CIA. Burke volunteered there, proving his mettle in fighting behind enemy lines in Italy and infiltrating into France, where he helped the resistance set the stage for the D-Day invasion in 1944.[4] He later headed OSS operations in London.

Burke returned to the United States where he ran the Ringling Brothers and Barnum and Bailey Circus before joining CBS in 1956. Although Burke had no experience in television, CBS sent him to Europe to find and develop programs for its network and coordinate program sales.

Merle Jones, president of our group, phoned Burke in London and told him I had just been appointed head of international sales and that henceforth he was to report to me on that side of our business. I called Mike and told him I was flying over, and asked that he set up appointments. I also asked him to have a car meet me at the airport and reserve a hotel for me in London.

Crossing the Atlantic overnight on British Airways' pioneering jet, the Comet, I arrived early in the morning in Britain. No car met me, so I took a taxi to Piccadilly, headquarters of CBS Europe. The office in the handsome brownstone was locked, so I waited until the first employee, a young woman, arrived to open the door.

"When will Mr. Burke arrive?" I asked.

"He's away on the Continent and won't be back for several days," she said. Obviously Mike was showing what he thought of my arrival on the scene.

"Is my hotel reserved?" I asked.

"Well, Mr. Baruch, spring is always terribly busy here in London. We had a great deal of trouble getting you a room, but we managed to get one at the Cadogan Hotel."

I checked in. They had indeed reserved a room, but the common bathroom was two doors down through a hallway. I cooled my heels for a couple of days until Michael finally appeared, explaining casually that he had been delayed on the Continent with CBS production matters. The next day we had drinks at his attractive rented home in the exclusive Belgravia section of London, where Michael lived with his wife Timmy, a former actress, and their four children. They had a cook and nanny.

We discussed CBS sales in Europe and agreed to take a hard look at Tony Bartley there in England, whose chief credentials, it seemed, were his war record as an air force ace and his marriage to Deborah Kerr, which was about to dissolve. I suggested that Bartley perhaps spent most of his time at the Royal Air Force Club. Michael agreed. He seemed to view Bartley as a production rival and to welcome the opportunity to get rid of him.

We went to Paris, where Mike had reserved rooms at one of his favorite places, the Hotel Vendome. After a pleasant dinner on the Ile de la Cité, with a CBS producer-friend of Mike's, we went back to the hotel and I retired for the night. To my dismay I found that Michael had booked me a room overlooking the corner of the rue Vendome and rue du Faubourg St. Honore, with a traffic signal right below. Throughout the night cars stopped, then revved up and took off. I tossed all night, calculating the method in Michael's madness.

Our agent in France, named Blondeau, was absolutely charming. But instinct told me he was a bit of a rogue. Later I discovered that, unbeknown to CBS, he had sold some of our made-for-television shows to French movie theaters. Obviously we had no rights for theatrical exhibition, and it became a great embarrassment.

A few days later we returned to London and I met Paul Fox, an exceptional television executive, later head of the British Broadcasting Corporation, and subsequently knighted. Based on discussions at Rediffusion, the private TV operation in London, I returned to New York and suggested to CBS's Merle Jones that Rediffusion might be interested in a business tie. I was confident it could prove very profitable for CBS.

Merle flew to Britain and met with Rediffusion's holding company executives. He returned and reported that the company was losing too much money for CBS to invest. A great mistake. Rediffusion became a mainstay of British commercial television, for many years one of the most profitable television franchises in the U.K.

After our shaky start, Mike Burke and I came to respect each other's abilities. Respect turned into friendship, and our families socialized. He was undeniably talented. Many Americans have trouble understanding Europe and conducting business in ways that work there. Not so Michael. He was a good manager and astute politician. Mike exuded charm, speaking excellent French and some Italian.

In the early sixties CBS recalled him to New York as head of corporate development. One of his acquisitions for CBS was the New York Yankees, where he became president in 1966.

Mike was a hero in the Big Apple after he got the city to refurbish Yankee Stadium and kept the team from moving to the New Jersey Meadowlands. Later he became president of Madison Square Garden. Mike retired from the Garden in 1981 and settled in Ireland, his ancestral homeland, on a five-hundred-acre farm. He died of cancer at the age of seventy in 1987. I was greatly saddened by his death.

On the home front, after years of scrimping and apartment living, our family was finally realizing the American Dream. In 1958 we bought our first home—a large English Tudor in the Long Island suburbs. After going seven years without another child—the longest they had been spaced—in July of that year Lilo gave birth to our fourth daughter, Michele. Our other girls were growing fast: Eve, fourteen; Renee, ten, and

Alice, seven.

I fervently hoped that this time, with adequate income and living in a lovely home to call our own, Lilo would escape the crippling depression that had visited her each time before. In the excitement of our new house things looked promising, as we planned some decorative changes—wallpaper and the like—and new furnishings. Weeks after Michele's birth, however, I came home to find Lilo wandering aimlessly around the house, crying. Postpartum depression had assaulted her again.

Lilo's life, it seemed, was destined to be dictated by reproduction. She had suffered three or four miscarriages in addition to birthing our four daughters. Strangely to me, Lilo had been happiest when carrying a new life inside her. It was after that life was lost or born that trouble set in.

It was obvious to me that we should have no more children, and I tried to impress that on Lilo. We discussed the issue but never firmly resolved it.

Australia, the sixth largest country, was the wild west of world television. With the possible exceptions of Canada and Latin America, it was more open to American TV interests than any other region. Australia welcomed foreign minority ownership of stations, and when television debuted there in 1956 ninety-three American-made TV series aired weekly—more than in any other foreign country. Seven years later only 10 percent of Australia's prime-time TV schedules were filled by local programs. The U.S. supplied nearly all the other 90 percent.

Australia invited the foreign invasion by inaugurating television service with an unusually large number of hours to fill and little ability to create local programming.

Unable to decide on the private American model or government-run European model, Australia adopted both.[5] The dual system included two commercial licenses each in the two largest cities, Melbourne and Sydney, along with a government network and public station in each city. The first commercial licenses went to syndicates dominated by owners of major newspapers, concentrating the mass media for decades to come.

With relatively few government restrictions across the vast, open country, media frontier brawlers slugged it out—figuratively and sometimes literally. When I began to focus on Australia for CBS, its leading brawler was big, blustery Frank Packer, who owned Channel Nine in Sydney. Our paths would cross repeatedly. His media empire, Consolidated Press, also had a radio network, published the *Daily Telegraph* and *Sunday Telegraph* in Sydney, and owned a number of magazines.

In 1959 I sent telegrams to potential Australian customers, offering a package of CBS News and public affairs programs. The government-run Australian Broadcasting Commission promptly accepted and we sold to them. Packer also replied by cablegram, saying he was "interested." I wired back that the programs already had gone to the ABC. Packer replied with a blistering telegram, followed by a phone call from his New York representative, Charles Michaelson, both outraged that the programs had been sold to someone else.

In September I went to Australia with a CBS vice president, William Lodge, to investigate possible investments in television stations. We flew to Sydney and went directly to Packer's newspaper building, where we were ushered into his rather seedy office, sitting on torn leather couches. Packer took pride in his Spartan surroundings. He kept us waiting for most of an hour, then stormed in. With no greeting, he turned to me and demanded, "Have I got it or haven't I?" meaning the news and public affairs package.

"No, you have not got it," I answered.

"Well, then there's nothing else to talk about!"

"Fine," I said. I picked up my coat and, to Lodge's dismay, was ready to walk out when Packer grabbed my sleeve and growled "Sit down." I didn't argue. Frank was well over six feet tall with a powerful build, and had been an amateur heavyweight boxing champion. His bouts had left him partially deaf.

Packer kept repeating that I asked for his reaction to my offer of CBS programs and he gave me the right one: "I am interested." But the best answer, I said again, was from the Australian Broadcasting Commission: "We accept."

Packer led me to believe the future of television in Australia was extremely bright. There were three mini-networks: the combined Channel Sevens in Sydney and Melbourne; Packer's Channel Nine in Sydney, affiliated with Channel Nine in Melbourne; and finally ABC, the government-underwritten radio and television network. ABC catered to elite viewers, similar to PBS in the United States, and attracted relatively small audiences.

Bill Lodge and I called on Charles Moses (later knighted to become Sir Charles Moses), head of ABC, in his modest office in Sydney. Moses was a large man with intriguing habits. On each birthday he stripped to the waist, took an ax, and chopped down the same number of trees as his age. He was fond of classical music and the ABC Radio Orchestra was his pride and joy.

Moses invited Lodge and me to lunch in his office. We had an excellent meal, including Australian wines Moses served in great quantities. We sat down to eat at 12:30, and nearly four hours later Moses was down on all fours, trying to find a rare bottle of port he had hidden too carefully. Fortunately it stayed lost.

The next day we met in the suburbs with Rupert Henderson, who ran the newspaper and television operations owned by the *Sydney Morning Herald,* the city's dominant newspaper. He was a pleasant old gentleman, skinny and bent over, with a taut face and raspy voice. In years to come I would deal repeatedly with all these gentlemen.

Lodge and I conferred at length about the future of television in Australia. A great majority of the population was centralized in urban areas along the southeastern and southwestern coasts. Most Australians had yet to buy TV sets, so the emerging market was large. In addition, station licenses were about to be granted in Perth, on the West Coast, and in Hobart, the capital of Tasmania, an island south of the mainland.

I argued that Australian stations would make great television investments for foreign companies, including CBS. Lodge disagreed. He believed the minority interests would be too small for CBS to bother with.

Lodge left Australia and I remained behind to further study the television landscape. In Hobart I met with Eric Macrae, a hard-drinking Aussie who was to run the station in Tasmania. It was surprisingly cold. The island is as far south of the Equator as New York is north. It was late winter in the southern hemisphere and central heating was uncommon in Australia. Although I had three blankets in my hotel room, the humid air chilled me to the bone. Finally I propped a small space heater on a couple of suitcases next to the bed, which thawed me a bit.

I returned to Sydney and embarked westward to Perth, three thousand miles across the continent. Jets were not used yet on the route, so it took about twelve hours. I was the first American network or program leader to visit Perth, a lovely city with subtropical climate and palm trees—a welcome change from frigid Hobart. I returned to the U.S. from Sydney.

Boarding the Qantas flight I saw that six seats were curtained off to make a berth in the first-class section. It was for Gretel Packer, Frank's wife. He was taking her to the Mayo Clinic for an undisclosed ailment. Frank himself could not get a first-class reservation and sat in the rear of the aircraft. During the long flight I exchanged seats with him so he could be with his wife. Not long afterward Gretel Packer passed away. She had been an elegant, attractive lady, and I felt most sorry for Frank.

Packer made yachting history in his late wife's name. In 1962 he outfoxed the British and took their customary place as that year's challenger for the America's Cup. *Gretel* was the first Australian yacht to mount the challenge. While not winning overall, *Gretel* made an excellent account of itself, encouraging Frank to return to Newport, Rhode Island in 1970 with *Gretel II*. The swift yacht nearly defeated the Americans. But for a highly controversial home club ruling against his yacht, the *Gretel II* might well have carried the Cup back to Australia.

On the return trip I faced the same exhaustion suffered by other visitors to Australia and New Zealand. We left Sydney in the evening, refueled in Fiji in the middle of the night, and landed in Honolulu around noon. I went on to San Francisco, arriving in the afternoon and just missing the last daylight flight to New York. Having flown one nearly sleepless night through, I faced the choice of staying over in San Francisco or catching the red-eye for a second night's flight to New York. Anxious to get home, I caught the night flight—setting a pattern I would usually follow on subsequent trips to Australia.

Further complicating my long trips was an attempt by Larry Lowman, a CBS executive bean counter, to force all employees to travel coach-class, no matter the destination. When I took the matter up with Lowman, he suggested that on future trips to Australia I could rest for a few days in San Francisco or Hawaii, then fly on to Sydney. I pointed out that this not only would cost more than a first-class ticket, but would be a waste of valuable time. He continued to stand on principle and I continued to fly first-class.

A mountain of work awaited me in New York. I routinely spent from early morning until late evening at the office, dealing with routine papers, program clearances, and other business affairs. In addition I was in touch with CBS's worldwide staff at all hours of the day, the evening, and sometimes the middle of the night. Having operations in many time zones killed any notion of regular business hours.

Bill Lodge and I gave CBS opposite assessments of the potential in Australia. Perhaps in part because I was newer, his judgment outweighed mine, and CBS declined to invest. It was another marvelous opportunity lost. By 1961 television had been extended to thirty-three country areas, and two years later the Australian government awarded a third commercial license in each of the major cities of Sydney, Melbourne, Brisbane, and Adelaide, and a second licence in Perth.[6]

While Frank Packer was content to rule the Australian media, his fellow countryman, Rupert Murdoch, would not stop until he had conquered the world. Then virtually unknown outside his country, Murdoch, whose family owned the *Adelaide News*, had purchased a television station in Wollongong, about twenty-five miles from Sydney.

Murdoch desperately wanted *I Love Lucy* for his station. He was using the Wollongong station to cover Sydney, charging advertisers accordingly. *I Love Lucy* already aired in Sydney, however, where it was a huge success. On a subsequent trip to Australia I called on Murdoch, then about thirty years old, and he repeated his request. "It's sold in Sydney, but my station is in Wollongong," Murdoch insisted. I held firm.

It was an early peek at the personality and persistence of Rupert Murdoch. Over the next few decades he would build one of the world's most powerful media empires, starting with little else but his family's modest newspaper. His News Corporation now assumes global reach, concentrated especially in Australia, England, and the United States, where he became a citizen in 1993.

Murdoch created Fox, the first successful fourth network in the U.S., and also owned such properties as Twentieth Century Fox, Harper-Collins, *TV Guide*, the *New York Post*, the *Star* tabloid, the *Boston Herald*, and the *Times* of London. I was to meet Murdoch many more times, including at his summer home in Chatham, upstate New York, and his apartment on Fifth Avenue. Aside from his reputation as a ruthless media baron and tabloid journalist, I have been impressed with his business acumen.

Fall was budget time at CBS. Each division had to prepare a written budget and present a verbal narrative to senior management. I was terrified. This was the first time I was to appear before the entire CBS management team, consisting of Chairman William Paley, President Frank Stanton, the general counsel, several vice presidents, and others in executive ranks.

We in senior management sat behind a long table at the back of the room, waiting our turn at the lectern. Managers of CBS-owned stations were up first.[7] Leading off was Jack Schneider, who ran the company's recently acquired WCAU-TV in Philadelphia. Jack, destined to climb nearly to the top of CBS, had a tough job. Channel Ten was not highly rated when he took over. It was a difficult station to manage, had public relations problems, and consistently ranked second or third in the market.

Schneider gamely plowed through his presentation, at one point saying brightly, "...and in October we really left the pack behind and became the number one station in the market." Stanton interrupted: "Jack, it seems to me that from January until October the competition sort of left you behind." Schneider, already with a reputation for shooting from the lip, turned toward us onlookers and said, "There's always a smartass in the crowd."

The other station managers followed, and then it was my turn. I launched into my prepared speech and was not through the first third, when I said, "In this two and a half network economy—"

"Hold it!" shouted Paley. "What do you mean by 'two and a half network economy'?"

"Well, there's CBS, there's NBC, and there's sort of an ABC," I answered. A lively discussion and mini-debate followed between Paley and me. I thought my boss, Sam Digges, would wet his pants. To top it all off, while I was talking, Cricket, Stanton's Irish fox terrier, dashed between my legs. The whole thing felt like a family affair, with me as the nervous beau dating a favorite daughter.

Starting the following year Digges insisted I submit to him a typed budget narrative, and the numbers to back it up, well in advance of budget day. He routinely changed my text to avoid having Paley, Stanton, or anyone else take issue with it.

But Paley remembered. Did he ever. Each year after our first encounter he relished taking issue with something I presented, and the same type of discussion followed. I began to enjoy the budget sessions as a sort of rite of passage I had surmounted to win the family's favor.

THE TRIP FROM HELL

On October 8, 1959, I attended a cocktail party in Manhattan at the invitation of Japanese television interests. While there I received a call from our teenage daughter, Eve. "Mummy is pretty sick, you'd better get home right away." I rushed home and found Lilo upstairs in bed, writhing in pain, barely able to speak. I quickly called her doctor-father, and told him something was drastically wrong. Lilo moaned that she was pregnant—the first I knew—so I also phoned an ambulance and her gynecologist.

As they lifted her onto a gurney and carried her downstairs to the ambulance, Lilo kept yelling "I don't want to die!" Throughout the night at the hospital the doctors looked increasingly grim, as Lilo's organs shut down.

At 6:30 a.m. Lilo died.

Doctors concluded that she died from sepsis—a deadly infection of the bloodstream caused by toxin-producing bacteria. How the bacteria had entered her body was a question serious enough that the coroner could not complete the death certificate until it was investigated. The cause remained a mystery. I did not know how much if any her personal demons had played a role in her death.

I was devastated with sorrow, mixed with terrible anger. The first love of my life was no more. Her parents lost their precious, precocious child. Our four daughters were motherless.

Suddenly I was a widower at thirty-six, with young children and a new job which required a great deal of time and off-shore travel. I hired a nurse for one-year-old Michele, and asked Rose, our cleaning lady, to work full time. Some friends and Lilo's family tried to help—her mother Lucy came over each Sunday, bringing fresh rolls or croissants, to relieve the nurse—but there was little else they could do. My two bosses, Sam Digges and Merle Jones, visited briefly.

I placed ads for a nanny in Switzerland. When there on business I interviewed applicants and hired a Helen Kaelin, a woman in her early thirties, who enjoyed music, spoke four languages, and seemed competent. She was not unattractive, but I had decided that this was to be strictly an employer-employee relationship. Miss Kaelin, however, arrived in New York bearing two fur coats as well as what seemed to be romantic intentions. I emphasized there would be nothing more than house and child care in exchange for reasonable compensation.

I immersed myself in work, trying to focus and function in spite of our great loss. It seemed a good time to organize or reorganize our various international offices. Latin America was up first. Cuba's leading broadcaster, Goar Mestre, was CBS's partner and the largest buyer of American television programs in the region. He bought the rights to CBS programs, had them dubbed, and sold them at substantial profit—a bad deal for CBS.

Late in 1959 I flew to Cuba to visit Mestre. After the stress of recent weeks I also looked forward to a short rest in tropical Havana. On New Year's Day that year, Fidel Castro and his fellow bearded rebels had seized power. They were well on the way to establishing a Communist dictatorship. The first evening at my hotel I went downstairs to eat. It was a warm day and a cold beer sounded good.

"What kind of beer do you have?" I asked the waiter.

"No *American* beer, only *Cuban* beer," he answered with a sneer. "Now what do you want?" Based on my wartime experience in Europe, I suddenly felt uneasy. If I were detained, what protection would I have? Would the U.S. intercede on my behalf? Unsure of the answer, I took the next flight out of Cuba.

I consulted with Merle Jones before negotiating a new contract with Goar Mestre. Merle insisted we remain with Mestre, and told me just to get the best agreement I could. With one arm thus tied behind my back, I sat down with Mestre. We agreed that CBS would share the profits from the programs we supplied. But then Mestre had second thoughts and went to Jones to get the agreement nullified. Merle called a meeting where Mestre—who had gone to Yale and spoke fluent English—claimed he had not fully understood the agreement. Merle caved in and I had no choice but to give Mestre a better deal.

Later CBS and Mestre—whose holdings in Cuba were seized by Castro—started a new company, ProArtel, and began broadcasting on Channel Thirteen in Buenos Aires. Since foreigners could not own television stations in Argentina, Mestre's wife Alicia, an Argentine citizen, held the license. ProArtel extended its television interests to Caracas, Venezuela, and Lima, Peru.

In Japan a trading company represented us at a commission of 30 to 35 percent. Since that just about wiped out CBS films' profits in Japan, a change was high on my list of priorities. I took my first trip there, but knew better than to take a heavy hand with the Japanese, whose approach to business affairs is much different than in the West. The contract with the firm did not end for some time, and my trip simply set the stage for later action.

In 1962 the U.S. television industry took in about $50 million from program sales to forty countries. Canada easily led all nations, buying $16.5 million worth. It was followed by Australia and New Zealand, $9 million; the United Kingdom, $7 million; Latin America, $6 million; continental Europe, $5 million; Japan, $3.2 million; Thailand, Hong Kong, and the Philippines combined, $2.8 million; and the Middle East and Africa, $1 million.[1]

As a native son of Europe, I was anxious for CBS to do well there. But the Continent presented stiff challenges for foreign TV interests. Nearly every European country had only quasi-government-run television, which usually expanded slower than commercial networks. At that time there was not much space for new programming. Great Britain bought more U.S. programming than all the countries on the Continent combined.

Only West Germany and Italy were making headway toward establishing a second channel. CBS and German partners attempted to establish a new commercial network in Germany, to be called *Freies Deutsches Fernsehn* (Free German Television). Unfortunately, shortly before broadcasting began, the German government ruled the network unconstitutional and we abandoned the project.

In the early sixties the German government established a solid second national network to compete with the many state networks loosely tied together as German television service. The new, all-UHF network was called *Zweites Deutsches Fernsehn*—Second German Television, though why anyone would call their enterprise number two was beyond me.

The government apparently first tapped a political appointee to head ZDF. When we met in New York, it was apparent he knew nothing about television. Tagging along, however, was a handsome young aide named Dieter Stolte. He did all the translating, and we hit it off from the start. After several executive moves, Stolte was named director-general of ZDF, a position he held for twenty years, building it into a true competitor of the veteran first network and sometimes beating it in the ratings. We remain friends to this day.

Nonetheless, knowing that far greater TV consumption in Europe was just a matter of time, I began to set up subsidiaries there. CBS already had an office in London to serve the U.K. For tax reasons I was told our headquarters for the rest of Europe had to be in Zurich, Switzerland. Years later CBS pressured us to abandon our office in Zurich and move European headquarters to Zug, Switzerland, which had an even lower tax rate.

A forty-minute drive from Zurich, Zug was a tiny town on a small lake. Because of its tax structure, Zug was home to a number of American companies, including IBM. But I worried. How could a large subsidiary operate out of that small village? I bought a postcard picturing a local couple in native dress, sitting by Zug Lake, and added a caption coming out of their mouths: "*Ach, wie wunderbar, die CBS is coming.*" I sent it to Frank Stanton with a note outlining the problem. To no avail. A year later we were forced to relocate to Zug.

Our staff there decided that when we had visitors we didn't particularly like, such as company auditors, we would put them up at the hotel in Zug rather than in Zurich. The church next door had a thunderous bell which boomed every half-hour. At midnight, for example, twelve enormous "bongs" were heard, and it continued to sound all through the night.

I wanted to open our own office in Canada, but was told no by the CBS tax department. With that I engaged our top salesman there, Ken Page, to represent us. Ken and I shook hands on a multi-year relationship, with contracts to be signed later. A few days later the CBS tax department called and said I was suddenly free to open our own office in Canada. But I was honor-bound to the hand-shake deal we had made. Ken Page named his new company Page One Ltd. and made a great deal of money representing us.

We fired Jean-Paul Blondeau in France—who had embarrassed us by illicitly selling TV programs to movie theaters—and hired a new organization to represent us there; engaged our own representative in Germany, and so slowly established ourselves across the globe.

My workload was enormous. I pleaded with CBS management to give me an assistant, but they balked at the cost. Finally, after considerable badgering, Sam Digges relented. I interviewed a number of candidates and hired a promising young CBS salesman in the domestic area, Willard Block, and began training him for international work.

Willard went to Japan, where we had established a close relationship with the Tokyo Broadcasting System, including its chairman, Junzo Imamichi. We were negotiating with TBS for purchase of CBS programs.

Several weeks after his arrival, Willard called from Japan. Bitter disappointment in his voice, he reported that Tokyo had turned down his proposal. I suspected the Japanese purposely were dragging out negotiations in hopes Willard would get tired and go home. I instructed him to go back and, in Japanese parlance, tell them that "CBS cannot accept your refusal." I also told Willard to tell them he was prepared to stay another three to four weeks to get the matter worked out.

"Another three or four weeks?" he groaned, understandably upset. "I've been here four weeks already."

"Look Willard, I didn't ask you to tell them you are *going* to stay. I told you to tell them you are *prepared* to stay. There's a big difference in

Japanese eyes." I pictured Willard at the phone, shrugging away what I was saying. But true to form he went back and did as instructed. Two days later the contracts were signed.

John Howell was my CBS counterpart for domestic sales as I headed the international team. John had known trauma. As a Marine in World War II, he saw some of the worst fighting against the Japanese on Pacific islands. He sold *Navy Log* after its run on CBS to the ABC Television Network—quite an accomplishment, since few network-produced shows could migrate to another network.

Following ABC's cancellation of *Navy Log* I noticed a downward spiral in John's demeanor. Early in 1960 he asked me to have a drink with him and his wife at a nearby bar. John complained bitterly, tears in his eyes, that he had difficulty making decisions and could not reconcile himself to being part of an organization. He mentioned various other problems.

As a recent widower I had my own difficulties, and was not as responsive as I should have been. I encouraged John to take a vacation, which he and his wife did, but they returned early. On St. Patrick's Day, March 17, 1960, I joined John and Jim Victory, our supervisor for domestic sales, for dinner at Christ Cella. We had a couple of drinks and ate large steaks. Before the end of the meal John suddenly announced "I gotta go," and rushed out. I had not finished my work for the day so went back to the office.

Next morning, as people filed in to work, I was asked where I had been last night, when they had tried to reach me at home. They did not think to call the office, where I worked late. That's when I learned that John Howell, after leaving us at dinner, walked underground to the subway and laid across the tracks in front of an onrushing train. They sought me to identify his body. That onerous task fell instead to poor Jim Victory, our third dinner companion.

John's death was a tough, timely reminder to keep things in perspective.

My own problems at home increased, especially with Eve, our oldest daughter and the child probably most affected by her mother's death. She was a pretty girl and brilliant student whose marks on standardized tests were off the charts. She skipped grades twice. I learned too late that younger students often have difficulty fitting in and making friends.

She was strongly set on the University of Chicago. I tried to dissuade her, because the school was very large and located in a fringe area of the city. But she was adamant, in part because of famous faculty members. Eve learned, however, that the best-known professors teach graduate students, not undergraduates. Nonetheless she enrolled at Chicago, probably hastening the unwinding of our relationship.

She was extremely antagonistic toward me, for reasons I have not understood to this day. I brought her a solid gold bracelet from Brazil and presented it to her in the campus cafeteria. She flung it away, calling me names. I was shocked. Perhaps Eve thought that I had indirectly caused her mother's death, because my business activities caused me to be away from home so much. Perhaps. I will probably never know.

The placid fifties turned into the turbulent sixties—hippies, drugs, the Vietnam War, the assassination of President Kennedy, his brother Bobby, and Martin Luther King. CBS chronicled it all, under the unblinking gaze of its television symbol—an eye backed by floating clouds, created by CBS's in-house graphic designer William Golden in 1951. It was also a time of transition at CBS. Famed Finnish-born architect Eero Saarinen was commissioned to design a spectacular new headquarters building, on Sixth Avenue between Fifty-Second and Fifty-Third Streets.

While CBS's image was rising along with its elegant new headquarters, the company lost a living prestige symbol in 1961 when Edward R. Murrow, the most celebrated journalist of his time, left to become head of the United States Information Agency (USIA) in the new Kennedy administration.

Murrow's departure for America's propaganda arm came after his relations with Stanton went from tepid to ice cold and his access to Bill Paley was sharply cut. Murrow strongly opposed the commercialism of television at the expense of news and public affairs, and had kept CBS busy putting out fires from his hard-hitting exposes.

He was tolerated—until his musing turned on broadcasting itself, including CBS. Murrow lectured that television "can teach; it can illuminate; it can inspire...otherwise it's just lights and wires in a box."[2] In a 1958 speech in Chicago, he called the broadcast industry "fat, comfortable and complacent," and criticized television for "being used to detract, delude, amuse and insulate us."[3]

Murrow asked the industry for a "tiny tithe" of its income to pay for occasional one-hour reports focusing on great issues of the day. Stanton and Paley were angered and offended by Murrow's attack on the hand that fed him.

I personally became involved in the last Murrow controversy at CBS that came back to bite him as well as the network. On the Friday after Thanksgiving 1960, his *CBS Reports* vividly portrayed the plight of America's migrant workers, a la *The Grapes of Wrath*. "Harvest of Shame" showed the deplorable living conditions and abject poverty of these workers on the bottom rungs of the nation's food chain as they harvested the fruits and vegetables others feasted on. Farm groups were enraged and demanded equal time to answer the indictment.

Weeks later in his USIA confirmation hearing before a Senate panel, Murrow pledged that the agency would "tell the bad with the good," and not try to hide the nation's failings.[4] "If the bad news is significant," said Murrow, "it's going to be reported abroad anyway. We should tell it accurately." Once in harness, however, Murrow did not always sing that tune.

I was in Los Angeles, and got a phone call at about six in the morning from Frank Stanton. He asked if we had sold "Harvest of Shame" to the British Broadcasting Corporation. I said yes. Stanton said he had just received a call from Murrow who asked him to call the BBC and request that they not broadcast the program, for fear it would embarrass Murrow in his new role as America's mouthpiece.

"Ralph, should I make this call?" asked Stanton.

I thought for a minute and said "No, I don't believe you should."

"Why not?" Stanton asked brusquely.

"Because the BBC considers itself an independent body of broadcasters, not subject to pressures from the British Government, and even less so to outside pressures. If you call them, they may or may not follow your advice, but certainly your call will leak out. No matter what they do, you will be embarrassed for having tried to pressure the BBC. That's my advice."

"I believe you're right, Ralph. I appreciate it."

Stanton told Murrow he would not call the BBC. Murrow made the call himself, asking them not to run "Harvest of Shame." The BBC promptly broadcast it—twice.

By then "Harvest of Shame" had been distributed in many countries and regions, including Japan, Australia, Canada, South America, and Europe. The networks, notably CBS, and my division particularly, were criticized by members of Congress and others in Washington for distributing abroad such warts-and-all programs. We tried hard to resist such pressure. I explained time and again that free expression is essential to other freedoms in a democracy.

America's Founding Fathers understood that fact so clearly that they enshrined it in the First Amendment to the Constitution. Thomas Jefferson, the author of the Declaration of Independence, once remarked that if he had to choose between government without newspapers or newspapers without government, he would choose the latter. That these kinds of programs could be broadcast, without fear of interference or censorship by the government, was a demonstration of true freedom.

It is also true, however, that the cost of public affairs programming often is borne by shows that are less critically acclaimed but far more popular. At the time Murrow left the network, CBS Reports was up against ABC's The Untouchables on Thursday night, and getting killed weekly in the ratings. CBS Reports had no sponsor. It and Face the Nation reportedly were costing CBS $250,000 a month to keep on the air.

James Aubrey, most noted for putting on the tube a bunch of lowbrow, commercially successful rural comedies, became president of CBS Television in December 1959. Aubrey personified the kind of TV critics detested. Big-money game shows, easy and cheap to produce, squeezed out more creative programs. In 1960-61, CBS's Andy Griffith Show was the highest-rated new series. Critics, notably the chairman of the FCC, Newton Minow, blasted TV programming. Variety wrote that television had sunk to "mediocrity and even less."[5]

But at CBS, ratings and profits rose faster than the criticism raining down. In 1960, CBS-TV netted $30 million and had six of the ten highest-rated evening programs and eight of the top ten daytime programs. Three years later CBS's dominance was even greater: nine of the top ten evening shows and all ten top daytime shows, while netting nearly $42 million. Someone said you could light a match between programs on CBS and the match-lighting would get an audience.

I continued to seek new or expanded markets for CBS programs abroad. Latin America still looked promising. Commercial television there had little government oversight. As in Australia, regulations in most of Latin America permitted minority ownership of radio and television stations. High rates of illiteracy meant relatively few customers for the printed word but a ready market for television.

Brazil looked especially golden to me. The world's fifth largest country (just ahead of Australia), it occupies nearly half the South American continent and has more than half its population.

In 1950 Brazil was the region's first country to get television. Viewers there, reported *Business Week,* "will watch anything so long as it is not highbrow," and even have a "high tolerance...for endless parades of commercials."[5] By the early sixties there were fifteen advertising agencies in Brazil, in good part to do the bidding of multinational companies. Increasingly they turned to television to get their messages out.

Others at CBS were not sold on Brazil. "Twenty-five years ago Brazil was considered the land of the future," said Merle Jones. "Today Brazil is still considered the land of the future and twenty-five years from now Brazil will *still* be considered the land of the future." I was not discouraged. Latin America as a whole bought more U.S. programs than Europe or Japan, and I was anxious to enlarge CBS's share. We found a person who worked for Sears in Brazil to represent us as well.

In November 1962 I went to Brazil. It was a trip that would have profound meaning for me, and make Thanksgiving from then on more special in its remembrance. I hired a new representative and we engaged a lawyer to help form the subsidiary. The three of us were in a restaurant discussing business.

As the evening wore on I said, "I must catch the Aerolineas Argentina evening flight home. Tomorrow is Thanksgiving and I promised the children I would be back for the holiday." Since we were not finished, however, the lawyer asked if I could return instead on a Pan-Am flight, leaving later from an outlying airport. Reluctantly I agreed, if he could get me a reservation. He telephoned Pan-Am and booked me on the later flight to New York.

I arrived home exhausted after the long trip, and told the children I would take a nap and then our housekeeper, Ms. Kaelin, would help us celebrate Thanksgiving with the traditional meal. I went upstairs to the bedroom and no sooner had laid down than the telephone rang. It was a man from CBS calling to say hello, which I found strange. He said he just wanted to make sure I was alright, which of course I was. I turned over and tried to go back to sleep, but forty-five minutes later a similar call came from another CBS associate. That ended my nap.

I went downstairs, turned on the news, and learned that the Aerolineas Argentinas flight I was scheduled on had exploded on takeoff and all aboard had perished.

The following year I was roped into an extended trip as a business advisor for Merle Jones and his wife Frances. While none of our flights crashed, almost everything else went wrong. Our destinations were Australia and Japan, where Merle wanted a first-hand look at the television potential.

Both Merle and Frances grew up in Iowa. Merle became an attorney, then got into radio and later television. Almost his entire career had been at CBS. Merle was fastidious about his appearance. He bought expensive, well-tailored suits, got his shoes shined from the CBS shine boy each day, and looked the epitome of a top leader—about six-feet-two, slim, silver-haired, suave. He ran the CBS-owned television stations and other businesses. Frances Jones was blonde, slender, and attractive, and they made a handsome couple.

My impression was that their overall knowledge of things cultural, in music and other fields, was quite limited. At any rate I had no choice but to say that of course I would accompany them to the other side of the world. Had I known what lay ahead I might have begged off.

On my first trip to Australia I met an impressive program leader named Bill Wells, and subsequently hired him to represent CBS down under. He would serve us well for many years. I called Bill and asked him to prepare the itinerary. I traveled ahead of the Joneses and Bill and I met them at the Sydney airport early one morning. Out stepped the Joneses, Merle white as a sheet and bristling, though reluctant to discuss why.

Later he told us that upon boarding the Qantas jet in Hawaii, their seats, 1A and 1B, were already occupied. He politely asked a man and his female companion to move, but the man, who may have been drinking, told them to get lost. Merle summoned the pilot, who shrugged and said he could not forcibly oust them. He asked the Joneses instead to occupy two other first-class seats. Merle was used to getting his way, and was furious. So began the trip from hell.

A car took us to the Chevron Hilton Hotel, where Merle and Frances had reserved a large suite. When we arrived the Joneses were told by management that the hotel was still partially under construction and their suite was not finished. Instead they were assigned a suite on the floor below. Merle had scheduled a noon press conference and sent his pants out to be pressed while he and Frances got a little rest.

While unpacking a suitcase, Merle stood up and banged into a cabinet, gashing his forehead. After the wound was bandaged, they lay down, soon to be disturbed by hotel staff at the door who wanted to show the suite to prospective guests. Merle refused to let them in and called the manager to complain. No sooner was he back asleep than the same thing happened again.

Bill Wells and I reappeared at their door at 11:45 a.m. to find that Merle's pants had not been delivered. Impeccable Merle, head bandaged, conducted the press conference in his robe.

Whenever we ate out at one of Sydney's better restaurants, it seemed, not far away sat the impolite gentleman who had refused to give up the Joneses' seats. When we ran into him for the third time he came over and identified himself as an executive of the Philips Petroleum Company. Merle, with glee, informed the man that he was well acquainted with his boss, the president of Philips, and would certainly inform him of his employee's misbehavior on the Qantas flight.

We visited with Frank Packer, who graciously asked us to dinner at his beautiful home, in the nicest part of Sydney overlooking the water.

We also visited the other Australian networks, and Jones, still simmering from his flight, lodged his complaint in an appointment with the head of Qantas. I thought little else could go wrong. How naïve I was.

Merle refused to fly to Japan on Qantas so we booked a KLM propeller-powered plane, which landed in New Guinea at one in the morning. When plane doors opened, a blast of suffocating air hit us. It must have been well over 100 degrees, with matching humidity. Small cots were set aside for rest until our connecting flight arrived. We left in a DC8 with sleeping berths.

At long last we landed in Tokyo and were met by Mr. and Mrs. Koreaki Takahashi. He had been a classmate of the Emperor, and now headed our new office in Japan. His wife was a daughter of Japan's first ambassador to the Court of St. James. They both spoke English, Mrs. Takahashi fluently. Mr. Takahashi was modest and awed by Merle.

Also at the airport to greet us was Peter Kalischer of the CBS News Tokyo office. Peter also had been reared in France and educated at the same school I attended, Lycée Janson de Sailly in Paris.

Mrs. Takahashi had a large bouquet of flowers. When Mrs. Jones alighted from the plane she handed her the beautiful bouquet. Frances immediately turned to Merle and in a loud voice said, "What am I going to do with these?" It was embarrassing to me and somewhat humiliating to the sensitive Japanese. The Tokyo Broadcasting System had made a Lincoln limousine and driver available to the Joneses. We set off for the Imperial Hotel in the center of Tokyo. On the way Frances Jones pointed to a building and asked Mr. Takahashi what it was.

"Just an office building, Mrs. Jones."

Twice more she asked the same thing of other nondescript buildings, getting the same response. Finally, Frances bluntly said to Mr. Takahashi: "You mean you've been living here all your life and you don't even know what these buildings are?" I wanted to sink through the floor of the car or be anywhere else. I think Mr. Takahashi was ready to fall on his sword.

We arrived at the Imperial Hotel—a beautiful structure designed by Frank Lloyd Wright—and Peter Kalischer asked us to join him and his wife for dinner at "a typical, old-time Japanese restaurant." I advised

Merle and Frances not to go, but they accepted and could not understand my reluctance. I explained that they were not yet used to Japanese food and this might be a mistake. They ruled that out of the question and because they went I had to also. That evening they ate hundred-year-old eggs, broiled sparrow, and other Japanese delicacies.

The next morning Merle and I were to visit the head of Dentsu Advertising, one of the largest agencies in the world. A shaky Merle came out of the hotel and got into the car, saying Mrs. Jones was in bed ill and they had called a doctor. We had a fascinating two-hour meeting with the president of Dentsu. On leaving, he handed each of us a small package which contained a Seiko watch, one of their accounts. We got back into the car and found that obviously the packages were mixed up, as I had been given the gold watch and Merle the chrome.

We then went to the American Embassy for a rather unproductive meeting with Ambassador Douglas MacArthur III. He draped his leg over the arm of the chair, used foul language, and generally was unimpressive.

The Joneses, avid golfers, were taken to the Tokyo Broadcasting System's own golf course in Hakone. It had a lovely country club and in the evening the dining room was empty, since TBS had reserved the entire place to host Mr. and Mrs. Jones, and to some extent the Kalischers and me. TBS was headed by Junzo Imamichi, whom I knew and respected from earlier dealings.

TBS's movie cameras followed the Joneses everywhere. Merle and Frances stayed in a small cottage on the course and the next morning Frances, in her nightgown, opened the door to check the weather. A camera was thrust in her face. The Joneses then played golf, a camera recording every stroke. Finally Merle asked a TBS executive to discontinue filming them.

Throughout the trip Merle kept an attaché case on his lap, guarded with his life. But it was awkward in the limousine that took us to an airport for a side trip to Osaka and Kyoto, so I suggested he put the case in the trunk. Merle was reluctant but finally did so. Later, as we alighted from the car at the airport, the chauffeur fumbled for several minutes, then confessed he could not find the trunk key.

Merle was furious. I offered to take a later flight and bring the case, but he said absolutely not. He had confidential papers in it and insisted that his case be retrieved immediately. With that, several Japanese men appeared with crowbars and forcefully opened the trunk to retrieve Merle's attaché case. I could not believe my eyes.

Shortly before leaving Kyoto, we visited art shops and I fell in love with some Japanese prints. The Joneses were waiting in the car, so I hurried with my purchases as the shopkeepers put them in the tubes necessary to transport them. When I got back in the car Merle was furious at my making him wait. It could not have been more than ten minutes. We returned to Tokyo and were picked up by the same limousine, all traces of trunk damage gone.

Next day the Joneses, without me, were scheduled to take off for Hong Kong and points beyond. I counted the minutes. We arrived at the airport to find that, through a mix up, Frances Jones's reservation had been canceled. The airline had difficulty accommodating her.

After phone calls and TBS intervention she boarded the plane with her husband. I sprinted up to the observation deck to watch it take off. I made dead certain they were on their way.

The following year I was invited to the Joneses' house for cocktails preceding a dinner for Junzo Imamichi and his visiting TBS entourage. When I arrived in Greenwich I noticed that Merle had a luxury car with license plate MSJ2. Being a young Turk, I asked, "Merle, who has MSJ1?" The room fell silent. Humor was not Merle's strong point. We had cocktails and then Frances Jones pulled out a large photo album and asked me to sit on the couch and go through it with her. She pointed out photos, asking where we were or what were we doing in most of them. Obviously the trip did not make a great impression and she could not remember much about it.

We then proceeded to La Crémaillère, a wonderful restaurant in Westchester County, for dinner in a private room. Duck was the main course. My luck with the Joneses hadn't changed. The duck was served bloody and had to be sent back for further cooking.

This time, for a change, *they* had made the arrangements.

9
JEAN

American television was much more interested in taking than in giving to its foreign counterparts. Our domestic industry—the eight-hundred-pound gorilla of world television—was anxious to sell programs abroad, but had little interest in buying or co-producing there. Offshore broadcasters were increasingly upset by our one-sided interest, and rightly so.

At CBS the vice president of programs, Michael Dann, was extremely apathetic to any TV produced overseas. To help calm the waters, I recommended two steps to CBS: first, institute an "International Hour," making an hour a week available for foreign programs on an exchange basis. Each participating country would produce a one-hour program suitable for airing anywhere in the world. For our one hour we would receive at least ten to thirteen hours for broadcast on CBS-owned stations. No money would change hands.

Top management endorsed the idea, so CBS produced *The American Musical Theatre*, which aired on WCBS in New York and was exchanged for foreign programs for several years, until interest finally waned.

The second step I recommended to CBS and other U.S. television colleagues was to form the International Council of the National Academy of Television Arts and Sciences, and award Emmys for the top programs produced overseas, just as the Academy gives Emmys for U.S. television. It was a difficult sell, but finally I got approval from the National Academy and we organized the first International Emmy competition.

Concerned about possible proliferation of Emmys, we restricted the awards to two categories: fiction and non-fiction. (Fears of proliferation were well-founded: The International Emmys now consist of fourteen categories and four special awards.) We organized a black-tie event where clips from the nominated programs would be shown and the winners announced. The first dinner was at New York's Plaza Hotel in 1963. As author of the event I wanted to make sure its launch was a success, and personally sold many of the tables.

We assembled the foreign program clips, which were to surround a half-hour of entertainment by Dudley Moore, then appearing on Broadway in "Beyond The Fringe." Through the show's producer, a friend of mine, Moore agreed to appear at no fee. He joined us right after his show's curtain came down.

A wonderful pianist, Moore began to entertain us. Suddenly, in the middle of his act, he stopped cold and declared that he was not properly "miked." With that he stomped out, not to return. I was mortified but made light of it. Everybody laughed and I continued the best I could to emcee the evening. I had organized the event, sold the tables, and now was the entertainment as well.

Today the International Emmys are the symbol of excellence in global television. Many of the competing programs have later been broadcast in the United States. The annual event takes place in a New York ballroom, where twelve hundred people pay homage to foreign broadcasting. The gala is the financial foundation of the International Academy.

I continued to focus on Australia, one of our fastest-growing areas. At one time all CBS sales were to one client, media mogul Frank Packer, through his New York representative. His agent later told me that when I appeared on the scene, he figured the end of that closely knit relationship was near, and I aimed to get the most dollars from that market. He was right.

Relations with Australian broadcasters continued difficult. Time and again we clashed as the Australians conducted business like the American robber barons when the U.S. was first becoming industrialized. June 1960 again found me in the Sydney office of Sir Frank Packer—he had been knighted by the Queen of England—as he talked spiritedly with his two sons, Kerry and Clyde, both, like him, well over six-feet tall and perhaps two hundred-fifty pounds.

A newspaper war was raging. The Packers, who owned the Sydney *Daily Telegraph,* and the Fairfax family, who owned the Sydney *Morning Herald,* had joined together to try to keep Rupert Murdoch, centered in Adelaide, from muscling in on the lucrative Sidney market. They sold Murdoch the Sydney *Daily Mirror,* apparently in the hope that the large debt would sink him. It did not.

At the same time, the Packer and Fairfax families started some suburban newspapers and thought they had a place to print them—at the Anglican Press in the grimy inner-city suburb of Chippendale. However, the press deal fell through at the last minute, leaving them stranded.

As I watched, spellbound, Sir Frank raged about the problem and ordered his two strapping sons to take over the press by any means necessary. That evening Kerry and Clyde, with their attorney and a couple of friends, went to the press facility, produced a document they said was a valid bill of sale, and occupied the building.

Meanwhile a local tough named Frank Browne reportedly was paid to stop the Packers. With his own gang of ruffians, Browne marched to the facility and a brawl broke out. It began in the building, then spilled out onto the street. A reporter said both sides carried monkey-wrenches, and at one time Clyde "was running around with a dart stuck in his shoulder and another two in his backside."

A photographer from Murdoch's *Daily Mirror* conveniently happened on the scene and recorded the chaos. Next day the *Mirror* ran a photo of Clyde Packer throwing the general manager of the Anglican Press out the door. Its lead story blared this headline: "Knight's Sons in City Brawl."[1]

Sources in Sydney say that one day Packer was in his building and rang for the elevator, but it did not come. He waited, punched the button again, and waited some more. Finally the elevator descended bearing a boy with papers under his arm, obviously a copy boy. "How much do you make a week?" Packer demanded. "Twenty pounds a week, sir," the boy reportedly answered. Packer handed him forty pounds and said, "You're fired." The boy took the money happily, since he worked for a competing newspaper.

Packer lost the Australian bid from CBS and my division for coverage of the 1960 Rome Olympics. With no communication satellites in those days, tapes were shipped solely to the winning bidder, the Australian Broadcasting Commission (ABC) in this case. Packer did not take this lying down. Unbeknown to us, he secretly sent crews to Rome to film events right from the stadium seating—strictly against International Olympics Committee rules, of course. Since he broke the exclusivity guaranteed in our agreement, we had to refund the ABC's money for coverage we had sold them.

The American industry's biggest challenge down under came after Australian broadcasters formed a buying pool—in essence a cartel—in 1962, formalized in a written agreement. It set prices for half-hour and one-hour television programs. Though highly illegal in our country, cartels at that time were permitted in Australia.

Jack Valenti's Motion Picture Export Association (MPEA) members—major Hollywood studios—eventually sold at the prices set by the cartel. Our own Television Program Export Association (TPEA), headed by John McCarthy and comprising CBS, NBC, ABC, and the William Morris Agency, refused to sell at cartel prices. We held together despite ABC's strong objection to our "boycott," and, as the weakest of the three networks, its particular need for the income.

In 1963 Bill Wells, the head of CBS Australia, quietly informed me that Reginald Ansett, founder and owner of Ansett ANA Airlines, had secretly applied for a Channel Zero in Melbourne. Ansett had already hired an old friend of mine, Len Mauger, to run Channel Zero. Wells urged me to come to Australia and meet with Ansett and Mauger. *This might be the key to breaking the cartel,* I thought.

Frank Packer reportedly received daily manifests of passengers arriving in Australia on Pan-Am or Qantas, the two overseas airlines then serving Sydney. Traveling directly to Australia would reveal my presence, with unpredictable results in the volatile climate. Instead I first flew to neighboring New Zealand, then on to Sydney, arriving early one morning after an exhausting thirty-hour trip from New York.

Bill Wells and I met with Len Mauger. Our talks about CBS programs for Channel Zero were animated and, at times, quite heated, but in a friendly spirit. We talked until way past midnight, then caught a seven o'clock flight later that morning to go see Ansett in Melbourne. I had been warned that if Ansett put a cigarette box on his desk or the dining-room table, I was to stop negotiating, as it may hold a recording device. That's how Australians did business.

Finally Ansett, Mauger, Wells, and I agreed that new CBS programs would be sold to the new network at prices much higher than the cartel offered. Ansett and Mauger also asked that every show we had on Packer's network be sold to them as well. This we refused, not wanting once again to put all our eggs in one basket.

We wondered how to tell Packer and Rupert Henderson, owning or running Australia's two commercial networks, that their cartel was broken and I was in Australia.

We returned to Sydney and learned that Bruce Gyngell, Packer's programming genius, was at a meeting upstairs in the Chevron Hilton Hotel. Bill Wells and I simply went there and sat on a couch facing the elevator, waiting for Gyngell to come down. He was surprised to see me, and I feigned surprise to see him. We met with Gyngell and told him we had established higher, more fair prices for CBS programs in his country. We said nothing about Ansett.

Gyngell told Packer and Packer called me at my hotel—and told me to get lost. He would not pay our "blackmail" prices. "You can dig yourself a hole and rot there for all I care," he added. I answered that *Gunsmoke* would soon end on his channel, and would be sold to someone else. He slammed down the phone.

Packer burned to know who or what was behind our bravado. For the next couple of days Bill and I were followed everywhere. I had to call New York to report our progress to Merle Jones and Frank Stanton. Just before placing the early morning call, I looked out my hotel door. There, sitting in the corridor, was a man with a briefcase beside his chair and a suction-like device attached to the outer wall of my room. I called downstairs and reported that he apparently was bugging me.

But the fix was in. The hotel manager replied casually, "Well, Mr. Baruch, is he bothering you?" With that, I turned on the television set to obscure my voice and, further, put my head and the telephone under a blanket. I called CBS in New York and got Merle Jones on the line. He calmly asked if I had been fair with Packer, so we could not be accused of shortchanging him. I assured him we had been fair, that we had bent over backwards to negotiate in good faith, and Packer had refused. Jones wished me well and we hung up.

What Merle did not tell me, I found out later in New York, was that Packer had sent him a vicious telegram, saying there was a supposed agent for CBS down here negotiating with him and other networks in a typical Jewish way. He added a few more gratuitous insults. Merle did not tell me about this telegram at the time, not wanting to upset me when I was negotiating thousands of miles from home.

A day or two later I met with media manager Rupert Henderson at his office. Henderson, a kindly older gentleman, in his raspy voice, said "Mr. Baruch, can I give you some advice?" I had a great deal of respect for him and said by all means. "You have accomplished what you wanted," he said. "Why don't you go home?"

I thought for a moment and said, "Mr. Henderson, you are absolutely right. I am going home." That was the beginning of free and open negotiation in Australia, which benefitted every foreign entertainment company.

I was proud of what we had done, even though the details were lost on some others. At an industry cocktail party, the head of international sales at Screen Gems—television subsidiary of Columbia Pictures—approached me.

"Ralph, how do you like the way I broke up the cartel?" he said. I could not believe it. Once film giants MCA and Universal sold their programs at prices set by the cartel, every member of the Motion Picture Export Association followed suit, including Columbia and Screen Gems. On the other hand, the members of the TPEA—CBS, ABC, NBC, and the William Morris agency—held out for everyone's benefit, and Australia once again became a free market.

At home things were going fairly well, but my youngest daughter, Michele, now four, had no children to play with in our neighborhood. I scouted around for a pre-kindergarten program. In August 1962, I visited yet another school, where the director received me early one morning. I explained our problem, but scarcely could concentrate as my pulse quickened.

The director was a stunning dark-haired young woman with green eyes and a heavy British accent. I instantly fell in love with Jean Ursell de Mountford. She was dressed in a sweater, plaid skirt, loafers and white socks. (*She* says she wore a pale blue dress that day!) We discussed Michele at length. I liked what I heard. In contrast to the psychobabble from other educators who insisted Michele needed professional counseling after being without a mother for three years, Jean said she would be fine after making a few friends.

Our mutual attraction unnerved us both. Jean led me into a faculty room to introduce her colleagues. "Mr. Baruch," she said of the first teacher, "this is Mrs. Smith." We approached the second teacher and again Jean said "This is...Mrs. Smith." And of yet a third colleague she said "This is...Mrs. Smith." Down the road Jean confided that she had been flustered in the school that day, much to the merriment of the other teachers, and her mind went blank. Only the first woman really was named Smith.

Jean was born in South Wales, in a small village nestled in the Rhondda Valley, a coal-mining region. Her father, Hector, served in World War I and was a powerfully built adventurer who played rugby and attempted several small businesses.

Jean's mother, Edna Mae, had deep-auburn hair, piercing green eyes, and was celebrated for her beauty. She died when Jean was three, of tuberculosis—a frequent killer in that mining region. Jean was born blonde, but had jet-black hair by age ten. Her parents were both taller than average, and Jean is five-foot-eight.

The Depression hit family finances hard, and Edna Mae was buried in a six-grave family plot identified only by numbers. Decades later, Jean returned to the Rhondda Valley with my daughter Alice. They tracked down her mother's grave through parish records, had the unkempt site cleared, and added a white marble tombstone.

Several years after her mother's death, Jean stayed with her maternal grandmother in Wales as her father, who remarried, left for a job at an automotive plant in England. Once settled, he sent for Jean, who joined her father and stepmother in Rubery, near Birmingham, Britain's industrial heartland. During the years without a mother, Jean had grown independent and daring. She was a gangly tomboy who climbed trees, pulled pranks at school—where she was the tallest girl in class—and later went on hundred-mile bike rides.

In the summer of 1940 Jean and I had something in common. As the Germans pursued my family on the ground in France, they pursued hers from the air over Britain. Industrialized Birmingham and nearby Coventry were set to produce a large share of allied planes, arms, machinery and military supplies—making them a prime target for the *Luftwaffe*. The Austin Motor plant where Hector worked converted its production lines to produce military vehicles and Spitfire aircraft.

Birmingham, just west of the geographical center of England, became the most heavily bombed city outside London. The German blitz—the period of fifty-seven consecutive days of bombing—began September 7. One of the worst attacks was on Coventry, Birmingham's neighbor city to the east. On the night of November 14, 449 German planes dropped 1,400 high-explosive bombs and 100,000 incendiaries. More than 500 people were killed, another 1,000 seriously injured, and 50,000 buildings destroyed.

Hitler hoped to shatter English morale and force Winston Churchill to surrender. Churchill had been named prime minister as well as defense minister earlier that year. The Nazis, as history attests, underestimated Churchill as well as Britain's people, and the bombing had exactly the opposite effect.

Although the country's air defenses were almost powerless at the start of the Blitz, Churchill rallied his countrymen as few leaders in history have done. His frequent speeches and public appearances strengthened Britain's backbone and steeled its people to withstand the onslaught.

Many families, including Jean's, painted their windows black to deny German planes nighttime targets. They took various other precautions, including crisscrossing windows with tape to stop deadly flying glass if they shattered. During nightly bombing raids, citizens in London, Birmingham proper, Coventry, and other cities took shelter in subway stations and warehouse basements.

Jean's parents built an air raid shelter under the back garden, furnished with food, water, bunk beds, and gas masks for each family member—including the dog. They first used it in late August 1940, as Jean turned twelve. She remembers the whine of sirens, her father rousting her out of bed, and the quick exit out the back door and into the shelter.

Hector was a volunteer fireman. Once his family was safely in the shelter, he reported for duty wherever needed. It was a routine repeated nightly across the country. After a tense night in their shelters, Jean and other children would saunter out the next morning, seemingly oblivious to the evidence of hell all around them, and pick up shrapnel for souvenirs.

Children carried gas masks wherever they went. "Each school day we had what our teachers called 'gas-mask play,'" recalls Jean. It was a friendly term with a lifesaving purpose. The headmaster decided which class they'd wear the masks in, and for the next forty-five minutes they were required to do so.

"I suffered from claustrophobia," says Jean, "so this was very hard for me. With the mask tight on my face, and the smell of rubber, I felt like I was suffocating." When sirens whined, her school would empty quickly but orderly, to an air raid shelter large enough to hold hundreds of students.

The Blitz lasted into May 1941, causing about 43,000 deaths across Britain—2,200 in Birmingham—and destroying over a million homes. But Hitler's strategy of knocking Britain out of the war or rendering it powerless to resist an invasion vanished.

Jean loved poetry, devoured books, and, like many others in her native land, loved to sing. She grew up innocent and shy. At sixteen going on seventeen she kissed a boy for the first time. "I ran home, crept into the kitchen, and washed my mouth." Jean enrolled in a government program at Edgebaston University and Birmingham University, studying child development and child psychology. She graduated and has her degree certificate, but not the records of her courses or class standing, which were destroyed in a fire.

Longing for excitement, Jean and a friend named Gwendolyn went to Helsingor, Denmark, for a year, to separate homes where they tutored young children in English. Helsinger, on the east coast of the Jutland peninsula, is known in literature as Elsinor, the setting for most of Shakespeare's "Hamlet." While there they partied with abandon—at the Kayak Club, Ski Club, Yacht Club.

Periodically they took a ferry to Helsingbord, Sweden, to buy clothes, returning that evening to throw out the old ones. One day fog rolled in to Helsingbord and the boat left early, stranding them. With no money, they were turned away at a hotel—"We don't trust Danes to pay it back"—and went to the police station. There they spent a sleepless night in a cell, Jean on the bottom bunk, as drunken sailors staggered into jail, many singing, until dawn.

In July 1949 Jean came to the U.S. She crossed the Atlantic on the *Mauretania,* a 1,200-passenger ship of the Cunard-White Star line. As a new ship a decade earlier, it had been the largest vessel ever to visit London. The crossing was "the greatest time in the world," remembers Jean. "Shuffleboard, movies, a library, all kinds of food."

Passengers included three Protestant ministers and a nun traveling together. Jean, who was fascinated by religion, became fast friends with the foursome. In the evenings, after her new friends had gone to bed, Jean and a young woman roommate quietly left their cabin for the ballroom, where they danced until midnight with members of an Italian soccer team also aboard.

Jean took an apartment in Manhattan and became head teacher, later assistant head mistress as well, at a Jewish community center in the Bronx. Later she became assistant head mistress at the Episcopal Academy on Seventy-Fourth street, an elite prep school supported by five parishes. On weekends Jean taught Sunday school at St. James Church on Madison Avenue.

Her interest in religion nearly set the future course of her life: Jean was actively considering becoming a nun. She had spent time at an Episcopal convent in Mendham, New Jersey, and had formed strong friendships with the nuns. Meanwhile, since the Episcopal Academy operated just eight months of the year, she took a summer job at another private school to supplement her income. That is where we met on the morning of August 9, 1962, when I sought a school for Michele.

I suggested we discuss Michele's schooling over dinner the next night. That was Jean's birthday, however, and she had other plans. The next day I sent her two dozen red roses. Much later I learned that mine was the third bouquet arriving at her apartment that week. During the daytime the yellow, white, and red roses sat together in the living room.

In the evening the only bouquet on display was the one sent by the suitor taking her out.

A few nights later I took her to the Penguin, a cozy little steakhouse with a fireplace. We drove out to the convent in New Jersey, where she introduced me to the sisters. Jean reported that they approved of me. Much as I was attracted to her, however, my family not only would have disowned me, they would have discarded me if I married outside Judaism after all we had sacrificed in Europe to stand up for it. And, of course, Jean had her own traditional Christian beliefs.

Jean faced a hurdle even tougher than religion. Actually four of them—my daughters, now ages eighteen, fourteen, eleven, and four.

I had occasionally dated other women during the years since Lilo's death, and the girls had their own ways of approving or disapproving. The biggest challenge was the "throw-up test." Four-year-old Michele had an unfortunate habit of getting carsick and disgorging. Her older sisters secretly conspired. They saw to it that Michele was always seated next to Dad's date. If their decision was thumbs down, they would tell Michele to heave—turning her head toward my unfortunate lady friend.

The girls first met Jean when we all went to the Bronx Zoo. Sure enough, going home, poor Michele threw up all over her little tan polo coat, trimmed in white fur. But not a drop on Jean. She had passed the throw-up test.

10
LOVE BLOSSOMS

Jean and I dated the rest of that summer, and in retrospect I'm amazed she put up with me. She had lovely long hair, often worn as a braid down her back. After she learned I preferred shorter hair on a woman, she went to a salon to have it chopped off. The hairdresser flat refused such butchery, so Jean grabbed his scissors and cut the braid off herself.

When she wrote me, I sometimes included a list of her misspelled words in my reply. Words such as the British spelling of "colour" instead of the American "color," sent with a smug little lecture beginning "When in Rome..."

I could envision Jean as my lifetime companion and mother to my children, so I began to include her in more family activities. The two youngest, Alice and Michele, were quite taken; the oldest, Eve, was not pleased, nor, to some extent, was fourteen-year-old Renee. My suddenly threatened housekeeper, Miss Kaelin, did not take kindly to her either. I asked Jean to stay with the children while I was on an overseas business trip. When she came home one evening Miss Kaelin had locked all the doors to keep her out. I knew then that Miss Kaelin's days with us were numbered.

That October, during one of my trips to Australia, the news from the United States was bleak. Tensions between the U.S. and Soviet Union were escalating ominously in what would become known as the Cuban missile crisis. I met with Sir John Williams, owner of Melbourne's leading newspaper and a television station there, expressing my fears. He had been seriously injured in World War I and part of his jaw was missing. Williams, a fine man, assured me that there was no need to go home; war would not break out. He put me at ease and, fortunately for the entire world, he was right.

From there Bill Wells and I went to Japan, then to Singapore where we had a lavish dinner for leaders of Radio Singapore. The station's staff, to reciprocate, insisted that they show us *their* Singapore. They took us to the Tiger Balm Gardens and then to eat at a typical Singapore restaurant. One dish of noodles was cooked before us, after which everyone dug in with their bare hands.

Early the next morning Bill said he was not feeling well, and went to see a doctor. I kept an appointment at the American Embassy, then returned to the hotel also feeling awful. I had just enough strength to call Bill on the phone and say "Please help me." Then I passed out. When I awoke an English doctor, sitting next to my bed, said, "Mr. Baruch, welcome back to reality."

"What day is it?" I asked.

"It's Wednesday afternoon. You've been pretty sick for the last couple of days." He said my temperature had gone to 105 degrees and, despite seven blankets, I shivered so hard the bed started to move across the floor. He asked where I was going from Singapore and I told him Karachi, Delhi, Beirut, Frankfurt, and then back to New York.

"Oh no, Mr. Baruch, you'll never make it," he said, "You'll be buried somewhere along the way. My advice is to go home as quickly as you can to see your own doctor." I had contracted paratyphoid, a serious contagious disease usually transmitted from animal products—similar to typhoid fever but milder. Bill Wells also was sick, both of us, we assumed, from our lunch in Singapore.

I went from Singapore back to Hong Kong to try to recuperate. While there, CBS Chairman Bill Paley wired, asking me to scout out the television landscape in Israel on my way home. CBS wanted to be a consultant for Israeli television, not yet on the air. We landed in Tel Aviv, but I became ill again and the hotel called a doctor. He was a German refugee who looked me over and, in a heavy accent, said, "Mr. Baruch, vat you need is schicken soup." Already nauseous, I nearly threw up at the suggestion.

I called the prime minister's office and made an appointment to see an official there the following afternoon. We traveled by private car to Jerusalem and I presented myself in the office at the appointed hour. The official kept me waiting more than an hour, then appeared and apologized. I handed him my card and explained CBS's interest in helping Israel initiate television.

He exploded with anger. What was I doing here? What did I want? He raved for five minutes or so, while I tried to calm him down and explain that I was simply fulfilling Mr. Paley's request. I could not begin to guess what provoked his outburst. The meeting ended as abruptly as it began, as he ushered me unceremoniously out the door.

Next day the fog lifted. In reading the *Jerusalem Post* it became clear that the official met with me right after returning from the Knesset, the Israeli parliament. There, on behalf of the central government, he proposed that television begin in Israel, and was soundly defeated. From this affront he had returned directly to his office, where Baruch and CBS offered to help start Israeli television.

It was a meeting I still remember with a smile. The official, incidentally, was Teddy Kollek. He honed his diplomatic skills and served as the highly regarded mayor of Jerusalem for nearly three decades, starting in 1965.

I flew from Tel Aviv to Frankfurt, where I became ill again, but not so seriously, and finally from Frankfurt to New York. Dutifully waiting at the airport was Jean. I had lost so much weight she scarcely recognized me. Jean took me to her apartment and called a doctor, who gave me belladonna for the pain. After a few hours of rest I went home.

My paratyphoid recurred annually for the next ten years, usually around Thanksgiving, and I had to be hospitalized twice. Not much could be done except give me standard remedies for the bouts of headache and fever. Eventually the illness subsided.

Days later, after I had recuperated, Jean told me she had converted to Judaism. She had looked into it carefully and decided she could accept its basic tenets. She had taken courses at a synagogue and later went through a ritual purification and cleansing bath called a mikva. It was a wrenching decision. Jean knew she would never sit in a church or celebrate Christmas again. While pondering her decision, she went to a chapel and cried for a long while.

We had a romantic courtship that Jean called "storybook." I loved making her happy, and took her dining and dancing at some of New York's best establishments. Two of her favorites were the The Columns at the Savoy-Plaza Hotel and the Forum of the 12 Caesars, where gladiators' helmets served as wine buckets, waiters wore togas, and the bar had a stunning floor-to-ceiling mosaic mural.

She was a great asset professionally as well as personally. Often I entertained clients, usually men, and Jean would engage their partners as we talked shop.

That fall, however, we started to grow apart. Perhaps it was the pressure I felt to make a lasting commitment, especially now that Jean had converted. I was swamped at work, and felt I did not have the time to carefully sort through my private life. It was easier to defer a decision. Jean and I both started dating other people. After a couple of months, I knew something was very wrong. I was seeing other women, but when alone, Jean's face was the only one I saw.

I called and she agreed to go to dinner. That night, at the Forum of the 12 Caesars, I asked her to marry me.

"Ask me properly," she rightly insisted. I got down on my knees and proposed again. She said yes. I gave her my mother's ring, and—a good omen—it fit. We planned to marry in June. Unfortunately that prospect caused consternation in my two older children, but I was confident they would eventually warm up to Jean.

The parents of my late wife also complicated our relationship. The Bachrachs were quasi-Orthodox Jews, never very pleased with our family's more casual approach to Judaism, and they did not welcome Jean. The first time we were invited to dinner at their apartment, Lucy Bachrach barely greeted Jean at the door. She marched past us and eyed her granddaughters carefully. "You poor things! You look like you haven't had a decent meal since your mother died."

Jean, who in fact loves to cook and is very good at it, was better prepared the next time we saw the Bachrachs. It was winter and the girls' skin was sallow from lack of sun. Jean fished into her makeup kit, got a tin of rosy blush, and brushed the girls' cheeks. Lucy had to admit they looked healthy.

Jean was wise and wonderful with my daughters. She spoke well of their late mother and did not force herself on them. They were starved for affection, and Jean supplied it in abundance.

"It was like being a bone between puppy dogs," she remembers. "You spent fifteen minutes talking to one, and the others insisted on their fifteen minutes." They argued over who got to sit by Jean in the car. We had a lot of fun as a family on weekends—traveling to points of interest, such as Amish country in Pennsylvania; swimming and picnicking at nearby lakes. We wanted the girls near us, and rarely sent them away, even to summer camp.

Unlike the Bachrachs, my father Bernard was thrilled with Jean. She was bright and spunky. He was often bored and found most of those around him ignorant, dull, and easily intimidated. But he and Jean hit it off from the start. She was an avid reader and a lively conversationalist with wide interests. Jean was wise enough to defer to Father's brilliance at the right moments, and he basked in her attention.

Probably no one but Jean would have put up with such shenanigans from Father as the time he called just as we were leaving for the opera. She answered the phone and told him where we were going. Father burst into an aria from that opera—singing on and on and on as I glared at poor Jean and kept pointing to my watch to emphasize we were going to be late.

The Bachrachs and my father and his second wife Elsie joined us each Thanksgiving. Jean learned to prepare kosher meals, using all acceptable ingredients, and everyone went away happy.

Father, now retired, continued to read voraciously. Early in 1966, as he returned from the library with a bag full of books, a truck brushed him and he fell, breaking a leg. From there his condition deteriorated rapidly. He had smoked one or two packs of cigarettes a day all his life, and had emphysema. A doctor at the hospital showed me an X-ray of Dad's lungs. I was appalled; it was a ghastly sight.

They operated on Father's leg and returned him to his room. He began to have difficulty breathing and the doctors performed a tracheotomy, frustrating him terribly as the artificial breathing hole prevented him from talking—one of his great pleasures in life. His aggravation led to a bleeding ulcer and other complications. The medical staff used an electric blanket to regulate his temperature; otherwise he was bare to the waist. Jean was horrified to see all the scars from his saber duels as a youth in Germany.

Dad and Jean had a longstanding bet of ten dollars over whether there was life after death. Dad did not believe in it, Jean did. They were less sure of how to collect on the bet.

Dad was dying and he fervently hoped Jean was right. "Will I see my Charlie again?" he asked her. My brother had passed away in Paris thirty years earlier. Jean assured him he would. She was disappointed that Father did not mention seeing me in any afterlife. On April 6, 1966, Father died, ironically from the same original cause that had taken my brother, a fracture of the femur.

As he lay dying he expressed the hope that, as his sole surviving son, I would restore the name Baruch to some form of prominence. But he had never understood nor showed interest in what I did for a living.

I had inherited his drive and ambition, which would serve me well in the years ahead. I tried hard not to emulate less admirable traits, especially Dad's harshness with me as a child. I never remember him hugging me or telling me he loved me. His absence of affection taught me the importance of giving these things to my own children, however imperfectly I have done so.

Early in 1963 I convinced CBS to enter the annual Montreux Festival, an international competition for programs of light entertainment. To the best of my knowledge no American program had ever won. The show I thought had a shot was "Julie and Carol at Carnegie Hall," a lengthy special at the famous venue featuring Julie Andrews and Carol Burnett in a brilliant, sparkling performance. The taped show was converted to the 625-line system prevalent in Europe, and then submitted. I flew to Switzerland to be on hand for the judging.

The contest was similar to the Emmys or Oscars in the United States. At stake was the top award, the Golden Rose of Montreux, along with silver and bronze awards. Among many other entrants were the

BBC and the Czechs, both on hand with a number of representatives lobbying for their respective programs. With the pressure I saw applied openly by contestants, I tried not to think about what was going on behind the scenes.

Award of the prizes was to be broadcast to countries throughout Europe over Eurovision, the television network of the European Broadcasting Union. To my delight, I was called by the organizers and told that "Julie and Carol" had won the coveted Golden Rose. It was to be presented by French actress Jeanne Moreau. The British Broadcasting Corporation and Czech contingents were furious at being upstaged in their own backyard, and by the arrogant, uncultured Yanks no less. But a vote is a vote, and CBS had won.

Officials told me I could not say anything when accepting the award. Organizers blamed it on time constraints, though I suspected it had more to do with the BBC and the Czechs. It would be the first time a Golden Rose recipient did not publicly acknowledge the award.

In that case, I told organizers, I would not come up to accept it. My threat caused consternation, as I hoped it would, but I simply was not going to stand by and accept the award on behalf of the American network, not say a word, and go back to my seat like a good boy. Finally they relented, but asked that I keep my remarks to thirty seconds or less. For me, that would have been another first.

The time of the live broadcast arrived. After the bronze and silver awards were given, the emcee announced that CBS and "Julie and Carol at Carnegie Hall" had won the Golden Rose. As I stood to approach Jeanne Moreau, radiantly holding our award, I was astonished to hear booing from the British and Czech tables—a heckling so loud it could clearly be heard over Eurovision.

I accepted the award from Ms. Moreau and—I assume to the great surprise of our detractors—briefly thanked the Montreux Festival in French, in German, and finally in English. On my way back to our table the booing resumed, but it rolled off my back, for we had won. A year later the British won the top award and CBS the Bronze Rose for *The Jackie Gleason Show.*

We decided on a small wedding in my home, with just close family members, and a luncheon afterward. We would then fly to Europe for a short honeymoon. CBS kindly arranged for me to represent the company at the European Broadcasting Union (EBU) meetings in Stockholm. I was delighted to do so, and after a short stay in Paris we would fly to Stockholm for the session.

My eldest daughter, Eve, home from college, was implacably hostile to Jean. I had given Eve a leased car of her own, but she insisted that while we were away she would drive mine. I refused. It was a big car and I felt that, being a novice driver, she should use her own. On June, 9, 1963, the wedding went off perfectly. As the limousine pulled up to the house to take us to the airport, Eve said "I hope the plane crashes." With those final good wishes we embarked on our honeymoon.

After Paris, Jean and I went to Stockholm for the meetings of the leading European broadcasters. American and other non-European networks paid a premium price to belong to the EBU, and even then could only be associate, non-voting members.

The Europeans treated themselves royally, in part at our expense. On opening night the big event took place at the Stockholm town hall. To the blare of trumpets, we were all escorted up the stairs of the splendid reception hall to an enormous marble-floored ballroom. There, nearly a hundred long tables had been arranged for a feast featuring a local delicacy, reindeer.

The head of Yugoslav television taught Jean how to skol, intertwining arms and looking into each other's eyes while downing drinks. Following dinner we were led to another large ballroom for coffee. Meantime the tables were cleared and we were escorted back to the cavernous dinner hall where champagne was served and a band played for dancing.

It was a wonderful experience. Early in the morning, when we returned to our hotel, the sun still had not set in that far northern part of the world.

The next day during its formal meetings the EBU voted to increase the dues of associate members, including the American networks, by nearly 100 percent, even though we had no formal say in its affairs. I sat next to Charles Moses, head of the Australian Broadcasting Commission, who joined me in vehemently opposing the increase.

Sitting nearby was the Yugoslav television representative who taught Jean to skol the previous evening. He vigorously backed the increase. When I asked why he said it was directed at the American networks "because that's where the money is." I told him that was the reason the American crook Willie Sutton gave when asked why he robbed banks. Our objections fell on deaf ears and the EBU voted for the exorbitant increases.

The following day we took a boat trip to a resort, where the head of the BBC sat opposite Jean at lunch. During World War II he was in charge of counterintelligence operations in Malaysia. To satisfy Jean's curiosity he explained it consisted primarily of offering rewards of about one pound for the head of a rank and file Japanese soldier, and substantially more for enemy officers. He described in detail how the heads were handled, costing Jean her appetite.

At the last plenary session I got an inkling of the BBC's power. EBU members voted to hold their next meeting in Central Europe on a certain date. The head of the BBC raised his hand and said he had a conflict that day. Members, perhaps not understanding him correctly, reaffirmed the same date. Again the BBC's hand went up: He would be tied up on that date celebrating the anniversary of his college. The entire EBU voted to change the date so he could attend. It was a telling demonstration of the BBC's influence on other European broadcasters.

On another occasion Jean and I were in California and had dinner at Dino's, Dean Martin's upscale restaurant, with the head of programs at the BBC. Across the room sat Rod Serling. I had gotten to know Rod when we were syndicating *Twilight Zone* abroad, which he wrote and narrated. Rod was a brilliant writer who later created "Requiem for a Heavyweight" and other award-winning dramas. He won many Emmys.

The BBC executive, who had a reputation for being bright but unpredictable, asked to be introduced. I took him over to Serling's table and they chatted awhile. Then, to my dismay, he said to Serling, in his clipped British accent: "You know, you're an intellectual phony!"

I was stunned and apologized to Serling. I never forgave the arrogant Brit, and do not know if he had had too much to drink or was touched off by something else. My relationship with Serling also was never the same again.

The BBC's reach extended to our own backyard. We had many requests from foreign broadcasters to buy excerpts of our news and public affairs programs. CBS News President Fred Friendly, a big bear of a man who had produced most of Ed Murrow's TV shows, decreed that CBS would not sell excerpts of our news and public affairs programs to anyone overseas. I agreed, because foreign broadcasters could change the editorial intent of a program or use it in one of their own without CBS's overview or control.

One day we received a call from our man in England, Bob Mayo, asking if CBS would sell a three-minute piece from one of our public affairs shows to the BBC. I reminded him of our policy not to do so. He said he knew the answer in advance but was just going through the motions to satisfy the BBC.

A few days later Mayo called me, irate and cursing. After turning down the BBC, they got the excerpt some other way and aired it. How did they get it? he demanded. I had no idea but also was anxious to find out. I called the CBS videotape department and learned that the excerpt in question was indeed dubbed—at the request of Fred Friendly.

11

TRAPPED IN TINSELTOWN

Hollywood was a weight I grudgingly bore. Marketing programs worldwide forced me to become better acquainted with Tinseltown. Television City is CBS's production and office facility in Los Angeles. The complex covers most of a city block and gives CBS a continuing presence on the West Coast.

Occasionally I attended the Golden Globe or Oscar awards. Before Jean entered my life I took a well-known woman to the Oscars. My date was interested in just two things—who she could see and by whom she was seen—and sulked after not being interviewed on the famous red carpet.

After the ceremonies we joined others at the Academy Ball at the Beverly Hilton. Many of the losers—though chin-up for the cameras—had left the scene immediately after winners were announced, and did not appear at the ball or elsewhere in public that night. (The Academy is well prepared for this and has standbys in formal clothes to fill in the empty seats of departing losers.)

Most members of Hollywood's creative community are a strange lot, suffering from equal parts narcissism and fantasy. Stars of television or the big screen often fall victim to their own inflated publicity. They have great difficulty returning to earth once their shows end, and try to coast on faded stardom. Their demands continue—from the best tables and immediate service in restaurants, to charging any expense in sight to their shows.

Monkey-business accounting is all through the movie industry. Routinely we saw an overhead factor of 20 to 25 percent added to expenses. When a studio is producing a series for a TV network, perhaps a car is written off as "demolished" in episode four. The studio might well charge the network the full value of the car, plus 25 percent overhead. Then, in a subsequent episode, voila! the same car, miraculously mended, might well be back on the road, ready to be demolished and fully written off again. Many a star or investor has sued a studio which reported a loss on a film that, by most reckoning, made money.

Bennett Newman, former head of taxes at CBS who later had his own consulting firm, told me of an audit he did on one motion picture. He went to a major Hollywood studio and sat down with his counterpart on a particular movie.

"I must object to Catherine Deneuve's expenses on this motion picture," said Bennett.

"Why is that?"

"She took a number of people to New York, and ran up an enormous cleaning bill as well as huge bills for limousines, hotels and other things. Then several round-trip Concorde seats to Paris, where she had even larger expenses for hotels and limousines."

"Catherine Deneuve likes to live well and there is nothing we can do about it," said the studio official.

"I still object," said Newman.

"Why do you keep objecting?"

"I keep objecting because Catherine Deneuve is not *in* this picture!"

"Well," said the other man with a laugh, "you can't blame a guy for trying."

Actor Raymond Burr, a good personal friend, was a pleasant exception to the usual Hollywood mentality. He gave back much more than he took. Ray had moderate success in motion pictures, then established himself after he was picked—over Fred MacMurray and Efrem Zimbalist, Jr., among others—to play Perry Mason in the TV show of the same name. *Perry Mason* was a big hit, airing on CBS from 1957 through 1966 and sold around the world.

A giant who sometimes ballooned to over three hundred pounds, Ray lived quite modestly—except for the time we sent him on a European promotion tour and he had a number of suits made in Italy and charged them to my department. When visiting New York, Ray stayed in a moderately priced hotel and was a gem to work with.

Perry Mason, for which he won two Emmys, was followed by another hit series with Ray in the title role of Ironside, a wheelchair-bound detective. It aired on NBC from 1967 to 1975.

Ray was part owner of the Fiji island of Naitauba, his pride and joy. He assisted its four thousand residents and arranged for dozens of children to attend school in the United States. Later Ray sold the island and bought a vineyard in Sonoma County, California. Ray's vineyard produced its first bottle of wine in 1995—the same year he died, at age seventy-six.

Andy Griffith was as pleasant off-camera as on. He and his agent Richard Linke were models of integrity and professionalism. *The Andy Griffith Show* was on CBS eight years, spinning off *Gomer Pyle* among other series. Clint Eastwood also was a pleasure to work with as his career was taking off.

After appearing in a half-dozen or so forgettable movies in the mid-fifties, Clint was picked to play Rowdy Yates in CBS's *Rawhide*, airing from 1959 to 1966. That led to his starring role in the big-screen spaghetti western trilogy, "A Fistful of Dollars," "For a Few Dollars More," and "The Good, The Bad, and the Ugly." They established Clint as a major star—a status he has maintained for more than four decades. We sold *Rawhide* across the globe for many years after its run ended on CBS.

Bruce Lansbury, Angela's brother, became CBS vice president of programs. Jean and I socialized with him and his wife Mary. Bruce helped CBS navigate around some shoals in our program distribution abroad. In 1966 he and Mary took us to the opening night of "Mame" on Broadway, starring his famous sister. Angela was wonderful. Bruce transferred to the West Coast where he produced and sometimes wrote for *Murder, She Wrote*, also starring his sister.

By 1963 about two-hundred thousand half-hours of CBS programs appeared annually on foreign television. We had a huge catalogue and I was constantly on the lookout for additional programming. But a rivalry between CBS's television network and its production activities complicated this effort.

When the network demanded domestic and international distribution rights—a demand usually enforced by network chief Jim Aubrey—producers and movie companies often sought extra money up front. Their special appeals to Aubrey, widely known as the Smiling Cobra, seldom were heeded. Aubrey thought nothing of having a producer cool his heels for half a day in his outer office, then dispatching a secretary to tell him to come back another time.

Program producers had only three American network prospects—CBS, NBC, and a much weaker ABC. This oligopoly control led the networks to demand all rights from the producer-suppliers.

Eventually producers were forced to actually sell programs for less than they cost to make, hoping the shows would be hits on television and that the investment plus a profit would be recouped years later in syndication. Program suppliers often had to find a big company willing to subsidize them in return for a share of the hoped-for profits down the road.

In 1963 CBS decided to have Judy Garland host and star in a weekly musical variety hour on CBS. Garland was a unique talent. With her global reputation I was sure it would be an easy sell, so my staff and I went to work to obtain worldwide distribution rights. It proved very difficult.

David Begelman, Garland's agent and confidant, called the shots on foreign distribution. Repeatedly I tried but failed to contact him. Then Sal Iannucci, head of CBS business affairs, said Begelman was coming to New York, and invited me to meet with them.

Over lunch in a CBS dining room, I outlined our successes abroad and why it was in his and Miss Garland's interest to have CBS Films handle distribution. Begelman seemed impressed. At the end of the luncheon we shook hands. "We have a deal," he said. I outlined several steps to take, for his benefit, to be sure residual payments and essential costs were covered. He agreed to send me a list of the items. After a few weeks I phoned Begelman's office and was told they were still calculating the residuals and would have them to me shortly. With that I informed all of our foreign offices that we would distribute *Judy*

Garland, and give it a first-rate launch.

Then we got a call from the head of our German office, Max Kimental, saying a new German TV network, ZDF, was about to start. It announced that its opening night of gala programming would include *The Judy Garland Show*. Kimental had assured ZDF that CBS had the distribution rights, and rightly was upset. "What happened?" he asked sharply. I was as stunned as he was, and promised to find out as soon as West Coast offices opened.

I called Begelman's office, telling them it was urgent. Begelman finally came to the phone. I reminded him of our meeting and handshake deal. He remembered. I told him of the telephone call from Max Kimental, and reminded him that we shook hands and he said "It's a deal." Begelman disputed none of it.

"David, what happened?" I asked.

"Ralph, I lie a lot."

If there was any poetic justice, perhaps it was that, despite its apparent potential, the Garland show was a big disappointment and lasted just twenty-six episodes on CBS—not even a full season. Observers blamed its demise on a poor format for Garland and too-stiff competition in its time slot.

Begelman went on to become one of the movie industry's top leaders, first as head of Columbia Pictures starting in 1973. His career path says a lot about what Hollywood values. Begelman's stint at Columbia ended after he forged Cliff Robertson's name on several checks made out to the actor, and paid gambling debts with money embezzled from the studio.

His actions shook Hollywood and inspired a best-selling novel, *Indecent Exposure*. Despite such deeds, Columbia considered Begelman a valuable money-maker and tried to keep him as head of its studio. But others clamored for a "Mr. Clean," and found him in Fay Vincent, Begelman's successor. Vincent had been head of the U.S. Securities & Exchange Commission and later would become commissioner of Major League Baseball.

Begelman received a suspended prison sentence and in 1980 became president and CEO of Metro-Goldwyn-Mayer. After producing several box-office flops, MGM showed him the door. By the mid-nineties, still wheeling and dealing as an independent film producer, he was in deep debt and declared bankruptcy. In August 1995 Begelman checked into a Los Angeles hotel and shot himself.

Distaste for the whole Hollywood scene, coupled with a lack of judgment on the creative side of television, prompted me to rarely review scripts, the "bibles" to be developed for one network or another.

Our staff, however, sometimes asked me to read scripts and respond. They figured, only half in jest, that I was a good barometer for a show's chance of success. If I liked a script or a description of a new program to be developed, they became concerned that the project would fail. If, on the other hand, I read the material and branded it "terrible," they felt it had a good chance to make it.

Joe Levine, president of Avco Embassy Pictures, needed funds to complete "The Graduate," starring Anne Bancroft and the rising but relatively unknown Dustin Hoffman. Levine, a rotund man with a cheerful disposition, was a typical old-time producer of what he called "fillems."

He and I met a number of times to explore CBS's potential involvement in this and other movies produced by Avco Embassy, including "Divorce, Italian Style." We agreed on distribution arrangements and the up-front payment by CBS that Levine needed to complete "The Graduate."

I advised CBS management of the deal and was called into Merle Jones's office. I explained what we had agreed upon. Merle's response: "CBS wants no part of distributing pornography." I did not understand what he was talking about. Merle said he considered motion pictures such as "Divorce, Italian Style" pornographic, and CBS would have no part in this and other "immoral" films in Levine's proposed package.

I tried hard to convince CBS leaders that motion pictures in the sixties had more leeway to tell their stories than those in earlier decades. But it was no use. I called Levine and offered some lame explanation. I did not dare tell him what I had been told.

"The Graduate" was a shadow of things to come at CBS. Unlike its news division, commercial programmers had difficulty adjusting to the reality that the sixties were a watershed decade. The nation was bitterly divided over Vietnam, the drug culture flourished, and "make love, not war" was on millions of adolescent lips.

Television had an obligation not simply to chronicle the tumult but to help citizens understand it. One way was through such shows as *The Smothers Brothers Comedy Hour*. Laced with political and social satire, it first aired in February 1967. The show gained a large following, especially among young viewers. But Tom and Dick's irreverence brought pressure from sponsors and unnerved CBS. Corporate leaders grew tired of the headaches and, despite continued strong ratings, canceled the brothers after two seasons.

During a trip to the West Coast Jean and I left our longtime housekeeper, Rose, in charge of the house and children. We called each day and, except for one, everything was fine. On that day Rose told us she had had a little auto accident and had hit some flowerpots, but everything was fine. I went on to Japan and Jean returned to New York, shocked to see that Rose had lost a great deal of weight but could not seem to explain why.

A few days later I called from Japan and Jean said that same morning a man came to the door and handed her two subpoenas. They were the result of Rose's "little" accident, in which a man was injured, and sought $1.5 million from each of us, a total of $3 million. I told Jean not to worry, that Rose drove her own car and we had no responsibility. Her insurance would have to step in. But it was not that simple.

When I returned from Japan I learned that the man Rose hit had had his leg amputated. I went to see a top CBS lawyer, who advised me to hire an expert defense attorney, because my insurance limit was $500,000. I might be held responsible, he said, because one of our children was in Rose's car at the time of the accident, and since I had left Rose in charge of the children, she could be considered my agent. If a jury agreed, anything over $500,000 somehow would have to come out of my pocket.

I secured a prominent, very expensive attorney for the ten-day trial. Counsel for the plaintiff even put five- and six-year-old friends of our youngest child on the stand to try to show that Rose regularly drove them or our children to school. They denied it. Fortunately a majority of the jury—sufficient in this case—voted in our favor. It was a harrowing experience.

Canada's traditional love-hate relationship with the colossus to the south was reflected in television. Canada bought the lion's share of American-produced programs, and was crucial to U.S. television interests. One of the first TV stations in the world was VE9EC in Montreal in 1931. There were almost no sets to receive its hazy, orangish picture, however, and the station folded during the Depression.

It would be two decades before Canadian television was on the air again. Meanwhile the void was filled by American stations near its border—in Buffalo, Rochester, Syracuse, Detroit, and Seattle.

Arguments over government regulation and cultural dominance from abroad have been debated more vigorously in Canada than anywhere else.

"Canada has long been aware of the potential of broadcasting to create a sense of nationhood in a society divided within itself and heavily influenced by its more powerful neighbor," noted one broadcast historian. "...For Canada national broadcasting was a chance to resolve a troubled national unity."[1]

By 1951 there were an estimated ninety thousand television sets in Canada—all tuned to American stations. The following year the government-run Canadian Broadcasting Corporation (CBC) went on the air in Montreal—the largest French-speaking city in the world next to Paris. Two days later the CBC signed on in Toronto, and a year later private stations began operating.

As Canadian television was born, its lobby group for private broadcasters opposed limits on the amount of foreign content allowed in programming. U.S. shows were available at about one-tenth the cost of Canada producing its own. The lobby group, called the Canadian Association of Broadcasters (CAB), was assailed by a member of Parliament:

It [the CAB] is a powerful propaganda agency, operating, as I believe, against the best interests of this country, and from my point of view likely to destroy the independence of this country and place it more and more under the cultural and economic control of the United States....I regard that as treasonable and subversive activity—just as treasonable and subversive as the activities of those who sell our country to a Communist power or to Russia.[2]

Government, however, proved as powerless in Canada as in other democratic countries to block the development of television or stop the flow of foreign programs demanded by viewers and the domestic TV industry. Even the government's own network could not resist American programs. A parliamentary study in 1955 indicated that about half of CBC programs originated in the United States.

As Canadians continued to argue over domestic vs. foreign content, we at CBS and at other American networks did a brisk business with Canadian TV program buyers. They visited Los Angeles, including CBS's Television City, early each year to audition new programs for their home audience. The screenings were an annual ritual.

CBC program chief Doug Nixon was gifted. In the spring of 1962 he and his staff again arrived in Los Angeles to preview new programs offered by the Hollywood studios and the networks. We showed pilots of all the new programs and I explained what to expect in future installments.

Then, with no introduction, I asked the control room technician to lower the lights to view a surprise entry. I was a bit embarrassed by the lowbrow fare. The screening ended and lights went up. Doug Nixon called out "I'll buy it!"

I was flabbergasted. The show was the original pilot for *The Beverly Hillbillies,* about a bumpkin family finding oil on their land and moving to a Hollywood mansion. "This will be a smash hit," Nixon predicted. In fact, he said he would schedule it on Saturday nights preceding hockey. Hockey in Canada is more than a sport, it is an addiction. To schedule a program ahead of hockey on the CBC national network was to express ultimate confidence.

When *The Beverly Hillbillies* debuted in September, television critics blasted it with both barrels. It had a weak story line and mindless dialogue, they said. Quietly I agreed—a sign it might well become a hit, given my notoriously bad sense of what the public will watch.

Viewers were far ahead of us detractors. Like Nixon, they considered *Hillbillies* outrageously funny, and made it a runaway hit in Canada as well as in the United States. It was the highest-rated show on American television during its first two seasons. *Hillbillies* stayed on the air nine years, almost always among the top twelve shows.

During the Canadian visit in 1965, CBS prepared to unveil *Green Acres.* It was a sort of *Beverly Hillbillies* in reverse, starring Eva Gabor and Eddie Albert as a wealthy couple who moved from the city to the countryside. We organized an evening at Eva's home. She lived in exclusive Bel Air in a mansion with a big swimming pool. It was cool so she had heaters placed around the pool. Eva billed us for the heater charcoal as well as the food, liquor, and the hired help.

A year later the party was at the home of Al Simon, producer of the show, and was also attended by Eva, her husband, and Canadian program leaders. Eddie Albert brought a guitar and accompanied his wife Margo as she sang Spanish-language songs. It was lovely.

Jean had a nice party dress made for the occasion at a little boutique in the East Fifties. It was off-the-shoulder and had long sleeves in cream and rose silk organza with flowers and a large silk cabbage rose at the bosom. Shortly after we arrived at Simon's house, Eva sauntered over to us. Looking Jean up and down she said, "Dahling, I vant your dress." Jean politely told her the shop where it came from, and that it had been custom-made.

"No, no, no, no, I vant your dress now!"

Jean didn't know how to answer. Finally: "But it won't fit you."

"I vill have it altered. I vant your dress!"

By now Jean had gathered her wits. "I'm sorry, you can't have it. It's mine." Eva did an about-face and didn't speak to Jean the rest of the evening.

Bernard Baruch, Ralph's father, drafted into the German Army in World War I.

Alice Gunzenhauser and Bernard Baruch on their wedding day. Note dueling scars, marking him as a German and aiding his return to the Third Reich years later as a French intelligence agent.

Family vacation, circa 1930. Back row, left to right: cousin, grandmother (later carried over Pyrenees Mountains to freedom by Ralph), father, mother, Ralph and brother Charles in front.

Ralph as a French Boy Scout. Setting trees ablaze and pitching tents on golf courses. (circa 1935)

Growing from boy to man.

Varian Fry's courageous undercover work in Vichy France saved the Baruchs and hundreds of others as Hitler gripped Europe. Fry has been called "America's Schindler." (courtesy of the International Rescue Committee)

As a U.S. vice consul in Marseille, Hiram Bingham IV disobeyed Washington and assisted Varian Fry's rescue mission. Bingham issued hundreds of visas beyond State Department quotas, and falsified other papers that helped hundreds of Jews, including the Baruchs, escape. (courtesy of Robert Kim Bingham and the U.S. Holocaust Museum.)

Elizabeth (Lilo) Bachrach Baruch, Ralph's first wife. In Pontresina, Switzerland, where the family often vacationed. (circa 1957)

With Eve, first of four daughters, 1945.

CBS representatives from across the world assemble in New York for the company's first international sales meeting, 1963. Company executives (from left): Ralph, head of international sales; Frank Shakespeare, Merle Jones, Sam Digges, Willard Block, Larry Hilford.

Ralph and former Secretary of State Henry Kissinger compare notes on world affairs. Both have served on the board of the International Rescue Committee, which assists refugees.

Rod Serling was one of many writers and producers whose creations Ralph sold across the globe.

Jean and Ralph on their wedding day, June 9, 1963.

The newlyweds at a garden party.

Honeymooning with 200 "friends" at a gala of the European Broadcasters Union in the Stockholm Town Hall. Next morning, over Ralph's strong objections, the EBU voted to increase the dues of CBS and other non-European members nearly 100%.

David Sarnoff led powerful RCA/NBC for half a century. Sarnoff and CBS's William Paley were fierce competitors. (courtesy of David Sarnoff Library)

William Paley in 1928 bought and developed CBS radio and later television into the "Tiffany Network." *Broadcasting and Cable* magazine called him the leading broadcaster of the twentieth century. (courtesy of CBS)

With Leonard Goldenson, founder and chairman of ABC, which got a later start than CBS and NBC, and trailed them for decades, finally reaching parity in the late seventies.

The trip from Hell, in 1963, guiding CBS executive Merle Jones (second from right) and wife Frances (center) through Australia and Japan. Others (from left): Koreaki Takashi, CBS's representative in Japan; Ralph, U.S. Ambassador Douglas MacArthur III, Mrs. MacArthur.

Jean teaching best pal Nim sign language for "love."

A weekend on Long Island Sound on *Calisto*, the Baruchs' forty-three-foot Camper Nicholson sailboat.

Jean at the helm, with Ralph on the *Calisto*.

With (from left) Federal Communications Commissioner Benjamin Hooks, Robert Lewine, president of the Academy of Television Arts & Sciences; and Richard Wiley, chairman of the FCC, who tangled repeatedly with Ralph.

With cable television pioneer Ted Turner, who put news and other cable programming on the map, as CBS's Bill Paley had done for broadcasting.

Pope John Paul II greets Ralph and Jean during a business trip to Rome. The Pontiff blessed a half-dozen rosaries that Jean gave to friends.

12
A VAST WASTELAND?

By 1960 about 90 percent of American homes had television, and it was viewed five hours a day in most of them. As foreign governments continued to fret over the impact of our programs on their citizens, public and private groups in the United States also turned up the heat on the networks. Violence was the biggest concern, especially its impact on children.

"If you came and you found a strange man...teaching your kids to punch each other, or trying to sell them all kinds of products," said noted child psychologist Jerome Singer, "you'd kick him right out of the house. But here you are; you come in and the TV is on, and you don't think twice about it."[1]

Congress began holding public hearings on television violence in the early fifties. Periodic hearings in the sixties, led by Senator Thomas Dodd, a Connecticut Democrat, got a lot of media coverage. Numerous studies suggested a relationship between aggression viewed by youngsters and copycat behavior. One specialist at the University of Wisconsin, testifying before Congress in 1992, summarized decades of research.

> There can no longer be any doubt that heavy exposure to televised violence is one of the causes of aggressive behavior, crime and violence in society....Television violence affects youngsters of all ages, of both genders, at all socio-economic levels and all levels of intelligence....a vicious cycle exists in which television violence makes children more

aggressive and these aggressive children turn to watching more violence to justify their own behavior.[2]

Television also stood accused of squandering its vast potential. The most piercing—and thereafter most-quoted—rebuke came from Newton Minow, chairman of the Federal Communications Commission. Minow, in a 1961 speech, said he had forced himself to sit before a television set, with no distractions, from sign-on to sign-off. He invited others to do the same.

"I can assure you that you will observe a vast wasteland...a procession of game shows, formula comedies, about totally unbelievable families, blood and thunder, mayhem, violence, sadism, murder...And endlessly, commercials..."[3]

Minow's "vast wasteland" stung. It led the networks to take somewhat more seriously their responsibility to inform and educate as well as entertain. The year before Minow's rebuke, John F. Kennedy and Richard Nixon squared off in the first-ever televised presidential debates. In 1962 the U.S. launched Telestar I, a communications satellite that made possible live transmission of events from across the globe. It put public affairs programming on a more equal footing with entertainment.

Among notable news-oriented programs, NBC one evening in 1963 turned over its entire three hours of prime time to a civil rights special. The next year CBS produced "D-Day Plus 20." Former President Dwight Eisenhower led CBS anchor Walter Cronkite on a tour of the beaches of Normandy where Ike commanded the Allied invasion of Nazi-held Europe in World War II.

Americans, for the first time, got more of their news from television than newspapers. News and public affairs, however, remained minor players in television programming. As the Kennedy-Nixon debates were taking place in the fall of 1960, television's first animated prime-time series, *The Flintstones*, began. Four years later, as television prepared to cover the Johnson-Goldwater presidential campaign, the Beatles debuted on *The Ed Sullivan Show*. The historic performance would be replayed numerous times in coming years.

Long after political coverage of 1960 and 1964 was history, *The Flintstones* and Beattles continued to help define American culture.

I continued to press CBS to consider programming from overseas. We sold shows all over the world, yet U.S. network doors were still shut to programs produced offshore. I was frustrated but made occasional inroads in nontraditional ways. First Lady Jacqueline Kennedy conducted a tour of the White House on CBS. At my suggestion, CBS Films distributed the program worldwide, for just the cost of the videotape.

In November 1963 President Kennedy was shot. I was in a restaurant around the corner from CBS headquarters, with a German television official. I rushed back to CBS and ordered that our television coverage be recorded for CBS's foreign clients. We stayed up most of the night, preparing material and sending telegrams and telexes alerting clients that the programming was available. I recommended—and CBS leaders agreed—that these tapes of the assassination, narrated by Walter Cronkite, be made available at cost worldwide.

CBS, ABC, and NBC were on the air covering every angle of the tragedy for four days as the President's body lay in state. None of us aired commercials or entertainment programming during that period. Our nation and much of the world came together as one, for a rare moment in history, to mourn and honor a revered world leader and his young family. None of us at the networks got much sleep. We felt that we were performing an important service for our clients overseas and for our country.

Complaints against American television continued to mount, and hit my international efforts directly. We were accused of distributing violence, sex, and banality, and of staining America's image across the world. We answered that in a free society we offered all our programs, uncensored, and it was the job of offshore broadcasters to decide which ones they should or should not broadcast. It was not our role to decide for them.

To help counter criticism, however, I proposed to CBS that we distribute worldwide a program that would be uplifting in any language: *Young People's Concerts,* featuring the New York Philharmonic, conducted and narrated by Leonard Bernstein. Maestro Bernstein led the music and explained the pieces and individual instruments. The shows cost a lot to distribute because of contractual arrangements. I finally convinced CBS to subsidize them, and I believe we about broke even. I was exhilarated.

We sold these programs worldwide, with wonderful response.

Our home, a three-story English Tudor in Holliswood, a Long Island suburb, was lively. It was large, with four bedrooms on the middle floor and another five or six upstairs. Jean turned one room into a studio where the children painted. She helped them build a little zoo with birds, gerbils, and other small animals. For Father's Day they presented me a do-it-yourself kit for making an alligator belt—complete with live alligator! I stuck with store-bought belts, however, and left the gator in our zoo, where, unfortunately, it eventually got caught between rocks and drowned.

Jean was still adjusting to managing a bustling household with four children, a husband often absent, hired help, and a large house to keep up. Family weekdays started at five-thirty in the morning when we woke Renee, enrolled at a private school in Manhattan. Jean fixed Renee's breakfast, then drove her to the subway to go to school. A half-hour later the routine was repeated for Alice, who also attended school in Manhattan. Finally came Michele, still in kindergarten.

With the girls' schooling, my work, and our social life all centered in Manhattan, we decided to move there. In 1964 we put our house on the market and it was bought by Nita Lowy, later to become a Democratic U.S. congresswoman from that district who still serves her country and constituents with distinction.

We moved to a duplex at One Gracie Square, facing the mayor's home, Gracie Mansion, and the East River. The three-bedroom apartment was on two floors, one of them shared with the Algerian Ambassador to the United Nations.

I returned home from a trip to be greeted by a surprise gift from Jean: a German shepherd puppy. Though we both love dogs, Watson complicated our lives with the early-morning walks and expensive boarding when Jean and I both traveled. Then there was the time the Ambassador accidentally opened the wrong door on our common floor, to find himself eyeball to eyeball with a growling Watson, now 130 pounds of tense muscle. The Ambassador did not repeat that mistake.

For weekend relaxation we bought a small home on Candlewood

Lake, Connecticut. The house was modern with lots of glass. We called it the "fish bowl."

I traveled a great deal, but tried to make it to our daughters' special events when home. Alice, thirteen, went to Nightingale-Bamford, an outstanding college-preparatory school for girls, where she excelled in her studies and took up the viola.

As the third child, Alice probably did not get the attention she deserved. I recall attending a concert of her school orchestra. The scraping of the strings hurt our ears. But we parents were proud of our daughters, of course, and applauded vigorously. Alice had three majors—Latin, chemistry, and science—and several years later graduated first in her class.

That summer Jean and I took the girls to Europe. We stayed in London and ended up in Pontresina, Switzerland, at our favorite hotel. Bill Wells, our CBS representative in Australia, and his family joined us in Pontresina, where we took them on a cable ride nine thousand feet up the Alps. It was the first time their children had seen snow.

The following spring, 1965, Eve graduated from the University of Chicago. Jean and I went out for commencement. The sixties' counterculture was on full display. Shaggy haired hippies paraded before us to slouch in their seats. Painted faces, torn clothes, little personal grooming. It did not inspire confidence in the coming generation. Eve returned to New York to look for work.

Broadcasting in color was a major milestone for television—one I had anticipated for years. I checked out different early versions of color TV at several television studios in Florida and at Japan's Tokyo Broadcasting System.

In the late fifties our family bought our first color television set from RCA. Three company men brought it to our home on Long Island. They muscled the unwieldy set into the house and—literally dressed in white coats—spent time "operating" on it to coax out a picture. The result was pretty washed out, but was undeniably in color.

CBS through the years had consistently led NBC and ABC in programming, but NBC under taskmaster David Sarnoff kept the edge in technology. Americans had purchased 5.5 million color TV sets—nearly

10 percent of all sets sold worldwide—but there were no CBS programs in color to watch. CBS and NBC had fought a titanic battle over whose color system the nation would adopt. Even the U.S. Supreme Court in 1951 tried but failed to settle the issue. Unlike at NBC, programs broadcast in color on the CBS system could not be picked up in black and white on the millions of sets already in American homes.

In the end, after losing tens of millions of dollars stubbornly backing its approach, CBS threw in the towel. The future of color television would be dictated by NBC and its parent, RCA. Grudging admission of that fact came in 1965 when CBS belatedly started broadcasting in color—on RCA's system.

Also at CBS that year it was out with the old—network president James Aubrey—and in with the new, CBS's impressive new headquarters building. Aubrey's liabilities at last outweighed his assets in the minds of Bill Paley and Frank Stanton—the only two company leaders who outranked him. Those hurt by Aubrey's ruthlessness—and they were legion—applauded his downfall. So did media critics, who blamed him for filling CBS's schedule with what they considered insipid, crassly commercial shows at the expense of more worthwhile programming.

Stockholders did not applaud. When Aubrey became network president in December 1959, CBS stock sold at about $17 a share. When he was fired six years later it was the equivalent of $42—thanks in good part to his usual genius for knowing what the public would watch. In the wake of Aubrey's dismissal, CBS stock dropped nine points—to $33.

Why then did CBS give him the boot? Perhaps only Aubrey, Paley, and Stanton knew the full story. Aubrey hit a rare dry spell in the 1964-65 season. He commissioned three new prime-time series from a personal friend, rumored to have less then savory connections, without requiring a customary pilot for any of them. All three bombed, at huge cost to CBS. Suddenly our network was in a tough fight—eventually won—to retain its longtime ratings lead over NBC and ABC.

Insiders hinted at a darker reason for Aubrey's ouster. Along with other CBS brass, he was in Miami the last weekend in February 1965 to celebrate Jackie Gleason's forty-ninth birthday. Aubrey was suddenly summoned back to New York by Stanton and fired that same weekend. Some observers alleged that Aubrey, a playboy whose life was the stuff of at least two novels (*Only You, Dick Daring!* and *The Love Machine*), roughed up some of the beauties he dated, and made the fatal mistake of mistreating the daughter of a station owner, who threatened to blow the whistle if CBS failed to act. Whatever the reasons, Aubrey was gone and his understudy Mike Dann took over as programming chief.

Some of Aubrey's duties, along with his title of network president, went to Jack Schneider, previously general manager of WCBS-TV in New York. The following year Schneider was named president of the newly created CBS Broadcast Group, which included the network, CBS-owned television stations, CBS News and CBS Radio. Schneider was a tough, self-important troubleshooter, somewhat in Aubrey's mold.

Little changed under Dann initially, as CBS continued to coast on Aubrey's rural comedies. But in February 1970 we trailed NBC in the crucial evening hours for the first time in years. Dann, an operator of the first rank, worked every angle with the media, preempted weaker shows, and replaced them with specials—including popular films "Born Free," "Hatari," and "African Queen"—and barely pulled CBS's chestnuts out of the fire.

In the process the barrenness of CBS's program cabinet became evident. Mike's reward for the come-from-behind ratings win was to be shown the door by CBS leaders bent on taking the company in a far different direction.

Veteran CBS manager Bob Wood, named network president in 1969, wielded the big broom that swept CBS's rural comedies out the door—even those still riding high in the ratings. Gone were *The Beverly Hillbillies, Green Acres, Petticoat Junction,* and other shows that appealed largely to older viewers.

Advertisers wanted youth, and Wood would deliver. He started, without fanfare, on January 12, 1971. That evening, a Tuesday, an adult comedy debuted that was unlike anything seen before on American television. *All in the Family*, produced by Norman Lear, starred two little-known actors, Carroll O'Connor as Archie Bunker and Jean Stapleton as his "dingbat" but lovable wife Edith.

Numerous sensitive subjects were about to be thrashed out in America's living rooms. The audience heard the toilet flush upstairs, and witnessed pointed debates between Archie and his "Meathead" son-in-law on prejudice, bigotry, abortion, birth control, homosexuality.

CBS executives held their breaths that first evening as Archie referred to African Americans as "black beauties." When son-in-law Mike (Rob Reiner) called him on it, Archie explained he got the term from "a black guy who works with me [who] has a sticker on his car that says, 'Black Is Beautiful.' So what's the matter with 'black beauties?'" Edith jumped in: "It's nicer than when he called them 'coons.'"

CBS hired extra switchboard operators to be on hand for the howls of protest that night. But not many calls came, and most that did were favorable. Critics, as well as rank-and-file viewers, liked the show. Corks popped on champagne bottles at CBS.

All in the Family started low in the ratings as an unsung mid-season replacement, and rose to become the most popular show on TV by May. It kept that coveted spot five years in a row. With a name change in 1980 to Archie Bunker's Place, it remained on CBS's prime-time schedule through the 1982-83 season, usually among the top fifteen programs, before petering out. Envy at the other networks was intense, especially since NBC and ABC had rejected All in the Family before it found a home at CBS. Analysts said it was the worst programming decision ever made by ABC chief Leonard Goldenson.

All in the Family paved the way for other "relevant" CBS comedies. They included The Mary Tyler Moore Show and two Lear creations: Bridget Loves Bernie, about the intermarriage of a poor Jewish boy to a rich Irish-Catholic girl, and Maude, an outspoken, strong-willed woman. A third Lear creation, Sanford & Son, was on NBC. That network also grabbed the brass ring with Laugh-in, which included numerous jokes about sex and spawned the careers of many stand-up comics and comic actors. Laugh-In aired from 1968 to 1973, and was television's top-rated show its first two years.

The age of innocence was over at CBS, and the other networks were not far behind.

CBS left Madison Avenue in 1965 and moved to its spectacular new corporate headquarters on what is now Avenue of the Americas. It was designed by famed architect Eero Saarinen. His creations also include the TWA Terminal at John F. Kennedy Airport, the General Motors Technical Center near Detroit, and Dulles International Airport outside Washington, D.C. CBS President Frank Stanton, a talented amateur architect, hovered over every detail, and the building is a monument to Stanton. Modern, stark, sleek. The thirty-six-story structure, covered in dark Canadian granite, soon became known as Black Rock. It is Saarinen's only skyscraper. Sadly he died in 1961, four years before it was completed.

Black Rock signified CBS's coming of age as a world-class corporation, and set it handsomely apart from the other two American networks. NBC was located a couple of blocks away in dowdy quarters at Rockefeller Center, and ABC rented space in a modern building a block north.

My office was across from a large room destined to be a screening room, with theater-style seating, projectors, and special technical equipment to conduct the kind of audience research that had helped put and keep CBS on top. Frank Stanton had pioneered the research at our old CBS quarters. Pilots of television shows were projected on a screen and audience members activated a green lever when they liked the show and a red one when they did not. Results, recorded on graph paper, helped guide program producers.

As we prepared to relocate, Stanton announced that all top managers would have the same Knoll Company furniture he selected, but a choice of color for carpet, couch, and chair coverings.

The new offices were modern, except for Paley's. Along with the board room it was done in more traditional style—French Impressionist art on the walls, a round antique card-table as his desk. Stanton's office had Corbusier chairs, a Henry Moore sculpture, a piece of brick from the old Imperial Hotel in Tokyo designed by Frank Lloyd Wright. A handsome, contemporary office. Nearly every major floor had a kitchen and dining room.

Paley and Stanton were on floor thirty-five. Elevators were rigged to go express to that floor or from that floor to the lobby anytime Paley, Stanton, or others on the floor were aboard. CBS didn't miss a stitch. Soon after CBS moved operations to Black Rock, its Madison Avenue building was gutted. During the transition Paley, still at 485 Madison Avenue, needed a screening room at Black Rock. Unfortunately the bare screening room next to my office was selected.

What Chairman Paley wanted, he got. His request came mid-week, for a screening the following Monday morning at ten. Late on Thursday afternoon dozens of workers descended on the empty room. They scurried in and out around the clock for the next three and a half days, looking like the Keystone Kops. The Kops installed two 35-millimeter projectors—no easy task—along with loudspeakers, screen, and all the seats, finishing at 9:30 a.m. Monday. The room was ready for Mr. Paley. Twenty minutes later he called and canceled the screening.

Stanton issued an edict that nothing was to be displayed at Black Rock—including in our personal offices—unless approved by a committee chaired by the head of CBS design. Virtually all photographs and other art were to come from CBS's own collection.

After we moved in, it was announced that Stanton was going to inspect the offices on our floor. Despite the edict, many of us displayed family photos. We were advised to take them all down for Stanton's visit. I had hired another assistant, Larry Hilford, a Harvard graduate who helped lighten my load. Larry flat told me he was not going to remove his family pictures from his desk and console.

I took the problem to my boss, Sam Digges. His reaction: "He's going to have to resign." I was dismayed. Here was a magnificent piece of manpower—a brilliant planner and a nice man, who was going to be fired over personal pictures. I went to see Merle Jones. He agreed to handle the matter, and convinced Stanton to visit a different floor.

Then there was the CBS flower lady. The Japanese woman reportedly had been found by Stanton in a flower shop he frequented. She was hired to tend all the greenery at Black Rock. A friend sent me a plant for my new office. The flower lady came in and watered my CBS plant. When I asked her to also water my personal plant, she pointed at it and said "No water, that's not CBS plant." She finally relented and gave it a trickle. It was another reminder that, at Black Rock, CBS called all the shots.

When CBS fired network president Jim Aubrey, his hand-picked assistant Frank Shakespeare was transferred to the division that included us. Frank, who later played an important role in the Nixon administration, oversaw a number of areas, including international investments. I was named a CBS vice president and my boss Sam Digges and I both reported to Shakespeare.

Frank was forty years old—two years younger than I was. He had red-blond hair and boyish good looks. Like most top company executives, he came up through sales at a couple of CBS stations. Shakespeare usually was a quick study and an excellent decision-maker. During our first meeting I explained the contract I was ordered to negotiate with Goar Mestre, our partner in Latin America, which disadvantaged CBS. Frank said to do only what was best for CBS. That was what I hoped to hear. It enabled me to form CBS Latino Americana to explore opportunities across the region.

Occasionally Frank tripped over his hubris. For some time I had talked with my friend Junzo Imamichi, chairman of the Tokyo Broadcasting System, about an ownership tie between our two companies. He was amenable.

My assistant Willard Block went to Japan and worked out a plan for CBS to purchase 15 percent of TBS. We considered this a marvelous opportunity, particularly since ABC was being wooed by Fuji at the time. CBS leaders agreed on a price for the 15 percent. All that remained was for Imamichi and his top lieutenants to come to New York to work out final arrangements and conclude the agreement.

Willard and I met with Merle Jones, Shakespeare, and others, and outlined the order of events which would take place during the Japanese delegation's stay. During our initial meeting, as is customary in Japan, we would exchange gifts, with Stanton presenting his gift to his counterpart, Imamichi, and so on. Someone asked, "Gifts? What for?" We explained that it is the Japanese way. We would purchase all the gifts from Tiffany's, to be given in descending order of importance, and the Japanese would give us their gifts.

The first meeting was set for the CBS executive dining room, with the Japanese facing the window view and us facing the wall. It would be a get-acquainted event, with strictly no mention of business. We would then suggest a luncheon, at which Merle Jones would outline the acquisition plan.

Shakespeare's body language said he thought this was all non-sense. He continued to question why it was necessary and we continued to explain it was the Japanese way—the only way they did business. To close the deal we had to do it in an upward, spiraling manner, leading to a final celebration dinner, held after both sides had signed the preliminary agreements.

The Japanese arrived, we received them in the dining room, and the gifts were exchanged. So far so good. Then Shakespeare, with a flourish, blurted out that CBS was delighted to be investing in TBS. Our guests looked at each other, bewildered. This was not the plan they had agreed to, and they were completely taken aback. The Japanese actually hissed in embarrassment. They mumbled that this was premature, and that they had to discuss the matter privately among themselves. From there the deal unraveled, not to return. I was crestfallen. This would have been marvelous for CBS, but it was not to be.

Shakespeare's genuine overall ability was tempered by a fierce, sometimes nutty conservative ideology. One day I was in his office when he closed the door and asked "Ralph, what are we going to do about Hunt-ley, Brinkley, Chancellor, and Cronkite?" All were broadcast journalists at the top of their profession. Chet Huntley and David Brinkley anchored the NBC nightly news, John Chancellor was an NBC correspondent, and, of course, Walter Cronkite anchored the CBS evening news.

"What do you mean?" I asked.

"Ralph, they are all a bunch of communists."

It was surreal. I shrugged, did not say another word, and left his office. I then understood better Frank's attraction to Richard Nixon.

During the 1968 presidential election Frank took a sabbatical from CBS to run the formidable television end of Nixon's campaign. The following January he was one of the new president's early appointees—to head the United States Information Agency, the same job that took Edward R. Murrow from CBS eight years earlier. Frank overall was given high marks for running the USIA fairly despite his strong views.

Bill Paley and some other company leaders wanted to get into the motion picture business. CBS showed movies several times a week, they reasoned. Why not produce our own, rather than buy from outsiders in expensive bidding? The company hired cigar-chomping Gordon Stulberg, a Hollywood attorney at Columbia Pictures, to head its movie-making. Stulberg wanted my division's name, CBS Films, for his new division, and, over my strong objections, company leaders acquiesced.

We were known as CBS Films throughout the world, and the name change required an enormous amount of effort and paperwork, costing about $2 million, for which I charged Stulberg $3 million. We had just finished when Stulberg decided he did not want the name CBS Films after all, because theater owners disliked the networks and he did not want a name associated with one. It was unclear why he did not think of that two million dollars earlier. He named his division "Cinema Center Films." We stayed with our new name, CBS Enterprises.

The first motion picture CCF launched was in 1968, "With Six You Get Egg Rolls," starring Doris Day in her last big-screen role. Stulberg organized a private viewing of another new CCF film for CBS executives, including Paley and Stanton, and we assembled in the theater to preview it. At the end of a picture, a certain amount of applause was expected and almost always accorded. In this case the room remained utterly silent. The film, "Boys In The Band," was about homosexual life in New York City. Stulberg forgot an old entertainment rule of thumb: If you want to send a message, call Western Union. CCF got a black eye as a result.

Other Cinema Center Films releases included "April Fools," with Jack Lemmon and Catherine Deneuve; "A Man Called Horse," Richard Harris; "Little Big Man," Dustin Hoffman; "The Reivers,"Steve McQueen, and "Royal Hunt Of The Sun," Christopher Plummer—a true financial disaster. The films were of mixed quality. After losing what some say was hundreds of millions of dollars, Bill Paley's ardor to make motion pictures cooled and then froze. Cinema Center Films was abandoned.

In 1967 Sam Digges went to CBS Radio and I was named head of CBS Enterprises, still reporting to Shakespeare. My portfolio included domestic and international sales, licensing and merchandising, Terrytoons, and other activities.

As head of a major division I was given one of the company's ninety-nine executive telephones. When in the office you were expected to answer that phone, whether you were Ralph Baruch, Bill Paley, Frank Stanton, or any of the other ninety-six who had them. When absent, a secretary was to answer your executive phone, not ask who was calling, and, in my case, say, "Mr. Baruch is not here, may I take a message?" In an age before email, it was an effective way to communicate internally with company decision-makers.

CBS Enterprises sold NFL football abroad, as an experiment. We sent broadcasts of games to Mexico, working with Emilio Azcarraga, the William Paley of Mexican broadcasting, and his company, Televisa. Live broadcasts of Dallas Cowboys games were a huge success.

I also decided to resurrect *What's My Line?* and sell it in syndication. The show had aired on CBS from 1950 to 1967—television's longest-running prime-time game show. Panelists tried to guess the occupation of the contestant. There was great chemistry among its intelligent, well-spoken regulars: moderator John Daly and panelists Dorothy Kilgallen, Arlene Francis, Bennett Cerf, and often Fred Allen.

We agreed on the royalty to CBS and now needed a producer. After a long search we engaged Mark Goodson-Bill Todman and their Gil Fates, who had produced the original *What's My Line?*

They suggested we play the "owl game" to find an emcee. Mark Goodson would suggest a name, and if we said "Whooo?" that would alert us that the individual may not be well-enough known. Goodson suggested Wally Bruner and I said "Whooo?" Despite losing the owl game, Bruner emerged as our emcee. The show returned to the air for seven years, until 1975, and was moderately successful in syndication.

13

ADVENTURES ABROAD

I n Australia our relationship with crusty media baron Frank Packer improved somewhat, thanks in good part to Bill Wells, our man there.

Jean and I had dinner with Sir Frank at "21" in New York. Even on our turf he was the same blustery bull I had watched rage down under. Frank ordered a rare vintage Bordeaux. The wine steward apologized and told Packer that "21" did not have that particular vintage. Packer insisted that they did and he wanted his wine.

Jerry Burns, an owner of "21," came over and apologized. "Sir Frank, I'm sorry but we're out of that wine." Packer: "I know you have it, I want it, and I want it now!" Jerry disappeared, then returned in a few minutes. "We're looking, but we don't have it." Packer continued to insist they did. Sure enough, ten minutes later, whether purchased elsewhere or found deep in their own cellar, two bottles of the wine arrived.

Jean and I went out to Australia and Packer invited us to his home. He liked to intimidate guests and before he appeared he let loose two of the biggest dogs I had ever seen. Jean and I owned a large German shepherd, so Frank's unique welcome was wasted on us—an obvious disappointment. "You're not afraid of my dogs, eh?" he asked Jean. "No, not at all," she answered.

Frank had remarried and he and his wife served an impressive dinner for twelve, with an enormous side of beef he carved on the sideboard. Guests included Australia's national treasurer, William McMahon, sixty, whose right-of-center Liberal Party was preparing for national elections. After the meal the women retired and the men went into another room for cigars and port. McMahon, a short man with piercing blue eyes and little hair save for bushy white sideburns, asked Frank casually, "Are you going to support us again in the election?"

"No way," answered Packer. "I will not support you."

"And why not?" asked McMahon, who hoped to become prime minister if his party won.

"Others who support you get something for it," said Packer. "My support is taken for granted and I get nothing."

McMahon asked what he wanted and Packer cleverly replied, "A television outlet in Canberra," Australia's capital. Only the public Australian Broadcasting Commission was there. "If you give me a license in Canberra, I will not be competing with any local media in the market and will not sell local ads. I will just make it a repeater station."

Packer in fact offered nothing in exchange for the license. A relay transmitter from Sydney into Canberra had no need for local studios, local news, or any other obligations. It would simply increase the warm bodies watching his Channel Nine and hence the rate he could charge advertisers. McMahon, probably ignorant of what was involved, agreed.

Packer supported McMahon, who became foreign minister. Later, after internal shakeups in the Liberal Party, McMahon became prime minister in 1971. Australia was the last industrialized nation without pay television, thanks in good part to the power of the Packer dynasty.

Frank's older son, Clyde, was being groomed to take over his father's media empire. But in 1972 they had an explosive falling out after Clyde assigned a Channel Nine reporter to interview Bob Hawke, a prominent leader of the trade union movement and Labor Party, and later prime minister.

Frank shamelessly used his print and broadcast outlets to campaign against unions and that party, and forbade the interview. Clyde resigned in protest, severing ties to his father, his brother Kerry, and their far-flung empire. Sir Frank died two years later at age sixty-seven, and Kerry inherited nearly everything, including his father's aggressiveness. By the end of the century Kerry had expanded into other industries—in the U.S., Europe, and Great Britain, as well as his native country. He was

Australia's richest person when he died in December 2005.

On that trip we visited in Melbourne with media owner Reg Ansett, an aviation pioneer and founder of Ansett Airways—Australia's most prominent airlines after Qantas. Ansett insisted that Jean and I go see the Great Barrier Reef and stay at his resort house nearby. We flew north to Queensland from Sydney. On our way up, in a World War II-vintage DC-3, we were surrounded by two kinds of lively cargo—a rugby team that had just won an Australian championship, and celebrated by downing every alcoholic drink aboard, and crates full of cackling chickens.

A car picked us up in Townsville. We did not know that Reg had also promised his house to two other couples, so six of us shared the small, rather primitive quarters. With a lack of culinary water we showered in a mixture of seawater and fresh water.

A helicopter had been shipped up and, unbeknown to us, was assembled next morning, just in time for sightseeing. It took us over the Great Barrier Reef, actually the world's largest collection of individual coral reefs, with a diversity of species rivaled only by tropical rain forests. It was a magnificent sight, the deep-blue tropical water turning turquoise and then dusty white in shallow water directly over the reefs.

Traveling the globe had its perks and its perils. CBS Sales was well removed from CBS News, but outsiders tended to lump us together. That was helpful if they liked what they saw on the tube, but unhelpful and even dangerous if they did not.

It was the middle of the Cold War and leaders behind the Iron and Bamboo Curtains tried hard to keep foreign television and radio from reaching the eyes and ears of their citizens. The typical approach was to jam signals—broadcast an irritating noise on the same frequencies used by foreign broadcasters—to smother incoming messages. That was increasingly difficult to do given new technologies, including satellites, which transmitted TV signals from the U.S. and western Europe all across the world.

CBS newsman Marvin Kalb did a documentary on the Volga, the longest river in Europe, which flows entirely within Russia. Russians have deep feelings for the Volga, romanticized in song and literature.[1] Volgograd—formerly Stalingrad—on the bank of the Volga was the site of the major Soviet victory over Germany in World War II. Kalb's documentary was not a sentimental journey, but a hard-hitting piece of journalism about the problems and challenges of the Volga and those who live along it.

Larry Hilford left my staff for another CBS division, and I replaced him with a man named Fred Gilson. Gilson, along with our European sales manager, Howard Karshan, decided to take an exploratory sales trip to the Soviet Union. They were met at the airport by an official from Russian Television, who gave them a lengthy lecture about Kalb's documentary and its characterization of the Soviet Union.

One night as Fred and Howard returned to their hotel, the attendant present on every floor in Russian hotels appeared to be asleep. Fred opened the door and entered an outer hall leading to his room. As he opened the door to his own room he was hit over the head from behind and knocked unconscious.

When Fred came to he was bleeding profusely and called Howard for help. A doctor sewed up the nasty wound. Next morning the same television executive who ranted at the airport called Fred about the incident.

"Will you report this?" he asked.

"No," Fred wisely answered. "I'm sure it was just a bunch of hooligans trying to steal something."

"Good, if you won't report it, we won't have to detain you," said the Russian. Fred and Howard left shortly afterward and I was relieved to have them back on American soil.

In the Philippines we did business with a television station and network owned by Andres Soriano. The Soriano family was and still is extremely well known there. They controlled the country's largest food and beverage company, San Miguel, as well as its largest newspaper, *The Manila Times,* shrimp fishing and processing factories, and other enterprises.

Soriano's wealth, however, was not reflected in the payments to CBS of his TV holdings for programs licensed from us. Accounts were far in arrears, so on one of our world jaunts Bill Wells, our man in Australia, and I took a side trip to Manila to confront Soriano.

We arrived and checked into the old Manila Hotel, once MacArthur's headquarters. There was a strike at Soriano's *Manila Times*, shooting had broken out, and an innocent bystander had been hit in the head. Soriano invited us to dinner at his home. They would send a car for us. Meanwhile trouble at *Times* grew, and the city was tense. Kidnaping for ransom was not uncommon.

That evening we went downstairs for our ride, casual and careful not to draw attention to ourselves for safety reasons. We quietly told the doorman that we were waiting for a car from *The Manila Times*. The doorman obviously took his job seriously. He yelled over the public address system: "Driver for *The Manila Times*, pull up please."

It got worse. An old beat-up Chevrolet, with a big crack on the passenger-side window, pulled up. The driver, in an athletic T-shirt, told us he was the driver for the *Times*. "I'm not getting in that car, no way!" I told Bill. He talked with the driver, who insisted that the *Times* had sent the old car instead of a limo to avoid drawing attention.

Reluctantly I got in and we drove and drove. I turned to my colleague, and—in a remark that became a classic between us—said "Bill, the neighborhood is getting progressively worse." Suddenly the driver took a sharp left turn and pulled up in front of an enormous iron gate, which opened and then closed behind us. A guard with an automatic rifle patrolled the courtyard, and another was inside the mansion. We were relieved to find it really did belong to Soriano.

Weeks later I visited Soriano at his New York townhouse, accompanied by a CBS attorney. Finally he paid his debt. At the end of the century his grandson, Andres Soriano III, headed the family's business empire.

Italy's rising media tycoon was Silvio Berlusconi. For five years, ending in the spring of 2006, Berlusconi was his country's George W. Bush and Bill Gates rolled into one: Italy's prime minister and its richest person by far, with a personal fortune estimated at $12 billion. Several decades ago as I crisscrossed the earth promoting American television, I simply knew him as a growing force in Italian television. That was enough to pique my interest and lead me to Berlusconi's doorstep.

We had business in Italy and I was asked to be a presenter at Italy's equivalent of the Emmy Awards. Berlusconi called and invited us to meet with him. Jean and I flew to Milan, where we were met by a driver in an enormous Mercedes limousine. We were bound for the Villa at Arcore, the castle Berlusconi had recently acquired. The limo took off at breakneck speed—a good one hundred miles an hour at times—through the pastoral countryside until we came to a huge gate. Beyond it lay a park and, finally, the castle.

Berlusconi, suave, slender, and surprisingly young for his substantial reputation, greeted us warmly and proceeded to show us his one hundred forty-five-room "home."

In a magnificent art gallery he exhibited old masters on movable panels, as one would display rugs. Shortly before our visit thieves had stolen a Rembrandt and other extremely valuable paintings from his collection. We followed Berlusconi into his personal chapel. He pushed a button and soft lights came on. Another button and the organ began to play. A priest came on Sundays to celebrate his private mass.

Our host led us to the basement where he had just renovated a private theater, furnished with plush armchairs and a small stage where Luciano Pavarotti recently had performed. There was a large indoor swimming pool and nearby offices. Berlusconi and his staff often worked around the clock. When tired, they took a quick swim to revive, then returned to work.

His small office was crammed with stacks of video tapes. In the far end, over his desk, was a portrait of a stunning woman with an angelic face, half hidden in shadows. The artist was Italian master Pietro Annigoni. The tragic story of the woman, as told by our host and confirmed by friends in Italy, suited her brooding portrait.

It seems the castle previously belonged to the woman and her husband, a titled Italian nobleman. One day the count returned unexpectedly from a trip abroad and surprised his wife and her lover. Instead of raging, he calmly told both of them to be in his office the next day. They appeared as ordered and, at gunpoint, he directed them to an adjoining bedroom. There he forced them to make love. As they did he shot them both. Italian friends of mine confirmed the story.

The castle was abandoned and fell into disrepair. Berlusconi bought and restored it to its former splendor, adding the modern touches he showed us.

We retired for dinner, exquisitely served, with his daughter by a previous marriage acting as interpreter, and one of his top executives in attendance. Berlusconi apologized for the absence of the woman destined to become his second wife, Veronica Lario, who had just given birth and was resting upstairs.

A German writer offers this insight into the union of Berlusconi and Lario:

> After years of marriage, he falls in love with a theater actress with long blond hair and together they have a love affair otherwise known only to the watchers of the soap operas shown daily on Fininvest's [Berlusconi's media conglomerate] channels. The Latin lover hides her for months in one of his office buildings until she gives birth to a son. Berlusconi then breaks up his first marriage and moves with his new family to a castle close to Milan, the Villa at Arcore, that he has bought for almost nothing under obscure conditions.[2]

A quarter-century later, according to reports, the couple's ardor has cooled considerably. But Berlusconi's media and financial empire has continued to blossom. He owns three television networks, as well as newspapers and magazines, a huge amount of real estate, AC Milan—one of Europe's best soccer teams—and other businesses.

By the time his center-right coalition faced reelection in the spring of 2006, Berlusconi had a huge number of detractors, evidenced by the fact he had been the target of more than ninety investigations and had been indicted more than ten times for one form of corruption or another. But like the cartoon character Road Runner, Berlusconi had yet to be caught and punished by Wile E. Coyote.

The pattern for Berlusconi's devil-may-care approach to life was reflected when he broke the government's television monopoly in the eighties. A federal law prevented the creation of private television networks that would compete with the government's RAI. Berlusconi simply bought local broadcast rights across the country, and his stations ran the same programs at the same time, thereby delivering a national audience to advertisers.

When judges in two cities ruled his arrangement illegal in 1984, Berlusconi appealed to Socialist Prime Minister Bettino Croxi, who overruled the judges and put Berlusconi back on the air. Craxi later served as best man at Berlusconi's second marriage.

RAI had been created as a public monopoly in 1954, making Italy a poor market for foreign TV programs. Finally, in 1976, a court decision cracked opened the floodgates to privately owned television. A pent-up reservoir of commercial TV interests swam through, led by Berlusconi. He built his empire primarily with American films and television series, including *Dynasty, Dallas*, and sitcoms.[3]

By 1987 Italian television imported $300 million worth of foreign programs, nearly half the European total of $675 million. About 80 percent of Italy's imports were from the United States.[4]

Following his election as prime minister in 2001, Berlusconi stabilized Italy's government as he had privatized and stabilized its media. Italy, with many political parties, has long suffered from political fragmentation. Berlusconi represented the fifty-ninth Italian government since World War II—and remained in power longer than any of his fifty-eight predecessors. But his long string of good luck ran out in 2006. Dodging various accusations of wrongdoing, Berlusconi himself became the chief issue in parliamentary elections.

Clearly frustrated at being an underdog, he unleashed one headline-grabber after another. He accused a German member of the European Parliament of acting like a Nazi prison camp guard, said the Chinese Communists, under Mao Tse-tung, boiled babies to make fertilizer—Italy's communists were part of his opponent's coalition—said he had accomplished more than Napoleon, and called himself the "Jesus Christ of Italian Politics."

More damaging than Berlusconi's rhetoric was Italy's sick economy, which grew slower than that of any other big industrialized country during his five years in office. The unemployment rate for Italy's working-age population at election time was 42 percent, the highest in Europe. Even Italians willing to forgive the Prime Minister's gaffes drew the line when they could not find jobs to feed their families. They booted

Berlusconi from office.

CBS expanded rapidly abroad. We formed CBS-Japan, with Ko-reaki Takahashi as chairman and two other highly competent men to as-sist him.[5] We engaged Jorge Adib, who had been in advertising, to head CBS-Brazil. In my entire career I believe he was the most able, hard-working sales executive I have encountered. Under Jorge we started to realize Brazil's potential at last.

In Israel, CBS signed a consulting agreement with the govern-ment to establish television service. Israelis came to New York to be trained, then a number of our engineers and other experts were stationed there.

We held our first international sales meeting in 1966, bringing our executives to the U.S. from throughout the world. They came from Australia, Brazil, France, Germany, Japan, Lebanon, Nigeria, the United Kingdom, and Miami where we maintained CBS Latino Americana. We started on the West Coast, where our guests toured CBS's Television City and met many stars of our shows.

In New York we took the group to a baseball game at Yankee Sta-dium, complete with beer and hot dogs. Most did not understand base-ball at all, but they seemed to have a good time.

The last evening was at the old Savoy Plaza Hotel, scheduled to be demolished right after our event. Frank Stanton spoke. He was fastidi-ous in making any technical arrangements. When he needed a projector it always had to be set up in duplicate in case of malfunction. I did not think the microphone also needed to be duplicated, but I was wrong. When Stanton stood to speak he grabbed the mike stand. A flash of fire and smoke shot out of the top. I thought, *Oh my god, we've electrocuted him!* The mike was dead, but fortunately Frank was not. He gave a good speech without it.

A highly prized item for CBS executives was a set of eighteen-carat-gold cuff links with the CBS eye logo in onyx and marble, designed and produced in Italy. Our top people wore them with pride, and they were greatly coveted. At a cocktail party the leaders of our offshore sub-sidiaries were presented these cuff links, and immediately put them on their shirts.

I gave Ken Page, our man in Canada, just one cuff link and announced that if Canadian sales justified it, he would get the other link the following year. He was embarrassed until he realized it was a joke.

Ken went on to bigger things for us, as head of CBS Europe. His predecessor, Bob Mayo, had relocated to CBS New York because his wife did not like shopping in Europe. Ken's new office was in Switzerland. But a few weeks after he moved to Zurich he came to me with another spouse problem. His wife Pat could not stand living where she did not speak the language. Ken said they would have to move to London. This was a major challenge and involved considerable cost and time of CBS employees, especially in our law, tax, and finance departments. But we made the switch from Zurich to London.

At the end of December that year, we received a letter from Ken, saying he was going to resign. After all we had done to accommodate him, it was a shock. I noted that Ken sent his resignation after his Christmas bonus check had cleared. Willard Block and I left the next day for London. We talked at length with Ken. He had been offered the same position he held with us at a competitor, Screen Gems, a subsidiary of Columbia Pictures.

We had dinner at Prunier's. I recall it well because it featured a rat that ran by on an enclosed ledge above us to entertain diners, and I pointed it out to my two guests. Our discussions seemed to bear fruit, and before we left Prunier's we shook hands on Ken's decision to stay at CBS. The next day in his office, however, Ken again expressed doubts. That did it. I turned to his assistant, Howard Karshan, and said "Congratulations, you're the new head of CBS Europe."

Ken did not stay long at Screen Gems, and eventually moved back to Canada. I will not claim that the rat at Prunier's was an omen, but I do wish I had kept Ken's other cuff link.

14
STORM CLOUDS FROM WASHINGTON

I n Washington, storm clouds gathered over ABC, CBS, and NBC. The government was concerned over the networks' considerable power. Part of the worry was political grandstanding and part was well-founded.

Their oligopoly enabled them to force unreasonable concessions from producers. Their position: For the privilege of getting your program on our air, the network will take all rights, including U.S. and foreign syndication, licensing, merchandising, and whatever else we want.

The networks wielded power unwisely, virtually inviting the Federal Communications Commission to step in. CBS insisted on keeping all rights to the shows they and most others produced for the CBS Network, and owning at least 50 percent of shows distributed by others and airing on CBS.

Late in 1968 a nervous Frank Stanton asked me to draw up a plan of what CBS should do if forced to stop syndicating and owning programs. After weeks of hard work I submitted a thirty-page document to Stanton. I proposed that CBS could form an outside company, using syndication rights as collateral to secure bank financing. Then I all but forgot about the report.

In 1970 the FCC adopted several rules that hit the networks hard. Under the prime-time access rule, stations in the fifty largest markets could not air more than three hours of original network shows or network reruns during the main viewing period each evening. The goal was to make room for new players to use the airwaves. (The FCC abolished the prime-time access rule in 1996.)

At the same time the FCC adopted Financial Interest and Syndication Rules (the "fin-syn" rules) that prohibited the networks from having a financial stake in programs they did not produce, and barred them from later syndicating reruns of programs they aired. The networks were also barred from owning cable systems.

The syndication rules were a severe blow to the networks and a disastrous development for my division, CBS Enterprises, whose bread and butter was syndication. Our future looked bleak.

The networks were particularly vulnerable to pressure from Washington at that time because of financial challenges beyond our control. A sluggish national economy, including a strike by giant General Motors, reduced the sale of commercial time. Congress banned cigarette advertisements on television and radio—CBS's number one source of ad revenue—which meant an annual industry loss of at least $230 million in gross sales, starting on New Year's Day 1971.

No one expected any favors from the Nixon administration, which took office two years earlier. Rarely if ever has a U.S. president and the national news media eyed each other with such mutual dislike. Richard Nixon had a visceral hatred of the media, thinly disguised by a veneer of politeness in public, but at times on full display.

He probably never forgave television for his loss of the presidency to John F. Kennedy in 1960 following the nation's first televised presidential debates. Surveys indicated the debates were about a toss-up on substance, but Nixon—then recovering from a knee injury and underweight—looked tense and pallid, and Kennedy healthy, handsome, and smooth. Two years later Nixon also lost the California governor's race and famously promised reporters "You won't have Nixon to kick around any more."

That, of course, was not true. In 1968 Nixon rose like the phoenix from his political ashes and the struggle was joined again. From his earliest days in the White House, archival records show, Nixon sought ways to get even with the media. The most damning evidence comes from his own mouth—in audio tapes produced by the system Nixon had installed in the White House in February 1971.

Two months later, in April, Vietnam Veterans against the War massed for the first time in Washington and marched to Capitol Hill. They included John Kerry, later a U.S. Senator from Massachusetts and the Democratic presidential nominee in 2004. Kerry and other veterans threw their combat medals or ribbons over a wall.

On May Day, student protesters threatened to shut down the capital by blocking the bridges over the Potomac River that connect Washington to Virginia and Maryland. District police took away tens of thousands of protesters—including many journalists—and detained them in a football stadium.

But Nixon was not satisfied. An Oval Office tape reveals Chief of Staff H.R. Haldeman telling the president that special White House counsel Charles Colson is having the Teamsters Union send "their eight thugs."

Nixon: "They've got guys who'll go in and knock their heads off."[1]

Haldeman: "We can deal with the Teamsters. And they, you know—"

Nixon: "Yeah."

Haldeman: "—it's the regular strikebuster types and all that and... they're gonna beat the shit out of some of these people, and, and hope they really hurt 'em. You know, I mean go in with some real—and smash some noses."

The biggest club Nixon held over ABC, CBS, and NBC was the threat of an antitrust suit or non-renewal of broadcast licenses of the stations they owned. "If the threat of screwing [the three networks] is going to help us more with their programming than doing it, then keep the threat," Nixon told White House Counsel Charles Colson on July 2. "Don't screw them now. [Otherwise] they'll figure that we're done."

Colson, Nixon's surrogate in trying to browbeat the media into treating the White House better, agreed: "...keeping this case in a pending status gives us one hell of a club on an economic issue that means a great deal to those three networks...something of a sword of Damocles."

Nixon: "Our gain is more important than the economic gain... Our game here is solely political....As far as screwing them is concerned, I'm very glad to do it."

Attorney General John Mitchell was set to file an antitrust suit against the networks to break up monopoly ownership of prime-time programs, Nixon said. He told Colson he would have Mitchell "hold it for a while, because I'm trying to get something out of the networks." Nine months later, in April 1972, the White House gave the signal and the Justice Department filed suit. The immediate issue was network ownership of prime-time programming, but that was only the start of the trouble.

Vietnam continued to divide the country. The time was ripe for a demagogue, and Vice President Spiro Agnew stepped forward. He tried hard—and to a degree succeeded—to hang the blame for America's anger and pain on the media's front door.

In a November 1969 anti-TV speech carried live to the nation by the same three networks he condemned, Agnew argued that "Nowhere in our system are there fewer checks on vast power."[2] He said a news commentator opined that, if it weren't for Nixon's fear of hostile reaction, he would follow "his natural instinct to smash the enemy with a club or go after him with a meat axe."

"Is it not fair and relevant to question [the networks' concentration of power] in the hands of a tiny, enclosed fraternity of privileged men elected by no one and enjoying a monopoly sanctioned and licensed by the government?" asked Agnew. "The views of the majority of this fraternity do not—and I repeat, not—represent the views of America." He concluded: "...we'd never trust such power over public opinion in the hands of an elected government. It's time we questioned it in the hands of a small and unelected elite."

Scary stuff. Such broad-brush rants are common in dictatorships, which always crush or coerce into silence the independent media. They are not common in democracies—especially the Republic with the world's oldest living constitution, whose foundation is a hallowed Bill of Rights which guarantees freedom of speech and the press.

At the time of Agnew's broadsides I was president of the International Council of the Television Academy. In introducing a speaker at an awards ceremony, I noted that the Nixon administration, including Agnew, was itself being widely investigated for corruption.

One of the trade magazines published my remarks. A few weeks later, for the first time ever, I received a letter from the Internal Revenue Service telling me to bring in a recent tax return for audit. My accountant in tow, I went down to the IRS. An agent went over my return and stamped it "accepted as submitted."

I breathed easier, but the IRS was not finished. Another notice soon arrived from the agency, ordering me to bring in my prior year's return. In that year Jean and I had been sitting in our car at a toll booth when a car slammed into us from behind. Jean spent nearly two agonizing weeks in the hospital, part of it in traction. Her physician prescribed a mattress especially constructed for her. In those days one could deduct this as a medical expense.

Again flanked by my accountant, I presented my return to an IRS auditor. I believe she was determined to find something wrong with my return. She would not accept the deduction of the mattress as a medical expense. Although my accountant advised me to forget it because an appeal would cost more than the deduction, I refused because of the principle involved. We won on appeal.

The House Judiciary Committee voted three articles of impeachment against Nixon in July 1974. He resigned days later. Agnew was already gone, departing the previous October after it was shown he had accepted illegal payments as governor of Maryland and as vice president. Michigan GOP congressman Gerald Ford replaced Agnew as vice president and, when Nixon stepped down, replaced him as president.

Fortunately for the good of the nation, most presidents have accepted and some even relished the essential role of the media in our democratic system. One such chief executive was Lyndon B. Johnson. CBS President Frank Stanton had a good working relationship with the garrulous Texan, as he had with a succession of other presidents.

When I came home one weekend, there was a message that Frank wanted me to call him. I phoned the CBS switchboard, whose operators were like bloodhounds in tracking someone down. After a bit of a wait a voice said "This is Frank Stanton." He had a question that I quickly answered. Then, out of curiosity, I asked where he was.

"I'm at the White House under President Johnson's desk," he answered. As he told me later, Johnson's desk was too low for his long legs.

LBJ knew of Frank's woodworking hobby and asked him to fix it. Frank sculpted and added one piece of wood under each desk leg.

On another occasion, Richard Salant, then president of CBS News, was asked by Johnson's staff to come to the White House to discuss some matters on LBJ's mind. In the middle of their meeting, the president suddenly stopped and suggested they all go for a swim in the White House pool. Salant, as he told several of us, said he had not brought a bathing suit. No problem, said Johnson. Led by him, they stripped off all their clothes and skinny-dipped.

Though extremely busy, I wanted to assist the International Rescue Committee, which helps refugees throughout the world and was instrumental in getting my family out of Europe.

Leo Cherne, a prominent businessman, was the IRC's longtime chairman. He advised nine U.S. presidents on humanitarian and intelligence issues. Leonard Marks, a prominent Washington, D.C. attorney, was the group's president. Over dinner we discussed the IRC, and Leo and Leonard appointed me to its board.

At any given time there are millions of men, women, and children wandering the earth—vagabonds abroad or displaced within their own countries because of famine, other natural disasters, or especially war. They are a poignant human wave lapping at the settled world's doorstep.

The United States historically opened its arms to refugees. But there are shameful chapters when America's compassion faltered, including World War II when only a tiny portion of those seeking safe haven here were allowed in, and perhaps again today as the fate of millions of illegal immigrants is debated, too often in harsh terms unworthy of a great nation.

As governments press their agendas, thousands of non-government organizations have risen to the humanitarian challenge. None is more effective or has a better track record than the IRC. Ninety percent of its funds go directly to refugee programs and services, just 7 percent to administration, and 3 percent to fund-raising. *Forbes* magazine calls the IRC one of three "broad, efficient charities" most qualified to make a significant difference in impoverished areas of the world.[3]

The IRC in 2006 was co-chaired by Tom Brokaw and U.S. diplomat Winston Lord, with Norwegian actress and director Liv Ullman as vice chair. Its overseers and directors included such figures as Colin Powell, Henry Kissinger, and Nobel laureate Elie Wiesel.

My first foray abroad for the IRC was to Hong Kong, then a British colony. Thousands of mainland Chinese each year escaped across the south China land border or risked their lives swimming the bay to Hong Kong. Those caught by the British were returned to communist China. We helped establish refugee camps. When I was there, however, the camps lacked tents, let alone more substantial shelter. After 1975, when communist North Vietnam defeated the U.S.-backed South, some 200,000 Vietnamese boat people also flooded Hong Kong.

IRC chairman Cherne organized the Citizens Commission on Indochinese Refugees—a cross-section of American political, cultural, and religious leaders. The Commission made many trips to Southeast Asia, and was the leading advocate for those fleeing Vietnam, Cambodia, and Laos.

During my tenure on the board, the IRC also helped resettle dissident refugees from the Soviet Union; aided Afghans fleeing to Pakistan after the Soviets overran their country, and when Afghans began to return home eight years later; created emergency programs in the Sudan for refugees fleeing Ethiopia and Somalia; helped Palestinian and Lebanese refugees uprooted by the war in Lebanon; began a health-care program in Poland in partnership with the Polish trade union movement, Solidarity; offered relief to Mozambicans fleeing to Malawi in southern Africa, and when they returned eight years later.

Like many non-profits, the International Rescue Committee was often short of funds. I suggested we raise its public image and more money at the same time, and called on some friends to help. Herb Strauss wrote and produced thirty-second and one-minute public-service spots for television. Our non-paid talent included Raymond Burr, Mary Tyler Moore, Eddie Albert, and Liv Ullman. A distribution firm sent the public-service ads to TV stations across the country. They aired many times, raising the IRC's profile and helping to fill its coffers.

My most satisfying mission was helping to establish a short-wave radio station in northern Honduras. It brought elementary education to

Indian children whose families had fled persecution by the Marxist Sandinistas in Nicaragua and now lived in camps.

After working hard to establish the station, I attended the inau-
gural ceremony in Honduras. We flew to Tegucigalpa, the capital, then
traveled by open-air jeep in sweltering heat for about two hours to a village
near the camp. I checked into a stable-like "motel"—bare rooms separated
by partitions that went about three-quarters the way to the ceiling. A radio played hot Latin music a few stalls away, making a nap impossible.

Next morning we showered with a hose, and breakfast was prepared on heated stones. Conditions in the camp were dispiriting. A mea-
sles epidemic had broken out and the camp was quarantined. A circle of
tents sheltered families who had been there for weeks or months with no
prospects of better housing. Most of the refugees were Mesquite Indians
who left Nicaragua without the skills, education, or, above all, help from
any country to begin a new life.

The guest of honor was the Honduran minister of culture. She
was charming and seemed competent, but arrived an hour late at a nearby
grass airstrip as we sweltered in a large tent. Everyone else drank a beverage of water and fruit, but I did not dare touch it, given the paratyphoid
I contracted in Singapore years earlier. Someone cracked open a coconut
and I drank the tiny amount of juice. By the end of the ceremony my lips
were blistered.

Several of us hitched a ride on the minister's plane back to Tegucigalpa, where I had an ice-cold beer that I can taste to this day. The
same IRC driver picked us up. His battered Jeep with perhaps a quar-
ter-million miles on it was parked next to a fancy four-wheel-drive air-
conditioned vehicle owned by the government Agency for International
Development.

The contrast symbolized the status and life possibilities of those
in the mainstream of the developed world and the teeming millions of
refugees clinging to the edge of life across the globe.

Israel launched television service late, in 1967, because of cost—
estimated at $200 million the first six years—and other factors. Its first
broadcast was live coverage of a victory parade celebrating the end of the
Six-Day War and reunification of Jerusalem. Kol Israel—"The Voice of

Israel"—hired CBS earlier to help plan its service, train personnel, and supply programming. Though on the air, they had not yet paid the required program license fees to CBS. On a trip to the region I tried to collect.

Making an appointment, I arrived right on time at Kol Israel and walked into the director's office. He looked up from his desk and said coolly "What can I do for you?" I answered as I had in similar situations: "The first thing you can do is offer me a chair." He did, then said "Our lawyers tell us—" I stopped him in mid-sentence. "Look, this was to be a business meeting. If you tell me that you want your lawyers involved, that's fine with me, I'll have the CBS lawyers contact your lawyers and let them work things out."

"Well," he replied, "I find your programs inferior and we want no part of them, and I will tell my lawyers so."

"Fine. I will tell my lawyers that you signed a contract and refuse to honor it." The meeting was over. Many months later the matter was straightened out, but that and similar personal experiences left a bad taste in my mouth for dealing with Israeli businessmen.

When Merle Jones retired from CBS in 1968 the Paleys threw a black-tie dinner for him at the St. Regis Hotel where they maintained a residence. Bill Paley and his wife Barbara were gracious hosts. (Once considered one of the world's most glamorous women, Barbara, known as "Babe," is best remembered for saying "you can never be too thin or too rich.")

Jean and I wondered how the sensitive seating of CBS's top executives would be handled. Who would get the coveted seats next to the Paleys and Stantons? Bill and Barbara handled it with typically perfect protocol. They had two bowls at the entrance to their dining room. One had blue numbered slips for the men, and the other pink numbered slips for the women. Guests picked a number and voila! seating arrangements were settled.

When we returned home our teenage girls asked us all about the party. We said it was nice, particularly the entertainment—two male singers in turtle-neck sweaters and jeans—featured on CBS Records. The girls, full of awe, said: "Could it have been Simon and Garfunkel?" "That's it!" we answered. They swooned.

It was not all that strange that I did not know of Paul Simon and Art Garfunkel, important as they were to another company division. CBS operated not as a united kingdom but a land of fiefdoms, each jealous of its prerogatives and too often loath to help one another.

Paley was king, of course. For decades Stanton was heir apparent—or so everyone, especially Stanton, assumed. In 1966, however, Paley stayed on past age sixty-five, mandatory retirement age for everyone else, dashing Stanton's ambition of heading CBS. In 1973 Stanton would retire with Paley still at the top.

The relationship between Paley and Stanton frayed somewhat after Paley's decision not to step down. Two other factors also may have contributed to the independence of CBS division leaders that enabled them to ignore the interests of other divisions: Paley's reluctance to involve himself in corporate details, and Stanton's preoccupation with a hostile Washington. He was the leading spokesman and defender of the broadcasting industry in the halls of Congress and at the FCC.

An example of an intra-division conflict costly to CBS occurred in the early seventies when Canadian television interests began to insist that filmed programs they acquired be released to networks or stations in that country before the U.S. Most Canadian stations were near the U.S. border, and they refused any longer to play second fiddle to American TV stations sending signals into Canada. On the other hand, of course, U.S. television stations near the border violently objected to a Canadian "pre-release."

The Canadian Broadcasting Corporation gave our office an order for Perry Mason for twenty-six originals and—providing we supplied all the originals—twenty-two repeats. At about that time CBS program chief Mike Dann decided to economize by having the network produce just twenty-two originals. I went to see Mike with the numbers and showed him that if he produced four more originals, we would gain several million dollars in repeats from the CBC.

"That's great for your budget," said Mike, "but not the network's budget, which is my budget." Not enough originals were produced to satisfy the Canadians, so we lost the entire order and CBS corporate lost a great deal of money. I was extremely disappointed.

CBS Laboratories, under Peter Goldmark developed the first home video tape recording system in the late sixties. Despite tremendous creative capacity, CBS released the hardware with almost no software. The CBS Network was interested only in developing its own software, taking the same position they did vis-à-vis CBS Films: Anyone else who developed software, including other CBS entities, was in competition with them, and that was unacceptable.

CBS attorneys, inside and out, likewise acknowledged only one client: the CBS Television Network. They cared little about any other division, including mine.

Once I was nearly thrown out of a lawyer's office when I urged that CBS give up some of the program ownership rights which yielded nothing for CBS, made my work more difficult, and had attracted the baleful attention of the FCC. It was useless. The network always prevailed, whatever the problems to others at CBS or the negative impact on the company's bottom line.

Early in 1970 Frank Stanton called me to his office. He said he had spent sleepless nights pondering the report I prepared in 1968 on what CBS should do if the networks were ordered by the FCC to stop syndicating and owning programs. When writing the paper I knew that ABC intended to sell its film division to its employees and NBC its similar business to a small distribution company. I instinctively knew CBS would be unwilling to sell to employees or a third party. The thirty-page report I wrote suggested CBS Enterprises go public, with its assets collateralizing a bank loan.

Stanton instead told me CBS was going to spin off its cable and syndication interests into a new company that also would belong to its shareholders. I would be part of the new company and Clark George, then head of CBS Radio, would lead it. I barely knew George but had heard his colorful nickname, "Chief Crazy Horse," and soon enough would know how he earned it.

George was standing by in another room and Stanton asked him into his office. The three of us chatted awhile and then George and I left. "Let's get together at the earliest possible time," I said.

"Oh, absolutely not," answered George. "We should not even be seen together."

Since the planned spin-off had not yet been announced, he probably thought it best not to have someone guess what we were up to. But to not even meet together was extreme, especially with all the planning before us. At Stanton's request I made an office available to George on my floor, so he could familiarize himself with our operation.

George was a trim six-foot-two with a white crew cut. Once a high-ranking Navy officer, he was known locally as a senior athlete who played bruising basketball at the City Athletic Club. His work habits were bizarre. When I arrived at about eight in the morning, Clark would already be in his office. Except to enter or exit, his door was always closed.

What he did in there was a mystery, partly solved after a few weeks when I started to find a daily trickle of what became an avalanche of paper under my door. Some were clippings from *Variety* with the notation: "RMB—did you know this?" I assured him that I routinely read *Variety*, the publication that most closely followed our industry, and was aware of whatever he had clipped from it.

A board of directors had to be formed. George and I and some other CBS executives were to be directors, with recent retiree Merle Jones as board chairman. I learned that Richard Forsling, CBS's former assistant general counsel, was to be a director and head up the new company's small cable operations. All contracts and other arrangements with CBS had to be negotiated and signed.

Our company needed a name. One day I discussed possibilities with Stanton. He ventured that all of our work would be in communications. I agreed. Frank then suggested ViaCommunications, but we both knew that was too long. He loved to dabble with graphic arts and said "We could abbreviate it and call it Viacom, starting with the V then the straight I, and then inverting the V to make an A."

"Frank, I think that's a poor choice," I said.

"I like it," he answered.

Viacom it would be.

15

CBS vs. VIACOM

O n June 29, 1970, CBS notified its forty-three thousand stockholders of the coming spin-off. "We have looked at other alternatives and concluded that this is the course which is best for the two businesses [syndication and cable] and thus best for our shareholders," said the letter, co-signed by Paley and Stanton.

They explained: "We have felt that cable television and syndication have a bright future. We still do. But the FCC restrictions are impairing these two operations just at the time when they should be taking advantage of bright opportunities for growth. It is neither wise nor fair to shackle their prospects during the inevitably long process of seeking more equitable rules."

Viacom would have about two hundred of the current CBS employees, and annual sales projected at about $20 million. They hoped Viacom would be listed on the New York Stock Exchange.

CBS shareholders would get one share of the new company for every seven shares of CBS they held. This meant Paley would own nearly 10 percent of our company and Frank Stanton 1.2 percent. The FCC ordered that these shares be put in a voting trust and be disposed of by a certain date.

Clark George (aka Crazy Horse) was preoccupied with finding a logo for Viacom, apparently trying to imitate the CBS eye. He turned to Lou Dorfsman, head of CBS design, and threw $30,000 at Dorfsman's artists to come up with a design. One day George asked all the new directors to assemble in the screening room. There, on the chairs, were displayed the proposed logos. Already impatient with this priority, given all the decisions we faced, I was not encouraged by the designs, which got progressively worse. George, I thought, picked the worst one of all, in which the V in Viacom could scarcely be discerned. In the end Viacom's logo—with a strong, simple V—was created by a graphics consultant after the company was independent.

Near the end of 1970, CBS hosted a Viacom news conference for business reporters in the cafeteria at Black Rock. George had been warned by lawyers not to discuss too many details of the new company, especially financial projections, since we were in the process of registering with the Securities and Exchange Commission. Schooled in the Navy tradition that loose lips sink ships, George scarcely answered anything at all.

When questions were directed at the Enterprises part of the new company and I stood to answer, he motioned me to sit down. A couple of reporters asked what good was the meeting if no questions were answered? The session was a disaster. We were off on the wrong foot with the media, who would pay us back in spades down the road.

George's wife Judy was going into the hospital for back surgery. "This is no time for a husband to be around," he announced. Instead he would organize a "safari" to visit all the cable systems Viacom would soon inherit out on the West Coast.

After the surgery, Jean visited Judy in the hospital. A few weeks later Jean picked me up at the office for a social engagement. Clark opened his door briefly, saw Jean, and closed it again. A few moments later he emerged and, without uttering a word, handed Jean a buck slip and disappeared back into his office. It said: "To Jean Baruch from CBG. Thank you for being so kind to Judy when she was in the hospital."

George must have had a bad experience with CBS News. He outlined a plan to go into competition with it. He thought our international offices could double as news bureaus. George consulted with Time Inc. and other media outlets about establishing a news operation, and even asked broadcast journalist Martin Agronsky if he would like to lead it. It seemed sheer folly for a commercial company with no expertise to consider gathering and distributing news—especially in competition with

CBS's vaunted news team. Fortunately the idea died of its own weight.

When George set up shop on my floor at Black Rock I had an Asian secretary, Vicki. She was a pretty young woman with long hair and nice figure, but was somewhat flaky. Whenever Clark came by my office he would stop and chat with her.

I returned from an overseas trip and found a copy of a cash advance, on which Vicki had signed my name. I knew nothing about it and immediately confronted her. Where was the cash? "I have it at home," she admitted. I fired her on the spot. A few days later Clark asked "Where's Vicki?" When I told him, he erupted. "The only attractive secretary we have, and you *fired* her?"

George hired a radio salesman with no public relations experience to promote Viacom. When Viacom was officially in business, said George, he would take out a large ad in the top fifty newspapers in the country, including *The Wall Street Journal*. I told him that would wipe out all our profits for the following year. He did not respond.

He asked for memo after memo on an array of issues such as contractual arrangements with CBS, relations with producers, and many other aspects of our operation with which he was unfamiliar. In a series of extremely frustrating sessions I tried to brief him on the importance of all the agreements and what they should be after the spin-off.

George then began to negotiate with CBS Inc. which held all the aces. Representing CBS was tough Jack Schneider, executive vice president, backed by Bob Daly, new head of business affairs. Many of the subjects were alien to George, which was to be expected, since he was from radio and knew little about our core businesses. Almost every point went to CBS by default.

Most CBS syndication agreements followed the industry pattern. The syndication division reported the financial status of shows once or twice a year and, based on actual receipts, remitted what was owed to CBS. But in Viacom's case CBS insisted that we report quarterly and pay CBS in advance, based on estimates. Obviously this would severely strain our cash flow, and I pleaded with George to resist it. He did not. CBS demanded all foreign tax credits. I urged George to appeal to Frank Stanton for fairness. He would not.

That fall Bill Paley arranged a lunch with three Viacom leaders. By now I was so used to CBS corporate clobbering us that the thought of even eating together gave me pause. But I told myself: What could possibly go wrong at a simple social function?

The lunch was set for one o'clock in Paley's private dining room. Three of us arrived shortly before one and waited in a reception area. It got to be ten past one, one-thirty, and finally at a quarter to two Paley appeared and ushered us into his dining room, apologizing profusely for being late. The head of network programming had just resigned, he explained.

Paley was famous for having the best of everything, including his own chef, and was a model of protocol and decorum. We chatted amiably, the appetizer was served, and Paley asked many questions about Viacom. We answered the best we could.

Then the thin beef steaks were served. They were cooked to be eaten at one-fifteen, had been kept warm, and were served forty-five minutes late. Now, I should explain that my European upbringing was fastidious, including strict table manners. No elbows on the table, chew with mouth closed, and handle utensils properly—never touch the knife blade nor the tines of the fork. If I did so at home my father would say, "If you want to eat like a peasant, go and eat in the kitchen with the help."

But here came the lingering CBS steaks. I tried mightily to cut into the shoe leather-tough meat using proper etiquette. No luck. Finally I pinned a piece with the knife and was able to pierce it, then tried by sheer force to separate it from the rest of the steak. Suddenly it skipped across my plate and across the table like a frisbee, landing near Paley. I thought it was funny. He did not. Chairman Paley, in fact, was dumbfounded. He threw a disparaging glance my way and did not talk to me the rest of the luncheon.

Viacom set up shop at 345 Park Avenue. It was an elegant building, extremely well run, and our space was excellent. The furniture remained, simple but functional and sufficient for my tastes.

Prior to the move some of my colleagues in the Enterprises division wanted to discuss issues with George. He called a meeting in our screening room and was the last to appear. At CBS Radio he began the day as he had in the Navy—with morning inspections of his salesmen, checking for proper attire, shined shoes, and clean finger nails. All through this Viacom meeting he addressed us military-style as "men."

Some of my managers were ready to give up on George. I tried hard to convince them that we could get along with him and that I stood between them to mitigate problems. I had no stomach for leading a revolution against George. But it was no use. Following that meeting a number of my top people resigned.

A former lawyer for CBS Radio was to be Viacom's new general counsel and secretary. He continued loyal to CBS ahead of Viacom. For outside counsel he chose a three-lawyer firm, one of whom had represented CBS for many years. George accepted another castoff, CBS's assistant general counsel Richard Forsling, making him president of the Cable division, and Jim Leahy, CBS controller, as our chief financial officer. I respected both of them.

Only later did I realize that some Viacom appointees were executives that CBS and Jack Schneider apparently wanted to get rid of. Some of my staff told me that key people at CBS tried to discourage them from joining the new company by saying Viacom was the repository for many CBS rejects and would not last long in the communications industry.

In the fall we moved into our new quarters. Afterward I had lunch at the Laurent restaurant with retired CBS executive Merle Jones, chairman-designate of Viacom. I was getting more and more concerned about our contracts with CBS, which greatly disfavored Viacom. Walking along Park Avenue back to our offices, I explained the dilemma to Merle. As Viacom's prospective chairman and a former top CBS executive, Merle certainly had the power to intervene and help.

"Ralph," Merle answered, "when a baby is born we must do nothing to hurt the mother."

"But Merle, what happens if, in the process, the baby dies?"

"Ralph, in the birth of a new child, one must do nothing to hurt the mother." His position was clear, as was his loyalty. The deck was stacked against Viacom top to bottom.

Late on a December evening we all met in the CBS law library. The new Viacom/CBS distribution agreement, codifying arrangements between the two companies, was put on the table for signing by Bob Daly, head of CBS business affairs. George pushed the document over to me and said, "Please sign."

"No, you sign it," I answered.

"No," said George. "You sign it."

My reply gave vent to months of frustration. "That piece of shit? I will not sign it."

"I'm ordering you to sign it," said George, voice rising. It was sign or lose my job. I signed.

For accounting simplicity, the spin-off was to take place at noon on December 31, 1970. But earlier that month three minority shareholders of CBS's San Francisco cable system brought suit against CBS and Viacom, claiming anti-trust and other violations. Just an hour before the scheduled separation the FCC notified us it was stopping the action. When he learned of the decision, George, cursing, literally punched a hole in his office wall.

The FCC said Viacom's corporate structure was unacceptable. Certain CBS officers and beneficiaries of various CBS deferred profit-sharing plans could not serve on the Viacom board. The agency insisted on a complete and absolute separation of Viacom from CBS. Merle Jones was suddenly stripped of the Viacom chairmanship. To add insult to injury, Viacom had to agree to indemnify CBS for all costs of the litigation with the minority shareholders, even though CBS's actions had brought the suit.

Life with Clark George became even more difficult after the FCC decision. He saw Viacom as a junior CBS, with all the accouterments it took its parent four decades to acquire. Viacom in fact was an emerging entity quite different in design and function from CBS. It had many financial problems that threatened to sink it almost before it left harbor.

Early in 1971 Forsling, Leahy, Paul Sternbach, who was to be general counsel, and I met several times, each doubtful of Viacom's viability under George. Our careers were at stake. Finally we took the issue to Frank Stanton. Either George went or all of us went. He could name any of us head of Viacom and the others would work under that leadership. Frank asked us to return the next day, a Saturday, when he would bring

CBS's assistant general counsel.

Next morning, after we had reassembled in his office, Stanton extended his hand to me. "Congratulations, Ralph, you are Viacom's CEO."

He chose me, I believe, because I was the only one of the four who had line experience. The others had worked as support staff—Forsling and Sternbach in legal and Leahy in finance. The other three congratulated me, then left. Stanton stressed the importance of getting along with Viacom's new board of directors—mostly his friends and blue-ribbon business colleagues, several of whose boards Stanton served on.

Board members included Paul Norton, a leader of New York Life Insurance Company; Najeeb Halaby, head of Pan American World Airways; John White, president of the Cooper Union, a local college for art, architecture, and engineering; George Harrar, president of the Rockefeller Foundation; Richard Schall, president and CEO of Jostens, a Minneapolis-based company that produced class rings and yearbooks; and finally—one of our own choices—W. Burleigh Pattee, managing partner of Chickering & Gregory, our law firm in San Francisco. This was to be my board, together with Forsling, Leahy, and myself. It felt like getting married to strangers.

After Stanton named me CEO I immediately asked him a number of questions, including if Viacom would have the syndication rights to motion pictures produced by CBS's Cinema Center Films. He confirmed it would. I also said I wanted to think about his job offer.

"Absolutely," said Frank, nodding his head. I started to get up from my chair.

"Where are you going?" he asked.

"I just said that I'd like to think about this."

"Please, take all the time you need," he said, motioning for me to sit back down.

That is how I became head of Viacom.

Stanton asked me to make Richard Forsling chairman of Viacom's board as well as president of its Cable division. I mentioned the difficulty of having a line officer serve as board chairman and said it might not work. "You make it work," he answered. No sooner had I returned to Viacom than Frank was on the line, asking me to please come back to Black Rock. He had been told by a CBS attorney that, since Viacom was to be an independent company, he could not appoint the board chairman. But Frank wanted my assurance that I would propose Forsling. I again noted my reservations, but assured him I would.

Many of the early headaches CBS gave Viacom seemed traceable to one man, Jack Schneider, executive vice president for all of CBS and, at the time, the leading candidate to replace Frank Stanton as president. Whether solving CBS personnel problems by shoving round employees into square Viacom holes, forcing oppressive financial conditions on the yet-to-be-born company, or withholding CBS assets that should go to Viacom—Schneider was never far from the levers being pulled.

This was the same Schneider who years before had called Stanton a "smartass" during a budget meeting for questioning the success of the television station Schneider managed. Mike Dann, then CBS program head, introduced Schneider to a publishing executive during a party at Dann's house. This exchange followed:

"What do you do at CBS?" asked the publisher.

"I reign," said Schneider.[1]

"You what?" repeated the publisher.

"I reign."

"Right," said the publisher, "And you snow too, I'll bet." Asked if he was powerful enough to fire the "most trusted man in America," CBS anchor Walter Cronkite, Schneider said "I could, but I wouldn't."

I met with Schneider one last time to try to win fairness for Viacom and to clarify what assets CBS had assigned us. He outlined briefly that they consisted of syndication and the company's cable operations. Did this include CBS's interest in a Canadian cable company? I asked. His answer: "Don't get greedy." I asked him to alter onerous conditions CBS had put in our distribution agreement, to no avail.

Schneider seemed miffed at all the problems Viacom, its proposed board, and, lastly, I presented him. On the bright side, since CBS was prohibited from the syndication business, it transferred all rights held in various programs to Viacom.

In retrospect, I believe Schneider came close to arranging for Viacom to be stillborn. How? By assigning Dr. Clark George to perform the

C-section. It is possible that the only two CBS executives who outranked Schneider at the time—Bill Paley and Frank Stanton—were not fully aware of Clark's idiosyncracies. Schneider could not have been unaware. When Schneider was president of the CBS Broadcast Group, George, then head of CBS Radio, reported directly to him.

After Stanton named me to head Viacom, our directors accepted Clark George's "resignation" at a board meeting. It must have been awful for him. To his credit, he took it calmly. I understand he became manager of a luxury hotel in the Caribbean. I heard later that the job did not work out and he then became a consultant on human resources on the West Coast. Perhaps there are still managers he trained out there, inspecting their employees' shoe shines and fingernails and addressing them as "men."

Shortly after I replaced Clark as head of Viacom I learned that in our new office space Italian marble tile was scheduled to be installed in the CEO's private bathroom. It was then to be covered with carpet. I checked to see what else George had ordered, and was dismayed. The list was long and luxurious. It included a stereo music system, in both his office and bathroom. Many items were coming from Knoll, CBS's elegant furniture supplier, including a six-figure order for George's own office. I was outraged. With difficulty I got the furniture and everything else canceled.

In February 1971 CBS announced my appointment as a CBS group president and CEO-designate of the new company to be spun off. Viacom would issue a little more than three million shares and have forty-three thousand shareholders—a daunting prospect as we considered the cost of annual reports and servicing their needs. (Our first annual report had no photos or graphic flourishes, and was printed on paper not much heavier than toilet tissue.)

Stanton, CBS general counsel Robert Evans, and I met on another issue. To my dismay, Evans insisted that before it could spin away, Viacom had to turn in CBS's microwave licenses to the FCC, and reapply for them. Signals to our cable systems were transmitted by microwave. This meant that, for an unknown period of time, service would be cut off to many of our cable subscribers.

I was devastated. This latest blow by CBS would damage our reputation and standing with newly inherited customers. But we were stuck. We ended up providing video cassettes of our programs to the cable systems, pending re-issue of the microwave licenses.

For working capital, CBS loaned Viacom $6 million at prime rate, although, with its financial clout, CBS almost certainly could borrow at lower rates. As soon as we were independent, we would have to secure new bank loans and repay CBS. To top it all off I was told that, in the interest of fairness, all employees transferred from CBS to Viacom were to receive the same benefits as at CBS. That benefits package was very generous, and a costly proposition for a small company such as Viacom. Our only choice was to agree.

So here was the deal: I was to lead a brand-new company whose board I did not know and did not choose, with an oppressive distribution contract dictated by CBS, with a number of executives (certainly not all) castoff by CBS, including an alcoholic in a key position; with a cumbersome number of shareholders, a complicated voting trust comprising shares of major stockholders, an outside law firm in which I had no confidence, and a costly employee benefits plan unsuited to a new company. Add an interruption of service to many of our cable television subscribers after forfeiting our microwave licenses, and an expensive lawsuit hanging over our heads which could prevent the spin-off entirely.

It was a daunting prospect which led me, in reflective moments, to seriously doubt that we could survive. Viacom would consist of two divisions—Cable, with about one hundred thousand subscribers, and Enterprises, the syndication arm.

Our two hundred-plus employees were an anthill compared with CBS's twenty-eight thousand souls. For 1970, as part of CBS, Enterprises had revenue of about $12 million and Cable about $6.5 million, for a total $18.5 million—compared with CBS's $1.2 billion in revenue.

I met with Viacom's general counsel and the three-man outside firm he had engaged, to plan the divestiture. One of the outsiders, supposedly a Securities and Exchange Commission specialist, arrived wearing a ghastly tie and a paisley silk handkerchief dangling a foot from a jacket pocket. It was a ludicrous sight and, we would learn, a harbinger of his judgment. As Washington counsel we engaged Arent Fox, which included Harry Plotkin, a former FCC official whose advice was sound.

Viacom, for tax reasons, was to be incorporated in Delaware. The microwave licenses were to be turned in to the FCC in Washington, D.C., and the shares of the new company were to be mailed from New Jersey so CBS would not have to pay New York transfer taxes. It was a logistical challenge.

We planned carefully for Viacom to spin away from CBS, knowing that a minority shareholder in our San Francisco cable system may well file an injunction again to stop us. Four telephones were installed on my desk anticipating a favorable FCC vote—one open to Sacramento, where CBS Enterprises was incorporated; another to Delaware; one to attorney Harry Plotkin in Washington, D.C., who would turn in the microwave licenses; and a final one to a Viacom attorney in New Jersey who would mail the shares. Once the shares were mailed, the deed was done.

The vote by the FCC was scheduled for June 4, 1971, at 10 a.m. our time—7 a.m. on the West Coast, where lawsuits against the spin-off had previously been filed. Since the courts in San Francisco had not yet opened, however, the FCC postponed the vote until 1 p.m. our time—10 a.m. on the coast. Shortly before one, I was told, an FCC clerk called the court in San Francisco to ask if there was any impediment to the separation. The court said there was none. FCC commissioners then voted to authorize it.

I immediately phoned the orders in to California and Delaware, then called Harry Plotkin in Washington. "Turn in the licenses," I told him, "and let me know when you have done so. " When Harry hesitated, I raised my voice several decibels: "Turn in the licenses immediately!" Harry did.

Then I called our general counsel in New Jersey, who dropped the shares in the mail. The entire operation took less than a half-hour. Soon afterward we learned how critical it was that we had moved fast. The FCC notified us that the court clerk in San Francisco had made a mistake and in fact there was an injunction against the spin-off. But now it was a moot point. The shares had been mailed, the deed was done.

Viacom was in business.

Executive Vice President Jack Schneider, who led the CBS charge against Viacom prior to spin-off, did not last long on his lofty perch. It seemed clear that Bill Paley had been grooming Schneider to replace him. But around the time Viacom became independent, Paley had second thoughts. Schneider lost his position and again became head of the Broadcast Group, later leaving CBS.

Several years later I got a bit of pay back for all the headaches Schneider had given Viacom and me. When my daughter Michele graduated from Sweet Briar, a women's college in Virginia, I gave the commencement address. In the audience was Schneider, whose own daughter was graduating. For once he had to sit still and listen while I got in the last word.

CBS's annual report for 1971 reflected how little Schneider and most other company chieftains thought of Viacom. The report devoted thirty-two lines to CBS Laboratories, twenty-two to the New York Yankees, and just twelve to Viacom. Parts of CBS Labs were sold and the rest given away four years later. The Yankees, in a historic slump, barely had a winning season in 1971. CBS sold them at a loss two years later.

Nearly three decades later, Viacom, the tiny outfit nudged out the back door with an assortment of people and plans picked by others, would return through the front door and *buy* CBS.

16

VIACOM MAPS ITS FUTURE

Evelyn Y. Davis, a petite but scrappy middle-aged woman, was perhaps America's best-known corporate gadfly. She owned stock in
CBS and scores of other blue-ribbon companies, and made it her
life's work to show up at annual stockholder meetings and raise Cain.

She once came to a CBS shareholders' meeting I attended wearing a football helmet and sweater emblazoned with "Give 'em Hell." From
the start she badgered poor Bill Paley, who did his best to keep cool amid
her constant interruptions. Finally, exasperated, he glowered down at her:
"Miss Davis, instead of just having it on your sweater, why don't you go
there?" The entire room, of course, burst out laughing.

Now, along with other CBS investors, Davis was also a Viacom
stockholder. And since I was the CEO who might have to deal with her
antics, suddenly she didn't seem so funny. A few days before our first annual meeting Davis called and asked if I was familiar with her book about
shareholder meetings. I said I was and she asked how many copies I wanted to order. "None," I answered. "Nine?" she said. "No, none." She replied
that I would probably change my mind after the meeting.

In truth I was nervous, though elated, as we put the finishing
touches on plans for our first meeting. It was set for the New York Hilton
on August 19, 1971. Our attorneys and I agreed that, with the proxy votes
in by then, Viacom management would have the power to proceed however we wished. Hence the meeting should be open and friendly. I would
encourage every shareholder who wanted to speak or ask questions to do

so.

Minutes before the meeting started I was told that one of the Gilbert brothers was in the audience as well. The Gilberts also attended corporate shareholder meetings and often asked what some considered embarrassing questions.

Immediately our outside lawyer with the paisley handkerchief told me, "Rule any of them out of order." I reminded him we had agreed that we should listen to anyone who wanted to be heard. "Rule them out of order, rule them out of order," he repeated. I silently vowed not only to ignore his nonsense, but to replace him right after the meeting.

I called the session to order and began to explain procedures for the meeting. Evelyn Davis stood and interrupted me. The question and answer period would follow my report, I said, but she interrupted twice more and insisted that her questions be answered immediately so she could go to another shareholder meeting.

Finally I offered a deal: I would let her ask three questions and would answer them promptly if she promised to then be quiet. She agreed. The first question was why Viacom held its annual meeting on the same day as Time, Inc., when Time's meeting was so much more important than Viacom's. Her second and third questions were equally trivial.

"In answer to question number one, Ms. Davis," I said, "no, their meeting is not more important, certainly not to the shareholders of this company. The answer to your second question is no and the answer to your third question is yes. Thank you very much, Ms. Davis, we will look forward to seeing you next year." The audience snickered as she left, never to reappear at a Viacom stockholder meeting.

That afternoon I called in our general counsel and told him I had decided to change outside counsel. He vehemently objected, leaving me no choice but to replace him as well. A head hunter was engaged to find us a new general counsel. I received the resume of Terrence Elkes, general counsel for a privately owned paper company. Elkes wore thick glasses and was overweight. But he had a degree from the University of Michigan and seemed competent. I interviewed Elkes several times, introduced him to other Viacom leaders, and recommended to the board that we hire him.

In those days executives had to pass a medical exam. The report on Elkes was mixed. At that some of our board members objected strongly to hiring him, especially Paul Norton, executive vice president of New York Life Insurance Company. I talked with Elkes, who acknowledged he was not in good shape. I felt this could be remedied and that he was the best choice for the company. The board relented and I hired Elkes as vice president, general counsel, and secretary of Viacom.

We held the first of what would become regular long-term planning meetings for Viacom's senior staff. Planning costs valuable time and brainpower, but I considered it indispensable. I had seen too many organizations—including major corporations—lose their way by blindly barreling straight ahead when they should have stopped and checked their bearings on occasion.

We went to a reasonably priced conference center outside New York City and explored a wide range of potential pursuits for Viacom.

First we decided to secure as many syndication rights as possible, and to also produce our own first-run programs for syndication or network exposure. On the cable side we explored every blue-sky possibility we could think of—even home burglar alarms provided by cable when this became technically feasible. We decided to provide motion pictures and other special attractions via cable at a monthly cost that was in addition to the basic cable fee. We called it "pay cable." We would offer motion pictures to individual homes on a pay-per-movie basis.

Once these audiences were exhausted we would offer the same programs on a dedicated channel (such as the present Showtime and HBO). Finally, we decided that, given our extensive collective knowledge of broadcast radio and television, down the road we should also get into those businesses.

Richard Forsling, board chairman as well as head of our cable division, began to concern me. Perhaps he was professionally frustrated. Richard had hoped to become CBS's general counsel and was crestfallen when that did not happen. Now, swimming in a much smaller pond, he was anxious to prove himself, to make things happen, no matter the risk or cost to Viacom.

A few months after we became independent, I asked our leaders to cut their budgets wherever possible. Instead, Richard proposed several hundred million dollars' worth of cable acquisitions. I knew a company our size could not raise such funds and, even if we did, our debt-to-equity ratio would be so high we could not make the interest payments.

I met privately with Richard and tried to dissuade him from presenting this untenable budget to our directors. He argued that as chairman he had the right to do so, and proceeded to put his budget demands before the board.

On the night before the next formal board meeting a director called at home, waking me out of bed. He said a number of board members were at the University Club and "urgently need your presence." I quickly dressed and went out into a ferocious thunderstorm, which seemed fitting for whatever awaited.

When I arrived at the club the directors had flushed faces, apparently the result of a good wine with dinner. They got right to the point: Force Forsling to resign because of his unreasonable demand for funds. I tried to dissuade them, arguing that our little company had plenty of challenges already. But they insisted. After a long discussion I said "Fine, you do it." Someone spoke for all of them: "No, you are the CEO, Ralph, you do it."

Next morning I asked Forsling to come to my office prior to the board meeting. There, I relayed the board's request for his resignation. Forsling was livid. He insisted that he again explain the merits of his proposal to the board. He did so but members were not impressed, and at the end of the meeting they still wanted his resignation.

I felt sorry for Richard, and decided on my own to have Viacom pay him one year's severance. I left the chairman's position vacant for the moment. Within a short time Richard landed the top job in a Denver cable company.

Early in 1972 Viacom bought its first cable system as an independent company, Com-Cable TV in the Cleveland area. We also bought cable systems in Seattle and Bellevue, Washington, from NBC, which, like CBS, had to dispose of its cable holdings. We secured a new outside law firm and Lehman Brothers as our investment banker. Lehman's Peter Solomon, later to become deputy mayor of New York City, was assigned to us.

We were now set to face the future. We had our long-range plans and expert legal and investment help. To set an example of frugality I decided my salary as CEO would be the same as when I directed CBS's Enterprises division—$70,000 a year plus profit sharing.

I wanted to settle the longstanding lawsuit—a real thorn in our side—filed by Marino Iacopi against Viacom. He and his son owned 19 percent of the stock in our San Francisco cable system.

CBS owned most of the stock and didn't even bother telling Iacopi when they gave the cable company to Viacom. I was sure CBS had put the squeeze on the smaller guy. Iacopi and his attorney had blocked the original Viacom spin-off in late 1970 and tried but failed to prevent it again in June 1971. He would be an obstacle to our plans until we settled.

Terry Elkes and I flew out to San Francisco. After preliminary talk, I met alone for lunch with Iacopi at the Clift Hotel. I put my cards straight out on the table and the matter was settled before dessert. Viacom paid him what we both considered a fair amount for the stock the Iacopis owned, and he was happy. One thorn pulled from Viacom's side.

But we were about to land in a thorn bush. The U.S. Justice Department summoned our lawyers to Washington and informed them that the federal government was filing an antitrust suit against ABC, CBS, NBC, and Viacom. They charged that all of us had "monopolized and restrained trade" in prime-time entertainment programs. We were ordered to fork over all financial interest in the programs, except profits from initial showings.

An official told us Viacom was included in the suit because "You're part of CBS." An incredible development, especially after all the grief CBS had given us. We tried to convince them of the truth, that Viacom was independent and that another federal agency, the FCC, had imposed stringent rules to ensure we stayed that way.

But Justice would not budge. Its officials were convinced, against all facts, that we were still part of CBS. The threat of the anti-trust suit frightened a pending merger partner, Columbia Cable, whose subscribers would have increased our cable base substantially. But they called off the deal.

It seemed obvious that Justice's quarrel was with CBS, not Viacom. Therefore CBS should hold us harmless from the suit and, at a minimum, pay our legal fees. Fat chance. We met with CBS's lawyers, who refused to do either. The suit hung over us for nearly the rest of the year.

Finally I went down to Washington with our attorneys, led by Jerry Shapiro, one of our outside law-firm partners, and met with government lawyers. After twelve hours of nonstop bargaining, we reached an agreement. If the courts eventually decided CBS acquired its syndication rights illegally, Viacom would remit the proceeds from the CBS programs not to CBS but to whoever the courts designated. In December the suit against us was finally dropped. It was a frightening example of how government run amuck can destroy organizations and lives.

The lawsuit had an interesting sidelight, which might have deprived the world of the famous Zagat Survey of restaurants and hotels. To fight the suit we had to sift through documents kept in scores of boxes in a warehouse. The boxes were stacked perhaps twenty feet high.

One of our attorneys, Tim Zagat, and an assistant went to the warehouse to search for files. Tim removed a box near the bottom of a stack. The tall column, like a giant domino, swayed and hit a second domino, which hit a third. They collapsed in a heap, Zagat and his assistant underneath. Fortunately neither was seriously hurt. Tim and his wife went on to found the Zagat Survey, which publishes America's leading guides to restaurants, hotels, and resorts worldwide.

The lawsuit rocked Viacom as well. But we, too, survived and, like the Zagats, we were just getting started.

Viacom could have consumed all my waking hours. But on most weekends, for relaxation, Jean and I took our girls to our second home on Candlewood Lake, Connecticut. It was a lovely lake about twenty miles long, bordered by rolling hills.

There was just one problem. Our next-door neighbor, a New York City school official, spent hours each day running various machines in his garage—lawnmower, trimmers, and heaven knows what else. In what I thought was a friendly way I suggested he might stop using the machines at some reasonable point on the weekend. He curtly told me that a man's house is his castle and he could do whatever he pleased.

I discussed the problem with another neighbor and good friend, David Rosen, a tall, athletic man who owned a fast-food franchise. Surprisingly he had not even noticed the obnoxious noises. Dave suggested I set up a hi-fi system on our porch, facing my obstinate neighbor, turn it to full volume on a Spanish-music station, and leave the house.

It seemed brilliant. One afternoon we set up the boom box, turned it to full volume, and were about to leave when the phone rang. The caller identified himself as our noisy neighbor and asked if I would please turn the music down. I exploded. A man's house is his castle, I reminded him, and I could do whatever I wanted. I became quite distraught. The caller, guffawing, interrupted my harangue. "Ralph, don't get so upset." It was David Rosen, who faked the call.

When I was out of patience and ideas, we sold the house on the south end of the lake and bought one on the north end, in Sherman, a couple of miles from the New York line. Not long afterward I got a call from a man who identified himself as the buyer of our southern house. "Mr. Baruch," he huffed, "you did not tell me about the man next door who makes so much noise with all his equipment on the weekends."

"What man?" I answered innocently.

"Come on now, you must have known this, and you didn't tell me when I bought the house." I was about to lose my temper again when the man identified himself once more as my fun-loving friend, David Rosen.

We assembled a family flotilla on Candlewood Lake—a motorboat for our daughters to water-ski, and assorted sailboats, including a large Hobie Cat which we loved to sail. But each fall the water crafts had to be cleaned and hauled into the boathouse, and each spring hauled out again. Often I asked our four daughters to help bring the boats in or out, but they always had something else to do. Their absence when needed gave me passing thoughts of selling the lake house.

Fortunately the girls were more conscientious about their studies than the family boats. They were growing up fast. Eve, the eldest, after graduating from the University of Chicago, became a writer, living in New York City. Renee got degrees from Wells College, a private school in upstate New York, and Albany Law. She became a corporate attorney with increasingly more responsibility. Alice, always a hard worker, went to Nightingale Bamford, a college preparatory school for girls in Manhattan, where she was valedictorian. She attended college at Mt. Holyoke, Massachusetts, graduated magna cum laude, then earned a Ph.D. and an M.D. from Columbia University.

Our youngest, Michele, finished secondary school at Chapin, an excellent girls' school near our apartment in Manhattan. She then graduated from Sweet Briar College in Virginia and earned a postgraduate degree in international communications from George Washington University.

At Viacom, support was tepid from some members of our board of directors. Najeeb Halaby, head of Pan-Am, was preoccupied with the airline's problems and rarely attended meetings. He was a Texas native, born to an American mother and Lebanese-American father. Given his frequent absences, Halaby said he wanted to be briefed by Viacom officers themselves, and asked that our division heads make presentations to the whole board. Some board members objected, led by Burleigh Pattee who bluntly told Halaby, "If you attended meetings, you'd know what is going on."

Prodded by that challenge, Halaby expanded his demand. He wanted division leaders to take two days to brief the board, infuriating Pattee even more. Nevertheless, a director had requested the presentation and it was scheduled for the next board meeting.

Everyone congregated, Patee flying in from San Francisco, and Richard Schall from Minneapolis. When the meeting convened Halaby was AWOL. Other board members were furious. Viacom managers gave their presentations. Halaby finally phoned in. He had been stuck on Pan-Am business in Tokyo and was on his way back.

Halaby, apologetic, finally arrived for the second day of the meeting. We proceeded with scheduled briefings. Most board members asked excellent questions. Halaby did not ask many. He had taken a red-eye flight from the West Coast the night before, and fell sound asleep in the meeting. Afterward some directors stayed behind. The situation with Halaby was intolerable, they said. I was delegated to ask for his resignation.

I called Halaby's office and made an appointment for breakfast a few days later in the Sky Club, a large members-only restaurant atop the Pan-Am building. I arrived promptly at our appointed hour, 8 a.m. The view of the city from the restaurant was superb. I had a lot of time to enjoy it because Halaby was forty-five minutes late. He had guessed the reason for the meeting. As soon as he sat down he cursed sharply and said he had to resign from the board.

"Very well," I responded, "when would you like me to date your resignation?"

"As of today."

I agreed. The meeting was over and I left, coffee cup still half-full. Halaby soon afterward stepped down as Pan-Am's chairman. Two decades later Pan-Am itself succumbed to years of crushing financial pressures and went belly up. More people no doubt know Halaby best as the father of Lisa Halaby, the beautiful Princeton graduate who married King Hussein of Jordan, reigning for two decades at his side as Queen Noor until the king's death in 1999.

George Harrar, another director, retired in 1972 as head of the Rockefeller Foundation. The Harrars and Stantons were close friends, so Frank organized a farewell social for him at the Rockefeller Foundation. Harrar helped develop agriculture in Mexico and had been honored by its government. Stanton hired a large mariachi band, handsomely outfitted in silver-spangled costumes.

Jean and I chatted with Stanton and the subject turned to the macramé wall hangings that decorated CBS's Black Rock. Stanton had helped select them. We left late in the evening when Stanton was still there.

Early next morning at home the doorbell rang and a messenger delivered a package for Jean. It was filled with magazines and articles on wall hangings, with a nice note from Stanton, typed and personally signed. How he accomplished it remains a mystery to us. It was that kind of class that made it impossible for me to dislike CBS, however many headaches it caused Viacom and me.

We decided at our first long-range planning meeting that pay-per-view would be a Viacom priority. Early on we signed a contract with Trans World International, a subsidiary of Columbia Pictures, to serve hotels in San Francisco, using our cable systems as a conduit for their motion pictures. We also acquired Petra Cablevision on Long Island, New York. The latter system had about twenty thousand subscribers and appeared to be an ideal proving ground for our pay-per-view experiment.

We had specially built boxes installed in two thousand homes of our Long Island customers to enable them to pay for and watch our movies. We called the service "Viacode." Our objective was to determine subscribers' willingness to pay for individual motion pictures delivered by cable. If it worked well, we planned to subsequently package many movies and air them in the form of a subscription service.

One of our first motion pictures was the original "Poseidon Adventure," about a cruise ship hit by a monstrous wave. Viacode's results were stunning. More than 60 percent of the two thousand homes ordered the movie, paying $3.95 each. Despite the tremendous promise of pay-per-view, however, it was not endorsed by the cable industry—nor even by the president of Viacom's own Cable division.

In fact it was an uphill fight to be accepted at all by the cable television industry. Since we came from CBS, some industry people still considered us broadcasters, and there was no love lost between broadcasting and cable.

That summer at the convention of the National Cable Television Association held in Anaheim, California, we were assigned rooms in a hotel twelve miles from the convention center. I decided that paying dues to an organization hostile to us—especially one that wore blinders in surveying the future—was fruitless. Viacom resigned from the NCTA.

We were aggressive. By 1973 our base of cable subscribers had nearly doubled, and we were a substantial cable system operator. But we lacked feature films, which we were prohibited from buying when we were part of CBS. (CBS's local television stations were the single largest consumers of motion pictures, leading its law department to bar us from acquiring films.) In the early period of independence, Viacom moved quickly to acquire movies for distribution to networks and individual television stations.

We also began to produce our own programs for the television networks. Our first network series was the *Melba Moore and Clifton Davis Show,* a musical variety show that had a short life but was critically praised. Viacom Productions also developed *The Harlem Globetrotter's Popcorn Machine*, a fast-paced comedy and musical variety show hosted by the Globetrotters and aimed at children. Our Enterprises division launched the syndication of *Hawaii Five-o*, at a program convention attended by its star, Jack Lord.

At the next Western Cable Show in Los Angeles, the NCTA's chairman, Alfred Stern, asked if Viacom would rejoin the association. I told him yes, on two conditions. First, we would have a representative on the association's board, and second, I would chair a new committee called the Pay Cable Committee, to fight severe restrictions the FCC had imposed on pay cable. We wanted to help shape the industry's future. Stern and his directors agreed to our terms and we rejoined the association.

We won the grudging respect of our cable peers the old fashion way: we earned it. Viacom had become too strong to ignore. Already we were the third largest cable company in the United States, with 255,000 subscribers—only 9,000 behind number two, the American Television and Communications Corporation.

But the tapestry of forces arrayed against cable itself was formidable. Prevailing there would prove far more difficult.

17
CABLE CLIMBS INTO THE RING

Ninety-eight percent of Americans had television by 1978, and average households watched it six hours a day. Historic events became global events.

On July 20, 1969 an estimated six hundred million viewers watched man step on the moon for the first time. Five years later one hundred million watched the impeachment hearings and resignation of President Nixon, and two years after that a billion viewers saw the Montreal Olympics.

The statistic of most interest to ABC, CBS, and NBC was this: Nine of every ten American television sets turned on in evening prime-time—the most watched portion of the day—were tuned to one of these three. Owning a network or even a single commercial TV station usually assured lavish profits of 40 to 50 percent of revenues and a life few others could ever live: limousines, chartered planes, weekend homes, exotic trips, mansions, six-figure salaries.

I knew that world well. I had just spent two decades there, helping television rise to dominate local, national, and world discourse and entertainment. When Viacom and I left CBS in 1971, little did I know that I would play a key role in helping a second television industry—cable—cut its shackles, soar, and return to go head-to-head with the networks.

Broadcasters were snug in their shells. Even in the biggest markets, viewers had access to seven channels at most, the VCR and video industry were years away, and cable had just started to flex its muscles.

In 1970 there were twenty-five hundred operating cable systems in the country, dividing a pie of $300 million in subscriber revenue—an average of $120,000.[1] CBS Inc. alone had more than $300 million in sales in just the first quarter of that year.[2]

Cable television was born as a direct result of the FCC's four-year freeze on licensing of new stations—1948 to 1952—and public impatience meanwhile with the lack of accessible programming.

John Walson, an ingenious appliance store owner in Mahanoy City, Pennsylvania, in 1948 may have built the first cable system. When people in the nearby mountains could not get clear signals from Philadelphia, ninety miles away, Walson solved that problem—and presumably the problem of selling TV sets—by stringing cable from a signal-receiving antenna to the homes.

Cable, also called community antenna television (CATV) was originally conceived simply as a way to deliver existing television signals to homes that could not get them clearly because of long distances or obstructions such as mountains or tall buildings. A powerful antenna is assembled on a hilltop or a skyscraper to receive signals which are carried by cable to individual homes.

Pioneers of the approach, in addition to Pennsylvania, included rural Oregon and Arkansas. Decades later cable would spawn a second powerful communications industry as cable companies created their own TV programs, rising to challenge the mighty broadcast networks.

Services offered by cable companies fall into three categories: basic cable, which is advertiser-supported and offered to individual homes at a monthly fee; pay or premium cable which charges an additional monthly fee, typically for movies or other entertainment costly to produce; and pay-per-view which charges extra for specific individual programs such as movies or boxing matches.

Cable has its own pioneers and giants, its Paleys and Sarnoffs, but most have toiled in obscurity. Broadcast television got a jump-start from related industries and investors with deep pockets. CATV was started at the grassroots by lunch-pail dreamers.

"There was a low degree of engineering sophistication," said an early cable pioneer. "It was truly seat-of-the-pants. It's amazing that this industry got started."[3] One of the first equipment manufacturers recalled that "I had inventions that nobody wanted. So I started in the basement of a building in New York City that had been a bookmaker's joint before I moved in. Police raided us our first day there."[4]

Some industry historians call Bill Daniels the father of cable television. Daniels saw television for the first time in a Denver bar in 1952. He worked in Casper, Wyoming, which had no TV, and wrestled with how to bring it there. Daniels talked some locals into putting up $5,000 each to build a system for Casper. Daniels was a superb promoter and deal-maker who inspired the start of many other cable systems.

Those whose businesses trace directly to Daniels read like a who's who of the cable industry. They include Irving Kahn, CEO of Teleprompter, which was the country's largest cable operator in the early years; Tele-Communications Inc. (TCI), the largest cable company from 1981 to 1997; Cox Communications, the third largest cable system operator by the early 1990s; and Time Warner Cable, the outgrowth of a company sold by Daniels and the largest cable system starting in 1997.

Technology drove the start of cable. Cable television grew for a decade before broadcasters and the FCC became concerned about it. By then, cable was entrenched across the U.S. as a signal-delivery industry. The networks, to their chagrin, had followed the famous advice of baseball's Satchel Paige: "Don't look back. Something might be gaining on you." Cable was gaining indeed.

If ABC, CBS, and NBC had perceived early on that one day cable would create its own programs and much more, in direct competition, they likely would have reacted sooner than they did. But they were asleep at the wheel. They dismissed cable as a crass pretender, a parasite that would be crushed in due time by friends in Congress and at the FCC.

By 1958 there were more than six hundred cable systems serving approximately a half-million homes in the U.S. That year a small television station in Montana shut its doors, blaming competition with the town's cable system.[5] Red flags went up at community TV stations across the country.

Station owners persuaded their industry lobby group, the National Association of Broadcasters, to put pressure on Congress to have the FCC fully investigate cable. The FCC was reluctant to do so, however. The agency said broadcasters had not shown that cable seriously threatened local television stations. In fact, the opposite was true: In most cases it added to a station's signal reception. In addition, cable was so decentralized that the FCC argued it was not equipped to regulate the rates and services of hundreds of CATV systems.

The broadcast industry and Congress forced the issue, however. It reached the Senate floor in 1960, where a measure directing the FCC to regulate cable was defeated by a single vote. Rarely would cable prevail again in Washington.

Instead of full-scale regulation, the FCC recommended that cable systems be required to carry the signals of local stations upon request, and get permission from originating stations before redistributing their programs to cable subscribers. Years later these rules—respectively called "must carry" and "retransmission consent"—were adopted.

Eight years after the Senate vote, the issue reached the Supreme Court, which gave the FCC full authority to regulate cable. With that mandate the FCC did a complete back-flip, systematically stripping away cable's rights on behalf of the networks and the rest of the broadcasting industry.

Gone was cable's right to import distant signals and sell ads on local cable. Other rules, said the FCC, would ensure that popular events and programs now offered "free" would not be "siphoned" by pay cable and viewed only by those who could afford them. (In reality there is no free television. People pay more for goods and services offered on TV to cover the high costs of advertising and marketing them.) One former FCC commissioner called the agency's assault on cable a "classic example of a watchdog out of control."[6]

Entertainment critic Clive Barnes in 1969 wrote that "Television is the first truly democratic culture—the first culture available to everyone and entirely governed by what people want. The most terrifying thing is what people do want."[7]

Barnes' definition of democracy was correct on what was in front of the camera, but not on what was behind it. Network and over-the-air commercial stations are ratings-driven and try to offer shows that appeal to the widest possible audience. Local-access cable, on the other hand, offers the opportunity for ordinary citizens and concerned groups to share in the actual selection and creation of programs. True television democracy.

After growing fast in the early years, largely unchecked by government, in the late 1960s and early 1970s a series of blows staggered the cable industry. They included increased federal, state and city regulation; heavy-handed FCC rules, higher equipment costs, and, especially, high interest rates. Cable construction slowed dramatically. In 1968 more than two hundred fifty new systems were started; in 1969 there were only ninety startups.

Another shadow fell over the industry, cast by the portly frame of Irving Kahn. To many observers, Kahn, a fast-talking showman, was synonymous with cable. He was co-founder and, for twenty years, head of what became the largest cable company, Teleprompter.

Kahn suffered a malady which often afflicts individuals of great wealth and power. He had no time or patience for piddling details, and gladly cut corners to avoid them. Thus when the city fathers of Johnstown, Pennsylvania, were considering renewal of Teleprompter's cable franchise, Kahn greased the palms of three of them with $5,000 each, to keep the franchise without having to actually leave New York and make his case there.

Kahn was charged with bribery but claimed in court that the money was extorted by crooked city officials. Our general counsel remarked that the difference between bribery and extortion is decided by who thinks of it first.

On the witness stand, Kahn went so far over the top touting his company that scores of perjury counts were added to the charges. In November 1971 Kahn was sentenced to five years in prison. His conviction played into the hands of cable's many enemies, who suggested Kahn was not a rare bird but rather a bird of the same feather as most other cable operators.

The Teleprompter mess, wrote one cable historian, "had convinced many analysts that the cable companies were shell games, that their talk of valuation on the basis of cash flow, not earnings, was just a sham to cover up phony accounting practices."

Kahn's conviction and imprisonment was the crowning blow for an industry already reeling. He was released after serving twenty months at a country club penal facility in Florida. A year later he was invited to speak to the Texas Cable Television Association, a meeting I also attended. I told convention officials it was inappropriate to have someone address our industry who had recently been in prison. Kahn heard of my objection and approached me during the convention.

"I understand you don't like my speaking here," he said.

"No, I don't. I think you should play it low-key for awhile."

"I've paid my debt. I can make any speech I want." And he did, bringing down the house with his opening line: "Now...as I was saying before I was interrupted."

Kahn was cable's crowning blow. By 1973 virtually all cable-television-related stocks hit record lows. The market for cable was not just bad, it did not exist. I believed the moment, however, offered as many opportunities as perils if we were energetic and smart. We aggressively increased our cable holdings.

Viacom shares, which traded at a high of 28½ the previous year, sank to a low of 2 5/8. I bought as many shares as I could afford for myself and my family. I was confident this was an incredible bargain for our stock. But only time would tell.

Viacom's problems with CBS continued. Richard Salant, president of CBS News, did not think his division needed Viacom or any other distributor to sell its news product overseas. We gave a series of presentations to show that, even after the 35 percent commission CBS paid us, this was a win-win relationship for both of us. While not a generator of substantial profits for Viacom, our distribution of CBS News film gave us a prestige we were anxious to retain.

At one point I called Salant to press our case. After a few minutes he said curtly, "Don't yak at me!" and hung up. Soon afterward CBS News terminated its distribution agreement with Viacom.

Some CBS executives, led by Bill Paley and Frank Stanton, at the time of the spin-off were ordered by the FCC to dispose of their Viacom stock within two years. The time was set to expire in June 1973. The stock represented a significant portion of our outstanding shares, and we were anxious for it to end up in friendly hands.

But two months before the original deadline, Paley's financial advisor, John Minary, called our chief financial officer and said Paley was considering a private placement and might not register the stock after all. Frank Stanton and perhaps others likewise were considering not registering. We had no idea where the stock would end up. The CBS executives' actions were shoddy at best.

In March I had received a call from Marvin Josephson, president of Marvin Josephson Associates, a talent agency whose clients included Robert Keeshan, CBS's Captain Kangaroo.

We met and Josephson outlined his company's assets. Josephson wanted to buy Paley's block of Viacom stock—and Stanton's if possible—then merge his company into Viacom. I said we were not interested because, under Justice Department restrictions, a merger with a talent agency could make it difficult for us to distribute television programs.

That same morning I called Frank Stanton and he invited me to his office. Over lunch he asked brusquely "Are you coming to see me on the Josephson matter?" Somewhat taken aback, I told him that Josephson's multiple for the stock of his company was nine, compared with Viacom's twenty-eight. Our future was far brighter than Josephson knew, and we had no interest in merging with him.

Stanton then explained, to my surprise, that meetings had taken place between Paley's attorneys and Josephson's. Stanton said Paley was assured by Josephson of getting the premium price he sought for his stock. I questioned whether Paley was that much in need of money.

"Ralph," said Stanton, "to him, a nickel is a nickel." Stanton assured me that "We would never do anything to hurt Viacom." The reality seemed exactly the opposite. After checking with our board I called Josephson and told him we were not interested in a merger.

As the sweet smell of success started to waft through Viacom, we were approached directly and indirectly by other companies casting a covetous eye our way. But we wanted to acquire, not be acquired. Our general counsel, Terry Elkes, suggested, and I heartily agreed, that we retain a veteran takeover attorney, Joseph Flom, of Skadden, Arps in New York, to represent us on a defensive basis if it became necessary.

Against all odds, just two years after striking out on our own, Viacom was a financial success. Revenues exceeded $31 million—30 percent over the prior year. Net income was sixty-two cents a share, and from the time we were spun off from CBS in June 1971, our per-share profit had grown at a compounded rate of 23 percent. Enterprises, one of Viacom's two main divisions—the other was Cable—was highly successful in placing programs for first-run syndication and reruns of CBS network programs. We started to distribute in the U.S. and abroad such shows as *Family Affair*, *Perry Mason*, and *Wild, Wild West*, and continued to distribute *The Twilight Zone* among other programs.

In mid-1973 we learned that producer Norman Lear would not relinquish tapes of CBS's *All in the Family*—then in a five-year run as the number one show on television—for domestic distribution. Viacom's agreement with CBS gave us the foreign syndication rights and, when its run on CBS ended, the domestic rights as well.

I liked Lear personally and understood his seller's remorse in having signed away what became a blockbuster property. But he left us no choice but to sue. The case came to trial that fall, and for once CBS was helpful. Business affairs chief Bob Daly testified that CBS clearly had the rights to *All in the Family*, and the right to assign them to us. The judge agreed and we began syndicating the program.

In 1971 CBS started to prepare for the end of the Paley-Stanton era. Stanton stepped up to vice chairman and Charles Ireland, senior vice president of International Telephone and Telegraph Corporation, was brought in to replace him as president. Months later, however, the stocky, red-headed Ireland had a fatal heart attack.

Paley and Stanton again reached outside CBS for someone to take the company into the future. This time they landed Arthur Taylor, thirty-seven, who brought a reputation as a hard-driving, innovative manager and financial wizard. Taylor, darkly handsome, came to CBS from the International Paper Company, where this sign hung on his office wall: "We are not here to do what we have done before."

Frank Stanton—Bill Paley's greatest acquisition—retired in March 1973. An aging Paley hung on for another decade. Stanton had been president and day-to-day leader of CBS since 1946. He also was broadcasting's leading voice in the halls of Washington, fighting for First Amendment rights and less bureaucratic interference. As young men, Paley and Stanton devoted their energies to building. The result was the Tiffany Network.

Taylor spent much of his time getting up to speed on broadcasting and attacking cable. He cranked up the networks' propaganda machine and urged Washington to tighten the thumbscrews on cable, especially pay cable.

The FCC considered relaxing its onerous anti-cable rules. But Taylor, in a 1973 speech in Arizona, said the rules already "offer grossly inadequate protection to both broadcasters and their public." Taylor proposed that owners of programs not seen on broadcast television the past five years be required to offer them to his industry before offering them exclusively to pay-cable systems.

Taylor issued booklets and gave speeches in which he said cable was expanding on the backs of broadcasters and that pay cable intended to outbid the networks for the rights to football games, movies, and other forms of entertainment. Then, he charged, the viewing public would be forced to pay for many things they now watch free.

CBS distributed 200,000 copies of a pamphlet over Taylor's name, titled "Does the American Family Need Another Mouth to Feed?"[8] A cartoon depicted a little boy saying "Dad, could I have a dollar to watch 'Gunsmoke'?"

Taylor argued:

[Cable] is sheltered from the normal American standards of fair competition. As a result, there is a real possibility that millions of American families will be denied the movies, sports events and other television attractions that now form an integral part of their lives. Millions of others will be allowed to view these attractions only at the expense of a large and continual drain on their family finances....What we are speaking of, in short, is less a revolution than a sneak attack on the family pocketbook.

The rhetoric from broadcasters, I believed, was a smokescreen to slow the overall development of cable. Taylor also appeared before the FCC. I was there one time when he came into the hearing room trailed by a small army of CBS staffers. He testified that "I got my knowledge of radio and television out of books"—a telling admission. Later, ignorant of procedures, he objected to one of the commissioners leaving his seat during witness testimony. The commissioner shrugged and, of course, left the room anyway.

The FCC clamped severe restrictions on pay cable's access to motion pictures. The agency inscrutably ruled that pay cable could not show films that were between two and ten years old. This essentially made it impossible for pay cable to present recent movies. Successful films remained in theatrical distribution for as long as two or three years. Then they immediately went to network television, to the exclusion of cable. After airing on broadcast television for two to three more years they again appeared on over-the-air TV in syndication.

By the time films were ten years old, television viewers could have seen them many times, and certainly would be reluctant to pay to see them again on cable.

After much lobbying in Washington we won a key ally in our fight against these rules—Jack Valenti, a seasoned political warhorse in the capital and head of the Motion Picture Association of America. He called pay cable "family-choice cable." Our moral position was also strengthened in 1973 by Rand, an independent, public policy research organization. In a twenty-fifth anniversary publication, Rand said plainly that "The growth of cable was retarded to protect an existing service."

"From the beginning," added Glenn Robinson, a former FCC commissioner, "the FCC has viewed cable not as a promise but as a problem...the regulatory task has not been how to secure the benefits of this new technology, but how to prevent it from supplanting the broadcasting system and the regulatory policies which nurtured that system." Robinson, who teaches telecommunications law at the University of Virginia, continued:

> To put it bluntly, the Commission has been not merely shortsighted but also cross-eyed. With one eye trained on broadcast interests while the other follows cable interests, the Commission has been unable to focus on the public interest in expanded communications service. Since the advent of cable, the Commission's first concern has been the impact of cable, not on the public, but on the broadcast industry.[9]

As head of our industry's Pay Cable Committee I testified in Washington, urging members of Congress to require the FCC to treat cable fairly. Eventually I helped win a key convert—the chairman of the House Communications Subcommittee, Lionel Van Deerlin from San Diego, California. Van Deerlin, a Democrat, and former journalist, agreed the pay cable rules were unreasonable. I also made some headway with a couple of the seven FCC commissioners, notably James Quello, a former Democratic congressman from Michigan.

In the spring of 1974 FCC chairman Dean Burch left the agency to serve in the White House. Commissioner Richard Wiley replaced him. Dick, forty, wore horn-rimmed glasses and looked like a bookish college professor. Like Burch, he had been active in Republican politics. Wiley had been general counsel of the FCC from 1970 to 1972. He was very tough in defending his views.

Wiley openly resented my efforts at persuasion. In April 1974 he told a group of cable executives that "I think it is time that you stop looking for advocates within the commission, or to put it more directly, regulatory security blankets."

The precise opposite was true: The FCC long since had thrown a security blanket over broadcast television. And, prodded by forces on every side of the issue, the commission at that moment was considering another set of rules which could make things even worse for pay cable.

That December, still awaiting the FCC's new rules, I was invited to address the Western Cable Television Convention in Anaheim. I took the occasion to answer Wiley.

All pay cable wanted were "regulations which are in the public interest," I said. I noted that a growing number of policy-makers called for relaxation or elimination of the FCC cable and pay-cable rules, including the U.S. Department of Justice, the White House Office of Telecommunications Policy, and at least twenty-five members of Congress, led by Senator Philip Hart (D-Michigan), chairman of the Senate Antitrust Committee.

"History teaches us that government will only respond when an entire industry shouts loudly enough," I said, urging my colleagues to become energized and help present our case to government leaders. One remark caused Wiley and other members of the FCC to come unglued: "At the recent Cable Association board meeting in Washington, we were reminded by the commission that its doors were always open. While their doors may be open, I believe that many of their minds are closed."

The following spring Wiley still steamed. His anger boiled over at a social event in Washington, sponsored by the California Cable Association. Jean and I were there. Wiley arrived, we shook hands, and then he began to lambast me for my pro-cable efforts. The entire room went silent as Wiley's tirade continued. Bruce Lovett, chair of our cable association, quietly said to me, "Ralph, we can't have this kind of discussion at an event like this. See what you can do."

Later I spied Wiley standing at the bar. Since it was March 17, I went over and said, "Dick, this is Saint Paddy's Day, let's have a drink." He started his harangue all over again.

During dinner Lovett told Jean, "Your husband is pretty abrasive, isn't he?" Her Welsh temper ignited, Jean wiped the floor with Lovett. She told him I was carrying the water for the entire cable industry and was serving it tirelessly, but the industry apparently did not care.

Wiley later apologized to me, but our relationship was never amicable again. That was proven when Viacom applied to the FCC to import Canadian signals into our Seattle cable systems. A cable company had to have FCC permission to import distant signals into a system serving subscribers.

Once we had the FCC's okay and began to import the signals, we could charge a dollar more a month per household. But each time this item appeared on the FCC's docket, Wiley refused to deal with it.

This went on and on. We were deprived of tens of thousands of dollars in additional revenue each month that would have gone right to our bottom line. Finally I contacted an attorney friend who also happened to be Wiley's tennis partner. I warned that if the FCC did not take up our request we would sue the commission. The attorney must have quietly passed this on to Wiley, and finally our proposal was acted upon and granted.

The pay cable wars got hotter. It was a struggle between television

broadcasters, led by the networks, and the comparatively tiny cable industry, supported by Hollywood. We sought freedom of choice and, we were
convinced, the best interests of the public. But we felt like David fighting
Goliath.

To further prevent pay cable from getting access to motion pictures, the networks began to warehouse them. We documented that of
142 films ABC agreed to purchase, 92 included exclusivity contracts to
keep them out of pay cable's hands. Of those 92 films, 71 were less than
two years old when the contract was signed. ABC secured other films even
before they hit theaters, with contract provisions that warehoused them
for a full three years following release.

All this was at a time when there were 65 million American homes
that received broadcast television and fewer than 75,000 homes subscribing to pay cable systems such as HBO or Showtime. (In 1973 about 7.3
million homes—10 percent of the nation—subscribed to basic cable.) The
networks' actions were ludicrous overkill. They were determined to exter-
minate cable. If they could not crush us they would starve us to death.

The struggle over pay cable was of great interest to other parties
as well, including Motorola. The head of Motorola Entertainment saw
pay television as a potential business using their technology. We met with
Motorola engineers and explained what we were doing, especially with
our pay-cable service "Viacode." Among other films on this system, we
released "Mame," with Rosalind Russell, which proved a huge success. We
again had the attention of our industry, including cable owners still reluctant to get into pay cable.

Motorola's interest in a possible merger led to a 1974 meeting in Chicago between its CEO, Robert Galvin, Sr., and his associates,
and Viacom represented by Elkes, Leahy, and myself. We explained that
Motorola's involvement might substantially benefit our shareholders and
their company, but we had to have complete autonomy. A few weeks later
we gathered for lunch in New York. We talked at great length, but were
somewhat discouraged because of the bottom-dwelling price of Viacom—
about five dollars a share.

Motorola was keenly interested. Obviously five dollars a share was
an extremely attractive purchase for them. But we explained to Galvin
and his colleagues that a cable subscriber was worth a minimum of $300.

(As this is written the attributed value of a cable subscriber is $3,000 to $4,000 or more.) That meant the cable business of Viacom alone was worth $90 million. If we assumed that the Enterprises side was worth no more than its debt of about $40 million, this would net a price in excess of $22.50 a share.

Galvin was floored. He said he was probably willing to offer us a 25 percent premium above our $5 price in the stock market, or a total of $6.25, but that even if he were to offer a premium of 100 percent, or $10 a share, we still would be unwilling to cut a deal. I agreed that we would not accept $10 a share. As we walked back to Viacom, Galvin said, "You know, you cable people are a strange lot. You have completely inflated ideas as to the value of your business." I called Viacom's board members individually and they all agreed with our position. That ended another possible merger.

Fighting for the entire cable industry while running Viacom was daunting, especially with a meager association budget and staff. I continued to meet with potential allies and contacts in Washington who might help put pressure on the FCC. What upset me most, however, was the myopia of our own industry. Too many of my colleagues discounted the importance of pay cable, either on a per-program or subscription basis.

I went before the NCTA's board of directors as head of its Pay Cable Committee and pled for $50,000 to publish booklets, push other educational efforts, and hire some help. I was dismayed by the board's lack of vision.

One female member, Pauline "Polly" Dunn from Mississippi, who operated small television systems in the deep South, said in a heavy drawl, "Ralph, pay cable isn't for us little guys who operate 10- or 20- or 30,000-subscriber systems; that's for you big boys." I tried hard to explain to her and other board members the importance of pay cable to the development of our entire industry. Finally they coughed up the $50,000.

In March 1975 the FCC issued its new cable rules. They made a few cosmetic adjustments but overall the changes were disappointing. The following month a subcommittee of the prestigious Committee for Economic Development said in a report on cable that "Program restrictions on motion pictures and series programs should be phased out gradu-

222 · Television Tightrope

ally and selectively." The CED is an independent organization of business and educational leaders.

There were a couple of dissenters on the CED panel. To no one's surprise they were broadcast executives—Wrede Petersmeyer, chairman of Corinthian Broadcasting, owned by Bill Paley's brother-in-law; and my old sparring partner Jack Schneider, president of the CBS Broadcast Group.

They offered this contrary view to the majority report: "Cable is basically a parasitic industry, living off the investment and knowledge of others."

Broadcasters continued a drumbeat of propaganda. The National Association of Broadcasters sent sample letters to local members, asking them to write similar, "original" anti-cable letters and send them to President Gerald Ford and the FCC. *The New York Times* reported that an NAB official told a member of Senator Edward Kennedy's staff that the Massachusetts Democrat would be labeled an "enemy" of broadcasting if he held hearings on cable before the Monopoly and Antitrust Subcommittee. Kennedy held the hearings anyway.

Our committee, on behalf of the cable industry, engaged attorneys in Washington and New York and prepared to sue the FCC. Committee member Jerry Levin, president of a still-young Home Box Office, and I met several times to plan our legal strategy.

Initially our lawsuit was to be titled "Viacom vs. FCC." However, considering my rocky relationship with FCC Chairman Wiley, it became clear to both of us that this time someone else should lead the attack. To the credit of Jerry and Time Inc., HBO's parent company, the lawsuit was filed as "HBO vs. FCC."

Eventually, in 1977, the courts ruled against the FCC. The agency appealed the outcome to the Supreme Court, which refused to overturn the lower court's ruling. Cable television finally had a legal mandate to spread its wings and fly.

In 1975 only 15 percent of homes had cable. By the end of the 1980s nearly 60 percent of households were connected to cable and it was available to 96 percent of all homes.

While awaiting the lower court ruling, the National Cable Television Association—I believe at Jerry Levin's suggestion—gave me a lovely plaque for leading the pay-cable fight. I thanked the dinner audience for the honor, given after we lost at the FCC, and said I would love to imagine what they would have given me had we won. In the end, thanks to the American legal system, we did.

FCC Chairman Richard Wiley stepped down from the commission in 1977 and later became head of a large Washington law firm. At this writing his Internet biography says that during Wiley's tenure at the FCC "he was a leading force in the effort to foster increased competition and lessened regulation in the communications field."

Go figure.

Two other of my sparring partners also moved on:

CBS Broadcast Group president Jack Schneider, who gave Viacom fits during the spin-off and in 1975 labeled the cable industry "parasitic." Two years later he left CBS and joined the parasitic cable division of Warner Communications.

CBS Inc. president Arthur Taylor, who led the network's charge against cable. One close observer of CBS writes that Taylor was considered pompous by his colleagues and "flubbed in attempting to emulate Frank Stanton as broadcasting's spokesman in policy matters and Washington appearances."[10]

Chairman Bill Paley abruptly fired Taylor in 1976. The man who wrote "Does the American family need another mouth to feed?" apparently decided the answer was yes. After CBS showed him the door, Taylor was hired by Rockefeller Center Inc. as the developer of RCTV, its new pay-cable division, which later became the Arts and Entertainment Network.

18

VULTURES EYE VIACOM

Then there were the investment bankers. I thought they were like doctors or clergymen. Tell them anything in confidence and they keep it that way. How naive I was.

Lehman Brothers was our investment banker, and Peter Solomon the partner assigned to us. In December 1976 Peter phoned to see if we could meet the following week. When the day arrived Terry Elkes and I were in my office when Peter walked in with Bill Michaels, chairman of Storer Broadcasting, and another gentleman. Peter had said nothing about bringing anyone.

After the usual pleasantries, Michaels, who had a slight speech impediment, said "Wouldn't it be nice if our two companies merged?"

"Why?" I asked.

"You have all these wonderful television programs and we have these great television stations. This merger would make so much sense for both of us. You would have a market in many cities for your programs and we would have access to programs at a good price."

Suddenly uncomfortable, I said, "Bill, are you suggesting that we make a sweetheart deal? We have a fiduciary duty to extract the maximum revenues possible from each of our programs. Any kind of a special deal would be contrary to our charter and we would not entertain it at all." Then I added, "But wait a minute. I know who Peter is and I know who you are, Bill, but who is this gentleman?"

"Well," said Peter, "this gentleman is also with Lehman."

"Good," I said, "then he represents us too."

"Oh, no, Ralph, he represents Storer," said Peter. I expressed dismay at this awkward situation as Peter added, "Well, you know Ralph, we have a Chinese wall between accounts."

"Chinese wall, my foot," I said. "This meeting is over."

As he was leaving, Michaels reached into his pocket and handed me a letter from Storer Broadcasting, offering us ten dollars a share for all Viacom's stock. It was what Wall Street calls a "bear hug"—an unnegotiated takeover proposal.

Shortly afterward Michaels phoned to say that there suddenly was considerable activity on the stock exchange in Viacom stock. I suggested that perhaps Storer was dealing with Viacom shares, which he denied. But it fit the pattern of bear hugs, in which the hunter tries to scare the board of the target company to sell, rather than be accused of not acting responsibly in the shareholders' interests.

I thought that when we had one member of an investment banking team on our side, we had the whole team on our side. But I had to assume that Peter Solomon and his firm were using information we had supplied on Viacom, including our long-range plans, to entice Storer to make an offer for our company. The "Chinese wall" metaphor is often used by investment bankers; I consider it transparent and disgusting, as it invariably masks a conflict of interest.

Angry at this plot in which our own investment banker had participated, I called Joe Flom, our attorney and a major partner at Skadden, Arps. Joe also was stunned at what he agreed was Lehman's and Peter Solomon's unconscionable behavior.

Flom came to our office that same day. In our board room he dictated one of the strongest letters I have ever read, from me to Peter Solomon at Lehman Brothers. Despite a blinding snowstorm early that evening, I personally delivered the letter to Solomon's apartment on East Seventy-Ninth Street.

The next morning Storer released a public statement saying it had offered ten dollars a share for Viacom stock. We were left without Wall Street representation because certainly we could not entertain having Peter Solomon handle this for us. We scrambled fast and began to engage Kidder, Peabody and one of their partners, Martin Siegel, for our defense.

That day and the next a large number of our shares were traded on Wall Street while we were still negotiating terms with Kidder, Peabody. Thirty-six hours after the Storer offer was made we reached an understanding with Siegel, who did a wonderful job reassuring investors and the business community of our solid standing.

We had no desire to sell Viacom, especially to Storer. I did not like what I knew about them. Years earlier George B. Storer was the reason an FCC commissioner was forced to resign in disgrace. While his company had a case pending before the commission, Storer hosted the commissioner on his yacht for a few days—a clear ethical violation.

I had been to Storer offices, and when I visited one in Miami, soon after lunch their executives all left to play golf. That was not my kind of work ethic.

Soon afterward Frank Stanton came to my office and urged me to make a deal with Storer. He felt certain that after a time I would end up running the entire operation. I gave Frank my opinion of Storer, and added that no Jewish person had ever worked in a top executive position there. Frank persisted, and asked that Viacom and Storer leaders at least get to know each other better.

To appease Frank I met with Storer executives at the City Athletic Club. Representing their side was George Storer, Jr., and Terry Lee, president of Storer Television. Within two minutes Lee handed us another piece of paper offering us fifteen dollars a share for Viacom—a cash sum of about $55 million.

"I thought this meeting was called so we could get to know each other," I said.

"Ralph," barked Lee, "this is all bullshit." The meeting was over.

I was determined that Viacom remain independent because the market assigned our stock a very low price-earnings ratio of four or five, while similar, better-known businesses had much higher P/E ratios, some in the twenties and thirties.

A company's P/E ratio is determined by dividing the current market price of one share of its stock by the company's per-share earnings. This is the common way the market places value on common stocks.

While generally reliable, new, cutting-edge companies in the 1970s such as Viacom, that were expected to grow and have higher earnings in the future, should have been given higher P/E ratios. We were undervalued, and I would not let anyone take advantage of our company.

I had tried desperately to raise our P/E ratio but met obstacles, particularly from people who did not understand our business. One leading analyst, who published newsletters on our industry, was present at many meetings. I asked him why he gave Viacom such a low P/E ratio. He said it was based on our cable television business.

What about our highly profitable syndication arm? I asked. His answer: "I don't understand your syndication business so I can't give it any value."

Other would-be analysts who wrote reports sold to prospective investors came to see us. On one occasion a young man representing one of the leading investment advisors came to Viacom and interviewed Terry Elkes and me. He asked the most foolish and uninformed questions.

Finally we challenged his knowledge of the industry and asked how long he had been with this investment counseling service. A few months, he said. And before that? "I was a tire salesman." So much for know-how in the industry at that time.

I thought my investment-banker experience with Lehman was unusual. Little did I know. After we retained Kidder, Peabody and were assigned Martin Siegel, things went well for awhile. As we had earlier with Peter Solomon, our staff spent considerable time with Siegel and his aides, laying out our long-range plans and goals and how we expected to attain them. We gave them every detail of our financial structure.

Siegel was strikingly handsome, able, bright. Early on we had his genuine attention and help. But as he became more successful, things started to change. Siegel began to arrive at meetings late, by as much as forty-five minutes. He would often come into the room and pick up a phone to make or receive calls. I left one meeting exasperated and was told he hadn't even noticed I had gone.

Siegel had married another executive at Kidder, Peabody. One day they invited Jean and me to lunch at the house they were building at

Green's Farms, an exclusive area of Westport, Connecticut. The house, an ultra-modern waterfront structure, was constructed around a large tree that was several stories high. It had a pool and tennis court.

The Siegels took us on a tour of the house, not quite finished. Mrs. Siegel was attractive and visibly pregnant. Their children would be two floors away from the parents' bedroom.

"What will happen if one of the children gets sick?" asked Jean.

"We'll have people for that," said Siegel. The reply astonished us.

In retrospect that conversation symbolized for us what the public would soon enough see: the arrogance, greed, and—not far behind— illicit behavior of some prominent investment bankers such as Michael Milken, Ivan Boesky, Dennis Levine, and, unfortunately, our own Martin Siegel. In the go-go '80s, they and other inside traders stripped billions of dollars from shareholders.

Siegel became increasingly prominent on Wall Street. He earned a great deal at Kidder as a specialist in mergers and acquisitions, at the same time becoming more distracted from Viacom. At Terry Elkes' recommendation, we ended our relationship with Kidder and Siegel and split our business between Donaldson, Lufkin & Jenrette and First Boston—two solid, well-established and reputable firms.

Years later Siegel left Kidder, Peabody and was hired by Drexel, Burnham—Michael Milken's firm, bringing the two future Wall Street thieves under the same roof. In 1990 Milken was convicted of insider trading, fined $600 million, and sentenced to ten years in prison. He served twenty-two months. Ivan Boesky, who had given Siegel suitcases stuffed with $700,000 in cash for secret information, was sentenced to five years and served twenty-one months.

Siegel proved more cunning than the others. By 1987 he had moved into a pricey Manhattan apartment. Just before his guilty plea in April of that year, he divorced his beautiful wife, sold his apartment and luxurious waterfront house in Connecticut, and bought an estate on the Atlantic near Jacksonville, Florida. The transactions neatly shielded Siegel's assets from possible creditors and still gave him his prized oceanfront mansion.

Siegel sang, and the government listened. He helped the Securities and Exchange Commission make its case against Kidder, which paid a $25 million fine, and supplied leads that led to the conviction of at least a half-dozen other traders. For his service, as Milken and Boesky were serving nearly two years each behind bars, Siegel served all of two months—and later remarried his former wife.

Investment bankers were only a small part, albeit a critical one, of growing a young company such as Viacom. While glancing their way as needed, we tried hard to stay focused on our ambitious goals. One goal was to greatly expand our pay-per-view service, Viacode, which began to perform extremely well starting in 1975.

But concern over our chief competitor, HBO, inhibited our plans. HBO favored a subscription service, with customers paying a monthly fee rather than paying for one feature at a time. HBO had begun to supply that service by microwave to cable systems in New York State from the Big Apple northward. If HBO, backed by the enormous resources of Time Inc., its parent company, maintained that approach, we felt their service would overshadow Viacode and make it a tough sell.

As we pondered the problem, we hired a president for that division, named it "Showtime," and began distributing programs on cassettes to our own cable systems.

Another goal was to somehow match or leapfrog the built-in advantage enjoyed by the television networks in distributing programs nationally. Their approach was made possible by a relay system established in the early years of television by American Telephone and Telegraph.

Video signals require a much broader band than radio signals, and coaxial cable was developed to carry them. AT&T was the only company equipped to deliver the required transmission over wires or sophisticated television relays, and the company took full advantage by charging what broadcasters considered exorbitant fees.

Following connections to eastern cities, in the fall of 1951 AT&T had inaugurated coast-to-coast television networking. For the next twenty-five years only ABC, CBS, and NBC could afford the high tariffs for interconnection. Although other companies occasionally attempted to form a fourth network, it was next to impossible for any newcomer to economically interconnect potential TV affiliates, even if they could be enticed to join a fledgling network.

How to compete? We simply had to look up—way up—for the answer: satellites.

In 1957 the Soviet Union had shocked the world by launching the first satellite, Sputnik. America raced to catch up, for national security reasons and, as a byproduct, commercial possibilities. The U.S. National Space Agency in 1962 launched Telstar I, the first global communications satellite. Three years later the Communications Satellite Corporation launched the first commercial satellite.

This was a once-in-a-lifetime opportunity for Viacom and the rest of the cable television industry. We believed the coming communication satellites could be the first step to a semblance of competition in television program distribution.

If enough downlink earth stations were distributed on a national basis at the head-ends of cable systems, satellite signals fed by third parties could be picked up on dishes and fed into the systems. This could be a reasonably cost-effective way to bypass the enormous charges paid by the networks for the AT&T landline system—truly a revolutionary development.

Obviously it would be light years ahead of how we were distributing Showtime, by shipping cassettes to subscribing cable television stations.

Early in 1975 we were jolted by an announcement out of HBO: The pay-cable leader was going to distribute its service through RCA's Satcom I satellite to cable systems throughout the United States.

I asked Jeffrey Reiss, head of Showtime, to brief me on our own satellite plans. Jeff told me he had requested such plans but that his boss, Larry Hilford, said to forget it because Viacom could not afford the multi-million-dollar commitment required by satellites.

I called Larry and Jeffrey into my office and told them we could not afford not to go on satellite with Showtime. If we were going to be in that business, we had no choice but to go head-to-head with HBO, despite the deep pockets of Time, Inc. We began to negotiate with RCA to secure two transponders—channels—on their satellite to transmit Showtime.

HBO's announcement was half bravery and half bravado. It had no authority at all from the FCC to begin a satellite service. Only after his declaration did company president Jerry Levin fly down to Washington to meet with the commission. "I assumed the networks, particularly CBS, would object," Levin said later. "All they needed to do was object and it would have been held up by a year. Time Inc. would have lost its nerve."

But broadcasters were asleep, no one objected, and the FCC gave the green light. The networks did not realize that satellites threatened their stranglehold on the distribution of television programs. In the not-too-distant future that stranglehold would be broken forever.

On September 30, 1975, HBO inaugurated its satellite service with the world heavyweight Muhammad Ali-Joe Frazier fight, the storied "Thrilla in Manila." It was uplinked from the Philippines to California on Westar, an Intelsat satellite. (HBO's original and eventual long-term choice, Satcom I, an RCA satellite, did not launch until December.) From California the signal went via AT&T landlines and microwave to HBO headquarters in New York. Then it was routed to Valley Forge, Pennsylvania, uplinked again to Westar, and downlinked to satellite dishes and delivered to HBO subscribers in Florida, Georgia, and Mississippi.

The signal had traveled 93,000 miles and instantaneously delivered a perfect picture of one of the century's great heavyweight fights, won by Ali on a TKO in the fourteenth round.

Cable saw its future. Viacom and other cable companies jumped into the satellite business big time. After years of stagnant growth, by the mid-1970s cable was booming. Our industry was the driving force fueling more and more communication satellites. Within a decade most TV stations received their broadcast as well as cable feeds by satellite, and many Americans without access to cable set up satellite dishes outside their homes. Cable at last was a force to be reckoned with.

Thank you, Sputnik.

China, the world's most populous country, inaugurated its first TV station, Beijing Television, in 1958. Nearly two dozen others sprang up over the next two years. During China's Cultural Revolution, starting in 1966, television's functions were narrowly defined to express and publicize "class struggles." In the chaotic decade of virulent anti-capitalism and anti-imperialism, Beijing Television almost ground to a halt, followed by local stations.

By the early 1970s television development began to pick up, accelerated by the end of the Cultural Revolution following the death of Mao Tse-tung in September 1976.

That fall the Chinese government asked me to review their telecommunications plans and help devise policies to expand television service. Jean and I traveled to China with a small group of Americans led by Dr. Samuel Rosen. Sam was an ear, nose, and throat specialist who had developed a breakthrough surgical procedure that restored hearing in some patients. He had traveled the globe teaching his technique, and was much admired in China. We arrived there shortly after Mao's death and the jailing of his widow Chiang Ching and three other revolutionary leaders for anti-government activities.

Also in our group were actress Nanette Fabray, a patient of Dr. Rosen's; her physician, the head of the Brooklyn Museum and his wife, and Craig Claiborne, food critic of *The New York Times*. We traveled through China.

One stop was at the archeological site at Shaanxi, where the Chinese were about to dig up a whole tera cotta army, buried centuries earlier. When we were there all they had found were a few statues of warriors and a horse. The pieces were displayed in a small corrugated iron shed. The Brooklyn Museum director tried to talk Chinese officials into loaning one of these outstanding statues to the museum.

The Chinese answer: "Why don't you do what the Japanese did? They bought a few." He was astonished as they explained that they would find thousands more statues.

Before leaving for China, a representative of Kodak gave me his company's latest Instamatic camera, Kodak's answer to Polaroid. We used it on many occasions. The Chinese at first were reluctant to be photographed. Then, astonished as the pictures came magically to life, they crowded around and begged to have their pictures taken.

At Craig Claiborne's suggestion, early one morning in Beijing we visited an open-air market. It was sparkling clean, with no garbage anywhere, a welcome contrast to many U.S. cities.

We visited a hospital in Beijing and observed patients, including one who had had surgery three weeks earlier to reattach fingers severed in a factory accident. Jean was asked to remove one of her hairpins and place it on the mattress. The patient, though with difficulty, picked up the hairpin with his reattached fingers. Acupuncture was widely used to deaden pain for surgeries and to quiet patients in a mental ward we visited.

Five years earlier, two prominent American visitors, James Reston of *The New York Times* and Secretary of State Henry Kissinger, brought acupuncture to the wide attention of the outside world. In July 1971, Kissinger was in Peking (now Beijing), laying the groundwork for President Richard Nixon's historic visit that reestablished relations with China the following year. Reston—perhaps the most widely read journalist of his era—was among reporters accompanying the U.S. delegation. While there, Reston suffered an acute appendicitis attack. Chinese doctors removed his appendix under local anesthetic.

Reston was in considerable pain following surgery, so doctors inserted three long, thin acupuncture needles into his right elbow and below his knees, manipulating them to relieve the pressure of his abdomen. Within an hour, reported Reston, the pressure started to ease and did not recur. Reston wrote about it in his nationally syndicated column and, more importantly, Kissinger mentioned it in a news briefing.[1] There was an immediate clamor for acupuncture, and practice of the ancient healing art took off in the U.S.

In a number of meetings with Chinese government officials and television specialists, I explained U.S. and world developments in broadcasting, cable, and satellites. A year and a half later Beijing Television became China Central Television (CCTV), which remains the country's primary national television network—with the world's largest audience. China now has more than three thousand television stations, four-hundred million television sets, and more than a billion viewers.

In 1975 Viacom signed a distribution agreement with Tomorrow Entertainment, a subsidiary of General Electric. As part of the agreement we got syndication rights to a movie made for television by

Tomorrow. It was called "Born Innocent," with Linda Blair—star of the motion picture "The Exorcist"—in the role of Chris Parker, a fourteen-year-old runaway who is committed to a juvenile detention home by her parents, where she is raped by a lesbian.

The show got excellent reviews in New York, Chicago, and Los Angeles, and won a hefty thirty-nine share in its first network telecast. (A share is the percentage of all TV programs watched at that time.)

Late that year the Gay Media Coalition spearheaded an effort to have Viacom stop distributing "Born Innocent." They offered us an alternative of editing the movie. Censorship was against our principles and we refused.

Shortly afterward, as I was sitting in my office, a group of three or four women suddenly appeared, unannounced, and said they were there to protest our syndication of "Born Innocent." They had appeared on our floor asking to use the ladies' room. Instead they crashed my office. I summoned one of our attorneys, who warned the women they were trespassing and that unless they left immediately we would call the police. Instead they staged a sit-in.

I wished our attorney good luck and left for lunch. In my absence the police came and arrested the women for trespassing. Later, when the matter came to court, we figured they had learned a lesson and dropped the charges. One of their members appeared at our next annual meeting and brought up the issue. Viacom's position remained the same. "Born Innocent" would not be censored.

Viacom also inked an agreement with ABC to broadcast a Viacom-produced three-hour special, "The Missiles of October." On December 18, 1975, the dramatic story of the Cuban missile crisis occupied ABC's entire evening schedule—a first for television and a wonderful demonstration of TV's potential to educate as well as entertain.

The superb cast included William DeVane as President Kennedy, Martin Sheen as Robert Kennedy, and Ralph Bellamy as Adlai Stevenson. The show was nominated for eight Emmy awards. Bellamy won as best supporting actor.

The following spring we held our annual leadership planning meeting at a small resort in the Florida Keys. A dozen or so executives attended, bringing their spouses or companions.

While we met one afternoon, four of the women, led by my adventurous wife, went on a sightseeing trip by car to the Everglades. They found more than they bargained for: an enormous alligator lazily sunning itself. The women got out of the car, approached the beast, and began throwing chunks of bread to it. Suddenly the huge gator lunged in their direction, obviously wanting more. The four took off running, jumped into the car, and sped away.

At this retreat we decided that broadcasting, both radio and television, was an expertise we possessed and ought to exploit. I asked the head of Viacom acquisitions to find potential stations to purchase. We focused on a television station that looked intriguing—Channel Thirty in Hartford, Connecticut. The UHF station was affiliated with NBC and owned by Herbert Scheftel, an absentee owner of retirement age who wanted to sell.

We believed the station had far more potential. I bargained long and hard with Scheftel, ending with Viacom's purchase more than a year and a half later. The price: $16 million.

The day the acquisition was publicly announced Scheftel and I flew to Hartford and visited the station, because I felt the employees deserved to hear it from the horse's mouth. The station manager met us at the airport. Scheftel turned to him and said, "Well, what's new?" I don't think the manager took kindly to the question. In a short pep talk I assured employees that Viacom was experienced in broadcasting and would make the station an even bigger success.

Weeks later I visited the station alone and chatted with the general manager, who had run it for many years. Together we watched its early-evening newscast. Part of the newscast was in color and, inexplicably, part in black and white.

"What happened?" I asked the manager. He shrugged and answered casually that "Probably something wrong with the projector." Eventually we appointed a new general manager and news director for WVIT (Viacom International Television), the station's new call letters, and infused new life into it. Its newscasts had been the lowest-rated in the area. Just one year after our purchase, WVIT received an Emmy for the best newscasts in the market. It is now owned by NBC.

Viacom began marketing reruns of *The Mary Tyler Moore Show*, whose seven-year run on CBS was set to end in the fall of 1977. Our Enterprise division wrote a detailed sales plan with dramatically higher prices than any show had ever obtained in syndication. We licensed the show to all NBC-owned television stations, which began to air it just as it ended on CBS. Other programs followed our lead in seeking and landing top prices.

I heard rumors that Mary Tyler Moore and her husband, producer Grant Tinker, were not happy with their return, given the high prices we obtained. I flew to Los Angeles and met with Mary and Grant. The president of our Enterprises division and I gave a detailed rundown of previous syndication prices, the prices we had achieved for their show, and how we were marketing and selling it.

Mary and Grant seemed pleased with our presentation. This was a pioneering effort in selling for syndication. In typical Hollywood fashion, shortly afterwards the rumors of their dissatisfaction once again circulated.

Around that time we were offered a series of four in-depth interviews of former President Richard Nixon, conducted by David Frost. Our staff felt the series would generate substantial revenues, and were eager to obtain syndication rights to the programs. The advance requested was quite large, however, and after internal discussions we decided not to proceed.

Since this was a decision that might cost us a substantial return, I informed Viacom's board of directors. To my surprise, some said that, had I decided to have Viacom distribute the interviews, they would have resigned from our board. I had no idea they felt that strongly about our disgraced former president. The four programs instead were distributed by Syndicast, garnering a great deal of publicity, including the covers of *Time, Newsweek,* and *TV Guide.*

Does the American Family Need Another Mouth to Feed?

By Arthur R. Taylor, President, CBS

CBS in 1976 distributed 200,000 copies of this brochure as part of a concerted effort by broadcasters to suppress the growth of cable television.

The first logo was proposed by Clark George for Viacom. Instead, the second version, chosen by Ralph, became Viacom's logo.

VIACOM

Viacom International Inc.

CBS executive Jack Schneider nearly strangled Viacom in its crib.

Viacom's first designated CEO Clark George, whose policies for the new company caused deep concern for Ralph and other top leaders. (courtesy of the Library of American Broadcasting)

Ralph, vice chairman of the International Rescue Committee, in Honduras in 1986 to inaugurate a short-wave radio station he helped establish. It brought education to refugee Mesquite Indian children whose families had fled the Marxist Sandinistas in Nicaragua.

With Raymond Burr, right, one of Ralph's closest friends in show business. Between them is Buddy Getzler, vice president of CBS Enterprises.

With (from left) Ray Timothy, president of NBC; producer Norman Lear; Jim Duffy, president of ABC. Viacom took Lear to court to secure its rights to syndicate *All in the Family*. Afterward Baruch and Lear became friends.

Testifying before a U.S. House committee against FCC rules allowing broadcast television networks to warehouse movies rather than permit pay cable television to show them. (circa 1976)

Dieter Stolte, longtime director general of German television network ZDF, and later publisher of the German newspaper *Die Welt*.

Junzo Imamichi, chairman of Tokyo Broadcasting System, worked with Ralph and CBS on various initiatives. (courtesy of TBS)

Silvio Berlusconi served twice as prime minister of Italy. He led the development of privately owned television, founding and owning Fininvest—three national channels, nearly half the Italian TV market. (courtesy of Dom Serafini of *Video Age*)

Frank Packer, Australia's most powerful media baron, tangled repeatedly with Ralph and CBS. An amateur boxer and yachtsman, he controlled the Nine television network and Australian Consolidated Press. (1953 photo by the *Sydney Morning Herald*, courtesy of Fairfax Photos)

In China at Beijing's request in 1976, to consult officials on telecommunications policy. China Central Television (CCTV) later began broadcasting to the world's largest audience.

Ralph, who gave the commencement address, and Jean with daughter Michele and Dr. Harold Whiteman, Jr., president of Sweet Briar College, Virginia, at graduation in 1980.

With Jean and daughters (left to right) Michele, Renee, Alice.

With Viacom's Terrence Elkes in front of the Christmas
tree at Rockefeller Center,
Viacom's headquarters. The
photo is from Viacom's 1979
annual report.

With (from left) Grant Tinker, president of NBC, and Bud Rukeyser, longtime
NBC executive.

Charles Wick, director of the United States Information Agency under President Reagan, in 1985 thanks Ralph for his volunteer service to the USIA during the Reagan years.

Joining forces to aid world refugees with (from left) Nobel Prize winner Elie Wiesel, humanitarian and actress Liv Ullmann, and Leo Cherne, longtime head of the International Rescue Committee, which helped Ralph and his family escape from Europe. (1987)

One of several letters from President Ronald Reagan to Ralph, thanking him for his professional, civic, and charitable contributions to the nation. On this occasion, Ralph was awarded the Gold Medal, radio and television's highest honor.

THE WHITE HOUSE

WASHINGTON

February 27, 1985

Dear Ralph:

Congratulations on receiving the Gold Medal from the International Radio and Television Society. This honor brings richly deserved recognition to your extraordinary leadership in the communications industry. Your dedication to excellence has earned the respect of your friends and colleagues alike. Also, I know that this tribute acknowledges your devotion to and efforts on behalf of many charitable and humanitarian causes. By sharing your gifts and your heart with your fellowman, you have demonstrated that the American spirit is one of caring and concern.

Nancy joins me in offering these good wishes. Again, congratulations and God bless you.

Sincerely,

Ronald Reagan

Mr. Ralph M. Baruch
Chairman
Viacom International
1211 Avenue of the Americas
New York, New York 10036

To Jean Baruch
With best wishes,
Nancy Reagan

Jean being greeted at the White House in 1985 by visiting President Raul Alfonsin of Argentina and First Lady Nancy Reagan. Ralph, a volunteer advisor to the USIA throughout the Reagan years, was ahead of Jean in line.

CBS's Frank Stanton (left) and Edward Bleier, president of the International Radio & Television Society, give Ralph the industry's highest award, the Gold Medal, in 1985. The citation, in part: "His is a success story with few equals in our industry. His is a life story which restores our faith in America's culture of aspiration."

With friend and former CBS president for a quarter-century, Dr. Frank Stanton.

Renowned violinist Isaac Stern, one of the most celebrated musicians of the twentieth century, saved Carnegie Hall from the wrecking ball, then became its president for the next four decades. Ralph, a longtime member of Carnegie's executive committee, raised millions to help fulfill Stern's vision for the famed venue. Flanking them at this black-tie event are Jean Baruch and Stern's wife, Linda. (Photo courtesy of Star Black)

To Ralph whose strong hands sent Viacom on its merry way.

Frank Stanton

CBS colleagues in 1999 honor former president Frank Stanton, center, with an Emmy for lifetime defense of the First Amendment, calling him "the greatest executive in the history of television business," and "the conscience of the broadcasting industry." Ralph is standing, third from the left. Among others: former CBS Anchor Walter Cronkite, seated second from the right, and, standing, three men from *60 Minutes*—Mike Wallace, sixth from the left; Andy Rooney, fifth to the right of Wallace; and Morley Safer, second to the right of Rooney. Stanton inscribed the photo: "To Ralph, whose strong hands sent Viacom on its merry way."

Presenting a special Emmy to Huw Weldon of Great Britain, a friend, former head of the British Broadcasting Corporation, and later director of the London School of Economics.

Former New York City mayors gather at an event chaired by Ralph and Jean Baruch in 1997 to raise funds for the city's award-winning Lenox Hill Hospital. Others in picture (from left) are former Mayor Abraham Beame, Joyce Dinkins and former Mayor David Dinkins, Mary Lindsay and former Mayor John Lindsay.

Jean with Matilda Cuomo, wife of former New York Governor Mario Cuomo, at a Broadcasters' Foundation event in 2006. The Foundation provides financial assistance to radio and television broadcasters in acute need. (Courtesy of Don Pollard)

With ABC News Anchor Peter Jennings, who served with Ralph on the board of Carnegie Hall before his death of cancer in August 2005 at age sixty-seven.

Welcoming Gloria and Jimmy Stewart to Carn-egie Hall.

Longtime friend and colleague Walter Cronkite presents an Emmy to Ralph in 1999, awarded by the International Academy of Television Arts and Sciences. (Courtesy of Agence France Presse)

Sumner Redstone helps honor the man he succeeded as head of Viacom at the Emmy Awards ceremony. "Ralph played a major role in the spin-off of Viacom from CBS," said Redstone, "and now sees his legacy come full term as Viacom buys CBS."

Ralph and Jean with two grown-up daughters, Alice (left) and Michele.

Seven Americans were inducted into the Cable Center Hall of Fame in 2006 for "significant and lasting impact" on the industry: (from left) James Robbins, Cox; Decker Anstrom, Landmark; Carolyn Chambers, Chambers; Robert Zitter, HBO; Ralph; Judy McGrath, MTV; Brian Roberts, Comcast. (courtesy of Cable Center/Rob Stuehrk, Agile Imaging).

19
VIACOM 'A COMPANY TO RECKON WITH'

I faced a dilemma: how to manage a fast-growing company, continue to foster the development of cable, and still have a life. As head of its Pay Cable Committee, I convinced the National Cable Television Association to let me hire someone to help produce written materials and lobby in Washington.

I interviewed and recommended Bob Johnson, an African-American who had been chief of staff to U.S. Congressman Walter Fauntroy of the District of Columbia.

Bob was highly capable and had excellent experience on the Washington scene. He came aboard as an NCTA vice president and we worked closely. Years later, in competition with Viacom and other companies, Bob obtained cable television franchises in the Washington area. He also initiated Black Entertainment Television, financed partly by cable companies. (Ironically, down the road Bob sold BET to Viacom, making him a billionaire.)

My load was heavy at Viacom, especially as our business expanded overseas. I traveled frequently and different time zones meant that I got phone calls at all hours, impacting my family as well. I wrestled with what to do and decided I must delegate more responsibility to other Viacom executives, especially general counsel Terry Elkes and the head of Viacom Enterprises, Larry Hilford.

I needed the approval of Viacom's board members, which by no means was automatic. Larry was well-regarded but some directors flat did not like Terry. He tended to mock their questions in board meetings, and smoked his pipe without ever asking if anyone minded. Leo Cherne and Allan Johnson especially objected to giving Elkes more responsibility.

But both Larry and Terry were talented professionals. I pressed our directors to name them executive vice presidents, splitting operational responsibilities. The board finally concurred, making the two men the leading candidates to replace me down the line.

As CEO, I considered Terry and Larry my right and left hands. Late in 1976, however, Larry resigned and went to Columbus, Ohio, to run QUBE, an innovative cable system owned by Warner Communications. Larry and I remained good friends. Years later he succumbed to cancer, and the industry suffered a great loss.

Terry was now my likely successor. Viacom moved to Rockefeller Center to get more space, and our offices were side by side. Throughout the day we visited each other, kicking around ideas. Our strengths complemented each other.

Terry's knowledge of finance, especially structuring debt, and his legal ability brought a lot to the table. I relied on his judgment in those areas, and my range of experience covered Viacom's other needs. I began to introduce Terry to the movers and shakers in our industry, as a friend as well as a professional colleague.

In 1977 we signed an agreement with RCA Americom to provide two transponders on its satellite to distribute Showtime. The cost was $7.5 million—a hefty $75 for each of our current 100,000 pay cable subscribers.

HBO had been on satellite for two years, and observers were amazed that a tiny company like Viacom had the audacity to go head-to-head with a subsidiary of giant Time Inc. But an important part of Viacom's future was in cable programming and pay TV. Our goal by the end of 1978 was to have Showtime available to more than one million cable homes and to triple our subscribers to 300,000.

RCA organized a big party at Cape Canaveral, Florida, and invited Viacom's assistant general counsel and me, with our wives, to watch the launch of our satellite. It would prove a painful experience. On the morning of launch day the big toe on my left foot had become infected and I went to the local hospital. A doctor briefly examined the toe. Then, to my shock, he grabbed a pair of scissors and plunged them into the front of my toe—with no pain killer. I screamed in agony. I still remember the pained look on Jean's face and tears that poured down her cheeks.

A nurse bandaged my foot, I was given a pair of crutches, and we were off to Kennedy Space Center.

At the viewing area, the wife of my Viacom colleague fell off a bleacher but fortunately was not injured. Nothing had prepared us for the launch. An enormous cloud of water-vapor shot from beneath the rocket, followed seconds later by a tremendous earth-shaking noise, un-like anything I had experienced. Watching the rocket lift majestically into the stratosphere was breathtaking. Aboard was our satellite, scheduled to separate from the rocket two days later.

After the launch it began to rain as we drove to a gala RCA had organized. After arriving, our wives got out and my colleague and I went to park the car. I hobbled back to the restaurant. As we entered, I noticed a lot of commotion, then was startled to see Jean on the floor, writhing in agony.

In the dark she had not seen a little step and had fallen. Jean thought she had broken her foot, but refused further attention and spent the evening with the foot in a bucket of ice water.

Next morning we returned to the hospital. Seeing my crutches, they wanted to care for me. Instead they took Jean in, and an x-ray re-vealed a broken toe. She was given a large sandal and a pair of crutches. Both of us limped out of the hospital and were driven to the motel.

When the maid saw us she asked "One bed to be made up?" In unison we said "Oh, no, two beds!" Jean's toe healed nicely. To this day my toe bears the scars of that painful procedure. And more trouble was to come.

The next day we returned to the satellite center. As a special priv-ilege, a NASA official invited me to press the button that would put our satellite into orbit. I pushed the button, the satellite separated from the rocket...and was never heard from again. So much for my luck in space. We never learned if the complete loss of signal was caused by a solar storm or some other identifiable problem.

Early on I instituted a company policy to close our offices at one o'clock on Fridays in the summer. However, I was lucky to get away by three or four. Jean and I usually took the girls to our weekend house on Candlewood Lake, Connecticut.

One day I received a call from one of my children, then in her late twenties, asking if she could use the lake house that weekend. I have learned with daughters that when one is asked a question, one must answer cautiously. The conversation went like this:

"Dad, I just want to know if you're going to use the house this weekend?"

"Why are you asking me?"

"I'd like to use the house, but wanted to be sure you're not going to be there."

That did it. Jean and I decided to sell that house and buy a sailboat. We inspected boats up and down the Eastern seaboard and purchased a beauty—a forty-three-foot Camper Nicholson in Annapolis, Maryland.

But how to get it to New York? One of Viacom's young salesmen heard of our need and claimed to be an excellent seaman who, with three or four friends, could help us sail it to New York. I accepted immediately. We all flew down to Annapolis and began our journey homeward on the *Calisto*. It was not as easy as I had assumed. Shortly after we set sail we hit a fog that plagued us for much of the three to four days back to New York.

We reached the D.C. Canal inland and the head of our crew figured there would be six to eight inches between the top of our mast and the bottom of the bridge—at low tide. We entered the canal, waited for low tide, and with a great deal of trepidation approached the bridge.

Calisto started through. A scraping sound pierced the air. My heart sank. Fortunately, however, it was the flexible radio antenna atop the mast brushing the bottom of the bridge. We barely squeaked through.

Jean was our indispensable sailor. She spent a lot of time in the galley, preparing great quantities of what our young crew called "monkey food," fresh vegetables and meat, all cooked together and eaten day and night. I took my turn at the bow in the dense fog to listen for boat horns and watch for obstacles. We traveled from buoy to buoy to mark our way, and as I kept watch I had the strangest experiences. I saw things in the fog that one could not imagine. One time I thought I saw an entire building; as I stared, it rose into the sky. I cannot explain what I sensed and saw, or why.

We sailed into New York under the Verrazano Narrows Bridge and stayed close to a Coast Guard buoy waiting for the tide to change. Finally we sailed up the East River and up Long Island Sound to Stamford, Connecticut, where we berthed at Yacht Haven.

The *Calisto* became the joy of our lives. The young Viacom salesman who was our skipper on that first voyage was Jamie Kellner. He continued to steer media people well. Jamie helped Rupert Murdoch launch the Fox Network, and later was head of AOL Time Warner's television networks. We trained him right.

I figured I had given my share of service as a good citizen of the cable industry, and looked forward to having less on my plate. But I learned that one who steps forward to answer the call of duty will be called on again and again. It was now more than forty years since the Communications Act of 1934 had been enacted. Congress had not touched it since. With the advent of cable television, the FCC had simply claimed jurisdiction and written the rules governing cable.

Early in 1977 I was asked to organize and lead a cable industry group to investigate possible changes in the 1934 Act and advise Congress how to amend it. Reluctantly I agreed, never imagining seven arduous years of work were ahead.

That November I addressed the Western Cable Show and Convention in San Diego. Although the Supreme Court had recently affirmed a lower court ruling largely freeing cable from discriminatory FCC rules, cable still had difficulty obtaining movies. I told the convention that "It is obvious that the networks are using their enormous economic power to extract from motion picture suppliers contractual exclusivity conditions which clearly discriminate against...pay cable. This is another matter we will have to take to the courts." I explained:

An industry must also establish its integrity and principles. I would like to see the cable television industry take the leadership in stating some of these principles....The new principles say simply this: Let those who advocate restrictions, regulation, or legislation prove that [they] are, in fact, in the public interest. Not in the cable television industry's interest; not in any other group's vested interest—just the public's interest.

I proposed five principles that also guided the work of our cable committee then engaged in helping to revise the 1934 Communications Act:

- All restrictions on the number and source of distant signals should be abandoned unless it can be shown they are in the public interest.
- Pay cable should not be regulated—in programming, rates, or other services and conditions.
- We should encourage the commercial use of unused activated channel time on cable television systems across the country.
- The FCC should encourage the use of cable to provide local community programming in the public interest, and require that moderate-size cable systems provide one equivalent channel for public-access users.
- The cable industry should be allowed to develop with less regulation rather than more.

We genuinely believed these principles were in the public interest, and invited the National Association of Broadcasters to support them as well. Bob Schmidt, president of the NCTA, wrote his counterpart at the NAB, Vincent Wasilewski, encouraging the NAB to do so. Wasilewski not only answered no, but hell no, and treated our olive branch with contempt. Clearly broadcasters and the NAB had no intention of burying the hatchet—unless it was in our heads.

Viacom revived and produced in syndication *The $25,000 Pyramid*. Taking great care to prevent any kind of rigging, we also created *The*

$128,000 Question in syndication—double its forerunner, *The $64,000 Question.*

While we did not hit home runs with every venture, our batting average was good enough that in 1977 Viacom declared its first cash dividend. Though small, five cents a share, it was a beginning. That year our revenues increased by 25 percent over 1976, profits by 47 percent—to $5.6 million—and earnings per share by 45 percent.

Rapid growth forced us to rent an additional floor at Rockefeller Center. Observers sat up and took notice.

"By most accounts," said *The New York Times,* "Viacom, the little-known enterprise that has become the world's leading independent syndicator of network television programs, is a company to watch....For six consecutive years, Viacom has achieved record revenues and profits."

That began a wide-ranging *Times* feature on Viacom, covering a third of a business page on May 19, 1978.

Reporter Edwin McDowell added that "the industry is in for radical transformation. Although the networks' influence and revenues have never been higher, many analysts predict that cable satellites and other technological marvels will turn the television industry inside out...[Viacom] is smart, the way it's diversifying, said one Wall Street analyst. It's soon going to be a company to be reckoned with."

A vice president at investment banker Goldman Sachs told the *Times* "[Viacom's] stock is doing well because for the first time the company's syndication business and cable business have come together. It did well even when one of the businesses was up and the other down, but now everything is pulling together."

Viacom was on the map. Like a blossoming debutante, our company had many suitors. One was John Kluge, president and a substantial owner of Metromedia. John had purchased the former DuMont television stations in New York and Washington, and bought other independent stations to create Metromedia. He wanted to buy Viacom as well.

But uncomprehending analysts still did not assign a value to Viacom's syndication operation, and our stock was depressed. As a result, I told John, Viacom was way undervalued and selling was not a viable option.

John tried to persuade me otherwise. He said I personally would be well taken care of. But I saw a big future for Viacom and told him my personal arrangements could not enter the equation. We parted as friends and he never raised the subject again.

Years later John paid me back at a social event in Washington. We shared a table as both of us were about to be inducted into the *Broadcasting and Cable* magazine Hall of Fame. John asked what I was going to say in my acceptance speech. I said I would praise those who had honored me while I was still alive, because many inductees were deceased, and I was pleased to receive the award while I could still appreciate it. John was called up first to accept the award and, rascal that he was, used my lines almost word for word. I was left to improvise.

Smiling Cobra Jim Aubrey called one morning. He had once been CBS Network president—behind only Bill Paley and Frank Stanton in the pecking order. Aubrey was ruthless but commercially talented and successful through never underestimating the public's bad taste.

After years of merciless treatment of subordinates and others, Aubrey had been fired by Paley and Stanton. He was now president of MGM, working for Kirk Kerkorian, who controlled the Hollywood studio, had extensive holdings in Las Vegas, and was known as the father of the megaresort.

"Kirk and I are here in New York and we have little time," Aubrey said. "We have to take the MGM plane back to L.A. no later than noon. When can you come over to our hotel?" It was a cheeky request and I had a busy schedule. I said I could not come to them, but if they wished to see me, I could set aside a little time in my office. Aubrey argued that their time was short, but I stood firm.

Shortly afterward they arrived at my office. I was surprised at their appearance. Aubrey was dressed in a gray jogging suit and Kerkorian in pants and jacket, no tie. They said they wanted to buy Viacom. I said we had no interest in selling, but that I would take the matter to our board of directors.

I discussed it with the board, who shared my feelings. We did not want to be involved with them, given Aubrey's checkered reputation and Kerkorian's ties to Las Vegas and his habit of buying, stripping, and then selling companies.

Guided by our long-range plans, we took aim at another possible acquisition, Sonderling Broadcasting. It was mainly owned by Egmont Sonderling, a former rabbi born in Germany, who was in his seventies. We signed a letter of intent in March 1978 and began a long, tough period of bargaining. Sonderling's properties included eight radio stations, a television station in Albany, and a couple of related businesses.

I visited most of the properties with staff and learned they were not well run. They offered great potential for improvement and added value under our capable people. After nearly two years of negotiations, Sonderling was merged into Viacom for just under $30 million.

The eight radio stations were an eclectic group, in some of the nation's biggest markets: New York, Houston, San Francisco, Memphis, and Washington D.C. KIKK in Houston played country music and was one of the most successful stations in that market. There were two radio stations in New York City, including an FM station with a jazz format and one AM in Queens formatted especially for African-Americans. There was a similar station in Memphis.

The transmitter for the New York jazz station was atop a church, limiting its coverage. We moved the transmitter to the Empire State Building and changed the format to country-western, then later to "lite" music.

Jazz enthusiasts were dismayed over the loss of their station. But with the latter format and the call letters WLTW, it became one of the most listened-to radio stations in the Big Apple. Years later it was sold for more than $400 million, compared with the less than $30 million we paid for the entire Sonderling group.

In visiting the Albany television station I got a strange feeling that things were not right, but we could not put our finger on the problem. We named a new manager. He suspected that drugs may have been sold and traded in the station and that the union representing technicians and engineers was tapping the station's phones.

We ordered a drug-free station and had the phones checked and rechecked, finding no bugs. That station too was later sold by Viacom for the equivalent of about $60 million.

We carefully studied each former Sonderling property and decided WWRL, the station in New York formatted especially for African-Americans, did not fit in our overall strategy. We decided to do a good deed and donate the station to a worthy cause. The NAACP, headed by my friend Benjamin Hooks, a former FCC commissioner, was a natural choice for this million-dollar-plus donation.

Ben came to my office and I outlined our plan: We would donate WWRL to the NAACP and they would have someone standing by to purchase the station at the same time. Ben argued vehemently that the NAACP did not need a radio station. I explained again that this would not be an NAACP-owned station. Rather, at the time of the donation, a buyer literally would sit on the other side of the table and would acquire the station simultaneously, putting a substantial sum of money into the NCAA's coffers. Ben shook his head, said he did not want to hear any more, and left.

Then I thought of Tom Murphy, CEO of Capital Cities/ABC. Murphy was a lanky, friendly guy—he often greeted you with "Hi ya, pal"—but was tough as nails in business. Tom was on the board of the United Negro College Fund. I called him and offered the donation.

"I'll come right over," he said. "No," I said, "we'll come to you." The station was donated to the UNCF, which found a simultaneous buyer at a substantial seven-figure price. That made Viacom one of the UNCF's largest donors that year.

As we absorbed Sonderling I was increasingly concerned about Showtime, our pay-cable service. Showtime had approximately 300,000 subscribers and projected substantially more by the end of 1978, compared with HBO's nearly two million subscribers.

At a budget meeting Jeffrey Reiss, president of Showtime, began by projecting a loss of tens of millions of dollars annually, starting in 1979. I stopped Jeff cold and told him this was unacceptable. We could not tolerate such losses, and they were to rework the numbers.

We decided to approach Teleprompter, the nation's largest cable television company, to see if it would buy part of Showtime. Jack Kent Cooke owned the NFL's Washington Redskins as well as Teleprompter. Our objective was to have the 300,000 HBO subscribers on Teleprompter's cable systems switched to Showtime—doubling our projected base overnight.

Another series of arduous negotiations followed. In September we reached agreement for Teleprompter to buy 50 percent of Showtime. Teleprompter would pay $3 million to $5 million, depending on Showtime's success in attracting subscribers, and would convert its 300,000 HBO subscribers to Showtime. The deal cost HBO 13 percent of its subscribers and brought Showtime needed capital and fresh fervor.

The Washington Post, reporting on the deal, called Viacom "one of the fastest-growing companies in the entire broadcasting industry." We syndicated television series worldwide, noted the *Post*, produced many of the game shows then on TV, and were "the sixth largest owner of cable television systems..."[1]

We began to hear rumors that Jack Kent Cooke wanted to sell his Teleprompter interests to devote more time to his beloved Redskins. I repeatedly asked Teleprompter managers about the rumors, and was assured Cooke would not sell Teleprompter. Soon after one of these reassurances Cook sold Teleprompter to Westinghouse Broadcasting, a subsidiary of Westinghouse Electric, in August 1981.

After the dust settled Dan Ritchie, head of Westinghouse Broadcasting, started to attend our joint Showtime management meetings. He was a slender man who spoke slowly and chose his words carefully. Ritchie had considerable wealth but drove a modest car and seemed approachable.

Unfortunately, his keen concern over what Westinghouse offered the public came to hinder Showtime. From the first meeting Ritchie attended he said we showed too many R-rated movies.

I told Ritchie that usually these movies did not air until 8 or 9 p.m., and they were what the audience demanded. Research showed these were our most watched films. Nonetheless he continued a drumbeat of objections. (Later, Ritchie's Westinghouse launched a competing cable subscription service with only G or PG films. It sparked little interest from viewers or cable system operators and folded after a short time.)

I suggested we buy back the 50 percent of Showtime Westinghouse had inherited from Teleprompter. Ritchie refused and, instead, suggested that Westinghouse buy our half of Showtime.

The end of this saga came a year later. After Ronald Reagan was elected President in 1980, our mutual friend Charles Wick was named head of the United States Information Agency. At Charlie's request I chaired the agency's newly created Private Sector Communications Initiative all through Reagan's eight years in the White House. Our mission was to promote the U.S. on radio and television worldwide, especially behind the Iron Curtain.

President Reagan asked select communication leaders, together with private sector members of the USIA, to an informal lunch in Washington. I attended and so did Robert Kirby, CEO of Westinghouse Electric. Still facing considerable pressure from Dan Ritchie, head of Westinghouse's broadcast subsidiary, I was at wit's end how to satisfy his opposition to R-rated films and still keep Showtime viable.

At the Washington event I made sure I sat next to Kirby. "You know, we have a common interest in a joint venture," I said casually.

"Oh, yes, what is that?"

" Showtime."

"Oh, that little thing," he said.

A bit disappointed, I answered, "What may be a little thing for you is a very big thing for us."

"Oh, yes, I realize that, but there are too many R-rated movies on Showtime."

Taking my courage in two hands I said "No, as a matter of fact, there aren't enough. The audience wants R-rated movies." Then, lying my head off, I added, "In fact, we are thinking of putting X-rated movies on Showtime at about midnight." I knew Viacom would never do that.

"Oh, no, you mustn't!" said Kirby, horror on his face.

"Well, we are thinking about it," I answered, enjoying his discomfiture.

Shortly after the Washington event Dan Ritchie called and asked me to lunch at the Manhattan Ocean Club. He said Westinghouse had decided to sell its interest in Showtime back to Viacom. Silently I thanked Robert Kirby.

By now I had cultivated a friendly relationship with Ritchie, which helped this set of negotiations. He owned an avocado farm in northern California, and built a gorgeous house atop a nearby mountain, where Jean and I visited. Ritchie was reputed to be second only to the U.S. government as the largest landowner in Colorado.

He was a fine, tough, thorough negotiator, as we learned in long bargaining sessions between Viacom and what was by then called Group W Cable.[2] In August 1982 Viacom bought back 50 percent of Showtime for about $60 million—more than twenty times what we had sold it for. It would anchor Viacom's future. By then Showtime served about 1,800 cable systems and had nearly 3.5 million subscribers. We were still number two to HBO, but closing steadily.

20

Networks Sleep
at the Switch

Whena you live in New York, London is a long way to go just for a meal. But when the head of our European office phoned and urged me to attend a dinner thrown by the British Broadcasting Corporation for program suppliers, I agreed to go.

Great Britain was the fourth largest market for U.S. television fare. Selling programs there and elsewhere abroad was a vital part of Viacom's business.

The BBC in its present form first aired on radio in 1927. It has long set the standard in international broadcasting. Britain's television system included two BBC networks funded by viewer license fees, and one commercial network. Throughout the 1970s its regulatory agency, the Independent Broadcasting Authority, had allowed the commercial network to use no more than 14 percent foreign fare. The BBC followed suit. In 1977, U.S. programs filled only 12 percent of the BBC's foreign quota. Viacom and other U.S. exporters had a lot at stake in England.[1]

Prices had risen sharply for our best programs. In the late 1960s, U.K. buyers paid up to $8,000 for a one-hour TV episode. A decade later they paid up to $25,000. Hollywood's price for feature films had risen even more sharply—quadrupling from about $25,000 to $100,000, with some blockbusters bringing $200,000.

The sumptuous dinner was in a private dining room at BBC headquarters. Served by white-gloved waiters, it featured a meal one could scarcely forget: vintage French champagnes, the finest of appetizers, and grouse, a delicacy, among other entrees, accompanied by the best Bordeaux wines. Dessert was followed by liqueurs and Cuban cigars. A grand affair, well worthy of the BBC.

Then, jarringly, Alisdair Milne, BBC Television's managing director, rose and gave a speech in which he outlined problems the BBC faced with American distributors. He said the BBC was in debt tens of millions of pounds, and we were charging too much for our programs. We were unnerved. As the senior American leader present, my colleagues looked to me to respond.

I felt it would be in bad taste to debate our hosts. Instead I stood and said that we greatly appreciated their hospitality in their lovely quarters, and realized their position regarding the debt.

"We also thank the BBC for this dinner. We understand that because of your financial situation, it is somewhat modest, and we hope in the not-too-distant future, when the BBC has regained financial stability, that you will serve us a really good meal." Guests roared, breaking the tension.

Nearly a decade later, Milne's candor and independence cost him his job. By then he was director general—top manager—of the BBC. To his credit, Milne insisted the BBC's news coverage follow the principles it publicly espoused—including nonpartisanship and journalistic integrity.

A board of governors appointed by the Queen regulates the BBC. Milne supported stories as critical of Prime Minister Margaret Thatcher's Conservatives as of Liberals and the trade unions. By January 1987, the Thatcher government apparently decided enough was enough. Milne "resigned" and was replaced by an accountant.

The U.S. government's involvement with domestic television has never approached that of the British government's. In Britain, each household is assessed a fee, essentially a tax, to pay for television. The U.S. role is through the Corporation for Public Broadcasting. It is a private, nonprofit organization, chartered and funded by Washington to promote public broadcasting. The CPB was created in 1967; two years later it inaugurated the Public Broadcasting Service.

In 2005 the PBS, headquartered in Alexandria, Virginia, was comprised of 169 noncommercial, educational licensees who operated 348 members stations. Station assessments accounted for nearly half the PBS budget, with a quarter of its funding coming from the CPB and federal grants. While federal money makes up a relatively small share of the budgets of major PBS stations, it is lifeblood to small stations.

Occasionally members of Congress get stirred up over PBS programming, deeming it too conservative or too liberal, and threaten to pull the plug on funding—sending shivers down the backs of small stations.

Through the years, PBS has proven its worth. What would children have done without *Sesame Street, Mister Rogers' Neighborhood,* or *Barney and Friends?* Adults looking for serious entertainment that also educated had such programs as *Masterpiece Theatre, Nova,* and *The American Experience.* And, at this writing, Jim Lehrer, who joined PBS in Washington in 1972, is the most solid, fair-minded anchor on television.

In 1978 Congress was locked in debate over another role of television in a democracy. Pressure was growing to allow cameras in its chambers. When televising the House of Representatives appeared inevitable, the debate turned to who would produce the coverage. The issue pitted the powerful broadcast networks against an unassuming young journalist, Brian Lamb, and cable television.

The cable industry was concerned that, should the networks be awarded the right to televise Congress, they would use only snippets of floor proceedings, since they obviously did not have a channel to devote to it. Networks would control the cameras and be the sole judges of what went on the air. If the opportunity arose, it was feared, they would likely use excerpts from floor debate to strengthen themselves and, if possible, harm their sworn enemy, cable.

As Washington deliberated, I got a call from Tom Wheeler, president of the National Cable Television Association. Over lunch Wheeler proposed that the cable industry devote an entire channel to cover the U.S. House and inaugurate the Cable Satellite Public Affairs Network, or C-SPAN, to produce it. To finance it, Wheeler suggested that Viacom and the rest of the industry contribute one cent a month per cable subscriber.

The idea was the brainchild of Lamb, then Washington bureau chief for *Cablevision* magazine. I immediately pledged Viacom's support.[2]

Lamb called and we met in Washington. A native of Indiana, Brian went to the capital as a young naval public affairs officer. Prior to *Cablevision* he was also a radio reporter, press secretary to a U.S. Senator, and staff aide at the White House. Years later Brian said he was scared the day he came to meet with me, that I had a reputation for being fair but tough.

I offered $25,000 a year for the next three years, and a continuing amount thereafter based on the number of our cable subscribers. Brian was thrilled. I was the second person to underwrite C-SPAN. The first was cable pioneer Robert Rosencrans, head of UA-Columbia Cable, who became C-SPAN's first chairman.

C-SPAN first hit the air on March 19, 1979, beaming floor proceedings of the U.S. House of Representatives into American homes and schools. Seven years later, in 1986, C-SPAN2 was born to cover all live sessions of the U.S. Senate. C-SPAN3 debuted in 2001 to offer other government-related events and historical programming from its archives. The three channels in 2006 operated around the clock and were available to more than eighty million homes on over six thousand cable systems.

C-SPAN Radio debuted in 1997, with coverage similar to its three television sisters, and migrated to satellite radio four years later. C-SPAN's live feeds are streamed free of charge and are available on its World Wide Web site. C-SPAN's ratings typically do not stack up against those of the networks, movie, or entertainment channels. But its viewers are uncommonly influential and active in the nation's political affairs; surveys suggest 90 percent of C-SPAN viewers vote.

On its twenty-fifth birthday in 2004, a study indicated 43 percent of Americans watched C-SPAN—12 percent regularly and 31 percent sometimes.[3] Six in ten regular viewers found it "very useful to the country," and 74 percent said they would miss it if it were no longer available. C-SPAN is the only television channel that carries the Republican and Democratic presidential conventions from start to finish every four years.

I value a letter from then-House Speaker Thomas P. (Tip) O'Neill, Jr. in 1979. It says: "On this historic day as the House of Representatives opens its chambers to the American people through television, I want to take this opportunity to commend you for the pioneering efforts of ...C-SPAN. It should give you and your fellow C-SPAN board members a great deal of satisfaction to know that the cable industry's decision to bring the televised sessions of the House directly into millions of U.S. homes will graphically enhance our democratic form of government."

C-SPAN indeed has enhanced our American system. An informed citizenry is essential to a healthy democracy. In the last couple of decades, cable news channels have proved vital in filling this role.

Newspapers and network evening news in the U.S. have suffered long-term declines. Citizens saying they read a newspaper "yesterday" fell from 58 percent in 1994 to 47 percent in 2000 to 42 percent in 2004. Newspaper readership is especially scarce among those under age 30, just 23 percent of whom reported in 2004 that they read a newspaper the day before.

Today C-SPAN is a crown jewel of cable. Its introduction marked a watershed in the broadcast networks' stranglehold on national and international public affairs programming. A year after C-SPAN began, Cable News Network hit the air. Within another half-dozen years, they had been joined by CNN Headline News, CNN International, and Fox Broadcasting. CNN and FOX are the most-watched cable news channels, each attracting about one in five viewers.

It was nearly time to roll out *All in the Family* in domestic syndication. We planned carefully to make the most of it. Years earlier we had to take Norman Lear to court to secure distribution rights. Since then we had established a good relationship with Lear and found him to be not only a talented producer but a fine person to deal with.

By the time *All in the Family* returned to the air we had $90 million in bookings. It was highly successful in syndication for many years. We partnered with Goodson-Todman to syndicate *Family Feud*, and resumed production of their *To Tell The Truth*.

Before Viacom and CBS split, company President Frank Stanton assured me we would have distribution rights to films produced by CBS's new motion picture division.

No doubt Frank believed this. But once again our mother company let us down. We negotiated hard for months and had to swallow a hefty guarantee before CBS gave us access to these films. We signed an agreement in July 1979 guaranteeing CBS over $30 million for twenty-eight films. They included such movies as "With Six You Get Egg Roll," starring Doris Day; "The April Fools," with Jack Lemmon and Catherine Deneuve; "Little Big Man," with Dustin Hoffman, two motion pictures starring John Wayne, and "A Man Called Horse," with Richard Harris.

Managing Viacom's swift growth was a challenge. We stepped up the purchase of related communication companies as I directed cable television's proposed changes to the U.S. Communications Act. Our newly acquired cable systems and radio and television stations required care and leadership, as did Viacom's well-established divisions. My office was busy and days were long. There was scant time for family, friends, or leisure.

In the late seventies, as every CEO should, I thought hard about who would succeed me if I were hit by the proverbial truck. Many a CEO has remained in the job too long and, by holding on, left little or no room for others in the organization to progress. That can cost a company the loss of its best and brightest, who are less likely to remain if they see little or no hope of advancing up the executive ladder.

Terry Elkes was now the only viable inside candidate. I felt strongly that, if possible, we should take advantage of experience within Viacom and not look outside for my potential successor.

But some directors firmly opposed Elkes. Terry, now a member of the board after years of attending meetings as secretary, had not endeared himself especially to Leo Cherne and Allan Johnson. When a director sought more than cursory information, Elkes had a tendency to deride the question, smirk, or even laugh, and give him a curt answer.

Most directors were busy with their own affairs and not able to follow the day-to-day activities of Viacom. No matter how elementary the question, they deserved a straight answer. Elkes' demeanor perhaps stemmed in part from the fact he was basically shy. He seemed uncomfortable in social situations, and his wife Ruth told Jean that she would not wear anything, even to formal dinners, that could not be tossed into a washing machine.

I spent sleepless nights pondering these issues, and finally decided Elkes deserved the opportunity to grow and aim for the top. I proposed that we create an Office of the Chief Executive. I would move up to chairman and CEO, and make Elkes president. I shared this plan privately with Johnson and Cherne. Though both had serious reservations, they agreed to back me.

Finally, late in 1978, the board approved my plan. Elkes never knew how difficult it was to clear the way for his ascent. I would come to regret this opening scene in a corporate drama that, before final curtain, would change Viacom and me forever. At the time, however, it seemed appropriate.

The business was all-consuming. I could not have done it without Jean, who patiently served late meals on a tray while I was on the phone at home, and tolerated my frequent travel.

On occasion I asked her to travel with me. Once was to Los Angeles to attend the Emmy Awards. Afterward we assembled at Chasen's with some of our creative people and Ed McMahon of NBC's *The Tonight Show*, with whom we were talking about hosting a new television program.

At the awards show Ed's boss, Johnny Carson, once more failed to win an Emmy. He sat at a nearby table, looking dejected. At our table Ed McMahon challenged Jean to a drinking duel of Pernod stingers while he recited Edgar Allen Poe. Both sides held up well. McMahon was in the middle of a Poe recitation when Carson came over to our table and nodded for McMahon to join him. Ed practically saluted and —midway through a quotation—abruptly left. The master had called. Our project with Ed never materialized.

I had a distaste for the whole Hollywood scene, and went out there as seldom as possible. Jean and I did not even watch the various TV series produced in Hollywood. I had notoriously bad judgment of which series were likely to succeed, and made it a point to not get involved in programming projects.

One year we were invited by the head of the CBS Television Network to a convention in Los Angeles of all its affiliated stations. At the final dinner we were invited to sit on either side of Greg Harrison. Jean turned to the handsome young actor, friendly-like, and said "What have you been in lately."

"I star in Trapper John." He neglected to add "M.D." Since its debut in the fall of 1979, we learned later, the medical drama series had been in the top twenty-five shows each year. Harrison played Dr. Alonzo "Gonzo" Gates.

"Oh, that's wonderful," said Jean. After a pause, she added "It must be very hard."

"What must be very hard?" asked Harrison.

"Well," said Jean earnestly, "it must be very hard to work with all those animals." She figured that's what trappers do—trap animals.

Harrison was visibly upset. He turned from Jean and began to chat with me. To smooth things over, I asked what else he had been involved in.

"I'm working on a project called 'The Enola Gay,'" he answered. The Enola Gay, of course, dropped the world's first atomic bomb on Hiroshimä. *Good,* I thought, *here's something we can chat about.* I asked for more details, which he gladly supplied. Then I made the mistake of asking, "What company are you doing this project with?"

"With your company!" he snapped. Harrison—make that Dr. Gonzo Gates—got up, stomped away, and did not come near our table the rest of the evening.

Days away from work were rare, but Jean and I made the most

of them by doing what we loved most: sailing. Weekends on the *Calisto* helped keep me on an even keel the rest of the week. We learned to navigate well, and had years of great fun on the water.

At mid-afternoon on Fridays I would leave the office and take the train to Stamford, Connecticut, where Jean would pick me up. She would have gone aboard the day before to replenish the boat with water, food, fuel, and all the other things one needs for a weekend on Long Island Sound. Even there I often kept in touch with the office by two-way radio.

Occasionally in the summer we took *Calisto* on longer jaunts, up to Newport, Rhode Island, or other places. One time we sailed from Shelter Island to Block Island and hit fog about an hour out. The fog thickened and after a few hours I told Jean "If we don't hit Block Island within the next half-hour, we'll have to turn around."

"Why?" She asked.

"Because the next stop is Portugal." Fortunately we reached Block Island and were only a couple miles off course.

The best way to clean dishes when sailing is to drag them behind the boat in a net, which you must retrieve before docking. On one trip I forgot about the net until we had anchored. It was still attached to the boat but was caught in the propeller and had sunk with our dishes to the bottom of the filthiest harbor one could imagine. As we got off *Calisto* I stared down at the water. I must have looked pretty helpless. Nearby sat a rough-looking character, disheveled and unshaven, wearing torn jeans and an undershirt.

"Would you like me to get the dishes out?" he asked.

I nodded sheepishly. I was not about to dive into that polluted water. He donned goggles, jumped in, and retrieved the net and dishes. Immensely grateful, I tried to give him a substantial tip.

"Oh no, that's quite all right," he said. He looked as though he could use it, so I insisted. "No, no, no, I won't take your money," he repeated, "but when you're through cleaning your boat, come on back and we'll have a drink on mine." He nodded toward a handsome craft that was half again longer than ours, and introduced himself as Dr. so-and-so. We all had a good laugh and enjoyed a drink.

Our guests on a long holiday weekend were Terry Elkes and his family. Although it was blistering hot, his son insisted on watching a televised baseball game down below. Occasionally his head would pop out of the hatch to announce the score. He persisted in drinking sodas with lots of ice until he emptied our ice chest. Afterwards we had trouble cleaning up because Terry had smoked his pipe, strewing tobacco all over the boat.

One day in 1981 we hit heavy weather and our forward sail, called a genoa, became tangled. I clamped myself onto the boat's lines and crawled forward to untangle it, while Jean held the wheel and, at the same time with considerable exertion, reined in the lines.

When we reached port in Stamford, Jean's arm hurt. The pain worsened. Days later we went to a doctor and found that she had torn all the ligaments in her right arm. That ended our adventures on the water, and we put *Calisto* up for sale.

We valued the privacy we had enjoyed on the boat, and searched for a weekend country house. At the same time, Meryl Streep, Dan Rather, and Henry Kissinger also were looking for summer homes in the region. We saw some houses after they did and some before, in which case Jean might say, "Don't bother showing this to them; they won't like it either."

A house caught our eye in Dutchess County, ninety miles north of New York City. It was built in 1760 with an addition a half-century later. An inspection company said it was in excellent condition, so we bought the house and its fifty acres. When it came time to paint, however, we found rotten soffits and other serious problems that required scaffolding around the house for over a year. I tried to sue the inspection company, but no local lawyer would take the case.

We fixed the house, put in a large swimming pool and tennis court, and built our girls their own private house and road to it on a nearby hill. We enjoyed the compound, hosting a big dinner there for Viacom leaders each year.

Although my expertise is the business end of communications, I have often said "He who owns programming owns the world." New modes of mass communication—notably the Internet at this writing—will continue to be introduced. People are largely indifferent to technology, however. What they hunger for is content that satisfies—emotionally, intellectually, culturally, spiritually. Sometimes they protest vigorously if deprived of their programming.

Viacom received bomb threats after one such loss. It came after properties of Sonderling Broadcasting were merged into Viacom in March 1980. They included New York radio station WRVR-FM, the area's dominant jazz station for almost two decades. Six months later, on the morning of September 8, listeners enjoying cool jazz on WRVR suddenly heard hot country instead.

Protests were immediate. About two hundred jazz musicians and fans picketed our corporate offices.[4] (*The New York Times* assisted protesters by running a pre-rally story that announced the event and gave them Viacom's corporate address, 1211 Avenue of the Americas.)

"We are protesting the loss of this station because it is vital to the jazz community," said the head of the Consortium of Jazz Organizations and Artists.[5] There were other jazz stations in the market, however, so enthusiasts were not left totally adrift. Two weeks later about sixteen hundred people gathered in the Beacon Theater on Broadway to vent feelings. Meanwhile a twenty-four-hour guard was posted at the station following several bomb threats.

Passion could not compensate for lack of practical support. Friends of jazz, no matter how spirited, were too few in number and had waited too long to whip up enthusiasm for the station. Radio is an extremely competitive industry, and about half the stations in the country were losing money. There were over seventy radio stations in the New York market, and WRVR ranked about fourth from the bottom, attracting at most 1 percent of the audience. A responsible commercial station cannot accept such numbers forever.

Country-western, not my own cup of tea, had been surging across the country. Viacom owned eight radio stations, including the number one country station in Houston and a successful country station in Washington, D.C.

Advertising revenues at WRVR had been less than $1 million a year. We threw more than that into promotion for the new format, including ads on TV, buses, and subway posters. The station's call letters were changed to WKHK (pronounced Kick, with a silent W). The campaign was headlined "New York is Putting its Boots On." It featured a picture of the Statue of Liberty wearing cowboy boots. Who says we had no sense of humor?

The station's new format succeeded, but not enough. Because of the huge population base, WKHK had more listeners than any other country-western station in the nation. By 1984 it ranked twentieth among stations in the New York area, according to the Arbitron rating service. But it still drew only 2 percent of the audience.

The urban cowboy phenomenon had passed, and it was clear WKHK had topped out. In 1984 it morphed into a light music/adult contemporary station with the call letters WLTW. Finally we hit the mark. WLTW became one of the area's most popular stations.

With regulatory roadblocks reduced, cable systems saw huge growth in the late seventies and early eighties. In 1975 there were 3,500 systems serving 10 million subscribers. Just ten years later 6,600 systems served nearly 40 million subscribers. Not far behind cable's fast growth as a signal-delivery system would be its blossoming as a program producer.

Television's annual Emmy Awards demonstrated broadcasting's deep-seated animosity to cable. The awards had long symbolized excellence in television. Cable, however, was not allowed to compete. Accordingly, I led a committee that established the ACE (Award for Cable Excellence) Awards, for the cable industry to honor its best programming. The first ACE Awards were given in 1979 in a small theater in Hollywood.

As cable programming got better and better, the ACE Awards became a close match for the Emmys. Our annual ceremony migrated to a 1,500-seat theater, followed by a ball in a huge tent next door. Broadcasters finally relented in 1988 and allowed cable to compete for the

Emmys. However, we continued to hold our separate awards ceremony for another decade, the last one in 1997. Today HBO dominates the Emmy Awards, outnumbering all other contestants.

Even the networks swallowed their pride and deep-seated animosity and explored cable investments. Cable television potentially had a big financial advantage over broadcasting: two sources of income—payments by subscribers and, in common with broadcasting, advertising.

In 1981 alone, California-based Getty Oil linked up with ABC to offer a sports channel, which became ESPN; ABC and Westinghouse attempted a twenty-four-hour cable news service which failed; CBS and NBC talked joint cable ventures with CNN's Ted Turner; CBS sought a cable TV franchise in Alameda, California; and Public Broadcasting Service announced plans to enter the pay-TV field with a performing arts and cultural programming service.

Cable's long journey was welcomed by broadcasters much as Napoleon's escape from the island of Elba and march to Paris in 1815 was welcomed in the press.

When the scourge of Europe stepped again on French soil, Paris newspapers blared headlines to the effect "The Monster Has Landed." As old comrades sent to capture him instead joined his ranks, it was "Danger, the Dictator Nears." By the time Napoleon had reached the outskirts of Paris, citizens were told "Our Beloved Leader Has Returned."

If cable—until then the ugly stepsister—was not beloved, one thing seemed certain: It was here to stay. Ted Turner put cable television programming on the map, much as Bill Paley had done for broadcasting. In 1976 Turner, a little-known station owner in Atlanta, bounced the signal from his station off a satellite and down to a small group of cable systems across the country.

WTBS, featuring Atlanta Braves baseball games and old movies, became the first Superstation. Over the next decade Turner launched, in order, Cable News Network, CNN Headline News, and CNN International.

As weakened broadcast networks cut staff and reduced news bureaus, CNN established a worldwide presence. When war broke out in the Persian Gulf in 1991, viewers quickly learned they were not hostage to the sluggish news schedules of ABC, CBS, and NBC. With correspondents already in place in the Gulf, CNN was quickest on the draw and won a large new audience throughout Desert Storm. (CNN lost most new viewers back to the broadcast networks at the end of the war.)

Another cable shot across network bows was fired in the fall of 1986 by Rupert Murdoch, whom I had dealt with since he was a tenacious young media mogul in Australia. Murdoch bought Metromedia's stations in Los Angeles, New York, and Washington, D.C., and created Fox Broadcasting.

The network, then headed by my former employee and fellow sailor Jamie Kellner, is available to most Americans and was the first full-service network since my old employer DuMont to successfully challenge the Big Three broadcast networks. Other cable networks followed, including, a decade after Fox, MSNBC (Microsoft and NBC), the other major English-language cable news network in the U.S.

The reaction of ABC, CBS, and NBC? Mostly derision. A brash, mustached sailor from the South and a nervy upstart from down under surely were not and could not be in their league.

"They failed to view themselves as programmers and instead saw themselves as broadcasters," noted cable's John C. Malone. Malone, then head of the nation's largest cable company, Tele-Communications, Inc. (TCI), added that the networks made "a classic error. They fought a new technology rather than try to own it."[6]

Over-the-air broadcasters, aligned with a compliant FCC, had opposed most cable developments tooth and nail. Their intransigence helped dry up venture capital to cable in the late 1960s and early 1970s, and kept cable from expanding as quickly as it would have otherwise. But cable's foes were doomed to failure. Progress desired by people in a free society cannot be blocked forever. As the tangle of anti-cable rules and regulations were hacked through—usually in court—cable became unstoppable.

In 1981 CBS, at the urging of Bill Paley, announced it would develop its own cable network, offering news, public affairs, dance, music, and serious drama—Paley's own tastes.

In CBS high fashion, its cable network was launched with a black-tie party on the *Queen Mary* in Long Beach, California, during a cable association convention. That brought chuckles. In those days many cable operators came to the convention without a tie, let alone a tuxedo.

CBS Cable hosted a second lavish launch back home in the New York Public Library, where string quartets played on several floors. As Jean and I walked down the stairs, Paley, now a widower, was coming up with an attractive young woman, perhaps a quarter his age, on his arm.

Transponder space—for electronic sending and receiving—apparently was unavailable on a satellite that gave full U.S. coverage. CBS Cable inexplicably wound up on a satellite that did not do the job. The new channel could not reach many cable systems, lost a great deal of money, and folded. The cable debacle joined a long list of non-broadcast businesses that CBS attempted over the years, many of which failed or were sold, often at considerable loss.

There was a simple reason why the networks cast about for a new lease on life. Their old lease—their once impenetrable security blanket of audience share—was slipping away.

For decades ABC, CBS, and NBC had been the only game in town—only they could afford to distribute TV programs nationwide on AT&T's coaxial cable system. Satellites made land lines obsolete and leveled the playing field. Media analyst Ken Auletta, looking back in 1991, described the change: "While the amount of daily TV viewing has varied little in recent years, what is being viewed has changed dramatically. In the past decade an earthquake that would register a 10 on the Richter scale has struck the television industry."[7]

New viewing choices fragmented the audience. *TV Guide* in March 1977 listed the following channels in New York City, the nation's biggest market: ABC, CBS, NBC, PBS, and three independents—seven stations. A decade later, in March 1987, broadcast choices were the same. But TV Guide also listed nineteen national plus twelve local cable channels. Add the seven broadcast channels and a New Yorker now had thirty-eight viewing choices—some five times more than a decade earlier. By 2002 most Americans had access to over one hundred channels—rising to five hundred in 2005.

The networks still had just one channel each. The VCR, generally unavailable for home use in the late seventies, was in 90 percent of American homes by 1990. The audience followed. In 1976 the networks had nine of every ten viewers each evening; by 1984, fewer than eight in ten, and by 1993, six in ten.

Contributors to network losses included the ascent of Fox as a fourth network, and the rapid rise of independent stations. But it was cable that really ate the networks' lunch. In 1976 only 15 percent of homes had cable, compared with over 60 percent in 1990. In the latter year cable companies had combined revenues of $17.8 billion, nearly double the $9 billion of ABC, CBS, and NBC combined. By the end of the century nearly 70 percent of American consumers got their television, including broadcast channels, through cable. And a powerful new player—the Internet—was siphoning away consumers from all other media.

As their fortunes shrank in the mid-eighties, each of the Big Three networks changed hands. In 1986 Capital Cities Broadcasting bought ABC, which in turn was gobbled up by Walt Disney a decade later. Also in 1986, General Electric bought RCA Corporation, keeping NBC and selling off the rest of the company. By September of that year, Loew's Corporation Chairman Larry Tisch owned 25 percent of CBS stock. He and company founder Bill Paley, who owned another 9 percent, ousted CBS Chairman Tom Wyman. Tisch took over as president and CEO with the aging Paley as chairman.

Near the end of the century three smaller English-speaking broadcast networks joined the Big Three and Fox: UPN, The WB, and PAX. They found it very tough sledding, however. Early in 2006 UPN and The WB announced they would shut down in the fall and funnel their programming into another network to be called CW, aimed largely at young and minority viewers, and now called MYTV.

Cable reached a major milestone in the 2003-04 viewing season. For the first time, the aggregate household share of the top sixty-plus basic cable outlets beat that of the seven broadcast networks. Nielsen Media Research reported that basic cable had an average share of 49.8 (percent of households watching TV), compared with a 47.2 share for broadcasters.

The major networks continue to be players, of course, but at shares of profits and viewers far below what they once commanded.

HOLLYWOOD TRIPLE-CROSS

O n June 4, 1981, Viacom as an independent company was ten years old. We had come improbably far from when we spun away from our corporate mother. CBS Inc. was anything but a nurturing parent. Indeed it had placed almost every conceivable road-block in our path. But a decade later not only were we still standing, we had confounded the skeptics and were soaring.

"A company born as a direct result of government regulation and which, at birth, was given little chance of survival, never mind success," said *The Wall Street Journal*, "has blossomed into the Cinderella of the U.S. entertainment industry."[1] It added that "In just 10 years, Viacom has stunned industry observers and even its own executives by becoming a highly profitable, well-positioned, diversified entertainment company... And Viacom's future looks as rosy as its brief but golden past."

In 1971 CBS stockholders were given one share of Viacom for every seven shares of CBS stock they held. One unnamed CBS executive told the *Journal*: "Most of us stupidly thought it was worthless and sold the stock right away."

Bad idea. In January 1976 Viacom's stock cost $8 a share. Less than five years later, when the news article appeared, it had rocketed nearly 700 percent to $55.50 a share. We had started in 1971 with 775 programs to syndicate. We now offered 3,100 programs in 109 domestic markets and 23 foreign markets. Mike Dann, once CBS's pint-size vice president of programs, told the *Journal*, "When Ralph Baruch was with CBS, I used to think he was the world's biggest pain...He'd come into my office and say 'Why did you cancel this or that show? I just sold it to Germany, or somewhere!' Nobody else cared about licensing shows overseas...Only what was on prime time was considered important."

Viacom began with about two hundred employees, including some CBS was glad to be rid of. Now we had more than three thousand. Back then our cable systems served 100,000 homes; now they served 480,000, making us the country's eighth largest cable operator. We had purchased two broadcast television and eight radio stations whose ratings and profits had risen substantially.

In sum, we had a lot to be grateful for on our tenth anniversary. To thank clients and others who helped us grow Viacom, we celebrated at a disco, Les Mouches, certainly a new experience for me. There were so many to thank that we hosted three evenings to accommodate everyone. We gave guests small glass vases from Tiffany's, each engraved with the name of the recipient, the Viacom logo, and "1971-1981."

I was especially pleased with the way Viacom had grown. We had not just taken, we had given much back. I felt strongly that, as a company and an industry, we needed to learn from and not repeat the mistakes that knocked the shine off the networks. Three lessons stood out in my mind: Take the long view and never rest on past or present success. Produce quality programming. Do not get greedy.

In 1980, as the three major networks were about to take a decade-long nosedive, Gene Jankowski, a well-regarded president of the CBS Broadcast Group, told *The Christian Science Monitor* that "Cable will have to bring something new and needed if it is ever to succeed...I don't think there are a lot of good [new] ideas except for some programs already available on PBS."[2]

Interviewer: "Then the president of the leading commercial network is convinced that the commercial networks are already giving the American public the programs it wants?"

Jankowski: "Absolutely. If we weren't giving them what they want they wouldn't watch it the way they watch it. When you get 40 percent of the audience, you've got to be doing something right."

There were in fact numerous programming ideas waiting to be

developed. They would cater to a great variety of interests: movies, sports, children's shows, discovery, the arts, comedy, weather, history, home and garden, shopping, animals, martial arts, science fiction, and the list goes on. Over two hundred cable networks based on such interests would be launched over the next couple of decades. As choices offered by cable and other new players increased, network audiences shrunk. The networks realized too late that they were in the fight of their lives.

A nationwide poll in 1979 found that a majority of respondents— 53 percent, the highest ever recorded—said they watched less television than five years earlier and often disliked what they saw.[3] The poll, said its sponsor, *The Washington Post*, suggested "that at least part of the reported decline in viewing is tied to... many who feel the quality of TV entertainment has been deteriorating."

Respondents also complained about the growing number of commercials and such "clutter" as network and station promotions. Television's creative community voiced similar concerns. "How can you put on a meaningful drama," asked writer-director Rod Serling, "when, every fifteen minutes, proceedings are interrupted by twelve dancing rabbits with toilet paper?"

Tom Shales, the Post's usually perceptive television critic, said his paper found that people are "tired of TV's monotone." Said Shales:

> Yet for almost every new or enhanced technology and its promise of increased variety, there is a bastion of well-heeled opposition within the broadcast and entertainment industry establishments ... In opposing such developments as cable and pay cable television, industry spokesmen invariably plead that they will not be able to face such competition and that the new wonders pose economic threats to them. Never is it alleged that the public will suffer, because it only stands to benefit."[4]

Concern over the banal, formula-driven shows on television was not new. Robert M. Hutchins, former longtime president of the University of Chicago: "We can put it in proper perspective by supposing that Gutenberg's great invention had been directed at printing only comic books."

But network leaders wore blinders. A short-term CBS President, John D. Backe, speaking in Los Angeles in January 1979, said "Spokesmen for special interests can hurl all the criticisms they want, can call it chewing gum for the eyes, can damn us from dawn on Monday to dusk on Sunday, but an honest poll of our fellow residents on this planet will find that their vote is for television." The honest *Washington Post* poll a month later was not the ringing endorsement Backe promised.

We were encouraged by what viewers said they were willing to do about it. Even at a time of economic turmoil, with double-digit inflation, 36 percent of respondents—another record number—told the *Post* that "I'd rather pay a small amount yearly if I could, to have television without commercials." Those welcoming pay TV were willing to spend an average $82 a year on it—nearly the same as the $84 the average pay-cable home then spent.

At Viacom we knew our long-term success depended on superior programming. While not good at guessing which weekly series might catch on with the public, I understood quality in the performing arts. From the time I was a boy growing up in Europe, I was exposed to great music and great theater. We directed leaders of Showtime, our pay-cable arm, to produce excellent arts programming for subscribers.

Among other offerings were The Peking Opera, Jules Feiffer's "Hold Me," a two-act play based on a series of his cartoons; "The Gin Game," a Pulitzer Prize-winning play by D. L. Coburn, about two elderly residents in a rest home, starring Hume Cronyn and Jessica Tandy; Eugene O'Neil's "Huey," starring Jason Robards; the musical "Pearly," and "Look Back in Anger," John Osborn's play about bored, disillusioned British youth in the postwar period. One trick to offering such quality programs was to keep a rein on the production budget. "Look Back in Anger," for example, cost us $300,000, a small fraction of what the networks typically spent.

Our programming efforts did not go unnoticed. Culture critic Leticia Kent wrote in *The New Times* that "Although ABC-TV, CBS-TV and the Public Broadcasting Service have all announced ambitious plans to mount arts-oriented program services for cable and pay television, Showtime has got the jump on the competition."[5] She noted our monthly series Broadway on Showtime, videotaped versions of Broadway and Off Broadway shows.

To broaden audience appeal, Showtime offered hot-ticket musical programs. They included Peter Allen and the Rockettes, taped at New York's Radio City Music Hall; Marvin Hamlisch and Liza Minnelli, Carly Simon, and Johnny Mathis in a celebration of Hamlisch's music; a live concert by The Grateful Dead; and concerts with such performers as Tom Jones, Barry Manilow, Paul McCartney & Wings, and Rick Springfield. Showtime was chosen as the only national pay-television service to carry Frank Sinatra's "Concert for the Americas," originating in the Dominican Republic in August 1982.

We co-produced an award-winning feature film for Showtime called "Come Back to the Five & Dime, Jimmy Dean, Jimmy Dean," with the original stars of the Off Broadway play—Sandy Dennis, Cher, and Karen Black. We also produced a television movie called "Thursday's Child," with Gena Rowlands and Don Murray, and another called "The Return of the Man from UNCLE," with Robert Vaughn and David McCullem reprising their spy roles.

Viacom's program development arm in 1982 had three one-hour, prime-time series on the networks. *Nurse* was on CBS, starring Michael Learned who won an Emmy in the title role. *The Devlin Connection,* a detective adventure series with Rock Hudson, was on NBC; and *An American Dream,* six one-hour episodes, was on ABC.

Our development division in Hollywood produced *East of Eden*, an eight-hour Emmy- and Golden Globe-winning series on ABC, starring Jane Seymour and Timothy Bottoms, and *For Ladies Only*, on NBC, with Gregory Harrison and Lee Grant. We began a popular series of children's programs, and each week distributed *Louis Rukeyser's Business Journal.*

On the home front Jean and I were disappointed that she had to give up her work with Columbia University's primate research project. Jean had majored in early childhood psychology and was part of a pioneering effort to teach chimpanzees sign language. They wanted to have the chimps communicate not only feelings but in more explicit terms. As part of a team, Jean had spent several years at Columbia with Nim, the chimp who understood two thousand signs and used about six hundred signs on his own.

Jean took Nim on trips, with him sitting in the car's front passenger seat. When she stopped at traffic lights, other drivers did a double-take, seeing a chimp riding shotgun. Nim loved to share Jean's lunch. He would wait patiently until she finished half a container of coffee and perhaps half a tuna sandwich. Since Jean did not use sugar, Nim would pour sugar into the container, stir it with a, spoon, and drink it with his half of the sandwich.

Jean let Nim try painting, even though chimps seem to have a limited sense of color. He would hold the paintbrush between his teeth, nod up and down and sideways, making original compositions, favoring reds and blues. His paintings were quite decorative and Jean kept them in our apartment.

One day a friend came to visit and brought a guest, the son of the ex-chancellor of Austria, Kurt von Schuschnigg. Jean pulled out some of Nim's paintings without telling our guests who did them. They were quite impressed. Young Von Schuschnigg said the paintings showed a very creative person with a good sense of color. We learned he ran an art gallery, and didn't have the heart to disclose the artist!

A few months later Jean was injured by Nim. It happened after he climbed a pipe and would not come down. Jean had been warned never to get physical with Nim—chimpanzees are incredibly strong—but at that moment she forgot. Jean tried to pull Nim down and he bit through one of her fingernails, causing a severe infection. That ended her stint at Columbia.

The leader of the chimp research wrote a book, reviewed by *New York* magazine. For the article they modified a picture of Jean with Nim, air-brushing Jean out and substituting Dr. Herbert Terrace's photo. After the review and photo appeared in *New York* I wrote a letter which the magazine printed. I said that while neither Jean nor I was upset with the substitution, the chimp went bananas.

Showtime had nearly 3.5 million subscribers in 1982, second most in the nation but still far behind HBO with 11 million. We faced two challenges: reduce Showtime's considerable debt and assure a constant supply of motion pictures. To tackle the debt we decided to sell portions of

Showtime to third parties, while retaining management control. But sell to whom?

The Hollywood studios seemed natural partners, despite my aversion to the "fill-em" business. If two major studios bought equity in Showtime, that might kill two birds with one stone—reduce the debt and assure a steady supply of films. The most logical partners seemed to be Twentieth Century Fox and Columbia Pictures. Fox had recently been bought by Marvin Davis, a wealthy oilman out in Denver who could make an immediate business decision. Columbia was owned by Coca-Cola and led by Fay Vincent.

We also thought it wise to have a broadcast network in the new consortium. An alliance with ABC, CBS, or NBC could bring a great deal of creative ability to Showtime, and a network's news and public affairs programming would help differentiate us from HBO. Network productions typically were much less expensive than those in Hollywood, which also could help our bottom line. I met separately with leaders of ABC, CBS, and NBC, and asked them to contact us if interested.

An executive at RCA/NBC called a number of times to suggest we make a "deal." We told him our price was firm and there would be no other deal. ABC's senior management also called repeatedly and took some of our leaders to lunch. CBS, in complete contrast, did nothing, even though its CEO since 1980, Tom Wyman, told me one of his division presidents would contact us.

Terry Elkes and I flew out to Denver to see Fox's Marvin Davis. He sent two large gentlemen with two-way radios and guns under their jackets to meet us at the airport. Terry and I were amused by the pretension. A personal bodyguard was a first for me, the reason for which I could not fathom.

They whisked us downtown and up to Davis's suite of garish offices on his private elevator. Davis was well over six feet tall and weighed three hundred pounds. Most of the men around him also were unusually large. Think of a half-dozen professional wrestlers in business suits.

Davis, then in his late fifties, felt strongly that two studios might not be able to offer enough films on an exclusive basis to a pay channel, especially if other Hollywood studios boycotted us because of Fox's ownership of Showtime. We agreed that we could later bring in a third studio if needed, so long as Viacom managed the operation. We were in a nice position and agreed that, with Twentieth Century Fox now aboard, we would approach Columbia Pictures.

We then discussed the broadcast network to be chosen. CBS had expressed no interest, yet, sentiment aside, my gut feeling was that it would be a good partner. Davis, however, tried hard to dissuade me from CBS. He said he owed Leonard Goldenson of ABC a great deal and this was a good way to repay him. The debate went on as Davis's position hardened. Finally he asked CBS's reaction since my meeting with Tom Wyman. I had to admit we had heard nothing. With that Davis had won his argument in favor of ABC. As we were about to leave Davis put a beefy hand on my shoulder and said "We've got a deal, baby."

Back in New York we met with Victor Kaufman, senior vice president at Columbia Pictures. Columbia was definitely interested. Over the following days the deal became firmer, until Kaufman assured us we had a rock-solid agreement. We also lined up ABC as our network partner.

As a courtesy, I felt obligated, perhaps wrongly, to let my former associates at CBS know they were out of the running. I tried but initially failed to make an appointment with Tom Wyman, and then had to fly to Europe on business. While there my office called and said the only time Wyman could meet was the afternoon of the following day. Next morning I returned to New York on the Concorde, went straight from the airport to CBS's Black Rock, and was ushered onto the thirty-fifth floor.

I simply told Wyman that we were in the process of making a Showtime deal with a different network. He asked why and I noted CBS's total silence since our meeting. Meanwhile the other networks expressed great interest in owning a piece of Showtime. Given CBS's silence, I was not sure company managers below Wyman would support such a deal.

Wyman's face reddened. "Are you telling me I'm a poor CEO?" I assured him that was not my intent. I was simply giving my perception of where matters stood. Wyman looked even angrier. I was puzzled, since the fault lay entirely with CBS. Perhaps he had slipped up and failed to brief his colleagues properly and now was angry at himself or someone else.

To calm his temper I said "I hope in the future our two companies can do some other business together." "I don't think so!" he snapped. Wyman brusquely ushered me to the door as I added a parting shot: "I've been thrown out of better places." It was another blow to any new business relationship I had hoped to build with my former employer.

Over that weekend I received a cryptic call at home from Marvin Davis. "Why don't you call Bill Paley and chat with him?"

"Why?" I asked.

"Well, he's pretty lonely these days and it would be nice for you to talk to him."

"But Marvin, as you know, I just had a nasty meeting with Tom Wyman. Why would Paley want to talk with me after we told CBS's CEO we were taking our business elsewhere?"

"Look, Ralph, Paley's an old man. It won't hurt you to call him."

"Marvin, if Paley asks me why I'm calling, I have no answer, except to say you told me to." Davis's strange request remained a mystery for the moment.

The day before Thanksgiving I met with Columbia's CEO Fay Vincent. We were all set, he said. Columbia looked forward to a good relationship with all the Showtime partners. ABC would host a celebration luncheon in its board room the following Tuesday. Vincent would attend, along with Davis of Fox, Donald Keough, CEO of Coca-Cola, parent of Columbia Pictures; Leonard Goldenson and Fred Pierce of ABC, two of my Viacom colleagues, and me.

We were ecstatic. After months of negotiations we were about to reap the fruit of our labors. It was a joyous Thanksgiving weekend.

But the celebration was not to be. On Monday, the day before the scheduled luncheon, Fay Vincent's office at Columbia called ABC's Leonard Goldenson and said Vincent and Keough would not be at the luncheon. We were puzzled. Then I learned that a press conference was scheduled that afternoon, at which HBO, Columbia, and CBS would announce the formation of Tri-Star Pictures.

We had been duped into believing we had an agreement. Instead, all during the Thanksgiving weekend Columbia Pictures was huddled with CBS and HBO, creating Tri-Star. All of us at Viacom were crestfallen.

Inside sources told me Tom Wyman engineered the switch. Apparently he reacted to my courtesy visit. I had made a mistake in sharing our plans with him. A very serious mistake. As they say, no good deed goes unpunished. When I read the details it was obvious the Tri-Star deal strongly favored Columbia and to some extent HBO, but was not a good business deal for CBS. Both CBS and HBO later bowed out of Tri-Star after losing a lot of money. CBS sold its one-third interest in 1985, declaring an official loss of $20 million.

The mystery of the weekend phone call from Marvin Davis was solved months later. Paley's office called and asked me to have lunch with him in his private dining room at Black Rock. After small talk, Paley said "Ralph, I hear you're the fellow who doesn't want to talk to me." I did not understand. He explained that after I met with Davis in Denver, Davis called him. He told Paley that it was I who had insisted on making the Showtime deal with ABC and that he, Davis, had tried in vain to get me to do it with CBS. Paley then suggested to Davis that I call him and he would try to convince me to make the deal with CBS.

I was thunderstruck. Davis had completely reversed the truth. It was he who had insisted that we have ABC and not CBS in our group. Then, talking with his old pal Paley, Davis made me the heavy who wanted no part of CBS. Our true roles were exactly opposite. I tried to convince Paley what really happened. But it was clear he did not believe me, perhaps because he and Davis had something in common—great wealth—and because my story just didn't sound plausible.

I learned afresh that, with many of those who pull the strings in Hollywood, normal standards of integrity have no place. We had been duped by both of our would-be Hollywood partners—Columbia Pictures and Fox's Marvin ("We've got a deal, baby") Davis. What a business!

Not long after our dealings, Davis moved from Denver to Los Angeles, where he was the city's richest resident for the next two decades. He sold Twentieth Century Fox to Rupert Murdoch, shed more than one hundred pounds, and raised tens of millions of dollars for charities. Davis died in September 2004 at his home in Beverly Hills at the age of seventy-nine.

One day Jim Rosenfield, president of the CBS Television Network, tried to phone me, saying it was urgent. I checked quickly and confirmed that the CBS affiliation of Viacom's TV station in Albany was up for renewal. The coverage area of our Albany station, Channel Thirteen, was limited, so I suspected CBS had struck an agreement with our power-house competitor, Channel Six.

I called Rosenfield back. Before he could say much I told him that if he wanted to cancel our affiliation agreement, I understood, especially if he was able to make a deal with Channel Six.

Jim, to this day a good friend, answered "Yes, we were able to come to an agreement with Channel Six. But Ralph, you don't seem particularly upset about this." I told him I was indeed upset but that if I were in his shoes I would do exactly the same thing. Viacom's Channel Thirteen had to affiliate with NBC, at that time the lowest-rated network by far.

To celebrate the NBC affiliation, poor as it was, we organized a reception at the television station for local advertisers, ad agencies, and others, and asked NBC to supply talent to add glamour. The network had Jessica Savitch of NBC News and Greg Gumbel of NBC Sports attend, along with the network president. They also furnished the RCA jet heli-copter to take us to and from Albany. We flew up and the reception went extremely well.

On the way back, however, the chopper was hit by two simultane-ous thunderstorms which tossed us up and down and from side to side. I suggested to the pilot and co-pilot that they may want to put down some-where, but they were confident they could fly through the turbulence. Jes-sica Savitch swore we were going to crash and all die. Fortunately she was wrong. We made it back to the city and landed in good shape.

Months later Savitch, whose life had been sadly chaotic, drowned when a car she was a passenger in accidentally drove into a canal near Philadelphia.

Jean and I also attended an NBC affiliates event in California. We sat with Thornton Bradshaw, chairman of RCA, and his wife, and Grant Tinker and his companion. Tinker, handsome and soft-spoken, re-cently had been hired by NBC to lead its television network. He had been divorced from Mary Tyler Moore for some time. Tinker faced the chal-lenge of rescuing NBC from its third-place position.

During the dinner Mrs. Bradshaw leaned over to Jean and said, "You know, Jean, we *love* showbiz." Jean and I smiled at each other. Fortu-nately she did not comment.

Alan King emceed the evening. He quipped that NBC had just

hired Grant Tinker to rescue it. "Now the question is, is it going to be Tinker's toy or Grant's tomb?" asked King. The audience roared, but the Bradshaws and Tinker and his companion didn't crack a smile.

NBC proved to be not Grant's tomb but his triumph. Tinker toyed with the network's programming schedule and lifted it with his golden touch. In the 1985-86 season, NBC beat both ABC and CBS for the first time ever in prime time. NBC remained number one for years. CBS's affiliation with Channel Six did not help it in the Albany market. But NBC's success nationally helped lift our Channel Thirteen. We re-named it WNYT and it became the highest-rated television station in the Albany-Schenectady-Troy market.

My Mistake: Terry Elkes

D r. Art Ulene, a medical commentator who appeared regularly on NBC, and Jeffrey Reiss, a former head of Showtime, approached with an idea. Would Viacom be interested in starting a cable channel on health?

They claimed connections with medical associations and pharmaceutical companies which could help sponsor the program. They also believed the cable network would be watched in every physician waiting room in the country—an idea which turned out to be mistaken. At any rate, we felt this had a real chance to succeed, though new cable channels, like most new businesses, sustain losses at first.

In July 1982 we inaugurated the twenty-four-hour Cable Health Network (CHN). The on-air talent included an interesting new face, Dr. Ruth Westheimer, a petite woman born in Frankfurt, Germany, my birthplace. She would become widely known as Dr. Ruth, the sex therapist. Ruth was an instant hit and Jean and I befriended her. Given her bantam size, Ruth had difficulty finding clothes. Jean often advised her about them.

It proved difficult to attract advertisers. CHN suffered substantial losses and was unlikely to be profitable in the foreseeable future. Two years after launch we merged it with *Daytime,* a four-hour daily weekday program for women, operated by Hearst/ABC Video Services. Under the new name of *Lifetime* it was programmed especially for women, offering features on personal and family health, fitness, science and medicine, and better living at home. The formula worked. Viacom invested just over $50 million in the venture and in 1994 sold its one-third ownership to Hearst and Cap Cities/ABC for a healthy $300 million.

In March 1982 *Barron's* editorialized that "When it comes to meteoric rises, there's no business like show business at Viacom International Inc."[1] *Barron's* credited us with "an entrepreneurial flair that is beginning to pay off. [Viacom] is managing to make popular shows and a profit at the same time—no small feat in the entertainment world. What's more, as the cable boom continues, the need for programming mushrooms, suggesting that Viacom knows where the future lies."

We had a library of over six hundred films and such popular syndicated television series as *I Love Lucy*, *The Honeymooners*, *Gunsmoke*, *Hawaii Five-o*, and *The Mary Tyler Moore Show*. The grand champion was *All in the Family*. Distributed in one hundred twenty markets, it had brought Viacom commissions of a tidy $100 million in the previous four years.

Barron's called the outlook for our pay-cable service Showtime "especially rosy." Subscribers shot up 75 percent to 2.8 million in 1981 alone. That gave Showtime its first profitable year, a milestone we had deferred by plowing funds back in to expand Showtime to twenty-four hours. Then, in August 1982, we took on a $75 million debt mostly to buy back the other half of Showtime from Group W Cable.

After our ill-fated attempt to sell ownership in Showtime to two Hollywood studios and a broadcast network, we looked for new partners. Enter Steve Ross, one of the entertainment world's most successful deal-makers.

Many years earlier Ross had married into a New York family that owned a string of funeral parlors. In off hours he used the limousines to start a car rental business. In 1967 Steve bought the Ashley Famous talent agency. Two years later he acquired the struggling Warner Bros studio and record business.

Warner Communications was the umbrella over his empire. In January 1983 we sought to enlist Ross and Warner Communications in a partnership to cut Showtime's debt and accelerate its growth. We believed Warner's own pay-cable service, The Movie Channel, was not well run and that we could soon increase its value. TMC ranked behind HBO and Showtime in subscribers. If we combined Showtime and TMC we would still be smaller than HBO, but in a better position to compete.

Steve and I hit it off. In a world of cutthroats, he stood out as a gentleman. Many deal-makers simply do not care what happens to the people affected by their grown-up Monopoly games. But Steve genuinely valued his people. We set up a joint-venture company called Showtime/ The Movie Channel. A couple of minor partners were involved as well. We retained our separate identities and TMC and Showtime each continued to offer twenty-four-hour programming. We were the managing partner, with 50 percent ownership.

Time's HBO was still king of the hill, but the gap had narrowed considerably. HBO had 13.5 million subscribers. Our new company had nearly 8 million—4.6 million contributed by Showtime, 2.6 million from TMC, and almost 800,000 from a small company we bought called Spotlight. We were now the second-largest pay cable service by far. The third, called Cinemax, had 2.8 million subscribers and also was owned by Time Inc.

We cut a $500 million exclusivity deal with Paramount for its movies over the next five years. The arrangement started to pay off quickly. Time's Cinemax had planned to feature Paramount's smash hit "Flashdance." Instead, On February 12, 1984, "Flashdance" aired first on The Movie Channel, followed the next night on Showtime.

In the early eighties the broadcast networks claimed that with cable at last healthy and ascending, there was enough competition to scrap the FCC's financial interest and syndication (fin-syn) rules. The rules had checked the networks' coercive power since 1971. Indeed, in a huge stretch, the networks said their survival depended on lifting the regulations. In truth, the networks were in fat city. During the eight years ending in 1984, ABC, CBS, and NBC had double-digit revenue growth every year, totaling more than 300 percent for the period.

Nonetheless the three networks began to lobby Washington, especially the Federal Communications Commission, to reverse fin-syn. If they succeeded, once again the networks could squeeze producers and demand that they be given a share of the financial success of programs. This was the start of a rough battle. Many of those who had promulgated the rules more than a decade ago were no longer around to explain their reasoning. Faces had changed at the FCC as well, and the agency seemed inclined to grant many of the networks' wishes.

As the leader of one of the major companies created as a result of the FCC rules, I felt a duty to defend fin-syn and confront the networks. This presented a serious problem for Viacom, since ABC, CBS, and NBC were also our clients. Our production staff in Hollywood worried that if we opposed changes in fin-syn, the networks might retaliate by refusing to buy Viacom programs. But our larger economic interests were paramount.

We rallied other syndication companies to our cause. I also turned to a relatively new Viacom director, Nancy Reynolds. She was once President Reagan's press secretary when he was governor of California, and had just moved to Washington to be half of a leading public relations firm, [Ann] Wexler & Reynolds. President Reagan, new to Washington, relied on a small group of advisers. One was his closest friend in Congress, Senator Paul Laxalt, a Nevada Republican. Nancy offered to have a dinner at her home, where Jean and I could meet Laxalt and Reagan administration officials.

We flew to Washington. Nancy had a lovely house with a large backyard where she had installed an authentic pioneer covered wagon. The guest list was impressive: Senator Laxalt, Jack Valenti, head of the motion picture association, and other entertainment and communication leaders. Nancy seated us at Laxalt's table. He agreed to meet with me within a few weeks so I could explain the problems we faced with the networks.

Friends on Reagan's staff arranged for Nancy Reynolds "by chance" to bump into the President himself. She used the occasion to ask him not to give in to network pressure to reverse fin-syn. My meeting in Laxalt's office also was productive. No doubt others, including Jack Valenti of the Motion Picture Association and Lew Wasserman, venerable chairman of MCA, also had a hand in the decision. At any rate we were successful and the fin-syn rules were retained.

I had now completed over thirty years in television and was ready to shift my load a bit. The last dozen years at Viacom were especially challenging, but exhilarating. Like a proud father, I had seen Viacom through its difficult birth, nurtured it through the early years, and now watched as it grew strong as an adolescent with a boundless future.

Viacom's fast growth required a lot of travel to visit our various businesses. I also volunteered service to various causes and lobbied in Washington. I was ready to let others make more of the routine daily decisions and share the traveling, freeing me to focus more on strategic issues at Viacom.

We had developed a fabulous cadre of managers and executives who were destined to become industry leaders. Every division at Viacom had capable young executives eager to move up. If they saw no room at the top they would begin to look elsewhere. This could hurt Viacom and I was determined not to let it happen. I started laying the groundwork for change in 1981. I told our directors, in one-on-one meetings, that I would remain Viacom's very active chairman, guiding the company in critical areas. I asked them to consider who should replace me as CEO, but they did little.

A failed effort at about that time was a sharp reminder of the high costs of bad personnel decisions. It involved the man I had chosen to replace Larry Hilford, former head of Viacom Enterprises, after Larry left us for another job. We had hired an executive headhunter to find us a replacement. The headhunter phoned one day and told me he had the perfect candidate. In fact the candidate was so good, he said, that the man had other offers, and we almost certainly would lose him if I didn't act immediately.

Foolishly I swallowed the bait, met with the man that weekend, and hired him. He did a passable job over several years, with other executives making up for what he lacked in initiative and creativity.

One glaring blunder, however, I could not overlook. Much as I personally disliked Hollywood, I could not ignore the fact that public interest in what goes on out there is considerable. I asked the head of Enterprises to create a program based on Hollywood stars and happenings. Months later I asked him how the project was coming. "Working on it," he quipped.

The idea continued to languish. Then, on September 14, 1981, it essentially died. On that day, *Entertainment Tonight* premiered in syndication. Several other shows have copied it over the years, none as successfully. A quarter-century later, *ET* remains television's most popular entertainment news program. Not long after the *ET* debacle, I invited the head of Enterprises for a walk along a California beach. During the walk I told him I was letting him go.

Increasingly, Viacom's top future leadership was on my mind. When should I step back, and how far?

I admired the grace with which Walter Cronkite, CBS's peerless anchor and a personal friend, had recently stepped aside. He concluded his final broadcast this way: "For almost two decades we have been meeting like this in the evening and I'll miss that .... This is but a transition, a passing of the time. Old anchormen, you see, don't fade away. They just keep coming back for more. And that's the way it is, Friday, March 6, 1981. I'll be away on assignment and Dan Rather will be sitting in for the next few years. Good night."

Our situations were different—by no means was I leaving—but whatever I did, I wanted to do it with class. At Viacom there was no Dan Rather ready to step in and assume all my roles. Running the company day to day was one thing. Having the respect and relationships with industry heavyweights to fashion deals favorable to Viacom was quite another.

One person I had seen as a possible successor was the whole package: Fred Pierce. Fred joined ABC in 1956 and moved up to president of ABC Television in 1974. He was a highly competent leader and years later I pondered how to woo him to our company. We met and chatted about Viacom. Fred seemed quite interested and asked for time to think about it. A couple of weeks later he called and said he could not accept what he agreed was a marvelous opportunity. His future would be with ABC, where he became president and CEO of the entire company in 1983.

Inside Viacom there was only one obvious candidate: Terrence Elkes. He was intelligent and knowledgeable about financial matters, and we had been a good team.

Yet he lacked wider experience in communications, was basically shy, and still had an offensive habit of talking down to our directors and others he considered not his equal. I had hired Terry over the objections of some board members, and had steadily advanced him in the teeth of opposition.

I also considered Terry a personal friend. Our offices were next to each other, and routinely throughout the day one of us would go into the other's, throw a leg over the arm of a couch, and chat. We solved Viacom's challenges—and devised answers to a lot of public problems as well, if only local and world leaders had been wise enough to consult us!

At a convention in Chicago, Terry broke his glasses and cut an eye lid. I administered first aid, and summoned the hotel doctor to patch him up. On another occasion Terry yelled for help from the men's room we shared. He was bleeding from hemorrhoids. I ran to a drugstore and got him bandages. Jean and I took Terry and his wife Ruth to industry functions.

I contemplated CBS's two longtime leaders, Chairman Bill Paley and President Frank Stanton. They are widely regarded as the best two-person leadership team television has seen, and both were vital to CBS's success. They had different strengths—Paley an entrepreneur and showman and Stanton a gifted stylist, organizer, and voice of broadcasting in corridors of power. The chemistry worked and kept CBS near the top for much of their quarter-century together. I believed Terry and I could continue to do the same for Viacom.

Early in 1983 I began to discuss the future with Terry. He said he had an offer from a major motion picture company on the West Coast and used that as leverage to negotiate.

We agreed that I would retain the top position as chairman and Terry would be CEO and president. He especially wanted me to handle government regulations, deal directly with other communications companies, and lead out in other critical areas. Years back I had created Viacom's Office of the Chief Executive, to be occupied by its top two people. Terry and I agreed we would both continue to occupy the office.

When we sat down to discuss details I was taken aback by Terry's demands. He handed me a three-page document. It included a clause that, at the expiration of his four-year contract, a new contract was to be negotiated or we had to go to arbitration. I had no objection to making Terry wealthy—which this proposal would do—if our major goals were achieved. We came to an agreement which I shared with Viacom's directors. As usual they had mixed feelings about Terry. In September 1983 we announced the change.

In 1977 I had chaired the National Cable Television Association's pay-cable committee that won a U.S. court decision deregulating cable programming. That same year the NCTA asked me to organize and lead an effort to establish cable's basic rights and responsibilities in U.S. law. I agreed, never dreaming how arduous it would be. Now, in 1984, I was in Washington still fighting for a comprehensive cable deregulation law.

The Communications Act of 1934 had not been altered in the half-century since. It was written before the advent of cable television, so obviously did not address challenges facing cable. In the absence of federal law, local jurisdictions had passed a hodgepodge of rules to regulate cable and keep its fees in check. Both the cable industry and local governments needed federal guidelines to establish their separate rights.

We got solid input from experts in key areas of cable—legal, engineering, programming, research. Karen Posner of the House Subcommittee on Communications was assigned by its chair, Congressman Lionel Van Deerlin, D-California, to lead our support staff. Karen proved bright, capable, and hard-working.

It was a tricky proposition. Congress was divided over the issue, as were cities and towns. Worst of all, the cable industry itself was deeply divided. With most of the industry at last doing well, major cable factions feared we would upset the apple cart. In an NCTA meeting as late as September, only three of thirty cable leaders backed the current version of the bill.

Other formidable opponents included the broadcast networks, telephone companies, and public interest groups including Ralph Nader's Congress Watch.

I spent a great deal of time in Washington lobbying for a bill—walking the halls of Congress, cajoling cable leaders, bargaining with powerful groups including the National League of Cities and U.S. Conference of Mayors.

At least four versions of a cable bill had been introduced in the 98th Congress. The one still alive in the House was H.R. 4103, sponsored by Congressman Tim Wirth, D-Colorado.

The companion bill in the Senate was S. 66, introduced by Senator Barry Goldwater, the Arizona Republican. Goldwater accused the cities of intransigence. On the House side, Congressman John Dingell, D-Michigan, who chaired the Energy and Commerce Committee, was sharply critical of cable. In a letter to the NCTA, Dingle blasted the industry for "greed and arrogance" and warned that "The ultimate victim will be the cable industry itself." That would prove prophetic.

Despite opposition by powerful interests, pieces began to fall into place. After years of bickering, close observers felt that at this moment in 1984 the political ducks were lined up for cable about as well as they ever would be. But it was now late September and members of Congress were hell-bent to get home and campaign for the November elections. Congress was scheduled to adjourn October 4. On Monday, October 1, H.R. 4103 passed the House on a unanimous voice vote. Goldwater's bill, S. 66, was poised for Senate passage.

But with just three days left in the session, conservative Republican senators blocked the bill because it included an equal-employment provision. As maddeningly close as we had come, it appeared there would be no cigar.

However, on the eve of its scheduled adjournment, Congress decided to stay in session one more week. We still had a chance. But more time invited more mischief. Some members of Congress, consumer advocate Ralph Nader, and others weighed in with additional objections to the legislation. As complaints were pitched, one by one, we helped our Senate supporters knock them out of the ballpark.

On Thursday, October 11, our bill still languished. Congress was certain to adjourn that evening or the next day. If members left without passage, it was dead.

At about two o'clock that afternoon Congressman Wirth and Senator Howard Metzenbaum, a liberal Democrat from Ohio, pressured the NCTA to accept another change. The cable industry refused. Fortunately, Metzenbaum backed off. The Senate, on a voice vote, passed an amended version of the House bill. The House immediately voted to approve the amended bill. And the White House signaled that President Reagan would sign it into law.

We did it! Along with most of our industry, I was ecstatic. Seven years of hard labor had ended in victory. The Cable Communications Policy Act of 1984 was about to become U.S. law. The landmark legislation for the first time established standards for local regulation of cable television. Cities could regulate cable rates for basic service only—transmission of signals from local broadcast stations—for the next two years. During that period, cable companies could raise rates up to 5 percent a year. After that rates would no longer be regulated.

I appreciated a resolution passed by the NCTA proposing that its board of directors "present a suitable memento to Ralph Baruch, Chairman of the NCTA Public Policy Planning Committee, 1977-1984, in recognition of his untiring efforts to obtain legislation establishing a national policy for the cable industry and expressing the heartfelt thanks of the officers and board of directors of the National Cable Television Association."

A few weeks later they gave me a reproduction of the first and last pages of the Cable Act, signed by the Senate president pro tempore—senior Republican—Strom Thurmond of South Carolina, and by President Reagan.

It would be pleasant to report that the cable industry has lived up to the trust implicit in the Cable Act, that it has not followed the networks' example of greed which led Washington to clip their wings over three decades ago. Regrettably, however, as many millions of cable subscribers know, history tells a different tale.

A string of congressional hearings documented unconscionable cable rate increases. By May 1990, for example, basic cable rates in Jefferson City, Missouri had risen 186 percent since deregulation took effect in 1986.[2] In Beverly Hills, California, rates rose 90 percent in one twenty-month period.[3] Paragon Cable in St Petersburg, Florida raised rates three times between May 1989 and December 1990.[4] A national survey released early in 1992 showed that, over one year, rates had risen three times faster than the cost of living.[5]

When the Cable Act became law in 1984, I knew first-hand that there was strong concern across grassroots America. Consumers and communities worried that cable firms would sharply increase rates as soon as local government controls were removed.

I tried hard to warn my colleagues that cable rates should only change gradually, and be reasonable, affordable, and based on the services provided. Otherwise, after coming so far, we risked re-regulation. In those heady days for cable, some of my cable colleagues thought I was a crank.

Congress hoped the Cable Act would encourage other carriers, including telephone companies, to compete against existing cable firms, driving down rates. That strategy was a bust, though it did foreshadow a future that started to unveil early in the new century. The overwhelming number of communities continued to be served by a single company.

As their consumer-constituents screamed at rocketing cable rates, members of Congress railed against our industry. Broadcasters predictably seized this issue cable had handed them, telling Congress the cable television industry had become a multibillion-dollar monopoly and—echoing an old theme—that cable should be re-regulated to ensure the survival of over-the-air TV.

The issue became a hot potato in the 1992 presidential election. That September, Congress overwhelmingly passed a bill to re-regulate cable, despite the threat of a veto from President George H. W. Bush, who argued that it was overkill. The bill gave local governments the discretion to roll back cable charges. Premium channels such as HBO and Viacom's Showtime were exempt.

Depth of feeling on the issue could be measured by this: Bush previously had successfully vetoed thirty-five bills in a row. Cable cost him that perfect record.

It takes a two-thirds vote in each house of Congress to override a veto. In a stinging election-season setback, the Senate voted 74-25 to override the President, and the House followed, 308 to 114. Bush, already trailing in election polls, played into the hands of populist Democrat Bill Clinton. The President appeared to back big business and oppose consumers at exactly the wrong moment politically. "Good for the House! Good for the Senate!" crowed Clinton. "This was a bill that was in the interest of the ordinary, average American."

Four years after the 1992 law failed to curb cable rates, Washington again deregulated the industry. The hope once more was that deregulation would stimulate competition; once more it did not happen. The dilemma of cable rates remains unsolved. Senator John McCain, R-Arizona, who chaired the Senate Commerce Committee, noted in 1999 that "We may now be facing the worst of all worlds, which is an unregulated monopoly."[6]

Basic cable rates in the six years from 1998 to 2004 rose at an annual 7. 5 percent—more than three times the 2.1 percent rate of inflation. Only effective competition—lacking in more than 90 percent of the nation's communities—slowed increases. Cable companies facing such competition in 2003 raised rates by an average of 3.6 percent, compared with 5.6 percent where there was a local monopoly.[7] Rates continue to rise, with Comcast, the nation's largest cable provider, saying it would increase rates an average of 6 percent in 2006.

At this writing, colossal competition to cable and broadcasting is in sight in almost every home in the nation. It is the giant telephone companies, which have suffered for years from the surging popularity of cellular phones and other wireless devices. Verizon, AT&T and others are poised to leap into television, making a splash that likely will swamp some lesser boats. What impact this will have on monthly television rates remains to be seen.

In 1988 I spoke at the annual Walter Kaitz Foundation dinner in New York, telling guests that "the cable industry needs to pay more attention to Main Street than to Wall Street, because every cable subscriber is a customer, while Wall Street not only can't be trusted, but only looks at the bottom line."

These additional observations sparked a standing ovation: "Don't consider broadcasters the enemy. We need to work together because they are the foundation of our business. Instead, watch out for the telephone companies. They are the real enemy. They are wired into nearly every home in the country, and eventually will compete with the cable industry. They have an enormous army of lobbyists, are well financed, and are 'wired' into the FCC and other regulators like no other industry."

That threat is now becoming a reality.

23

JACKIE GLEASON AND
BILL COSBY

Viacom's new leadership formula with Terry Elkes as president and CEO and me as chairman worked well. Shorn of a lot of travel and day-to-day management details, I had more time to concentrate on the most critical concerns and opportunities facing Viacom. Over the next three years we scored some of our biggest triumphs, solidifying Viacom's foundation for decades to come.

Viacom's next coup was with The Great One, Jackie Gleason. Our paths had crossed through the years. We were at the DuMont Television Network at the same time, and later at CBS together. Gleason hosted and performed on DuMont's variety show, *Cavalcade of Stars.* It was there that Gleason previewed his greatest characters—Reginald Van Gleason, Poor Soul, Joe the Bartender. The blockbuster of them all, *The Honeymooners,* also debuted on DuMont.

Gleason started on *Cavalcade* in 1950 at $750 a week. He had unusual star power. As ratings rose, so did Gleason's salary. DuMont paid him $1,600 by 1952 when his contract was up for renewal. As often before, however, a larger network snatched yet another DuMont star. CBS offered Gleason a weekly salary of $8,000—five times higher than DuMont. That was just for starters. He would own and have total creative control of the weekly hour-long variety show, hiring the cast members, writers, dancers, and orchestra.

The production cost to CBS: at least $50,000 a week. What really gave CBS heartburn was that Gleason approached the network shortly before his DuMont contract was set to expire. If CBS wanted him, they would have to sign a contract immediately for thirteen weeks guaranteed, even before trying to sell the show to a sponsor. CBS swallowed hard and signed. Weeks before the show first aired on CBS in September 1952, three advertisers each bought twenty-minute segments. CBS's gamble paid off. Gleason became the most watched man on TV in the 1950s.

Jackie Gleason would be a Saturday night fixture on CBS for the next twenty years. He created and starred in *The Honeymooners* as bus driver Ralph Kramden. Art Carney was his zany Brooklyn neighbor Ed Norton, a sewer-system worker. They were the only two major characters to last the entire two decades.

Each had four different wives over that time, though the first two—Audrey Meadows as Alice, married to Kramden, and Joyce Randolph as Trixie, to Norton—are probably best remembered. *The Honeymooners* at first was a weekly segment in CBS's *The Jackie Gleason Show*, then got its own half hour starting in the fall of 1955. It was the inspiration for a somewhat similar show in later years, *All in the Family*, with Carroll O'Connor.

The Honeymooners was always done before a live audience. Gleason scoffed at memorizing his lines and was a master improviser. If Alice often looked surprised by what Ralph said, it was probably because she, along with the audience, was hearing it for the first time.

Gleason's trademark line could have been recited by most grown-ups in the fifties and sixties: "One of these days, Alice, one of these days—pow! Right in the kisser!" It evoked a more innocent time, when few took his threat seriously. Today the same line probably would not pass censors. His other threat to simply send her to the moon seemed more benign.

Gleason originally contracted with CBS to do seventy-eight half-hour episodes of *The Honeymooners*, but after thirty-nine—just one year's worth—he decided that was enough.

Gleason himself canceled the show, explaining in later years that he didn't think the writing could continue at the same level. Those episodes, considered classic television situation comedy, were shown over and over through the years—ninety times on one New York station alone by the mid-eighties.

But there were only thirty-nine episodes—that is, until 1985 when Gleason went into his vault and came out with enough fresh material for over fifty more. Apparently he had been saving the personal copies for a rainy day. They were nearly three decades old, from the 1952-1955 *Honeymooners* segments of CBS's *Jackie Gleason Show*. Gleason's interest in resurrecting them apparently stemmed from a showing of three old *Honeymooners* episodes at the Museum of Broadcasting in Manhattan in 1984. Lines stretched around the block waiting to get in. "They were being received so well, I figured there must be a market for these somewhere," Gleason explained.[1]

At Viacom we got wind that the episodes existed and began talking with Gleason's attorney. We struck a deal to air fifty-two half-hour episodes on Showtime from September 1985 through August 1986, then offer the programs to broadcasters in syndication. Gleason himself would introduce them.

On February 6, 1985, we held a news conference with Gleason, resplendent with a red carnation in his lapel, to announce the discovery and the deal. The event, in a small third-floor room at Viacom, turned into a mob scene, with about a hundred reporters trying to outshout each other.

Fans of *The Honeymooners* learned such things as these in the new segments: Ralph and Alice, childless in the other series of episodes, once adopted a baby girl. Ed Norton's middle name, which he tried to hide, was "Lillywhite." He survived as an "engineer of subterranean sanitation" in part because he had lost his sense of smell.

Unfortunately Jackie did not live to see a full year of the new segments in syndication. He died of cancer on June 24, 1987, at his home in Fort Lauderdale at seventy-one.

Big as the Gleason deal was, in the wings for Viacom was an even bigger blockbuster involving America's favorite father, Bill Cosby.

In the spring of 1984, Marcy Carsey and Tom Werner, two former ABC programming leaders, submitted an idea to the networks for a program called *The Cosby Show*. Situation comedies had not done well recently, and only NBC showed serious interest. Carsey and Werner took second mortgages on their homes, but still needed a company to underwrite production costs. We took a gamble and furnished the funds in exchange for syndication rights.

Cosby is a marvel. Whether pitching pudding in commercials, doing stand-up for a benefit, or making a best-selling comedy album, he has a wry, gentle humor that puts audiences in the aisles without resorting to the crude jokes that prop up so many lesser talents. Former NBC news anchor John Chancellor called Cosby the nation's most effective communicator.[2] In 1984 it had been thirteen years since he had appeared on another NBC series, *The Bill Cosby Show*, and eight years since *Cos,* an ABC variety show.

Cosby was ready to return to the airwaves, in part because of disenchantment over current TV fare. "When it comes to situation comedies, a lot of the jokes have to do with the breasts or the behinds, or situations involving people's forgetfulness," Cosby told an interviewer, "things that don't cause anyone to say, 'That was a wonderful, warm story'...And if there's a black in the show, he will be either the detective sergeant or the pimp...nothing in-between."

In contrast, *The Cosby Show* offered what Coretta Scott King called "the most positive portrayal of black family life that has ever been broadcast."

Yet Cosby transcends racial lines and stereotypes. In 1965 he became the first African-American to star in a weekly TV drama series. *I Spy,* with co-star Robert Culp, mixed danger and humor and the two stars had engaging conversations—often unscripted, driving editors nuts—rather than just one-liners.

In the new show Bill played Cliff Huxtable, an obstetrician whose office was beneath the family's brownstone in Brooklyn, New York. He and his lawyer-wife, played by Phylicia Ayers-Allen, had three daughters and a son. Cosby was deeply involved in creating each episode. He is a genuine student of parenting. In real life he has five children, and returned to college at the University of Massachusetts, where he earned a doctorate in education in 1976.

The Cosby Show debuted on NBC on September 10, 1984, to universal praise. Compared with what else was on the tube, wrote the *Washington Post's* Tom Shales, "...*The Cosby Show* is the best, funniest and most humane new show of the season."[3] Sally Bedell Smith of *The New York Times* said the show "is this season's prime-time phenomenon" which "attempts to echo reality. It is filled with small moments that prompt chuckles of recognition in the viewer."[4]

The accolades, along with the ratings, only went up from there. *Cosby* was first in its time slot the first evening and stayed there for more than two years straight, even in NBC summer reruns. It became by far the most popular show on television, and got stronger the longer it was on. In the 1984-85 season, 38 percent of all households watching television in its time slot were tuned to *Cosby*. That rose to 49 percent the next season, and 56 percent the next.

We decided the selling of the show for syndication would be as extraordinary as the show itself. In October 16, 1986, we unveiled our sales plan at a reception in New York for four hundred advertising executives. *Cosby* did its part: On the night of the reception, the show led NBC to its highest rating for a regular evening of television in more than ten years.

Ratings measure the percentage of all possible households whose TV sets are turned on and tuned in to a particular program. (A share is the percentage of all actual sets that are on and tuned to a given program.) Advertising rates are based on ratings—on how many potential product buyers are actually watching. A single ratings point means many millions of dollars to a network.

Highly rated shows usually boost the ratings of other shows airing before or after them on the same network. On October 16, 1986, *The Cosby Show* had a 37 rating. Over that entire evening, NBC's rating was 27, swamping CBS with 14, and ABC with 10.

In essence, *Cosby* was going to be auctioned off for syndication, to start airing in 1988 like a first-run show, even though by then it would have been on NBC for more than four years. We offered it not for a per-episode fee, like other syndicated shows, but for a weekly reserve cash price, with a minimum bid to be set in each market. Winning stations could only run one episode of *Cosby* once each day for 182 weeks—three-and-a-half years.

It was bold, brave, brash. Did stations buy it? Did they ever. We hired Price Waterhouse to handle the bidding process, and began the road show in the greater New York area. Our minimum asking price there was $182,000 an episode. Sealed bids were collected by Price Waterhouse, and the highest bid was that of WOR-TV, located in Secaucus, New Jersey, at $240,000—nearly $60,000 above our minimum. It took our breath away. It was, in fact, nearly two and a half times more than the previous record in the area, held by *Cheers* at $100,000 an episode. *Cosby* sold in Los Angeles for about $300,000 an episode and in Chicago for $225,000.

Not everyone cheered our success. *TV Guide* ran a story under this headline: "The Cosby Push Wasn't Going for Laughs: 'We Gotta Confuse 'Em and Scare 'Em.'" The story said we browbeat television stations into taking *Cosby* by warning that those who did not would be at the mercy of competitors, whose programs surrounding *Cosby* likewise would rise in the ratings.

TV Guide called our marketing the "most shamelessly arrogant exercise in hardball salesmanship the television industry had ever seen."[5]

Arrogant? Perhaps. But, without question, effective. By the time *The Cosby Show* went into syndication in 1988, 187 stations had bought it, mostly at unprecedented prices. Overall sales totaled more than $600 million. Viacom kept a third of that, about $200 million, with the rest split between Cosby and Carsey-Werner.

In 1985 our stock traded at a record-high 66 1/4, even after we issued 5.2 million additional shares of common stock. To continue such gains, we sought a close relationship with a motion picture company to feed our distribution organization. We linked arms with Ted Turner to look at possible joint purchase of MGM. Our experts went to the West Coast to examine the studio and consider every aspect of the prospective purchase.

To acquire the MGM library and continue to produce motion pictures, Turner and Viacom each needed to put on the table $350 million. Turner decided he did not have the cash. I suggested Viacom buy the library alone, but the decision was Terry Elkes' to make as CEO, and he disagreed, so the entire deal fell through.

Later, Turner returned and acquired the MGM library, which was the foundation of many of his new cable network ventures, including TNT, Turner Classic Movies, and others. Some analysts maintained that he overpaid for the library. I disagreed. Motion pictures are a long-time resource that generates substantial funds. Whoever owns such programming owns the future.

We continued to seek additional content. We also looked for the rare opportunity to buy a good television station. Such a station became available that year, indirectly because of Ted Turner's audacious attempt to buy CBS. He offered $5.4 billion in stock and debt securities, but failed to purchase the company.

CBS had become vulnerable under CEO Tom Wyman, who arrived there five years earlier with no trace of broadcast experience. He was the catalyst who killed Viacom's deal to merge Showtime with two Hollywood studios and a broadcast network.

To fend off Turner, Wyman initiated a billion-dollar stock buyback plan at a substantially higher price than CBS traded for on the New York Stock Exchange. Larry Tisch, head of Loews Corporation, seized the opportunity to purchase large amounts of stock. CBS, anxious to reduce its huge debt, was then forced to sell various non-broadcast assets. CBS sold its toy business, some publishing interests, and its ill-fated venture in Tri-Star—the movie-production company it owned with Columbia Pictures and HBO.

CBS also owned five television stations. We at Viacom saw a golden opportunity to perhaps buy one—KMOX in St. Louis. I met with Gene Jankowski, head of the CBS Broadcast Group, who was receptive. Our experts negotiated. Late in the year, we came to a firm agreement, subject to approval of the transfer by the FCC, usually a formality.

Jankowski, a cheerful sort, had a reputation for seeing a silver lining in the darkest clouds. Still I was amazed at an answer he gave when speaking at a monthly industry luncheon at the Waldorf-Astoria. Asked about Tisch's plans for CBS, Gene said they included buying more television stations.

At that same moment our people were in a room at Black Rock with their CBS counterparts to sign the agreement for Viacom to acquire KMOX—later renamed KMOV. Resentment against CBS among station personnel was such that they sent the station manager their business cards with the CBS eye cut out.

We paid a little over $120 million for KMOX—a super buy. St. Louis was the country's eighteenth largest TV market and now Viacom's largest. Our other television stations were WVIT in New Britain/Hartford/New Haven, Connecticut; WNYT, Albany, New York; WHEC, Rochester, New York; and KSLA, Shreveport, Louisiana.

KMOX was a worthy addition to Viacom's other television stations, all of which shined. Our Albany station became the number one outlet in its market, while those in Hartford, Connecticut; Rochester, New York, and Shreveport, Louisiana, achieved record revenues and earnings. Viacom radio also excelled, including WLTW in New York which became the number one station in the key 25-54 age group.

After Ted Turner failed in a frontal assault on CBS, Tisch succeeded methodically to take over the company. He bought large chunks of stock, all the while assuring CBS directors he was simply a white-knight investor. Tisch promised to help CBS maintain its independence from the likes of Coca-Cola, which coveted the company.

By 1986 the tightfisted Tisch owned 25 percent of CBS stock. Joined by Bill Paley with 9 percent, he pushed embattled Tom Wyman out the door. CBS directors named Tisch acting CEO and brought Paley—two weeks shy of his eighty-fifth birthday—back as acting chairman. Later, against all previous statements that CBS was not for sale, Tisch sold CBS to Westinghouse.

At the invitation of President and Mrs. Reagan, Jean and I attended a formal dinner at the White House in March 1985. It was to honor President Raul Alfonsin of Argentina. We were greeted at the entrance to the executive mansion by a man and woman in formal Marine uniforms, the woman in a formal-length skirt. The handsome male Marine escorted Jean as the woman escorted me through corridors lined with white-blossom trees and elaborate floral arrangements.

The Marine Band struck up "Hail to the Chief." The Reagans entered with President and Mrs. Alfonsin. In a reception line President Reagan, briefed by a staff member behind him, thanked me for the service I had given the USIA. I thought to myself, *Look where I started from, and here I am being thanked by the most powerful man in the world. Only in America.*

Also that year the International Radio and Television Society presented me its annual Gold Medal, considered the most prestigious award for a radio or television professional. Recipients in other years included General David Sarnoff, President John F. Kennedy, Frank Stanton, Bob

Hope, Lucille Ball, Roone Arledge, Norman Lear, and in the prior year, Carol Burnett.

Bill Cosby, dressed in green fatigues and smoking a cigar, entertained at my award dinner, held in a packed Waldorf-Astoria ballroom. Congratulations included a nice videotaped one from President Reagan.

Frank Stanton, my former boss at CBS, presented me with the Gold Medal. Viacom's Terry Elkes also asked to offer remarks.

A transcript of what Terry said on the evening of March 8, 1985, includes: "[Viacom] achieved what we did because of three distinct qualities which Ralph brought to our executive office and which provided the leadership and stimuli for growth. First, Ralph has commitment...Second, beneath Ralph's patina of steel lies a heart of velvet....Finally, Ralph is a realist who is careful not to believe in his own publicity. He puts the organization first...he allows people room to grow." A little more than a year later, Elkes would sing a different tune.

The Gold Medal citation read by Stanton:

> The International Radio and Television Society, Inc. is pleased to award its highest honor, the Gold Medal, to Ralph M. Baruch, for what he dared, what he achieved, and how he did it...for not forgetting, along the way, that others need guidance, or counsel, or a helping hand. His is a success story with few equals in our industry. His is a life story which restores our faith in America's culture of aspiration.

A singular triumph for Viacom—its biggest deal to date—was on the horizon. After we had operated the joint venture Showtime/The Movie Channel for a couple of years, Warner Communications issued about 30 percent of the shares of its MTV Networks Inc. on the open market. Warner chairman Steve Ross and his colleagues were smarting from huge losses the year before when Atari, Warner's crown jewel, fell into a financial black hole.

Warner sought more cash as we sought more cable networking. The potential of adding a number of blue-ribbon acquisitions that could multiply Viacom's annual revenue was like a shot of electricity through our company. Warner's two pioneering cable networks had already carved out their own substantial niches among viewers—MTV and Nickelodeon—and a new programming service, VH-1, also showed great promise.

MTV (Music Television), the rock music video channel, was widely regarded as the most inventive new form on television. In 1984 it beat all other cable TV programmers in advertising revenue. The network's revenue that year was about $110 million—more than double its 1983 figure of $50 million. During the same year, MTV's reach increased a whopping 37 percent, to 25.4 million households.

Nickelodeon premiered in 1979. It was TV's only channel devoted exclusively to children—until 1985 when it expanded to twenty-four hours a day and catered to grown-ups overnight as well. Nickelodeon had won a trophy-case full of educational and broadcasting awards, including the only Peabody ever given to a channel for all its programming.

A few months before we sought to acquire Nickelodeon, it added *National Geographic Explorer* to its already impressive offerings. Nickelodeon reached about 25 million homes. VH-1 (Video Hits One) first aired on January 1, 1985. It is a twenty-four-hour music channel with contemporary performers, aimed at viewers aged 25 to 54. It reached about 8 million households.

For good measure, we also hoped to retrieve the 50 percent of Showtime/The Movie Channel we did not already own. Altogether it was a daunting prospect that filled us with awe and trepidation. The deal would involve what was for Viacom a huge amount of money. But it was a big step toward a new benchmark of success in cable television programming.

Terry Elkes and I set the stage for negotiations by making a courtesy call on Steve Ross one morning at his Park Avenue apartment, just a couple of blocks from where Jean and I live.

We were having coffee when a short, bearded man appeared from a back room. "This is Steve," said Ross. It was Steven Spielberg, apparently a guest at Ross's apartment. Spielberg was an example of what Ross was especially noted for—lavishing favors on producers, actors, and other creative types who typically have enormous egos that require constant stroking. Spielberg had made several films for Warner, including "The Color Purple," and "Gremlins."

Like our Lifetime network, MTV, VH-1, and Nickelodeon were non-subscription cable services which got revenues from two sources: advertising income and a monthly fee paid by individual cable systems. We predicted MTV and Nickelodeon were going to be huge successes because they were unique in their fields. Attempts to imitate them have been made, but never as successfully.

Our respective staffs bargained. The two sides hit a brick wall, however. I was asked to join our negotiating team to discuss the acquisition face-to-face with Steve Ross. His decision for Warner was to be final. We met in the elegant Warner Communications board room around an enormous table, with leather swivel chairs for directors and a telephone tucked into a drawer before each chair.

Ross demanded $600 million for MTV, VH-1, Nickelodeon, and the one-half of Showtime/The Movie Channel subscription services we did not own. As a matter of principle, I was determined not to pay $600 million. We inched closer, but came to an impasse at $590 million, when we broke off negotiations. I got up and started to walk out, heart in my stomach, when Steve put a hand on my shoulder and asked me to sit back down.

"I'll buy some warrants from you for Viacom stock," he suggested. "That will reduce the cash you have to pay." Warrants enable one to buy stock at a later time at a price that is set up front. We agreed on the number of shares, the price—$70 a share for one set of warrants and $75 for another—and a five-year window of time in which the shares could be purchased. Viacom was then trading at around $50, so we knew Warner was unlikely to exercise its purchase rights immediately. Steve and I shook hands.

The deal was done. We left our staffs to work out the details. Warner's stock closed down twenty-five cents that day, at $29.75. Viacom's stock rose twenty-five cents, to close at $50.75.

The next challenge was to convince Viacom's own directors to approve our action. By no means was that automatic. The next board meeting, in fact, was difficult. Elkes, as CEO, presented the acquisition. Board members, not without good reason, were nervous about the enormous debt we would incur. Ken Gorman, a Viacom executive, and I jumped in, urging the board to support this once-in-a-lifetime opportunity. Finally the board voted unanimously to approve it. By the end of 1985 the complicated transaction was essentially complete.

I considered the sky the limit for our latest acquisitions. They were the best services in their respective fields. Not only did we have the right networks, we had the right people leading them. Tom Freston and Robert Pittman headed MTV, and Geraldine (Gerry) Laybourne, a former educator and one of the nation's most acclaimed developers of children's programming, headed Nickelodeon.

Viacom's acquisitions in 1985, noted the *Los Angeles Times*, put us in "the major leagues of TV programming."[6] We now had five strong cable services—all of Showtime/The Movie Channel, MTV, VH-1, Nickelodeon, and a third of Lifetime. We also owned eight television and radio stations and were the tenth largest operator of cable television systems, the largest non-network syndicator of television programs in the U.S., and one of the largest distributors abroad.

We had an all-time record in programming backlog of nearly a quarter-billion dollars. *The Cosby Show* alone would add another quarter-billion to that. We had under distribution over 5,000 half-hour and one-hour episodes and more than 1,000 feature movies made for television and mini-series. In 1984 Viacom's total revenue was about $109 million. In 1985—the year of the acquisitions—it leaped to $444 million. In 1986 it was $919 million. In 1987, for the first time, we would be a billion-dollar company.

The dizzying climb proved costly. No longer was Viacom like a Stealth bomber, unnoticed on the radar screens of major corporate takeover artists. Wall Street sang our praises, and suddenly we were on a short list of rumored targets.

24

'RALPH, YOU ARE DEAD MEAT'

I had no one but myself to blame for Terry Elkes. From the start of our association and his tenure at Viacom, I championed and promoted him against the better judgment of others. In the end he threw it all in my face and imperiled Viacom.

As the reader may recall, Terry came to Viacom as general counsel in 1972 with no experience in communications. He had been an attorney at a private paper company. Some Viacom directors strongly objected to hiring him after learning the results of a physical examination—a routine requirement for key applicants in those days. Elkes was overweight and had associated health problems. Those would be overcome, but it proved hopeless to rid him of arrogance.

Elkes came aboard as vice president, general counsel, and secretary of Viacom. Whatever our individual failings, the two of us proved a good business team. I had industry-wide experience in communications, especially television, and Terry understood legal and financial matters. Together we secured outside counsel, investment bankers, and others needed to help Viacom grow. I often took Terry with me when dealing with industry heavyweights.

Meanwhile, Jean and I went well out of our way to befriend Terry and his wife Ruth, and help them navigate socially in the world of communications and entertainment. It was not easy. Terry was basically shy. Ruth, a short, stout woman, likewise barely tolerated the social obligations that went with marriage to an executive husband.

We had taken the Elkes family sailing. When one of their sons was turned down by the London School of Economics, I believe because of a late application, Terry asked me to help. I telephoned Sir Huw Weldon, a friend who was formerly head of the BBC and then directed the school, and pled the young man's case. He was admitted.

Terry had what seemed a nervous habit. As soon as he sat down at a business or social function, out came his pipe and pouch of tobacco. A minute later, Terry, not bothering to ask if anyone minded, would fill the air with a cloud of acrid smoke. His pipe was an irritant to some Viacom board members, and no doubt offended many others.

What bothered Viacom's directors most, however, was not Terry's pipe but his patronizing. Our directors were men and women of real substance—leaders in their own companies and industries. They did not have the time to keep up day to day with our swift-growing company. Too often Terry responded to their questions with a smirk.

For many years I had encouraged Terry to get out of the office and mingle with leaders in the industries represented at Viacom. As CEO he finally showed interest in doing so. I invited Ted Turner over. Before Ted arrived Terry asked "What do I say to Turner?" I told him he did not have to say anything, just watch and listen. Turner breezed in, greeted us with "Hi fellas," delivered a fifteen-minute monologue on his latest ventures, did not ask or wait for a response, and departed with "Well, fellas, nice to see you."

Elkes also wanted to meet Rupert Murdoch, whom I had known professionally and socially since the time I was head of International for CBS and periodically visited him in his native Australia. I arranged with Murdoch for Terry and me to have two nice luncheons with him in his office at the *New York Post*.

Jean is unusually observant and a good judge of character. Occasionally she dropped hints of concern about Terry. In retrospect, two incidents stand out.

On my sixtieth birthday Viacom threw a lovely party for me in the Starlight Room at the top of Rockefeller Center. Prior to the party, Jean and Terry went there to test the food and drink. On their table was a magnum—a double-sized bottle—of champagne. "Terry poured himself three glasses, and I had one," recalls Jean. "When I asked Terry for another, I saw that he had tucked the champagne in a briefcase under his chair, ready to take it away."

In 1985, soon after the International Radio and Television Society awarded me the Gold Medal, Terry and Jean were seated together at a luncheon. Midway through the meal, Terry leaned over and said "If you think Ralph's Gold-Medal party was something, wait until you see mine." Terry's boast was not tested, as he never got the award.

Viacom's success continued to attract major investors. They included National Amusements, a chain of movie theaters; a group in Chicago called Coniston Partners, and, our worst fear, Carl Icahn.

"Except possibly T. Boone Pickens, who seems to have lost interest in attacking corporations," said *The New York Times*, "no single corporate raider these days comes close to Carl C. Icahn for an uncanny ability to terrorize corporate chieftains by the simple act of buying stock and, one way or another, emerging with a profit."[1]

Icahn grew up in nearby Queens, and studied philosophy at Princeton. He began as a stock broker, then became an arbitrager, buying stocks of takeover targets and peddling them to the highest bidder.

Icahn's pattern was set in 1979 when he won a proxy fight for Tappan, which manufactures stoves.[2] Icahn bought enough stock to put himself on its board, where he forced Tappan's sale to a Swedish firm. Icahn pocketed $3 million from that transaction. Like it or not, Icahn was the raider who bought our stock from the Chicago group and had Viacom in his gunsight.

By May 1986 Icahn had accumulated a lot of Viacom stock. Elkes was asked to negotiate with him regarding his plans for the shares. After long discussions, Viacom agreed to purchase Icahn's shares of stock. We ended up losing tens of millions to him. In return, Icahn agreed not to seek control of Viacom for at least eleven years. We were the sixteenth corporation to pay him off in the past seven years.

After his last meeting with Icahn, Elkes made a presentation to our board. From out in left field he suggested that Viacom and Icahn form a joint venture, capitalized on a 50-50 basis, to explore businesses together. Our company had just been pillaged by Icahn, and Elkes wanted us to join his band of pirates. His suggestion was unanimously voted down.

Once the Icahn matter was behind us, I noticed a substantial change in Elkes' demeanor. Now fifty-two, he had long since lost the extra weight he brought to Viacom, and jogged almost fanatically. Several times a day he stood before the mirrored column in our outer office, combing his thick dark hair. Elkes often had spoken down to others, but not to me. Now he began to address me with the same smirk he used when answering directors' questions.

I was not invited to the next long-range planning meeting, but did not take it personally. Elkes was CEO and I understood that to have the former CEO present might be distracting. But he did not even have the courtesy to tell me why I was not invited. Elkes and our financial staff also organized meetings with our investment bankers and other outsiders. Again I was not included.

I felt entitled to an explanation about these meetings. But Elkes became reclusive and difficult to pin down. We had had adjoining offices for many years and never bothered making appointments with each other. We just walked into the other's office, put our feet up, and discussed whatever was on our minds. Overnight, it seemed, things had changed. His door was shut to me. Three times I made appointments to meet with Terry, and each time his secretary canceled for him.

Finally we met. Elkes said he planned to do a leveraged buyout of Viacom, using the assets of the company to raise the funds. This seemed a good idea in view of everything that was going on with National Amusements, Coniston Partners, and others who had accumulated Viacom stock.

"We know the company better than anybody and know just where to cut without harming the core of Viacom," I said. "This is a great opportunity; we can do it extremely well." His reply stunned me.

"Ralph, you use the word 'we' all the time. I have formed a group of insiders and you are not part of it. There are seven of us who are going to do this, and you're not one of them."

My mind raced as he added, "You should realize you are dead in the water and have absolutely no power base. You are dead meat."

Elkes added, "If I were in your place, I wouldn't even come in." Then he strongly advised me to cooperate with his group. I had a long-term consulting agreement with Viacom after retirement, he noted, and it is was in my best interest to not rock the boat: "If you and I have a problem we may not want to honor the agreement and you may have to sue. The company certainly has the resources to carry a suit five or ten years. I'm not sure you do."

To hear this from the mouth of one I thought of as my friend as well as my business associate all these years was surreal. It was the ultimate in betrayal and greed. I was to be locked out of the company I had led almost from the start.

A few days later Jean blew a tire coming home from the countryside. The car bounced from one side of the thruway to the other and was about two feet narrower when she finally came to a stop. The car, furnished by Viacom, was totaled.

I reported this to Elkes and said I would have to purchase a new one. He said I was only entitled to one car under my employment contract. I had anticipated his response and prepared for it. I showed Terry a legal opinion written by Viacom's general counsel, affirming I was entitled to another car. Elkes reluctantly agreed.

I had been quiet about the takeover attempt, but no more. I initiated a meeting with Ken Gorman, one of the seven in the Elkes clique, who was personally close to Terry. Gorman, forty-seven, was a small man with a sharply chiseled face. He had been with Viacom from the start, first in finance, then as a senior officer. Recently he had become executive vice president.

I told him I was offended and disappointed that I was not included among insiders who likely would decide Viacom's future.

"Ralph, don't push it. You have a lot at stake," said Gorman, again referring to my consulting agreement.

I had hired most of the seven, and got along well with them. But now Elkes was CEO and their ticket to continued lucrative employment as well as a share of the spoils at Viacom.

At a board meeting on September 16, 1986, Elkes outlined the conditions of their leveraged buyout (LBO). They offered $2.7 billion for Viacom. Holders of Viacom stock would receive $37 in cash for each share they owned, plus a fraction of a share of exchangeable preferred stock of the new partnership, called MCB Holdings. The partnership stock was expected to have a market value of $3.50 a share, bringing the price per share to $40.50.

On advice of counsel, the board of directors elected a special committee comprised of all eight outside directors to eventually decide the issue. A subcommittee, chaired by one of them, Allan Johnson, would consider the matter in detail and advise the special committee.

Elkes wanted it both ways with me—use my name publicly to assure investors all was well at Viacom, while knifing me privately.

Broadcasting magazine reported that Viacom's top management "but not including its chairman and founder, Ralph Baruch" were part of the deal. It added that another group of executives "definitely including Baruch, will continue in their present posts and have some 'participation' in the LBO."[3] Any participation was news to me.

Allan asked me to meet with him. Allan was a gracious man of seventy. He had been a director for seven years and was a former chairman and CEO of Saks Fifth Avenue. Allan asked why I supported the leveraged buyout by Elkes and cohorts even though I was not part of their group.

I repeated Elkes' comments, including his threat to make my life difficult if I did not cooperate. Allan was appalled. He passed this information on to other outside directors and they too were outraged. Nonetheless, their responsibility was to protect the interests of Viacom's shareholders, not those of any one individual.

Elkes, I learned, had been meeting with investment bankers and other financiers for nearly six months. The venture of the seven Viacom executives was backed by three leading investment banks—Donaldson, Luftin & Jenrette; First Boston; and Drexel Burnham Lambert—and by the Equitable Life Assurance Society.

"Given the formidable ensemble [of investors], I don't think there will be a competing bid," said Mara Balsbaugh of Smith Barney, Harris Upham & Company. However, Balsbaugh added, the $40.50 a share price "is at the low end of the range."[4]

Logic said the analysts were right. Who could hope to prevail against such an imposing group? It would take someone tenacious enough to walk through fire and live to tell about it. As it happened, someone was in the wings with precisely those credentials: Sumner Redstone.

In the same conversation when he told me I was "dead meat," Terry Elkes also had Sumner Redstone, a potential long-shot rival for Viacom, on his mind. "Redstone is smart but crazy," said Elkes. "He goes to bed at seven o'clock and gets up at two."

Redstone, sixty-three, was a prosperous but little-known businessman from Boston. As a youth he graduated first in his class at Boston Latin School and earned a degree from Harvard in less than three years. During World War II he helped crack Japanese codes for Army intelligence, then graduated from Harvard Law.

After practicing in Washington and Boston, Redstone in 1955 entered business with his father, who owned a chain of movie theaters called National Amusements Inc. By 1967 Sumner was president and CEO of NAI.

Twelve years later, in the early morning hours of March 29, 1979, Redstone was awakened by a fire alarm and a woman's screams on the third floor of Boston's Copley Plaza Hotel. He ran to the door, threw it open, and was engulfed by flames. Nearly half his body broiled, Redstone retreated to the window, crawled out onto the ledge, and held on with his smoldering right hand until rescued by firemen on a ladder.

He was not expected to survive sixty hours of surgery, but he did. He was told he would never walk again. In time he was on a treadmill and playing tennis, a leather strap holding the racquet to his gnarled right hand. Such was the resolve of Sumner Redstone.

As he recovered from burns, Redstone began to buy stock in the Hollywood studios that produced films shown on his theater screens, which numbered nearly 400 by 1987. He made millions betting on Columbia Pictures, Twentieth Century Fox, MGM/UA, and Orion. By September 1986 he also owned about three million shares of Viacom—nearly 9 percent of our company.

On the seventeenth of that month Redstone awoke to this headline in *The New York Times:* "Viacom Chief Leads Group's Buyout Bid."

Redstone read that the management team offer was $2.7 billion—$40.50 a share, $37 of it in cash. His conclusion: "Terry Elkes was trying to steal the company."[5] Neutral observers concluded the same thing. In an article in *Barron's*—called "Buyout or Sellout?"—economist-lawyer Benjamin Stein called the Elkes offer "extraordinarily low."

Even Goldman Sachs & Company, the investment banker retained by Viacom's outside directors to assess offers, concluded that management's bid of $2.7 billion, as well as a later bid of $2.9 billion, were "outside the range of fairness."[6]

Since the Elkes group altogether owned less than 5 percent of the equity in Viacom, their LBO was to be financed by the sale of junk bonds—high-interest bonds graded low by rating agencies because they have a greater risk of default. Viacom already had about $1 billion of debt following all our recent acquisitions.

Once the Elkes group controlled Viacom, reckoned Redstone, "they would have to sell off its assets [to pay the debts], essentially destroying the company."[7] Benjamin Stein concluded the same thing in Barron's: "Viacom's management LBO group will be 'forced' to liquidate most of the company (presumably in order to save it) and in short order."[8]

If Elkes prevailed, a lot of good, talented people would lose their jobs and the Viacom we had built so carefully over the years would be history. It was painful to stand by and watch the culmination of my life's work headed toward the auction block.

Analysts concluded that Redstone's interest also was to make a windfall profit, not to actually own and run Viacom. But they were wrong. The more Redstone learned about Viacom the more convinced he became that we had built a uniquely valuable enterprise whose full worth could only be realized by keeping it intact.

Elkes and cohorts ordered a code of silence at Viacom to keep Redstone in the dark. But a few of our gutsy middle managers confided in Redstone, convincing him his instincts were totally on target.

"So I was going to go after it," he recalls. "I must say I enjoyed the idea. Why? First, because the prize was of real value. This would not be a battle over a trifle. Viacom was a company worth fighting for. Second, it's fair to say that I would enjoy the contest." Redstone's tenacity was suggested in the title of his subsequent autobiography: A Passion to Win.

The day after reading about the offer by the Elkes group, Redstone bought more Viacom stock. He believed the company's outside directors were "plenty inside," and warned that a lawsuit would follow if they did not faithfully exercise their fiduciary responsibility and accept the best bid on merit. Redstone had $400 million in cash—the value of his theater chain and other holdings—plus nearly $500 million in Viacom equity.

Elkes staked his bid largely on junk bonds, secured notably through Drexel Burnham and its junk-bond king Michael Milken, who would be indicted two years later and sent to prison for insider trading.

To make Viacom less attractive to Redstone and other outsiders, the Elkes group had put a clause in their proposal that, if the board did not go with them, an outside buyer was obligated to pay a "breakup fee" of $50 million to their investment bankers, in addition to the other costs of the deal. At the time $50 million was considered a large breakup fee.

Early on, Redstone met twice with Elkes and went away convinced that his allegiance was not to Viacom's shareholders but to his own pocketbook. Elkes tried to keep Viacom's internal records away from Redstone, but Redstone forced him to give them up for due diligence. Redstone knew he was making headway when Viacom's Ken Gorman refused to shake hands with Kenneth Miller of Merrill Lynch, Redstone's primary investment banker.

In the early months of 1987 Viacom was auctioned between the Elkes group and Redstone's company, National Amusements. Marathon meetings produced a blizzard of new proposals.

Finally, in a session that lasted all day March 3 and until four o'clock the next morning, Viacom's outside directors voted to sell the company to Redstone. His offer was $3.4 billion, well above management's original offer of $2.7 billion and higher than management's final offer—built on a financial house of cards—of $3.2 billion.

"It's a shocker," said analyst Kenneth F. Berents of Legg Mason Wood Walker, a global financial services company. "It was a war of attrition, and Redstone finally wore them down."

Berents and others believed the Elkes group might well have won if they could have closed the deal earlier. One obstacle was the insider-trading scandal that had started to rock Wall Street and depress the junk bond market which was critical to management's proposal. "They snatched defeat from the jaws of victory," quipped Berents.[9]

Redstone's bid, all told, was about $55.50 a share—a substantial $15 more than Elkes' original offer. A little more than ten years earlier I bought as many shares of Viacom as I could, at $2 5/8 and $3 a share. Since the stock had split twice, its current value was more than $220 a share—a terrific investment for our stockholders.

On June 3, 1987, I presided at a special meeting of shareholders in which they approved the sale. For me it was a sad day. With the help of a lot of good people, I had built the company from practically nothing. At birth it was not much more than a shadow of what it had become and would yet become. Had the Elkes clique solicited my help, and that of other experienced board members, Viacom's future might have turned out otherwise. But there it was.

Sumner Redstone and National Amusements now owned most of Viacom. Redstone told me that, while struggling for control of our company, he met with Elkes in the latter's office. Elkes offered him substantial equity for only $25 million, if he agreed to be a totally passive investor.

Redstone was not interested. As he was leaving, Elkes said, "Incidentally, Sumner, you call it 'Vie-a-com,' around here we call it 'Vee-a-com.'" The gratuitous remark stuck as Sumner was shown the door.

Redstone felt isolated. Elkes had assigned him an office the size of a broom closet, and told him he was not welcome at staff meetings. "You know, Ralph, I can't live with that," Redstone told me. Then we discussed my future. Redstone understandably wanted to be chairman. I could do one of two things: resign and trigger a parachute, which might be financially attractive, or stay on as a consultant and Sumner would name me chairman emeritus. He offered me a spacious office, on my floor or elsewhere in the building, at my choice. I was to discuss all this with his attorney, Philippe Dauman.

The following day I met with Elkes. "For whatever reason, Redstone wants to be chairman," said Elkes. "He does not feel the office I assigned him is appropriate." Elkes again suggested I resign and begin consulting. "Go home," he said, "you have an overlap of two years during which you will get paid both your consulting agreement and your salary. You no longer have a place here."

Redstone and I agreed he would take my title and office. I told him I could not remain under the same conditions, especially if he wanted my title. But I assured him I was willing to assist at any time. I would certainly stay active in the industry, and it was important for Viacom that we part in a friendly manner, each side speaking highly of the other. He strongly agreed.

Redstone asked what I thought of various staff members, and said he could not talk to other company leaders because Elkes had asked them not to see him. "I'm being treated like I work for Terry Elkes and he wants me to be an absentee owner." I suggested he write a memo to Elkes saying he wanted an appropriate office and would meet with anyone he chose. I also suggested he sign his name and under it write "Owner."

After Sumner completed the takeover of Viacom, he wrote the memo as I suggested, called Elkes in, and handed it to him. As Elkes was leaving, Redstone said, "Incidentally, Terry, around here we call it 'Vie-a-com.'" Immediately Redstone had the tails of every show changed. The old logo was gone, a new logo inserted, and a voice-over now said "Vie-a-com."

Redstone asked me to suggest a CEO. I did not know that Elkes already had informed him who it should be: Elkes himself. Terry had relayed this to Redstone through attorney Philippe Dauman. Elkes told Dauman he already had a fortune of $30 million and did not need to work.

"However," says Redstone, "he and his management team were willing to stay on one condition. He demanded that I give him personally 20 percent of the equity in Viacom...Elkes told [Dauman] I had no choice, and that 'Sumner needs me to run this company.'"

Elkes was trying to cut his other management team members out the way he cut me out. It was the mind-set of one who would tuck a magnum of champagne into his briefcase and leave others thirsty. When Dauman relayed the ultimatum, Redstone exploded. Elkes' "greed had taken a quantum leap," wrote Redstone. "Now he was going to get nothing."[10]

The company picnic was the following week. I had just come back from a business trip but decided to attend. I rented a small black car and drove out alone. Elkes had asked Redstone not to travel there with me, even though our Manhattan apartments were just two blocks apart. At the picnic I saw Elkes waving his arms as he talked to Redstone, obviously trying to convince him of something.

I was depressed. I saw the end of what I had built—not of the businesses per se, but in terms of my role and contributions and those of people I had hired, trained, and in whom I had placed so much confidence. We had built something special. Then, soon after reaching Viacom's highest summit together and viewing a fabulous future for our company, they had turned mercenary and were fully prepared to butcher Viacom for their selfish ends.

I walked around a little in the picnic area, said hello to a few people, then decided to drive back. I took Sumner with me.

During the drive he said he had to change CEOs. I suggested several names including Frank Biondi, CEO of Coca-Cola Television and former chief executive of HBO. I also stressed the importance of trying to keep Jules Haimovitz, president of Showtime, and senior vice president John Goddard. Both were part of the Elkes group but were talented executives.

Then Redstone forcefully said he wanted me to stay and work full time at Viacom. It was hard to drive and discuss my future at the same time, so I tried to change the subject. Elkes had suggested to Redstone that all of our radio and television stations be sold. "It could well be another plot," Sumner surmised, "to make a leveraged buyout of the radio and television stations by Viacom executives."

I suggested a transition of Elkes out of the organization might be in order. Redstone then mentioned he might be acting CEO himself. I told him that would be a mistake, especially in the beginning, since he was not familiar with our various businesses.

The next day I told Sumner that Jean and I wanted more time to enjoy life a little more, so I would not be working full time. I added, however, that I would be available practically full time anyway for him and the company. My recommendation of Frank Biondi—along with those of others who also suggested him—fell on fertile ground. Redstone appointed Biondi as Viacom's new CEO. When Biondi came aboard, Terry Elkes left.

Showtime offered me office space at 1633 Broadway, and I moved into a nice corner office there on July 28, 1987.

SUMNER REDSTONE
FOILS THE PIRATES

A t Viacom, Sumner Redstone started at the top—and went up. He kept his word and did not sell off Viacom's most valuable properties, as surely would have happened had the Elkes group prevailed in their struggle for the company.

We provided a solid foundation and lower floors at Viacom. Redstone proceeded to build a skyscraper. He echoed my mantra that content is nearly everything, and set out to create or buy more production capability, cable networks, and other programming outlets. He reduced debt by selling businesses that were not central to Viacom's core interests of creating and presenting programs.

Gone were a TV station and some local radio stations and cable systems. They brought a princely price. Cablevision, for example, bought our cable systems on Long Island and in Cleveland for nearly $3,000 per subscriber, I believe a record high to that time.

Among radio stations sold or swapped was WLTW in New York, the lite music station at 106.7 FM. We had bought it in 1980, along with seven other radio stations and a television station in Albany for less than $30 million. Redstone sold WLTW alone for what was estimated to be more than $400 million. He sold the Albany TV station for nearly double what we paid for the whole group.

Viacom's other pre-Redstone acquisitions also have done extremely well. By 1989, proceeds from syndication of *Cosby* had put $500 million in Viacom's bank account—more than anyone had ever made from syndicating one show. Topping them all in value are the cable networks we bought from Warner: MTV, Nickelodeon, VH-1, and the other halves of Showtime and The Movie Channel. We paid Warner less than $590 million for them in 1985.

The value in 2006 of all Viacom properties acquired during my tenure ranged as high as $100 billion.

Redstone retained and filled key slots with some of our best people. We had hired Tom Dooley as a budget analyst; Redstone named him Viacom's treasurer and later deputy chairman. Tom Freston continued as president and CEO of MTV Networks, and was bound for the top of Viacom. Other Viacom veterans who helped Redstone take the company to new heights: Matt Blank, who succeeded Jules Haimovitz as president of Showtime; George Smith, an accountant who became chief financial officer; and many others.

A number of Viacom leaders went on to make distinguished marks elsewhere in the industry. Gerry Laybourne continued to lead Nickelodeon—garnering a larger share of child viewers than the children's programs offered by ABC, CBS, NBC, and Fox combined. Gerry became vice-president of Disney/ABC Television, and today heads Oxygen Media, a twenty-four-hour television network for women which she helped found, along with a handful of partners including Oprah Winfrey.

In 2006 Peter Chernin, once head of Showtime, was president of News Corporation, Rupert Murdoch's company. John J. Sie, also formerly at Showtime, founded and led Starz, a major pay-cable service. Jim Robbins, our senior vice president of operations, joined Cox Communications in 1983, rising to CEO in 1995.

James (Jamie) Kellner was the young Viacom salesman who was the skipper on *Calisto* when we first sailed our new boat from Annapolis to Connecticut in 1977. He helped Rupert Murdoch launch the Fox Network and became its leader; later he was named head of all television for the merged AOL-Time Warner.

Viacom's biggest deal yet was for Paramount Pictures and the rest of the Paramount Communications empire. Years earlier we had tried to acquire another Hollywood studio, MGM, but could not convince a partner to go all the way with us. Now Redstone eyed Paramount and the incredible package of properties that came with it. He was about to touch off the nation's biggest takeover battle to date in the nineties.

Paramount was one of the original studios, created in 1916. Under the legendary Adolph Zukor, it was the most profitable studio in the 1920s and became the home of such stars as Bob Hope, Bing Crosby, and their "road" pictures, the Marx Brothers, Gary Cooper, W.C. Fields, and Claudette Colbert.

The studio fell on harder times in the 1950s and 1960s, and was bought by Gulf & Western in 1966, beginning a trend of large corporations gobbling up studios. The conglomerate then grew stronger under excellent leadership.

In 1993 when Viacom eyed Paramount Communications, it had been led for nearly a decade by Martin Davis, a former publicist and friend to Sumner Redstone. His relationship with Davis opened the door to a genial Viacom-Paramount merger agreement, announced in September.

Eight days later, however, Barry Diller, head of QVC, the home shopping network, made a hostile bid for Paramount. His backers included John Malone, longtime leader of TCI, the world's largest cable television company. A court ruled that Diller's bid was stronger, and directed Paramount to merge with him.

But Redstone had not played his last card. He was as determined to prevail as he had been in the struggle for Viacom. A marriage of Viacom and Paramount Pictures, he reasoned, would be a merger of equals, and "would create exactly the company I had originally envisioned." As months went by, and the bidding and subsequent debt rose, Viacom's stock plummeted.

"I know there is concern about the stock price," said Redstone. "But we and others have staked our personal economic lives on the commitment that it's going to work...The pain will be worth it. " He added that "there are not eighteen Paramounts floating around out there; there's only one, and it's the last of the great studios."

Media analyst Stuart Rossmiller at Fitch Investors Service, said "You miss the whole point of this takeover battle if you just look at Paramount's current track record. What this whole thing is about is the future and its potential."

The issue finally was decided after Blockbuster agreed to merge with Viacom and brought an additional $1.25 billion cash to the table. By February 1994 Viacom's bid for Paramount approached $10 billion—nearly $2 billion more than the price Redstone and Martin Davis had originally agreed upon. Diller threw in the towel in perhaps the shortest concession speech in the annals of major takeover attempts: "They won. We lost. Next."[1] The London Observer headlined its story on the outcome "Killer Diller Loses Thriller."[2]

The merger made Redstone the most powerful American in entertainment, and for a time the wealthiest in entertainment. He controlled over 60 percent of the Class A voting stock of the merged company. In 2005 *Forbes* magazine listed Redstone as the forty-second richest person in the world, with a personal fortune of $8.8 billion.

Paramount brought these assets to Viacom: Paramount Pictures studio, Paramount television production, including such shows as *Frasier, Cheers, Star Trek: The Next Generation,* and *Entertainment Tonight;* a library of 900 films, a thousand movie screens, Simon & Schuster publishing, Madison Square Garden, the New York Rangers and New York Knicks, the MSG cable network, part of USA Networks, seven television stations, and Paramount Parks—five regional theme parks across the nation.

In coming years it would add such properties as BET (Black Entertainment Television), UPN, now merging with the WB network; Comedy Central, and CMT: Country Music Television. More recently, Paramount acquired Dreamworks.

As Viacom was becoming a global powerhouse in the 1990s, my former employer CBS was searching its soul to find what it had become and where it was going.

ABC, NBC, and CBS all changed hands in the mid-eighties. With stiff competition from cable and other sources of information and entertainment, the new corporate owners set out to increase network profits by cutting costs. The sense of higher mission that especially had imbued CBS News, the company's crown jewel, was eroded and then largely lost.

CBS's mandatory retirement age of sixty-five—from which founder Bill Paley exempted himself—in 1973 had cost CBS its brilliant day-to-day leader, Frank Stanton. He stepped down with considerable regret, and for good reason, because Frank still had so much more to give. We continued to get together socially. He was very down to earth. Occasionally he came to dinner at our apartment in New York. Frank insisted on eating in the kitchen, I suppose to make it easier on Jean. Frank had many interests, including woodworking and sculpting in wood and metal. His hands were those of a workman, strong and calloused.

Paley installed a succession of presidents and CEOs, and showed them the door when they did not measure up to Stanton: Arthur Taylor, John Backe, Tom Wyman. The leadership turmoil sapped CBS's spirit and strength and left it vulnerable. When Ted Turner tried to buy the weakened CBS, Larry Tisch, the company's largest stockholder, stepped in and installed himself as president in 1986.

Tisch's budget and personnel cuts were bitterly resented by CBS veterans. The rumbling inside CBS started to be seen outside. The *CBS Evening News* had been the leading network newscast for eighteen years straight with anchor Walter Cronkite. It retained that spot for a number of years under Dan Rather, who succeeded Cronkite in 1981.

But by 1990 *CBS Evening News* had sunk to number three in the ratings. That year Rather wrote a blistering opinion piece for *The New York Times*, called "From Murrow to Mediocrity."[3]

"CBS Inc. is a profitable, valuable *Fortune 500* corporation whose stock is setting new records," wrote Rather. "But 215 [news] people lost their jobs so that the stockholders would have even more money in their pockets...Our new chief executive officer, Laurence Tisch, told us when he arrived that he wanted us to be the best...Ironically, he has now made the task seem something between difficult and impossible."

The article incensed Tisch, but Rather was under contract so there was little he could do about it.

Walter Cronkite, a CBS board member, made a determined effort to save its news operation. In a long, impassioned plea to fellow directors, Cronkite noted that in most firehouses most of the time, ten firemen can be found sitting around playing checkers.

"But when the fire comes," noted Cronkite, "you'll wish you had thirty in there, not ten. And you find out that you've gotten down to ten because that's all you think you can afford to pay. This is journalism.

We're not a production line. It doesn't work that way."[4]

Other CBS directors listened politely—and did nothing. After a short-lived resurgence with the 1992 Winter Olympics and the luring of *The David Letterman Show* from NBC the following year, CBS again took some hard body blows.

It lost the bid to air NFL Football to the young Fox Network, and then watched helplessly as a dozen affiliated stations defected to Fox. In 1995, after repeated denials that he would sell CBS, Tisch did just that, to the Westinghouse Corporation. That ended CBS's long and distinguished history as an independent company.

Tisch and other network leaders had fought a losing battle to maintain dominance in the face of forces largely beyond their control. The media and entertainment market increasingly was fragmented—by powerful new broadcast and cable networks, pay cable, independent stations, VCRs and the huge videocassette industry they spawned, and a healthy big-screen film industry.

In 1976 the Big Three networks—ABC, CBS, and NBC—enjoyed more than 90 percent of TV viewers each evening. That fell to 68 percent in 1989 and to 43 percent in 1999.

In 1997 Westinghouse/CBS purchased an aggressive radio network called Infinity Broadcasting. Its president and CEO was Mel Karmazin, 55, a native New Yorker and born street fighter. Karmazin grew up on Long Island. His late father drove a taxi and his mother worked in a factory. Karmazin rose fast through CBS's ranks and, in January 1999, muscled aside its CEO to take the top job as chairman.

As the reader will recall, Viacom was created in 1970 and spun away from CBS the following year, under conditions that led most observers to doubt it could survive. The parent company loaded tiny Viacom with a big backpack of bricks, then nudged it out the back door without another thought. Viacom had long since become a player with or without CBS's notice. And in September 1999—at the agile age of twenty-eight—the circle was closed. Viacom returned home, this time through the front door, and bought CBS.

"Viacom's $37 billion acquisition of CBS has exquisite symbolism," noted one columnist. "That an offspring with such meager prospects could grow into so strapping a force certainly reflects the new balance of power in the entertainment world."[5] Another reporter suggested the network had turned dowdy, and in merging with Viacom, "CBS paired up with a lively young dance partner that could teach the old network some new steps."[6] A wag on CNBC described the merger simply as "Beavis and Butt-head meets Dan Rather."

It was the largest media marriage to that time. Viacom paid $37.3 billion for the CBS Corporation, to create the nation's second largest media empire. The largest was Time Warner, with a stock market value of $80.5 billion; the new Viacom was right behind at $72 billion.

Overnight, Viacom grew from 49,000 employees to 95,000, and from $12 billion in revenue to nearly $19 billion. The new Viacom was the nation's number one company in cable programming, radio, outdoor advertising, and as a creator of programming for the networks, cable television, and syndication.

Despite its size, the Viacom-CBS merger held almost none of the trauma that accompanied Redstone's purchase of Viacom in 1987 or Paramount Communications seven years later.

His talks with Karmazin followed an FCC ruling in August 1999 that allowed a company to own two television stations in the same market. Viacom and CBS owned stations in a half-dozen of the same major cities, and the possible savings from swapping stations or running them jointly appealed to both Redstone and Karmazin.

A few weeks after the FCC action, Redstone invited Karmazin to Viacom. In a dining room off Redstone's office—with no attorneys or investment bankers to gum up their talks—the two men began the negotiations that led to the merger. A joint news conference in September 1999 announced the marriage. Karmazin joked that it was "a deal I wanted to make probably from the time I was bar mitzvahed."[7]

In the new Viacom, Redstone remained chairman and CEO, and Karmazin was president and chief operating officer, apparently poised to replace Redstone. In June 2004, however, Karmazin abruptly resigned. His departure followed a frustrating year of fighting a weakening stock price, and reports that Redstone and Karmazin did not see eye to eye.

Redstone named two well-regarded Viacom executives, Tom

Freston and Leslie Moonves, to share day-to-day leadership duties. Viacom's stock, however, like that of other large media companies, continued to languish.

Redstone's solution: split Viacom into two companies—against conventional Wall Street wisdom that says the way to grow is to multiply, not divide. By the first of 2006 the split was accomplished. Freston became CEO of the new Viacom and Moonves the same for CBS Corp. Redstone remains chairman and majority stockholder in both companies, with voting control.

Near the end of 1999 I was awarded an Emmy for lifetime contributions to television. Sumner Redstone took that occasion to publicly note that Viacom had come full circle. "Ralph is a leader among leaders, a giant in our industry," he said generously. "Ralph played a major role in the spin-off of Viacom from CBS, and now he sees his legacy come full term as Viacom buys CBS."

Viacom became exactly the right company for its time. It helped create and then rode a wave of opportunity borne of emerging technologies, services, and especially programming. After a lot of rough and tumble in the surf, that wave ultimately carried Viacom triumphantly to shore as the once impregnable broadcast television networks were being pummeled on the rocks.

The good news, for the industries as well as the viewing public, is that both cable and broadcast television survived, the latter humbled a bit. Newer players are also on the scene, including portable satellite receiving dishes, the Internet, and television delivered over telephone lines.

Probably close behind will be a convergence of communication technologies, in which the computer, television set, Internet, and telephone will all be available in one appliance. It remains to be seen if the federal government will hinder such innovations as it obstructed development of the broadcast television industry and, later, cable television.

This much won't change: Whatever the mode of delivery, programming will continue to call the shots. Whoever owns programming owns the future.

I deeply wish I could end this journey through commercial television by expressing unbridled optimism in its future. Based on current offerings, however, I cannot. Television has sunk to a terrible low. *Stacked.* *Joe Millionaire. Fear Factor.* These and other so-called reality shows prove not how civilized people can be, but how uncivilized. A flood of situation comedies are so vapid that the only laughs they get are for crude double entendres. Where are today's brilliantly written and acted *Cosby, All in the Family, M*A*S*H ,* and *The Honeymooners?*

I have hope that viewers will yet rise up and say "Enough!" But meanwhile, a generation has grown up that doesn't care about serious television. Jean and I recently saw a brief TV news report showing destitute children in Pakistan walking in the snow without shoes. Instead of in-depth features on such misery, which might stir the world's conscience to act, we are fed mind-numbing documentaries on the latest grisly sex attack/murder.

The number of commercials has increased tremendously on both broadcast and cable. They are interminable. Except for PBS, broadcast television is no longer a public service, operating in the public interest, convenience, and necessity. It is a moneymaking machine, still driven almost completely by newly developed rating services. Broadcast networks continue to exist largely as a convenient way for advertisers to gain immediate national exposure.

For all my disappointment in today's television, I must acknowledge that quality remains in the eye of the beholder. Thanks to the hundreds of cable networks, there are a myriad of choices available. Television entertains us, every age and every taste, with a breathtaking variety of programs.

Many homes receive dozens of channels and networks, and a growing number receive a hundred or more. In this vast marketplace of competing ideas and artistry, television producers, networks, and stations will create programs that appeal to a market, however thinly sliced, or they will be off the air. True television democracy.

Television has not done all that its inventors and dreamers hoped. Philo Farnsworth, the Idaho farm boy-genius who enabled television's last leap from the laboratory to the living room, believed that television would wipe out illiteracy and war. As viewers learn more about people in other countries, he reasoned, differences and misunderstandings will melt away and war will be wiped from the earth.

Instead, war itself is fodder for television. In 2006, the quagmire for the U.S. in Iraq and Afghanistan oozes into our homes daily. America, it can be argued, is hated in some places not because people know too little about us but because they know too much—or, more accurately, because they know too much of what is worst about us and not enough of what is best.

I acknowledge a hand in feeding both perceptions, through extending American television across the globe.

Television has changed the world, mostly for the better. It has not conquered illiteracy. It has, however, helped level the education playing field for hundreds of millions across the globe. It has been a companion to countless lonely souls. It has helped produce an era of unequaled prosperity in the United States and other industrialized countries.

It has the power to rivet a nation and a world—during Olympics competitions, when a President is assassinated, or when terrorist-piloted planes slice through buildings, dooming thousands of innocent people. In the end, television and other media reflect who we are as individuals. In them we will find what we seek, for both the sordid and the sublime are readily accessible.

"I believe television is going to be the test of the modern world," said E.B. White of the new invention nearly 70 years ago, "and that in this new opportunity to see beyond the range of our vision, we shall discover a new and unbearable disturbance of the modern peace, or a saving radiance in the sky. We shall stand or fall by television—of that I am quite sure."[8]

I would like to believe that television continues to test us, and that we will yet get it right. The final exam is still to come.

Broadcast journalist Edwin Newman wrote of his career: "Enjoyment? Sometimes. Gratification? Sometimes. And over the years, along with the letdowns and disappointments, a sense that I should count myself fortunate to have worked in television, and for all its faults, more fortunate still to have seen it."[9]

I don't believe I can say it any better than that.

EPILOGUE

I am still active in television as a member of the board and executive
committee of Public Broadcasting Service's flagship station, Channel
Thirteen/WNET in New York City. The switch from commercial to
public television felt natural. Although my career has been in commercial
television, Jean and I most enjoy the type of fare produced by PBS stations.

After becoming a consultant at Viacom, the Gannett Center for
Media Studies at Columbia University, now called Freedom Forum and located in Arlington, Virginia, offered me a senior fellowship. Its director, Dr.
Everett Dennis, asked me to join them for a year and write the first scholarly
treatise on cable television. The Center assigned a research assistant to the
project, and we worked hard, producing a television white paper.

Some of my fellowship colleagues were Reuven Frank, a former
president of NBC News, and Kati Marton, a journalist who spent the year
writing a book on the 1948 murder of George Polk, a CBS News correspondent killed in Greece under mysterious circumstances.

My paper documented the vacillation and indecision of the FCC,
and how wrongheaded many of its edicts have been. In the early days of
cable television the FCC decided it had no jurisdiction. Later, doubtless at
the urging of broadcast television, the agency reversed itself and opposed
any possible expansion of the budding cable industry. Many of the FCC's
rulings were later reversed, either by the agency or by the courts.

As cable television applied for franchises in various cities, it became subject not only to federal regulations but also, in most cases, to local and state regulations. So cable television, alone among telecommunications systems, was usually regulated by three layers of government, not infrequently with different and sometimes contradictory rules.

While I labored at the Gannett Center, the television broadcast networks mounted another assault on the Financial Interest and Syndication (fin-syn) rules adopted by the FCC back in 1970. The rules sought to curb imperious practices of ABC, CBS, and NBC by prohibiting them from owning cable television and, more importantly, from having a financial interest in programs they aired or the rights to syndicate the programs or sell merchandise spun off them.

A small group of producers was formed and, in agreement with Viacom, I headed the group in vigorously opposing changes in fin-syn. This time we failed. The FCC gave in to broadcasting pressure, first relaxing and then scrapping the regulations.

I have enjoyed opening doors for minorities. Earlier in my career I was elected to the board of the International Radio & Television Society. Each month the IRTS held a luncheon at New York's Waldorf-Astoria Hotel, where industry leaders addressed people from media companies. I immediately noticed there were few racial minorities at these events, reminding me that communications as a whole lacked minority representation.

With the approval of other board members, in 1983 I spearheaded a minority career workshop, held at the Viacom Conference Center on West Forty-Third. We advertised the event, inviting interested minority men and women to attend.

For a couple of days before companies arrived, we instructed applicants on how to dress and conduct themselves in interviews, how to write resumes and fill out application forms, and other tips to winning a job. A dozen or so communication companies had booths at the event, where their human resources personnel interviewed applicants and hired a number of them.

The expanded career workshops continue to this day—the 2006 event was in April at the New York Marriott Marquis. Those eligible include college juniors, seniors, and recent graduates. They attend free of charge, and hundreds of African-Americans, Latinos, Asians, and others have landed communications jobs through the workshops.

At about the time of the first IRTS workshop, I was asked to organize the first cable television fund-raising dinner to develop minority managers for that industry.

The event was started as a memorial to Walter Kaitz, a cable pioneer in California, at the suggestion of his son Spencer. About two hundred people attended our first black-tie dinner in 1984. It has continued ever since, with more than a thousand now attending each year. Proceeds underwrite minority careers for promising individuals.

Television today is not far from when the monopolistic power of ABC, CBS, and NBC froze other TV interests out, leading to federal regulations that gave birth to Viacom and other cable and syndication companies. Now, however, a few decades later, the shoe is on the other foot. It is the cable giants such as Comcast and Time Warner that are making it difficult for independent networks to get on the air.

The United States has a creative community second to none, brimming with proposed innovative programming begging to be allowed on the air to compete for viewers. But these ventures are at the mercy of cable conglomerates which, in many cases, will not include new networks in their packages unless the conglomerates own an equity or financial interest in them.

This seems to duplicate exactly how the broadcast networks once operated, leading to the FCC's fin-syn rules some three decades ago. I believe this is worthy of an investigation.

While cable and broadcast companies continue to duke it out, as always, most are comparative lightweights alongside a true giant now entering the ring: telephone companies, which already are wired into 99.9 percent of the nation's homes and businesses.

Cable companies have had to apply for franchises one community at a time. Telephone companies increasingly are finding ways around this burdensome process. Courts in Texas recently ruled that Verizon, a huge wireless company, can offer statewide video services. AT&T, the largest telecommunications company in the U.S. and one of the largest in the world, has also begun providing video services in Texas, as a springboard to the rest of the nation. At this writing, bipartisan legislation is before Congress to allow phone companies to offer nationwide the same video services offered by cable.

When at the helm of Viacom, I warned cable colleagues that our real enemy was not television broadcasting, but telephone companies. Their competitive threat was a dream for many years.

Now, the advent of fiber optics combined with newly emerging IP—Internet Protocol—technology has enabled telephone companies to begin providing numerous services besides phones to the home, including Internet, wireless, and video. These companies are bent on overriding cable television, as satellite services have done, except far more thoroughly.

Turnabout is fair play, and some major cable companies, in turn, have begun selling telephone services in large cities. Will they also wise up and begin operating more in the public interest—keeping rates reasonable and facilitating rather than blocking new cable networks? Stay tuned.

On a personal note, walking and exercising have kept me in fairly good health. I choose to wear out rather than rust out. There is no end of good causes, and I have served a number of them.

I'm adept at fund-raising—an onerous chore to most people, but one I rather enjoy. When leading other funding volunteers, I give them a simple formula: get, give, or go. With rare exceptions, I do not believe in "honorary" volunteers. If a cause is worth serving, it is worth serving with all of our combined, vigorous efforts, including our personal resources.

The late CBS chairman Bill Paley asked me to help raise funds to build a new museum to replace the Museum of Broadcasting he founded a decade earlier. Paley donated the land on West Fifty-Second Street in Manhattan, and Frank Bennack Jr., CEO of the Hearst Corporation, and I raised the needed $40 million. After I badgered him quite mercilessly, Paley agreed to rename it the Museum of Television and Radio, to encompass cable as well. The seventeen-story building opened to the public in 1991 and is nearly four times larger than the original museum. It has two theaters for seminars, ninety-six TV consoles, and twenty-five radio consoles.

A close friend, Herb Strauss, had a daughter named Lauri, who was stricken with leukemia when she was just twenty-five. Laurie, bright and beautiful, died shortly after Jean visited her for the last time. I helped Herb organize the Lauri Strauss Leukemia Foundation, and chaired it for several years. We have held benefit concerts at Carnegie Hall for sixteen years, bringing in $5 million to fight leukemia. Foundation grants have gone to medical investigators, who have used it to leverage an additional $50 million from other sources.

For two decades I have been on the board of Lenox Hill Hospital, a superb 650-bed acute care institution on Manhattan's Upper East Side. Lenox Hill, named by the AARP as one of the nation's top twenty hospitals, has an outstanding reputation for minimally invasive cardiac surgery, a new spine center, a world-renowned sports medicine center, among many other programs.

Jean and I have chaired or co-chaired the hospital's annual fund-raising event, the Autumn Ball, four times, raising over $2 million each time. Our biggest thrill, however, was reading the inscription on one of Lenox Hill's ambulances: "A gift to the community from Jean and Ralph Baruch."

Jean has also been active in the New York City chapter of Junior League, a national women's organization that does a lot of charitable work. The 2,800 members in our city collectively contribute about 250,000 hours of volunteer service annually. They serve more than two dozen community projects in four areas: domestic violence, healthy foundations—teaching pregnant teenagers to care for themselves and their babies—family life skills, and cultural enrichment of youth.

Listening to classical music has been a favorite pastime since childhood in Europe. So when I was invited to become a member of the board of Carnegie Hall, I welcomed the opportunity to help direct the affairs of the famed music venue. Carnegie has a blue-ribbon board of some seventy members, including a seventeen-member executive committee I have sat on for more than a decade and a half. I also served as vice-chairman.

Carnegie Hall, more than a century old, came close to being leveled by developers in 1960. Isaac Stern, one of the greatest violinists of the twentieth century, also proved a man of iron will as he rallied an array of forces that save the great hall. Isaac was Carnegie's president for the next four decades, and it was my privilege to work with him and to become his friend. Soon after I joined the board, Isaac helped preserve and renovate the hall a second time. I helped raise $16 million to add air-conditioning and other upgrades.

Some anxiety accompanied the changes. Carnegie Hall is reputed to have the best acoustics in the United States, if not the world. Would it be harmed by the work?

The hall closed for seven months, reopening in December 1986. The verdict? "Rest easy, Andrew Carnegie," wrote *The New York Times*, "Your great music hall has survived another crisis." The Times added that "the best news of all was that in view of the extensive and ambitious refurbishing, the famous sound was so little changed."[1]

Isaac Stern, who spoke very movingly at our wedding anniversary celebration at Carnegie Hall, in 2001, died that September, at the age of eighty-one, just eleven days after the terrorist strikes that leveled the World Trade Center. His health had been somewhat fragile following heart surgery the previous year, and he was no doubt affected by the disaster in the city he loved and served for so long. Jean and I miss him greatly.

Jean and I have now been married forty-three years. She was a godsend to me and my daughters, and has been a full partner and my best friend in everything I have tried to accomplish. We divide our time these days between our apartment on Park Avenue and a newly acquired home in Bedford Hills, a suburb of New York City. We enjoy traveling, and have seen much of the world. Our greatest pleasure is being with our children and grandchildren, and watching them grow.

Our daughters have achieved a great deal in publishing, the law, medicine, and advertising. Renee is general counsel for a company in Connecticut and has one daughter, Rebecca, who recently graduated from Skidmore College. Alice has diplomates in internal medicine and infectious diseases, and is a senior executive at Pfizer Pharmaceuticals in New York. Michele worked for Italian television in New York, and later for Grey Advertising. She chose to be at home after the birth of her second child. She and her husband, Jim Jeffery, an asset manager, have a daughter, Jane, eleven, and a son, Charlie, from Michele's previous marriage. Charlie is a sophomore at a college in Rhode Island.

The pioneer era in broadcasting ended with the death of William Paley at the age of eighty-nine in October 1990. His fellow pioneer and nemesis at RCA/NBC, General David Sarnoff, died nearly two decades earlier. While Paley sometimes had feet of clay, especially in his lusty private life, he was a bold visionary with an infectious sense of class and style. He had an uncanny eye for the talent and entertainment his countrymen and millions of others continue to feast on today.

Dr. Frank Stanton deserves nearly equal credit for building what was once widely called the Tiffany Network. Frank was my boss at CBS and remained a friend until his death on Christmas day 2006 at age 98. He was a pivotal figure in the development of broadcast television and was the industry's primary spokesman, notably in defending the First Amendment.

I sometimes worry over the college training—or lack of it—offered to young people today who aspire to a life in broadcasting or cable. Where will the new Frank Stantons come from? Too many schools of communication, I fear, plant dreams of stardom in our students, and fail to train them for the rewarding and far more numerous jobs likely to be available to them.

What I tell communication students is that, whatever position they take, especially in their first job, they should wake up each day and not dread going to work. Rather, they should find a job so challenging and stimulating that when they arrive at the office, they feel like rubbing their hands together and shouting "Watch what I accomplish today!"

In my experience, many of those teaching our young people gleaned their knowledge from books and have little real-world experience. Too often they offer theory with no practical application, or teach skills no longer of value. Some years ago I was asked, along with the Pulitzer Prize-winning editor of the Philadelphia Inquirer and the foreign editor of *The Wall Street Journal* to evaluate the communications curriculum of a large state university.

Among courses, I was amazed to find a three-credit class in "Writing Radio Drama," eagerly pursued by the students. Radio, as surely everyone in the country except that faculty knows, has become nothing more than a jukebox, a distributor of national news and call-in shows. Parents were paying hard-earned money to prepare their children for the real world, and students were studying a course that would have been just as relevant if called "Living with Dinosaurs."

On another occasion I gave a talk to students at another state university. At the end I asked those students anxious to get a job in front of the camera to raise their hands. Practically every hand shot up. I asked how many would like to be directors or producers, and again almost every hand went up. Finally I asked for those who wanted to be in sales. One lonely hand slowly went up.

Yet a roster of leaders in cable, broadcasting, or other segments of the communications industry will show that most of them began their careers as I did, in sales. I believe the distaste for marketing and sales can be traced directly to educators, who infuse students with a feeling that this "dirty" side of our business is unworthy. Marketing and sales can be so productive, enjoyable, and rewarding when learned and practiced properly. Students and our industry would be better served if teachers taught this reality.

I wish I had kept the name of the one young man who wanted to be a salesman. Someday all the others may be working for him.

It has been six decades since the *Nyassa* limped into New York harbor with our family aboard. Another French expatriate—the Statue of Liberty—welcomed us that cold December morning, as she has welcomed countless others who were also "tired...homeless, tempest-tossed..." We were part of a vanguard of refugees that would become a steady stream into the U.S. through the rest of the twentieth century.

I will always be in America's debt. Over the years I have tried to repay a little of that debt through professional, public, and charitable service. In 1940, at a time of world crisis, the U.S. had all but stopped admitting refugees. An exception was made for my family and a relative handful of other men, women, and children. Otherwise we surely would have perished in Europe. Many of us came here for safe haven. A promising new beginning and equal possibility with native-born citizens also awaited us.

Television, in good part an American invention, became the ship that carried my own ambitions. I was young and so was it. We grew up together. In the process I took television to much of the world. Each time I returned home more certain that I was blessed to live in the greatest land on Earth.

Thank you, America.

Editor's Note

Ralph Baruch has given an unusually large amount of volunteer service to professional, civic, and charitable causes. In addition to activities discussed in the Epilogue, he founded or co-founded C-SPAN, the International Academy of Television Arts & Sciences, and the National Academy of Cable Programming.

He chaired the USIA Board of Advisors on Private Sector Telecommunications for seven years under President Ronald Reagan, and was a member of the President's Council on the International Youth Exchange Initiative. He was vice-chairman of the International Rescue Committee. Mr. Baruch was given the American Jewish Committee 75th Anniversary Human Relations Award and the United Hospital Fund's Distinguished Trustee Award. He has been honored by his peers with television's highest awards, including:

- Emmy Award, International Academy of Television Arts & Sciences
- Gold Medal of the International Radio & Television Society
- *Broadcasting and Cable* magazine Hall of Fame
- National Cable & Telecommunications Association: Vanguard Award (NCTA's highest), three President's Awards, Chairman

- Silver Circle Award, National Academy of Television Arts & Sciences
- Library of American Broadcasting: A Giant for All Time
- The Cable Center: Hall of Fame

SOURCES

To my knowledge and belief, everything in these pages is true. Directly quoted conversations to which I was a party have been reconstructed to the best of my memory. I have been aided by files full of correspondence and other documents and a sizable collection of pocket calendars which I have routinely carried and made notes in for decades. Where I was not personally involved in significant events that will be new to the general reader, I have tried to supply an independent source in the text or below.

As noted in the Epilogue, after stepping down from Viacom, the Gannett Center for Media Studies at Columbia University, now called Freedom Forum, offered me a senior fellowship. Aided by a research assistant, I spent a year writing the first scholarly treatise on UHF and cable television. Highlights of the white paper, called *How Broadcasting and Cable Happened (In Spite of the FCC)*, are distilled in this book.

INTRODUCTION

1. Vladimir K. Zworykin with Frederick Olessi, *Iconoscope: An Autobiography of Vladimir Zworykin* (Princeton University, Princeton, N.J., unpublished typescript, 1971), Chapter 8.
2. Scott Taggart, "1937 British Report: 'Television in America,'" *Popular Wireless*, August 14, 1937.

3. Arthur Chandler essay on "The Exposition Internationale des Arts et Techniques dans la Vie Moderne, 1937," *World's Fair* magazine, Volume VIII, Number 1, 1988, World's Fair, Inc., Corte Madera, California.

CHAPTER 1 · EUROPE IN TURMOIL

1. A modern medical doctor writes: "'First blood' (Mensur) student blade duels persisted in Germany long after most countries had eliminated duels of honor." James R. Keane, MD, "Dueling Doctors," *Southern Medical Journal*, September 2000, 869.
2. Ernest Hemingway, *A Moveable Feast: Sketches of the Author's Life in Paris in the Twenties* (New York: Charles Scribner's Sons, 1964), preface, taken from a letter to a friend.
3. William L. Shirer, *The Rise and Fall of the Third Reich* (New York: Simon & Schuster, 1960), 434.

CHAPTER 2 · NAZIS ON OUR HEELS

1. The IRC's pivotal role in saving prominent Europeans targeted by Hitler is recounted in Aaron Levenstein, *Escape to Freedom: The Story of the International Rescue Committee* (Westport, Connecticut: Greenwood Press, 1983). Many years later the author helped direct the committee, whose name change reflects its worldwide humanitarian work.
2. One of the books on Fry is by Sheila Isenberg, *A Hero of Our Own: The Story of Varian Fry* (New York: Random House, 2001).

CHAPTER 3 · STARTING OVER IN AMERICA

1. Some stores put lawn chairs on the sidewalk to help potential customers watch their TV sets. Taverns, on the other hand, found that many patrons were so riveted by TV that they forgot to buy drinks. Many tavern owners converted their TVs to coin-operated.

CHAPTER 4 · EARLY TELEVISION

1. Daniel Stashower, *The Boy Genius and the Mogul* (New York: Broadway Books, 2002), 81.
2. Larry Lessing, *Fortune* magazine, November 17, 1949.

3.   John Kenneth Galbraith, *The Great Crash: 1929* (New York: Mariner Books, 1955) 171.

4.   Bernard Schwartz, "'Headless Fourth Branch' Denounced by FCC Prober," *Harvard Law Record*, April 3, 1958.

5.   DuMont obituary in *The New York Times*, November 16, 1965.

6.   Michael Winship, *Television* (New York: Random House, 1988), 17.

CHAPTER 5 · DUMONT AND CBS

1.   Conversation between Ted Bergmann and the author.

2.   *Advertising Age*, online at adage.com/news_and_features/special_reports/tv/1940s.

CHAPTER 6 · THE TIFFANY NETWORK

1.   *Broadcasting and Cable*, December 20, 1999, 21.

2.   Ibid.

3.   Robert Metz, *CBS: Reflections in a Bloodshot Eye* (Chicago: Playboy Press, 1975), 173.

4.   The History of Film & Television (Boca Raton, Florida: High Tech Productions), online at <http://www.high-techproductions.com/whoweare.htm.>

CHAPTER 7 · SELLING CBS ACROSS THE GLOBE

1.   Kerry Segrave, *American Television Abroad* (Jefferson, North Carolina: McFarland & Company, 1998), 19.

2.   Ibid., 20.

3.   "TV abroad thrives on U.S. ways," *Business Week*, September 3, 1960, 105-06.

4.   *The New York Times*, obituary, February 6, 1987.

5.   *American Television Abroad*, 18.

6.   Anthony Smith, *Television: An International History* (Great Britain: Oxford University Press, 1995), 334.

7.   They became top company executives. Jack Schneider, WCAU-TV in Philadelphia, became executive vice-president of CBS Inc.; Robert Wood, KCBS-TV in Los Angeles, became president of the CBS

Television network; Clark George, WBBM-TV in Chicago, became president of CBS Radio and the first designated chief executive officer of Viacom.

CHAPTER 8 · THE TRIP FROM HELL

1. *American Television Abroad*, 36.
2. *Television*, 211.
3. Murrow speech to the Radio and Television News Directors Association, *Encyclopedia of Television* (Chicago: Fitzroy Dearborn Publishers, 1997), 1104.
4. Alexander Kendrick, *Prime Time: The Life of Edward R. Murrow* (Boston: Little, Brown and Company, 1969), 457-58.
5. *Business Week*, June 17, 1967, 87-88.

CHAPTER 9 · JEAN

1. *London Sunday Telegraph*, July 30, 1960.

CHAPTER 11 · TRAPPED IN TINSELTOWN

1. Anthony Smith, "Television as a Public Service Medium," in *Television: An International History,* edited by Smith (New York: Oxford University Press, 1995), 65.
2. Canadian Parliament member M.J. Coldwell, quoted in T.J. Allard, *Straight Up: Private Broadcasting in Canada: 1918-1958* (Ottawa: Canadian Communications Foundation, 1979), 225.

CHAPTER 12 · A VAST WASTELAND?

1. Jerome Singer, online at <http://www.brainyquote.com/inquire/inquire.html>.
2. Leonard D. Eron, Ph.D., representing the American Psychological Association before the Senate Committee on Governmental Affairs, June 18, 1992.
3. Newton N. Minow, speech to the National Association of Broadcasters, May 9, 1961.

Chapter 13 · Adventures Abroad

1. Kalb turned the documentary into a book: *The Volga: A Political Journey Through Russia* (New York: MacMillan Company, 1967).

2. Stefan Krempl, Europa-Universitat Viadrina, Frankfurt (Oder), "Metamorphosis of Power: The meaning of popular role playing for Berlusconi on his way to the top," paper delivered at a meeting of the International Society of Political Psychology, 1999, in Amsterdam.

3. *American Television Abroad*, 221.

4. Ibid., 206-07.

5. The other two executives were Jiro Sugiyama and Miki Itasaka. The latter still worked for CBS News at this writing.

Chapter 14 · Storm Clouds From Washington

1. Nixon tape transcript, May 5, 1971, 9:55 a.m.—, Nixon Presidential Materials Project, 12, at National Archives, College Park, Maryland. Subsequent quotes from the White House tapes—including those of H.R. Haldeman and Charles Colson—likewise are in the National Archives at College Park.

2. Speech delivered live on the ABC, CBS, and NBC television networks, November 13, 1969, from Des Moines, Iowa.

Chapter 15 · CBS vs. Viacom

1. *CBS: Reflections in a Bloodshot Eye*, 342.

Chapter 17 · Cable Climbs into the Ring

1. *Broadcasting*, July 4, 1971.

2. Ibid., April 20, 1970.

3. Archer Taylor, quoted by Craig Kubl, "50 Years of Technology," *CED Magazine*, June 1998, Introduction.

4. Ike Blinder, Ibid.

5. *Television Digest*, April-May, 1958.

6. Glenn O. Robinson, "Regulatory Mischief: Cable Television Regulation," *Virginia Law Review,* March 1978, 245-46.

7. Clive Barnes, *The New York Times*, December 30, 1969.

8.	Copy of Arthur Taylor brochure is in the author's files.
9.	Glenn O. Robinson, *Virginia Law Review*, March, 1978, 245-46.
10.	*CBS: Reflections in a Bloodshot Eye*, 342.

CHAPTER 18 · VULTURES EYE VIACOM

1.	James Reston, *The New York Times*, July 26, 1971.

CHAPTER 19 · VIACOM 'A COMPANY TO RECKON WITH'

1.	*The Washington Post*, September 14, 1978.
2.	In 1989 Ritchie became chancellor of the University of Denver. He refused a salary, instead donating $50 million to the school.

CHAPTER 20 · NETWORKS SLEEP AT THE SWITCH

1.	*American Television Abroad*, 147.
2.	Looking back, Lamb said his main goal "was to open the process up so everybody could be heard." *The Baltimore Sun*, March 5, 2001.
3.	"The C-SPAN Audience After 25 Years," Pew Research Center for the People & the Press, March 2, 2004.
4.	*The New York Times*, September 10, 1980.
5.	*The New York Times*, September 11, 1980.
6.	Ken Auletta, *Three Blind Mice* (New York: Random House, 1991), 33.
7.	Ibid., 3.

CHAPTER 21 · HOLLYWOOD TRIPLE-CROSS

1.	*The Wall Street Journal*, December 19, 1980.
2.	*The Christian Science Monitor*, quoting CBS's Gene Jankowski, November 6, 1980.
3.	*The Washington Post*, February 28, 1979.
4.	Tom Shales, Ibid.

CHAPTER 22 · MY MISTAKE: TERRY ELKES

1.	*Barron's*, March 29, 1982.
2.	*St. Louis Post-Dispatch*, March 30, 1990.
3.	*The Los Angeles Times*, May 1, 1990.

4. *St. Petersburg Times*, December 18, 1990.

5. *Chicago Sun-Times*, January 15, 1992.

6. Senator John McCain, *The Wall Street Journal*, April 1, 1999.

7. Associated Press, December 2, 2005.

CHAPTER 23 · JACKIE GLEASON AND BILL COSBY

1. *The New York Times*, January 26, 1985.

2. *The New York Times*, September 20, 1984.

3. *The Washington Post*, September 11, 1984.

4. *The New York Times*, September 11, 1984.

5. *TV Guide*, May 7, 1988.

6. *The Los Angeles Times*, September 22, 1985.

CHAPTER 24 · 'RALPH, YOU ARE DEAD MEAT'

1. *The New York Times*, **June 4, 1988.**

2. See Connie Bruck, *The Predator's Ball* (New York: Penguine USA, 1989).

3. *Broadcasting*, September 22, 1986.

4. Mara Balsbaugh in *The Washington Post*, September 17, 1986.

5. Sumner Redstone with Peter Knobler, *A Passion to Win* (New York: Simon & Schuster, 2001), 109.

6. Ibid., 114.

7. Ibid., 129.

8. Economist Benjamin Stein, *Barron's*, October 6, 1986.

9. Business analyst Kenneth F. Berents in *The Los Angeles Times*, March 5, 1987.

10. *A Passion to Win*, 144.

CHAPTER 25 · SUMNER REDSTONE FOILS THE PIRATES

1. *The Los Angeles Times*, July 14, 1994.

2. *London Observer*, February 20, 1994.

3. *The New York Times*, March 10, 1987.

4. Walter Cronkite, quoted in Peter J. Boyer, *Who Killed CBS?* (New York: Random House, 1988), 333.

5. Neal Gabler, *The New York Times*, September 9, 1999.

6. *The Boston Globe*, September 8, 1999.

7. *The New York Times*, September 8, 1999.

8. E.B. White, *Harper's Magazine*, October 1938.

9. *Television*, Introduction.

EPILOGUE
1. *The New York Times*, December 16, 1986.

INDEX